The Research Process

Books & Beyond

THIRD EDITION

Myrtle S. Bolner • Gayle A. Poirier

Louisiana State University   *Wayne State College*

KENDALL/HUNT PUBLISHING COMPANY
4050 Westmark Drive   Dubuque, Iowa   52002

Book Team
Chairman and Chief Executive Officer   Mark C. Falb
Vice President, Director of National Book Program   Alfred C. Grisanti
Assistant Director of the National Book Program   Paul B. Carty
Editorial Development Manager   Georgia Botsford
Developmental Editor   Liz Recker
Prepress Project Coordinator   Sheri Hosek
Prepress Editor   Angela Shaffer
Permissions Editor   Renae Heacock
Design Manager   Jodi Splinter
Designer   Suzanne Millius

Printed in the United States of America
10   9   8   7   6   5   4   3   2

ontents

Preface

The beginning of a new century provides us with an opportunity to reflect on how we have arrived at where we are today. The evolution of civilization is really the story of learning. Beginning with the infancy of the universe, the first inhabitants gathered and used information just as they gathered food and other essentials of life. With the knowledge they gained, they were able to create and provide information that resulted in the creation of new knowledge and in advancements that changed the way they lived. Information handed down through the ages enlightens us as to the physical environment, the political and social order, the scientific and technical accomplishments, and, indeed, all aspects of life. Viewed in that light, it is clear that learning to access and use information is an essential part of one's education.

The last decade of the twentieth century and the beginning of this century were marked by tremendous changes in the way information is stored and retrieved. Information media, once consisting only of materials printed on paper, now includes a wide range of different formats ranging from film to information in electronic format. It has become increasingly important that individuals recognize how information is created, organized, and disseminated and that they develop the ability to conduct research in a variety of media. As the knowledge base has grown, so has the complexity of the *research process*—the process by which information is stored, retrieved, and used in the creation of new knowledge. Technology has played an important part in simplifying the way we locate information. At the same time it is quite easy to be overwhelmed not only by the sheer volume of information but also by all the tools of research—especially those in non-traditional formats such as the Internet.

The purpose of this book is threefold:

☐ to make you aware of the different kinds of information that are available in libraries and beyond;

☐ to provide you with a guide to the means of accessing information;

☐ to help you evaluate and use information productively.

The authors recognize that along with basic retrieval skills you must acquire what is the most important ingredient for effective research—the ability to analyze, evaluate, and use information critically. Critical thinking in the context of research involves a certain attitude and disposition on the part of the information user, a willingness to challenge the propositions and assertions encountered as one examines information. Most importantly, critical thinking calls for the testing of values and beliefs in the light of knowledge and evidence discovered in the course of research.

The book introduces you to the materials and services available in a typical library and discusses the ways information is organized. It covers the principal tools for accessing information—library catalogs, the Internet, reference books, indexes, government publications, statistical sources, biographical sources, book reviews, literary criticism, and literature in collections. We have included many Internet sites and titles of reference books, indexes, and electronic databases on a variety of subjects. The more frequently used sources are described in some detail; others are simply listed. The book includes examples for documenting sources using both the MLA and APA styles.

The second edition of this title was published in 2001. Electronic technology is changing so rapidly that much of the information in that edition is already out of date. This third edition reflects changes that have taken place over the last two years in information storage and retrieval, particularly on the Internet.

cknowledgments

We wish to thank the reference staff at Louisiana State University Libraries and at Wayne State College for suggestions. In particular, Marilyn Liedorff, Technical Services Librarian, and Maria Johnson, Reference Librarian at Wayne State College, were extremely valuable in offering their expertise for several chapters. Special thanks are due Denise Sokolowski, Librarian, University of Maryland, European Division, and her staff for their many excellent suggestions and continuing interest in the book.

How to Use This Book

One of the most important skills you can acquire is the ability to find and use information. This is not only essential to achieving success in the classroom, but also necessary as part of the overall preparation for a lifetime of continuous learning. Recognizing that one of the best ways to acquire research skills is through specific instruction, many institutions provide formal courses designed to familiarize students with library resources and research techniques. In many instances, librarians and instructors cooperate to design research strategies that support classroom instruction.

This book is designed so that it may be used as a text in a formal course on developing research skills, or in connection with independent study. While the chapters are arranged in a step-by-step progression that the authors have found useful in teaching research skills, they may be used out of sequence to suit individual needs and learning styles. The book is comprehensive enough to be used by graduate students and others who just want a guide to research.

The book begins with an introduction to libraries and their resources and services, followed by a discussion of the research paper in Chapter 2. This is not a detailed guide for writing a research paper; rather, it gives an overview of the steps usually followed in the process. It also contains explanations of plagiarism, copyright, and documentation forms. The next three chapters are "how to" chapters. Chapter 3 shows you how to search electronic sources. The search techniques introduced here are generic in nature—that is, they can be applied when searching online catalogs, bibliographic and full-text databases, and Internet sources. This foundation prepares you for the next two chapters, which show you how to locate information in the online catalog and on the Internet. Chapter 6 covers an all-important step in the research process—evaluating information. The remaining chapters introduce you to various information sources: reference books, periodicals, government publications, statistical sources, biographies, book reviews, literary criticism, and literature in collections. Appendix A provides examples of documentation forms using MLA and APA styles. The Glossary in Appendix B will help you with terms you are likely to encounter in the course of using the materials covered in this book. Appendix C contains assignment sheets for guided research projects.

The exercises at the end of each chapter are designed to provide a review of the material covered in the chapter and to reinforce learning by providing hands-on experience with the information sources essential to successful research. Some chapters contain several exercises. It is expected that your instructors will choose those exercises that they think are most appropriate. The authors use the topic "Effect of TV Advertising on Children" to illustrate the many facets of information retrieval. Where that topic is not appropriate to the sources under discussion, other subjects are used.

This book provides you with the opportunity to acquire basic research skills—that is the ability to collect, evaluate, organize, and use information. Once you have mastered these skills, you will be able to vary your research activity according to subsequent demands, regardless of the topic involved.

About the Authors

Myrtle S. Bolner

Myrtle S. Bolner is Librarian Emeritus, Louisiana State University. Before her retirement in 2001, Bolner served as Head of Reference Services at Louisiana State University Libraries. Prior to that she was Head of the Business Administration/Government Documents Department at the LSU Libraries. Her professional experience includes four years as a teacher of high school English and twelve years as an instructor in the use of libraries at LSU. She holds a Bachelor of Science in Education and a Master of Library Science from LSU. Bolner is the coauthor of *Library Research Skills Handbook* (Kendall/Hunt, 1991) and *Books, Libraries, and Research* (Kendall/Hunt, 1979; 2nd ed. 1984; 3rd ed. 1987). Other publications include the *LLA Intellectual Freedom Manual* (Louisiana Library Association, 1986, 1994) and articles in the *LLA Bulletin* and *Government Publications Review*. During her long career as a teacher and librarian, Bolner participated in a wide array of workshops, symposia and conferences about bibliographic instruction, online processing, documents in the online catalog, managing a documents collection and similar topics. Bolner was awarded the 2001 James Bennett Childs award by the American Library Association/Government Documents Round Table (ALA/GODORT) for her leadership role in providing improved access to government information. The Louisiana Library Association honored Bolner with their 2001 Essae M. Culver Award, their highest award, for her lifetime contributions to the library profession in Louisiana. In 1990 Bolner was the co-recipient of the CIS/ALA/GODORT Documents to the People Award for her work on the MARCIVE GPO Database, a project to edit and upgrade the cataloging records of the Government Printing Office. Bolner is a member of the American Library Association, the Association of College and Research Libraries, and the Louisiana Library Association.

Gayle A. Poirier

Gayle A. Poirier is Documents/Instruction Librarian at Conn Library, Wayne State College, Wayne, Nebraska. At WSC she initiated a one-credit-hour course entitled Basic Research Skills, patterned on the Library Research Methods and Materials course she previously coordinated and taught at Louisiana State University. She has developed two Web-based courses using this text and plans to have additional courses in the future. Before moving to Nebraska, Poirier served as Head of the Library Instruction Unit at the LSU Libraries. While there, she developed an independent study course using this text. Prior positions include Adult Services Librarian, Columbine Public/School Library in Colorado; Head, Learning Media Center, Memphis State University; and Government Documents Librarian, Memphis State University. Poirier holds a Master of Library Science degree from the University of Oklahoma and a Master of Science in Curriculum and Instruction from Mankato State College. She is a member of the American Library Association, the Association of College and Research Libraries, the Mountain Plains Library Association, and the Nebraska Library Association. Poirier has published several articles in *Research Strategies* and other periodicals in addition to co-authoring *The Research Process: Books and Beyond*. She has spoken at several annual library conferences, including LOEX (Library Information Exchange), the American Library Association, Nebraska Library Association, and the Catholic Library Association.

Libraries:
Materials and Services

"I find that a great part of the information I have was acquired by looking up something
and finding something else on the way."

Franklin P. Adams

Introduction

From the beginning of civilization, humankind's learning about the physical environment, the political and social order, the scientific and technical accomplishments and, indeed, all aspects of life have been systematically collected and organized in libraries. Today there are many who believe that with the advent of technology, libraries no longer serve as the repositories and disseminators of the world's knowledge. Over the last two decades technology has drastically changed the way we think of libraries. For many, the traditional notion of libraries as storehouses for books has been replaced by the image of a "virtual" library in which all information is available electronically. In this image, if a building exists at all it is only to house computers and to provide a laboratory in which librarians, acting as information specialists, are engaged in creating information in digital format. Neither the traditional notion of a library as a storehouse for books nor the image of a virtual library is entirely true today. However, there is a certain amount of validity in each of these images. The library you are using may no longer have a card catalog. Many libraries have canceled paper subscriptions to indexes and abstracts, replacing them with electronic versions. Although libraries have become automated, they continue to retain and purchase materials in traditional formats: paper, microfiche, microfilm, video cassette, and the like. And while it is true that technology has improved the ways we retrieve information, it has also added levels of complexity that require a more educated approach to finding and using information. As an information seeker, you will find it is helpful to know:

- ☐ how materials are organized and arranged in libraries,
- ☐ what materials are available and in what format, and
- ☐ how to retrieve those materials.

Although library arrangements, materials, and services vary from library to library, there are many elements that are common to all of them. This chapter gives an overview of the formats and arrangements of library materials and describes the various services typically found in libraries. Although the focus is on academic libraries, the materials and services are typical of any large library. In describing the formats of materials, the parts of a book are analyzed in detail; other information sources are treated with sufficient detail to provide you with an understanding of their physical properties.

INFORMATION SOURCES

Information is not only available in great quantities, but also in a variety of formats. The term *format* refers to the general physical quality or appearance of an information source. Thus, book format refers to printed pages of paper that are bound together. The book is still the most extensive way that information is stored, and it is the source that many of us still find the most "friendly." Other formats, such as photographs, magnetic recordings, video tapes, laser disks, CD-ROM, DVD (Digital Versatile/Video Disk), online databases and catalogs, and information from the Internet are being used with increasing frequency. You may not feel as comfortable with these sources as you do with books, but understanding the formats of the various information sources will help to dispel some of your fears about unfamiliar formats. Beyond that, developing skills in the intelligent use of information sources will save time and result in a more effective use of the source.

Books

The traditional book printed on paper consists of pages fastened together at one edge and covered with a protective cover. The first printed books consisted only of the cover and the text of the work. There were no title or introductory pages as in modern books. As printing evolved, publishers developed a uniform way to arrange the contents of books that greatly enhanced their usability. The most significant features are discussed in Table 1.1. (Some books may not have all the different parts described, and the order of their appearance may vary.)

E-Books

E-books are texts of books which are published in electronic format and made available on the Internet. Many e-books are available for free, but others require a subscription. Most of the e-books that are free are books that are in the *public domain*; that is, they are not prohibited from publication because of copyright restrictions. This includes works published prior to 1923 and certain other works that are free of copyright limitations. Project Gutenberg (http://promo.net/pg/) has in excess of six thousand books freely available on the Internet. The University of Virginia's Electronic Text Center (http://etext.lib.virginia.edu/) has an extensive collection of e-books, many of which are available to the public. NetLibrary, a subscription service, provides a type of lending service for viewing rights to its e-books. Access to NetLibrary is usually through a subscription held by a library, although individuals may purchase a personal subscription. Individual titles of e-books are also available from an online bookstore such as Amazon and Barnes and Noble. E-books can be viewed on a desktop (PC) or a laptop computer or on a handheld computer such as Palm Pilot, Rocket, Softbook or any other device that is specifically designed for reading electronic documents. Although e-books will not make traditional printed books obsolete, they are growing in popularity. The advantages and disadvantages of e-books are listed in Table 1.2.

CD-ROM and DVD Books

Books in electronic format are available in CD-ROM or DVD format. They may be purchased or created "in-house" by libraries. This often serves as a means of preserving the paper copy of a book.

Table 1.1　Standard Features of Books

☐ **BOOK COVER:** The cover of the book holds the pages of the book together and protects them. The edge of the cover where the pages are bound together is called the spine. The short-title of the book, the author's name, the publisher, and, in the case of library books, the call number are printed on the spine. The front of the cover is often decorated. It may also give the author's name and the short-title of the book.

☐ **INTERIOR PAGES**

Preliminary Material

☐ **Title Page:** The first significant page in the book. It gives the following information:
- *Title:* Gives the full title of the book, including any subtitles or descriptive titles, e.g., *The Book: The Story of Printing and Bookmaking.* (Note: The title from the title page should be used in bibliographic citations.)
- *Author:* The author's name and sometimes a list of credentials such as degrees, academic position, and, occasionally, the names of other works.
- *Edition:* Given if the book is other than a first edition. (All copies of a book printed from one set of type make up an edition. Reprints are copies of the same edition printed at a later time. When any changes are made, it is a revised edition or a new edition.)
- *Imprint:* The place of publication, the publisher, and the date of publication. These are usually found at the bottom of the title page although the publication date is sometimes omitted. The publication date tells when a book was published. Only the place of publication, publisher and date are needed for identification purposes in a bibliography. If there is no publication date, the copyright date is used in a bibliographic citation.

☐ **Copyright and Printing Information**
The back of the title page contains the following information:
- *Copyright:* Legal rights granted to an author or publisher to sell, distribute, or reproduce a literary or artistic work. A small © before a date identifies it as the copyright date.
- *Printing history:* A list of different editions and printings of the work.

☐ **Table of Contents**
A list in order of the chapters or parts of the book and pages on which they begin.

☐ **Preface or Foreword**
Statement of the author's purpose in writing the book and acknowledgment of those persons who have helped in its preparation.

☐ **Introduction**
Descriptions of the subject matter of the book along with a preliminary statement leading into the main contents of the book.

☐ **List of Illustrations**
A list with page numbers of illustrative material in the book. Illustrations might include pictures, maps, charts.

Text and Notes
The main body of printed matter of the book. It is usually divided into chapters or separate parts.

End Matter

☐ **Glossary**
A list with definitions of the special words or unfamiliar terms used in the text, usually at the end of the text.

☐ **Appendix**
Supplementary materials following the text such as tables, maps, questionnaires, or case studies.

☐ **Bibliography**
A list of all books, articles, and other materials the author used in writing the book.

☐ **Index**
An alphabetical list of subjects covered in the book.

Table 1.2 The Advantages and Disadvantages of E-books

Advantages

- ☐ There is no need to go to the library or the bookstore to retrieve a book. It is possible to download an entire book almost instantly.
- ☐ Many e-books include multimedia capabilities such as music, games, and interactive activities.
- ☐ Search engines make it possible to locate words or phrases from the book quickly and easily.
- ☐ It is possible to navigate from one section of the book to another quickly and easily—no more flipping back and forth through pages to find certain chapters or sections.
- ☐ E-books are portable; it is possible to put several books on one small device.
- ☐ The print size can be adjusted to accommodate different user needs.
- ☐ E-books save paper and ultimately space in libraries or on home bookshelves.

Disadvantages

- ☐ E-books are not easy to hold while reading.
- ☐ The equipment to read e-books can be expensive.
- ☐ Some technical knowledge is required for downloading and using.
- ☐ Available publications are not as extensive as traditional formats.
- ☐ Not all e-books are free; many require subscriptions or fees to download.

Serials

A *serial* is a publication that is issued on a continuing basis at regularly stated intervals. The publication frequency varies: some serials are published each day (daily); others, once a week (weekly), every two weeks (biweekly), once a month (monthly), every two months (bimonthly), every three months (quarterly), twice a year (semiannually), or once a year (annually). Serials include periodicals (magazines and journals); newspapers; annuals and yearbooks; and the proceedings, transactions, memoirs, etc. of societies and associations.

- ☐ *Periodicals* are numbered consecutively and given volume designations so that several issues make up a volume. In many libraries, when a complete volume of a periodical has been accumulated, the issues are bound together in hard covers. These bound volumes may be shelved with other books by classification number, or they may be shelved in a separate periodical area. Some libraries acquire the current copies of periodicals in paper and the back issues on microform. *Periodicals* include *magazines* and *journals* that are issued at regular intervals, usually weekly, biweekly, monthly, bimonthly, or quarterly. *Magazines* contain popular reading, while *journals* are more scholarly.

- ☐ *E-journals* (electronic journals) are defined very broadly as those journals or magazines that are available over the Internet. The first e-journals appeared in the early 1990s and have proliferated at a phenomenal rate; currently there are thousands of journals and magazines available in electronic format and the trend for electronic publishing is expected to continue. Some of these are available exclusively online; others may have a print counterpart. Many libraries subscribe to e-journals and make them available through their home pages and in their online catalogs. The advantage of e-journals is that users do not have to come to the library in order to read available articles; rather they can access the journals from their home or office as long as they have a valid authorization to get to the database.

- ☐ *Newspapers* are usually published daily or weekly. They are printed on a type of paper called *newsprint* that does not last. For this reason, they are usually preserved on microfilm. The paper copies of newspapers are kept only until the microfilm copies arrive. Many newspapers are available on the Internet, some by subscription, others for free. For example, the electronic edition of *The New York Times* is available at: http://www.nytimes.com/.

☐ *Annuals* and *yearbooks* are treated much as other book materials and shelved in the general collection or in the reference collection in a library. The proceedings, transactions, memoirs, etc. of a society or association are considered serials because they are usually published at regular intervals. The serial titles owned by a library are usually listed in the library's catalog but may also appear in a separate serials list that identifies those titles and issues that have been received in the library.

Dissertations and Theses

A *dissertation* is research that is conducted and written in partial fulfillment of the requirements for the doctoral degree at a university. A *thesis* is a research project completed in partial fulfillment of the requirements for the master's degree. At least one copy of the original of all the dissertations and theses written at a university is usually kept in the university library. Many libraries acquire microfilm copies of the theses and dissertations in order to preserve the original. Libraries may acquire dissertations and theses from other universities or from a provider service on microfilm or online. A number of universities now belong to the Networked Digital Library of Theses and Dissertations (NDLTD) which requires students at member institutions to submit their theses or dissertations in a prescribed digital format. Theses and dissertations from all the member institutions are then available online for public access.

Archives

Archives consist of both unpublished and published materials that have historical value, such as the public and private papers of notable persons or the records of an institution. The format of archival materials varies: for example, archives might include original manuscripts, letters, photographs, diaries, legal records, books, etc. The materials found in archives may be likened to the items one frequently finds in the attics of old family homes: birth and marriage certificates, letters, and newspaper clippings that tell that family's story. Archives require special care and handling, and it is not unusual to find that access is limited to only serious researchers. Archival materials are also being preserved on microform, magnetic tapes, CD-ROM, DVD, and in digital form stored on computers. Many of the digitally stored materials are available over the Web. A notable example is the Library of Congress' *American Memory: Historical Collections for the National Digital Library*. As of this writing there are seventy archival collections that have been copied and stored in digital format. These collections can be accessed at: http://lcweb2.loc.gov/ammem/amhome.html

Vertical File

The vertical file (or pamphlet file) consists of pamphlets, brochures, newspaper and magazine clippings, pictures, maps, and other materials that are not suitable for cataloging and shelving along with the regular book collection. Vertical file materials are usually placed in manila folders and stored alphabetically by subjects in filing cabinets. The material placed in the vertical file is ephemeral in nature—that is, it has little, if any, lasting value and will soon be out-of-date. Therefore, the vertical file must be weeded, or cleared, from time to time to get rid of dated material. Much of the information kept in the vertical file might never appear in any other published form. Some libraries maintain a separate index of vertical file material.

Audiovisual (A-V) Materials

Audiovisual materials include audio, video, and microform formats.

☐ *Audio* materials—records, audio cassettes, CD-ROM, DVD, and reel-to-reel tapes. The audio materials in most libraries include musical as well as spoken records.

☐ *Video* materials—microforms, video cassettes, slides, synchronized slide-tapes, CD-ROM and DVD.

□ *Microforms*—printed materials that are reduced in size by photographic means and that can only be read with special readers. There are several types of these photographically reduced materials.

   □ *Microfilm* is print that is reproduced on a roll of 35 or 16 mm film.

   □ *Microfiche* is a flat sheet of film, usually measuring four by six inches, on which separate pages of text are reproduced.

   □ *Microprint* is the reproduction in positive form of a microphotograph. Microprint is printed on opaque paper, unlike microfilm and microfiche, which are printed or reproduced on film.

   □ *Microcard* is a form of microprint, but its reduction is greater.

  Microprints and *microcards* are no longer being distributed because of the difficulty in reproducing them on paper.

Libraries purchase microform materials in order to save valuable space and to acquire material not available in any other format. For example, the early census records containing the names of persons are available from the National Archives and Records Administration only on microfilm. Other materials that are usually in microform include newspapers, periodicals, archival materials (manuscripts, family records, personal journals, etc.), and even books, especially out-of-print ones.

Audiovisual materials require special equipment for their use and are usually housed in separate areas of the library.

Electronic Sources

Information in electronic format is available in a variety of formats—radio, television, video cassette, CD-ROM and DVD, etc. For the purposes of this discussion, electronic sources will be discussed only in the context of computer-assisted technologies. That is, to access information in these formats requires a computer and appropriate software.

The kind of information available in electronic format includes bibliographic information such as descriptions of books, periodical articles, and other literary works; raw data (e.g., statistics, census data, voting records); the full text of periodicals, books, and reports; and illustrative material such as maps and photographs. Telecommunications equipment is required for online databases, online catalogs, and Internet access. The equipment used to store and access information in electronic format consists of microcomputers, computer terminals, and disk players. In addition, software (computer programs) is necessary to run the various programs.

Following are descriptions of the various electronic sources:

□ *Online catalog,* also known as the OPAC (Online Public Access Catalog), is a computerized version of the traditional card catalog; it lists all of the items housed in the library or made available remotely through the Internet. The records are created in machine-readable format and are accessible by computer both within and beyond the library walls.

□ *Online database* is a term used to describe information that is stored in a computer and retrieved by other computers through telephone lines and communication networks. There are thousands of online databases, providing nearly every type of information, both bibliographic and full text.

□ *Internet* is a global telecommunications network that links computers together by a unique IP (Internet Protocol) address, and that allows for the free exchange of information among them. The Internet contains all types of information: online catalogs, electronic journals, periodical databases, personal messages, and, in fact, any information that is computer generated can be found on the Internet. (For a full discussion of the Internet, see Chapter 5.)

□ *CD-ROM* (Compact Disk, Read Only Memory) is a small (4.75 inches in diameter) plastic coated optical disk on which information can be stored. One disk is equal in contents to approximately 250,000 printed pages, or about 300 books. The information stored on a CD-ROM cannot be erased or altered, although it can be transferred to another utility such as a floppy disk or the hard drive on a computer. CD-ROM requires a microcomputer with appropriate software and a disk player to run the program. There are thousands of CD-ROM databases available. These include indexes, census data, corporation records, encyclopedias, government documents, statistics, maps, journal back files, and other literary works.

☐ *DVD* (digital versatile disk or digital video disk) is similar to a CD-ROM, except that it holds much more information—a minimum of 4.7GB (gigabytes) all the way up to 17GB, or enough for a full-length movie. Many experts believe that DVD will eventually replace CD-ROMs, as well as VHS video cassettes and laser discs.

ARRANGEMENT OF LIBRARY MATERIALS

While there is some uniformity of arrangement of the materials among libraries, there are also many variations. Differences in arrangement among libraries is governed by a number of factors: size of the institution, mission, and availability of resources. Some schools have separate libraries for undergraduates; other schools have only one central library; many universities have a central library as well as branch libraries that serve various colleges or departments within the university.

In addition to locating library facilities for maximum use, librarians are also concerned with arranging materials within the library. Most libraries arrange materials by function or by service provided. Typically, all the books are shelved together on shelves in what is called a stack area; non-book materials such as microforms and audio materials, are housed in other areas; and access services such as reference assistance, circulation, and interlibrary borrowing are provided at specially designated service desks. Many libraries provide guides to their collections and services; others have self-guided tours; and still others offer a computer-assisted or "virtual" tour of the library. These provide a good starting point in learning where materials are located and how they are arranged. The departments and areas listed below are typical of those found in most college and university libraries.

Stacks

The library's main collection of books is arranged by call number on rows of shelves called *stacks*. Libraries with large collections will have miles and miles of stacks. Some libraries have "closed" stacks to which only library staff and those with permission have access. Patrons present a "call slip" to a library attendant who gets the material. Having closed stacks reduces the loss of library material by theft and mutilation. It also reduces the number of books that are out of order in the stacks. In most libraries, however, books are shelved in "open" stacks where users are free to browse and select materials for themselves. Browsing is helpful in locating materials that the user might not have discovered in the library catalog. Some libraries have a combination of the two systems—the general stack areas are "open" while special collections are "closed." In some college and university libraries, stacks are open to faculty and graduate students, but closed to undergraduates.

The key to locating materials in the stacks or in other areas of the library is the *catalog*. When a library acquires a book or other information source, it is assigned a call number that determines where it will be located in the library. A catalog record is created that includes call number, author's name, title, publication information, and a note giving the height of the book and other descriptive information such as availability of maps, illustrations, and/or bibliographies. Subject headings are assigned in order to help the library user locate the book by its subject. The catalog record is placed in the library's catalog where it is available to library users.

Reference Department

One of the most useful collections in any library is the reference collection. This collection consists of encyclopedias, dictionaries, almanacs, handbooks, manuals, and indexes that are frequently used for finding information. It also contains reference tools in other formats such as CD-ROM and computers for accessing the Internet and specialized electronic databases. The reference department typically has open shelves that are systematically arranged, although some materials such as indexes may be shelved on separate index tables to facilitate their use. Highly used reference books may also be shelved in an area near the librarian's desk. Reference librarians familiar with this collection are available to help patrons find information in the reference area. As a rule, reference materials do not circulate and must be used in the reference area.

Reserve Department

The reserve department consists of materials that circulate for limited time periods, usually two hours or overnight. In many libraries, materials that can be copied, such as periodical articles and chapters or parts of books, are digitized and made available online. Students who are taking the courses for which the materials are reserved access the materials through secured Internet accounts.

Periodical Department

In many libraries periodicals (magazines and journals) are shelved together in one area for convenience of use. Other libraries have found that it is more desirable to have only the current periodicals in one area with the bound volumes in the stacks with other materials on the same subject.

Newspaper Department

Current newspapers may be housed with other periodical literature or kept in a separate area. Print copies of newspapers are kept for a limited period of time because they are printed on paper that does not last. Older copies are usually stored on microfilm.

Media Center

The audiovisual materials described on pages 5 and 6 and the special equipment needed to access them are often housed together in a *Media Center*. Some libraries have separate departments for microforms (Microform Department) and for other types of audiovisual materials (Audiovisual Department). Other names for areas that house audiovisual materials are: Instructional Media Center, Instructional Resource Center, and Learning Media Center.

Government Information Department

Many university libraries serve as depositories for state, local, national, and international documents. These publications are frequently shelved together in a separate area. Some libraries locate state and local government documents in a documents room with national and international documents, but it is also quite common to house these materials in a distinct "state" room designed to preserve materials dealing with the particular state. Documents housed in separate areas are usually arranged by classification systems designed especially for those systems. For example, U.S. government documents are usually shelved by the Superintendent of Documents classification system. (See Chapter 9 for a discussion of government information.)

Archives and Manuscripts Department

The archives department houses records and documents such as letters, manuscripts, diaries, personal journals, photographs, maps, and other materials that are of historical value. This area is staffed by archivists who are specifically trained in methods of acquisition and preservation of historical materials.

Rare Books Department

It is not unusual to find among the library's collections books that are valuable because of their artistic and/or unique qualities or because they are old and no longer printed. Such books need protection and care in handling. They are housed in rooms or in branch libraries and are not allowed to circulate. Some libraries house archives, manuscripts, and rare books together.

Special Collections

In fulfilling its research mission, a university library frequently has a number of highly specialized collections. The advantage of such collections is that they support the university's effort to become a center for research in particular subject fields. Examples of such collections might be African-American history, women's studies, or Asian studies.

Branch Libraries

Branch libraries are located away from the main or central library and house subject collections such as agriculture, business, chemistry, engineering, music, law, or architecture. Usually they are conveniently located in buildings that serve the needs of students and faculty in a particular discipline.

LIBRARY SERVICES

While the introduction of computer technology into information handling has resulted in more efficient and faster methods of storing and retrieving information, it has not eliminated the need for basic library services. The services outlined below are representative of services offered in most academic libraries.

Librarians

An important and indispensable resource in any library is the librarian. In order to acquire, maintain, and disseminate the vast amount of information that is stored in libraries, trained personnel are needed. Most libraries require that their professional librarians have a master's degree or the equivalent from an American Library Association (ALA) accredited institution. Persons trained in librarianship or information sciences perform a variety of services: administrative, technical, and public.

- ☐ Administrators are concerned with the overall operation of the library and with the budget, staff, and physical plant.
- ☐ Technical service librarians are concerned with the acquisition, preparation, and maintenance of library materials. They are in charge of ordering and cataloging materials, checking in serials, sending materials to be bound, repairing damaged books, etc.
- ☐ Public service librarians are those who serve the patron directly as at a reference or circulation desk. Library patrons are more familiar with public service librarians because these are the individuals with whom they come into contact when seeking assistance. Reference librarians are available to answer questions about the collection, to assist in using electronic reference tools, to help with search strategies, and generally to help locate and sort out information. They also select materials for the collection and provide outreach and instruction for the students and faculty. Many reference librarians provide virtual reference services by responding to reference queries posed via e-mail. Other virtual reference services include online chat and links to reference sites on the Internet.

Not everyone who works in a library is a professional librarian. Support staff such as clerks, paraprofessionals, and technicians help to maintain the library's services.

Getting Help

When reference librarians are approached for assistance with a question that involves research, whether in person or online, they conduct an informal reference interview to determine:

- ☐ the purpose of the research;
- ☐ the type of information desired (e.g., statistical, historical, etc.);
- ☐ specific questions to be answered, limitations (e.g., date, geographical, etc.);
- ☐ extent and findings of preliminary research.

It is important to ask appropriate questions during the reference interview and to be as specific as possible.

> **Example**
>
> "Where can I find factual information on computer crimes among government workers?"
>   **NOT**
> "Where are law books located?"

It is beneficial to conduct a preliminary search, such as searching the catalog, browsing, or looking up material in reference books, before approaching the reference desk for help. This enables you to focus on the type of information needed to deal with various aspects of the topic and then ask specific questions. It also gives the librarian a starting point from which to proceed in directing you to appropriate sources.

Electronic Reference Services

The library provides electronic reference services in a variety of ways:

(1) by acquiring and making available indexes and abstracts, reference books, and journals in electronic format;

(2) by identifying and providing access to free materials and services on the Internet; and

(3) by providing workstations, usually with print capabilities for accessing electronic information.

Most of the materials to which the libraries subscribe are now available over the Web, but some are in CD-ROM format. Reference librarians are responsible not only for selecting materials for purchase, but also for providing instruction and assistance in using the electronic resources.

Library Instruction

Library instruction is a service usually provided by reference librarians. It might include formal (for credit) courses, general orientation sessions, subject-related instruction, computer-assisted instruction, and individualized instruction. The reference librarians also prepare printed and online guides to the collection and to sources available on the Web.

Circulation   *desk*

Books and other materials are usually checked out from a centrally located desk that handles all matters dealing with the lending of library materials. In most libraries the circulation desk is located near the entrance or the exit of the library. Information regarding lending policies, fines, and schedules is available at the circulation desk. Many tasks such as checking books out and in, verifying circulation status, and sending out overdue and recall notices, once performed manually at the circulation desk, are now automated.

Interlibrary Loan

The rising costs of library operations and acquisitions have forced more and more libraries to seek co-operation with other institutions in order to serve their patrons. Libraries lend each other books and other materials that are unavailable at the local library. The loans are for limited periods, and the costs of borrowing material (postage, handling, and duplication) are generally borne by the patron. If a lending library does not circulate an item, it may send photocopies. Patrons borrowing books are required to fill out forms giving accurate and complete information on the item they would like to borrow. This usually includes the author, title, publication information and a reference showing where the citation was found. Interlibrary loan is for specific titles only and not for subject requests such as "all the works on the Cold War."

Document Delivery

Document delivery is a library service that provides copies of materials from other libraries or vendors to users, usually for a fee. It is usually administered by the interlibrary loan department. In some libraries, document delivery consists of the physical or electronic delivery of materials to the office or place of business of a library user. The term is also used to refer the concept of "documents on demand." Rather than subscribing to costly, low-use journals, the library subscribes to services that promise fast delivery of the articles. One of the largest document delivery services is Ingenta, formerly CARL UnCover. Ingenta is a database containing the full text of articles from several thousand journals. There is no charge to search the database, but if an individual or a library wants a copy of the article there is a charge, which includes the cost of reproducing and sending the article plus a copyright fee. The articles are usually sent by facsimile transmission (fax) to the individual or library requesting them.

Library Cooperatives

A practice that is prevalent among libraries today is that of forming cooperatives for the purpose of making holdings and services available to members and their patrons on a reciprocal basis. These groups are known by various names: library networks, information centers, or consortia. Some groups share general printed materials while others share specialized materials such as computing facilities, databases, periodicals, films, slides, and other audio-visual material.

Regional and state library systems, in which libraries in a geographical area share resources, are widespread throughout the United States. There are also national library networks in which members from different libraries all over the country cooperate to share resources. OCLC (Online Computer Library Center) is a national network with a variety of services ranging from shared cataloging to bibliographic searching. Members of OCLC may use its services to handle requests for interlibrary loan material, to catalog materials, and to help identify and locate materials.

Exercise 1.3

Instructor: _____ Course/Section: _____

Name: _____

Date: _____ Points: _____

E-Books

1. Each of the Web sites listed below provides links to e-books. Go to each of the sites and answer the question.

   a. http://www.bibliomania.com/ Approximately how many titles of books are available at the site?

   b. http://chaucer.library.emory.edu/wwrp/ What subject is covered by the books on this site?

   c. http://www.infomotions.com/alex Name three titles that are available from this site.

   d. http://digital.library.upenn.edu/books/ Name two titles from the banned books section at this site.

2. From one of the sites in Question 1 select an e-book. Name the parts of the book described in Table 1.1 that are included in the online book you selected.

Exercise 1.5

Libraries: Materials and Services

Instructor: _____ Course/Section: _____

Name: _____

Date: _____ Points: _____

Virtual Library Tour

Using the Google search engine (http://www.google.com/), search the Internet to locate a "virtual library tour" on the Web. Use the term "library virtual tour" for your search. (Note: Select a library other than your own.) Answer the questions below.

1. Indicate the name of the library you select.

2. Is there a library map on the page?

3. Name the first four departments indicated on the tour.

4. Is there is a page describing the periodical collection?

    If so, how are the periodicals arranged in this library? Are they cataloged? Shelved alphabetically? Another system? All in one area, or shelved by call number within the stacks?

5. Based on what you have seen on the Internet tour, how does this library compare with your library? (For example, does it provide more materials? More services? Is it more attractive?)

21

The Research Paper

"The most original authors are not so because they advance what is new,
but because they put what they have to say as if it had never been said before."

Johann Wolfgang von Goethe

Introduction

Do you know what the Iditarod race is?

Or have you ever wondered where you would find information on making cheese?

Or, where you should go on your next vacation?

Or, whether UFOs really do exist?

Whether you go to an encyclopedia or other reference book, or you surf the Internet to find answers to these questions, you are doing research. Regardless of the objective, the research process consists of a systematic investigation to find information. For most of us, research consists of seeking out recorded knowledge—knowledge that is found in libraries or on the Internet. Most new knowledge is created by highly trained personnel in universities, in government, and in industry who conduct experiments or other types of original investigations. For the college student, research is an integral part of the learning process. Students are expected to prepare themselves for living by learning how to access information and how to use it efficiently and effectively. Instructors seeking to develop their students' information skills usually rely on some type of formal research project—usually a formal essay requiring the student to use recorded knowledge. This can be a daunting experience, especially in light of the tremendous changes taking place in the way information is stored and retrieved. Some of the apprehensions related to doing research can be allayed once students learn how the research process works—how to organize and analyze information needs, how to locate and evaluate information, how to synthesize what is learned with original ideas and interpretations, and finally how to write and document the paper. This chapter will introduce you to the steps involved in researching and writing a research paper. Later chapters will concentrate on developing skills for finding and evaluating information in different types of resources.

WHAT IS A RESEARCH PAPER?

The most common type of research project is the research paper, usually a formal essay based on an accumulation of facts and ideas gathered in the research process. The research paper offers the researcher an opportunity to examine issues, locate material relevant to an issue, digest, analyze, evaluate, and present the information with conclusions and interpretations. In preparing a research paper, you will do practical research in the library or on the Internet. You will not be expected to do the type of original research usually done by more advanced researchers. But your research paper will have an element of originality in that you will be putting together pieces of information from various sources in order to present a new view of a topic.

Example

Most people believe that the Democratic Party is more inclined to favor gun control than is the Republican Party. But what is the official view of the two parties on gun control? Are they in general agreement about the issue? And, if so, what does each espouse? Or is there disagreement among the members of each party on any aspects of gun control? Someone interested in this topic could examine the platforms of each party, look at the voting records and the arguments on the floors of the House and Senate, and find out what others outside of Congress have said on this topic. The writer of the paper would gather information from both primary and secondary sources and reach conclusions that would, in a sense, be new and original even though he or she used only recorded information.

Steps in Preparing a Research Paper

It is helpful to approach the research paper assignment as a series of stages or steps. Some rather obvious steps are:

1. SELECTING A TOPIC
2. FORMULATING A THESIS
3. PREPARING AN OUTLINE
4. FINDING INFORMATION: THE SEARCH STRATEGY
5. EVALUATING RESOURCES
6. TAKING NOTES
7. WRITING THE TEXT OF THE PAPER
8. DOCUMENTING THE SOURCES

Selecting a Topic

Sometimes the initial step in the preparation of a research paper is the most challenging one. The selection of a topic is also the most crucial step in determining the success of the research paper. If your instructor assigns a topic, you need only determine how to proceed with the research. In most cases, however, you must choose your own topic. While this might tend to increase your apprehensions about the research paper, it also affords some exciting and rewarding possibilities. After all, research is about acquiring new knowledge and looking at information in new ways. The trick is to focus on a topic that interests you and to discover all the aspects that you want to work with. The best way to do this is to examine several possibilities systematically. Several overriding principles that should be considered in selecting a research topic are shown in Figure 2.1.

Selecting a Topic	
Initial consideration	*Beware of topics that may be too*
☐ prior understanding of topic	☐ recent
☐ manageability of topic	☐ regional
☐ length of assignment/project	☐ emotional
☐ due date of assignment/project	☐ complex
☐ type of assignment/project	☐ broad
☐ availability of research materials	☐ narrow

Figure 2.1 Selecting a topic.

Most college research papers are fairly brief, usually between five and ten pages or roughly between 2,000 and 3,000 words. Thus it may be necessary to narrow the focus of an overly broad topic because it would not be possible to cover a broad general topic in so few words. Topics such as civil rights in the United States, World War II, and the pros and cons of abortion are much too broad to be covered in a short paper. The topic, "The Incidence of Divorce in My Home Town," is probably too narrow and too regional. It is best to focus first on a broader concept of a topic, then to narrow it to a manageable level. Often a preliminary search in one or more of the sources listed in Figure 2.2 will help you narrow the topic and at the same time help you determine if there is sufficient information available.

Formulating a Thesis

After you have become somewhat familiar with the topic selected, the second step is to determine the *thesis* of the paper.

Ask Yourself

☐ What is the purpose of the paper?
☐ What will be the focus?
☐ What is to be proven or shown in the paper?

+ Clear + (gramatically correct)
+ wording matters + give (facts as fact)
your opinion + give examples (be specific)

The thesis statement is a concise statement of two or three sentences that provides a framework for the paper. The *search strategy*, or process to be used in locating information, is determined by the thesis since the information located must support the thesis. Some preliminary reading from one or two sources such as an encyclopedia article or a periodical article is probably sufficient to help formulate the thesis statement (see Figure 2.3).

Sources for Preliminary Search
☐ the *Library of Congress Subject Headings (LCSH)*—for narrow subject headings under a broad topic
☐ general encyclopedias—for overview of a topic
☐ the library catalog—to see what books and other background material are available on the topic
☐ periodicals—magazines, journal and newspaper articles for ideas on limiting a topic
☐ the Internet—for varying opinions on a topic

Figure 2.2 Sources to consult for a preliminary search on a topic.

Formulating a Thesis

Developing a Thesis

☐ Begin with a question—not an opinion. Do not just give the purpose of the paper.

☐ Conduct preliminary research to look for points that will shape or form an opinion.

☐ Prepare a final statement that indicates that the thesis is supported by evidence. (A thesis statement should be brief—no more than three sentences.)

Sample Topic

Effect of Television Advertising on Children

Initial Question

Are children under the age of eight adversely affected by advertising they see on TV?

After Further Research

What is the purpose of TV advertising that is directed toward children?

Do advertisers use tricks or unfair practices to influence children?

What are some of the parental concerns relative to TV advertising directed toward children?

Is there evidence to show that children and families are adversely affected by TV advertising?

Should there be an outright ban of advertising on children's TV programs?

Should the government regulate TV advertising on children's programs?

FINAL Thesis Statement

Numerous studies have found that TV advertising directed toward children can adversely affect their mental and physical health. The two most advertised products on children's TV are toys and food–toy commercials cause children to place undue emphasis on consumerism; food advertising encourages poor eating habits resulting in obesity and other eating disorders. Although there have been attempts to regulate TV advertising directed toward children, parental intervention seems to offer the best solution for countering the adverse effects of TV Advertising on children.

Figure 2.3 Formulating a thesis.

Preparing an Outline

The third step in the process is to prepare a working outline that includes all facets of the topic to be investigated. The same preliminary sources used as a guide to narrow the topic and formulate the thesis statement are also helpful in compiling the outline. To be useful the outline should divide the thesis into a number of major points; each of the points should be further divided and subdivided until the writer can visualize the outline as a guide for research and as a skeleton for the final report. The process of subdividing should follow a logical sequence with related points grouped together (see Figure 2.4). The major points should be parallel, just as the subdivisions under each heading should be parallel. The main points in the outline should support the thesis statement. These should be assigned Roman numerals. The first subdivisions are given capital letters; the second, Arabic numbers; the third, lower-case letters. Use Arabic numbers in parenthesis if it is necessary to subdivide any further than this. Since each heading or subheading in the outline denotes a division, there must be more than one part if it is to be logical. Thus, if there is a I, there must be a II; if there is an A, there must be a B. The working outline is important to the search strategy since the search should be directed to the relevant points in the outline.

In the process of locating information, it is probable that other aspects of the topic not included in the working outline will be discovered and that the final outline will be changed and improved. As information is gathered the outline can be revised and new headings or subheadings added.

Preliminary Topic Outline

Topic: The Effect of Television Advertising on Children

  I.   TV advertising aimed at children
       A. Purpose
       B. Statistics
           1. Viewing time by children
           2. TV advertising time directed toward children
 II.   Adverse effects of TV advertising on children
       A. Research findings
           1. Exploitation of children
               a. Children tend to believe advertising claims they see on TV
               b. Children under eight are unable to make critical judgments about products advertised
           2. Special tactics used by advertisers to appeal to young viewers
       B. Products
           1. Toys
               a. Promote undue emphasis on consumerism
               b. Children emulate characters they see in ads
                   (1) Barbie
                   (2) GI Joe
           2. Food
               a. Types of food advertised
               b. Health consequences ·
III.   Regulations
       A. U. S.—Children's TV Act of 1990
       B. Total ban—Denmark, Switzerland, Belgium
       C. Great Britain—Independent Television Commission (ITC) regulations
 IV.   Parental Intervention

Figure 2.4   Example of a preliminary topic outline.

Finding Information: The Search Strategy

Developing a Search Strategy

A search strategy is a plan of research. It involves two distinct phases:

1. analyzing the information you need (see Figure 2.5), and

2. determining which search terms you should use to guide your search.

   ☐ Consult your thesis statement and outline to come up with a list of key terms.

   ☐ Add related terms that are not apparent in your thesis and outline but which might lead to more information.

   ☐ Include words that have narrower or broader meanings than your original terms (see Figure 2.6).

   ☐ Use the sources listed in Figure 2.2 to help you select keywords. *The Library of Congress Subject Headings* (*LCSH*) would be especially helpful for finding appropriate terms.

Locating Information Sources

Finally, you need to locate information sources that support your thesis and outline. For this, you need to be somewhat familiar with the vast array of information sources that are available to you. Some of the ma-

What Do You Need to Know?	
Level of specificity	Do you need facts? opinions? background information? analyses? How much information do you need?
Time line	What is the time line of the information you need? Do you need an account of an event recorded at the time it happened? Does timeliness matter? Do you need current information? Or do you need a more historical presentation? Look at the date of the publication to determine currency and relevancy. For example, if you need information on the race riots in Tulsa, Oklahoma, in 1921, do you want newspaper articles written at the time of the event, or do you want articles written at any time since the event?
Focus	Do you need to focus on a specific subject area or discipline such as humanities, social science, or science? For example, if you were researching the causes of eating disorders among teenagers, would you look for information in scientific resources or would you look in the social sciences?
Level of scholarship	Do you need background information, or brief facts not backed by research? If so, you should use **popular** sources. If you need a more in-depth treatment, you should consult a **scholarly** source. (See Chapter 6 for a discussion of popular and scholarly sources.)
Type of information	Do you need an account of an event as it happened? **Primary** sources allow you to get as close to an event or an account as possible. And although it does not provide analysis or interpretation, a primary source may be more factual. **Secondary** sources provide analyses, explanations, or descriptions of primary sources. For a research paper, a good rule of thumb is to choose both primary and secondary sources when you have the opportunity. (See Chapter 6 for a discussion of the differences between primary and secondary sources.)

Figure 2.5 Analyzing your needs.

terials you use will be located in the library in various formats such as paper, microform, CD-ROM and DVD. Others will be on the Internet. Figure 2.7 provides helpful information on selecting appropriate sources. Later chapters of this book are devoted to analyzing the major sources to consult in the search process:

☐ the library catalog,

☐ the Internet,

☐ BROAD TERM—ADVERTISING

☐ NARROW TERM—TELEVISION ADVERTISING

☐ NARROWER TERM—TELEVISION ADVERTISING AND CHILDREN

Figure 2.6 Determining search terms.

Guide to Selecting Sources

Information	Sources to Consult	Finding Aids
Preliminary Ideas	*Library of Congress Subject Headings* magazine and journal articles	consult reference staff browse current periodicals Internet
Overview of Topic	general encyclopedias books periodicals	consult reference staff library catalog indexes and abstracts
Definitions	dictionaries	library catalog
Primary Sources	newspapers research reports manuscripts (archives) government publications	library catalog databases (e.g., *LexisNexis Academic*) Internet
Secondary Sources	books magazine and journal articles subject encyclopedias	library catalogs indexes and abstracts databases
Facts	almanacs and yearbooks statistics government publications	library catalogs statistical indexes Internet
Current Information	newspapers magazines and journals	indexes and abstracts databases (e.g., *InfoTrac*)
Historical Information	books encyclopedias and reference books periodicals	library catalog browse reference shelves indexes and abstracts
Evaluative Sources	book reviews biographies	indexes to book reviews Internet

Figure 2.7 Selecting appropriate sources.

☐ reference books,

☐ indexes and databases for periodical articles,

☐ government publications,

☐ statistical sources,

☐ biographical sources.

Asking for Help

Reference librarians can provide valuable assistance with research questions if they know what you are looking for. The key to getting assistance is asking the right questions.

Evaluating Sources

Evaluate each source that you locate for its suitability and reliability.

Ask Yourself

- ☐ Is the information relevant to your thesis and the points covered in your outline?
- ☐ Is the information sufficiently up-to-date?
- ☐ Is there a later edition of the work?
- ☐ Is the source reliable?
- ☐ Does the work reflect a particular bias or prejudice?

Use the criteria listed in Chapter 6 to evaluate the information you find.

Taking Notes

As you examine each source, you should take notes on all the important facts and opinions you might want to use in your paper. The best way to take notes is to use separate note cards or uniform sheets of paper for each topic that you locate. (If you are using a word processor, you need only create a separate document for each topic.) Each note card or note document should contain a heading that is keyed to a heading in your outline. As you take notes, it is best to paraphrase or summarize the words of the author, although sometimes direct quotations are needed for emphasis or for authoritativeness. In either case it is important to retain the author's intended meaning. Note the page or pages on which you found the information. Include all the essential bibliographic information: author or editor's name, title of the work, series (if any), publisher, date, and place of publication. It is helpful to include the call numbers of books and periodicals and the URL (Internet address) of materials found on the Web in case you need to go back to these.

Writing the Paper

Once you are satisfied that sufficient information has been gathered to support all the points in your outline, you can begin to write a first draft of the paper. Sort the notes so that they are grouped under topics that fit the headings in the outline. The research paper, by definition, is based primarily on evidence gathered from other sources. It demands a great deal of creativity to assimilate evidence and present it so that it gives the reader a new perspective. Allow yourself sufficient time for the actual writing. It may take several drafts to achieve the well-written research paper. As you write the paper, pay careful attention to all the elements of good writing: effective phrasing of ideas, good paragraph development, and logical flow of the paragraphs into a unified paper.

Documenting the Sources

It is expected that a research paper will be documented since by definition it includes ideas and facts gathered from other sources. To *document* a research paper means to acknowledge, or cite, the sources used or consulted. Failure to do so constitutes *plagiarism*. Another pitfall associated with research is the violation of *copyright* laws.

Plagiarism

"Plagiarism" is defined as the unacknowledged inclusion of someone else's words, structure, ideas, or data. When a student submits work as his/her own that includes the words, structure, ideas, or data of others, the source of this information must be acknowledged through complete, accurate, and specific references, and, if verbatim statements are included, through quotation marks as well. Failure to identify any source (including interviews, surveys, etc.), published in any medium (including on the internet) or unpublished, from which words, structure, ideas, or data have been taken, constitutes plagiarism. (Louisiana State University. Code of Student Conduct. *Section 5.1:16)*

In most universities plagiarism is considered academic misconduct and has serious consequences, including expulsion; recently some renown authors have had their reputations tarnished by revelations of plagiarism. Today more than ever, it is easy to plagiarize. The Internet makes it possible to retrieve information from various sources, cut and paste, and come up with a paper that is completely taken from other sources. At the same time, plagiarized information from sources on the Internet is also easy to detect. It is possible to type a single word or phrase into a search engine and locate the original source.

How to avoid plagiarism

☐ Acknowledge any sources that you use with proper documentation.

☐ Put in quotation marks and document the source of all the exact words or phrases that you get from another source.

☐ If you paraphrase, that is, put into your own words or rearrange the words of another, you must acknowledge the source.

☐ It is not necessary to document facts considered common knowledge. Ordinarily you should not have difficulty determining what is common knowledge. Some facts, even though they may be new to you, appear over and over in the readings and do not require documentation.

Example

```
Congress voted to declare war on Japan on December 8, 1942.
```

This is a well-known fact that needs no documentation; however, the following sentence should be documented.

```
When Congress voted to declare war on Japan on December 8, 1942,
there was one dissenting vote-that of Representative Jeanette Rankin,
who had also dissented against a declaration of war against Germany
in 1917(Facts 325).
```

don't need to document common knowledge

☐ It is preferred to attribute ideas which might be controversial or authoritative, whether you agree or disagree, to the author in the text of the paper.

> ### Example
>
> ```
> Fawn Brodie, in her biography of Richard Nixon, claims that self-decep-
> tion and lying to others was a part of Nixon's basic character(503).
> ```
> **NOT**
> ```
> Self-deception and lying to others were a part of Nixon's basic char-
> acter (Brodie 503).
> ```

☐ Avoid unintentional plagiarism. In research it is easy to get caught up in the ideas that you are trying to prove or the points you wish to illustrate and then appropriate them as your own. Reread the original to make sure that you are not guilty of plagiarism.

☐ As you gather information keep track of the sources. Be sure to include all the information needed to cite the source accurately and completely: author's name, title, publication information, and page numbers and, for Internet sources, the location of the site and the date on which you accessed the site.

☐ Become familiar with the various nuances of plagiarism. An excellent definition of plagiarism, along with questions and answers and examples of plagiarism can be found at: http://www.learningcommons. uoguelph.ca/writing/plagiarism.htm

Copyright

Copyright is the legal provision that guarantees owners the exclusive right to reproduce, sell, distribute, or display a work that they have created, including any published or unpublished literary, musical, dramatic, pictorial or other audiovisual work, and postings on the Internet. No one else may make a copy or use any copyrighted works without explicit consent of the owner, except for "fair use" in education, research, and news reporting. Even so, there are limitations as to what can be copied and the extent of use of copied materials. For example, it is okay to copy an article for personal use; however, it is not okay to make multiple copies of the article for distribution. Works that are not copyrighted are said to be in the *public domain*. That is, anyone has the right to reproduce or use them without restriction. Certain government publications and works produced before 1923 are usually in the public domain. The terms of the copyright vary but most works produced after 1978 may be copyrighted for the life of the owner plus 70 years.

Copyright has taken on new significance with the advent of computer technology and the Internet. It is extremely easy, and tempting, to copy text and images from Web pages and to paste them into a document you might be creating. It is also tempting to use existing HTML coding to create Web pages. While you may use parts of a text if you document your sources properly, you may not use the entire pages, or images, or HTML text without permission of the owner of the copyrighted material.

Forms of Documentation

While there is no one "correct" form for documentation, convention dictates that in a formal research paper the writer must follow a prescribed style—one that is consistent throughout and that communicates clearly and accurately the sources that are being documented. Your instructor may require that you use a certain style to document research for a particular assignment. The library has style manuals that provide models for documenting research. Many English composition textbooks contain a section on writing and documenting a research paper. You can also find style manuals on the Internet. The style manual that is recommended by disciplines in the arts and humanities is the *MLA Handbook for Writers of Research Papers* (MLA style). The *Publication Manual of the American Psychological Association* (APA style) is preferred by scholars in the social and behavioral sciences. Other fields, particularly in the sciences, use documentation styles adapted for their particular needs. Table 2.1 is a selected list of style manuals useful for documenting research.

Table 2.1   Style Manuals

The Bluebook: A Uniform System of Citation. 17th ed. Cambridge, MA: Harvard Law Review Association, 2000.

The Chicago Manual of Style: The Essential Guide for Writers, Editors, and Publishers. 15th ed. Chicago: U of Chicago P, 2003.

Council of Biology Editors. *Scientific Style and Format: The CBE Manual for Authors, Editors, and Publishers*. Bethesda: Council of Biology Editors, 1994.

Garner, Diane L., and Diane H. Smith. *The Complete Guide to Citing Government Information Resources: A Manual for Writers and Librarians*. Rev. ed. Chicago: ALA, 1993.

Gibaldi, Joseph. *MLA Handbook for Writers of Research Papers*. 6th ed. New York: MLA, 2003.

Li, Xia, and Nancy C. Crane. *Electronic Styles: A Handbook for Citing Electronic Information*. Rev. ed. Medford, NJ: Information Today, 1996.

Publication Manual of the American Psychological Association (APA). 5th ed. Washington: APA, 2001.

Stewart, Mark D. *Citing Electronic Documentation. APA, Chicago, and MLA Styles*. 2000. Online Writing Center, Dept. of Rhetoric, U. of Minnesota. 21 Jan. 2003 <http://www.rhetoric.umn.edu/Student/Graduate/%7Emstewart/citations/>.

Turabian, Kate L. *A Manual for Writers of Term Papers, Theses, and Dissertations*. 6th ed. Chicago: U of Chicago P, 1996.

Uncle Sam: Brief Guide to Citing Government Publications. 16 July 2002. Government Publications Department, Library, U. of Memphis. 21 Jan. 2003 <http://exlibris.memphis.edu/govpubs/citeweb.htm>.

The citations used in documentation sources generally appear in two places in a research paper:

1. within the text, immediately following the quotation, phrase, or sentence to which the citation refers, and

2. at the end of the paper in a list of "Works Cited" (MLA style) or "References" (APA style) (see Table 2.2 and Table 2.3).

Citations within the Text

There are several methods of acknowledging the sources used within the text.

1. parenthetical references,
2. notes (footnotes or endnotes), and
3. full bibliographic citation within the text.

Parenthetical References

The use of parenthetical references in which citations in the text are keyed to a list of *Works Cited* (MLA) or *References* (APA) is the preferred method for documenting sources used in a research paper. The entries in the *Works Cited* or *References* list contains full bibliographic descriptions of each of the sources that were used and acknowledged in the text. The source in the text is identified by a brief reference in parenthesis to the corresponding reference in the list. The examples below are typical of parenthetical references in the MLA and APA styles.

MLA Style

In the text of the paper:

"Women at the highest levels . . . comprise only 10% of senior managers in Fortune 500 companies" (Meyerson and Fletcher 126).

The author's last name and the page cited in the text is sufficient for identification.
If the author is mentioned in the text, it is not necessary to repeat the author's name in the citation.

Meyerson and Fletcher contend that it took a revolution to get women where they are today, but now a softer approach based on "small-wins" or incremental changes that chip away at biases is needed to shatter the glass ceiling (126).

If the parenthetical reference is to a work that is listed by title in *Works Cited*, use the title or a shortened form of the title. The reference "World" is sufficient to identify the title and page reference for the article cited below.

Figures show that British women have made little progress in breaking into professional ranks in the 20th century ("World" 42).

In the Works Cited *list:*

Note that in research papers and unpublished manuscripts, words that are normally in italics, such as titles, are underlined.

Meyerson, Debra E., and Joyce K. Fletcher. "A Modest Manifesto for Shattering the Glass Ceiling." Harvard Business Review 78.1 (2000): 126-36.

"A World Fit for Women: Changes Affecting the Role of Women Over Time." The Economist. 31 Dec. 1999: 41-42. ABI/Inform Global. ProQuest Direct. Louisiana State University. 22 Feb. 2000 <http://infotrac.galegroup.com/>.

APA Style

In the text of the paper:

Note that in APA style, the date of the publication is considered to be important and is given prominence in both the citation within the text and in the references list.

"Women at the highest levels . . . comprise only 10% of senior managers in Fortune 500 companies (Meyerson & Fletcher, 2000, p. 126).

The citation gives the authors' last names, the date of the publication, and the page number which is referenced.

When the author is mentioned in the text, it is not necessary to repeat the author's name in the citation. The date of the publication should follow the author's name.

Meyerson and Fletcher (2000) contend that it took a revolution to get women where they are today, but now a softer approach based on "small-wins" or incremental changes that chip away at biases is needed to shatter the glass ceiling (p. 126).

If the parenthetical reference is to a work that is listed by title in References, cite in parentheses the first few words of the title and the year of publication.

Figures show that British women have made little progress in breaking into professional ranks in the 20th century ("World," 1999, p.42).

In the **References** *list:*

Meyerson, D. E., & Fletcher, J. K. (2000). A modest manifesto for shattering the glass ceiling. *Harvard Business Review, 78*(1), 126-136.

A world fit for women: Changes affecting the role of women over time. (1999, December 31). [Electronic version]. *The Economist,* 41-42.

Notes

Some scholars, particularly in the arts and humanities, prefer to use *notes* to document sources used. Notes cited in the text may appear at the bottom of the page (footnotes) or at the end of the paper (endnotes). When notes are used for documentation, the documented material is indicated in the text with a *superscript* (a raised Arabic number) placed after the punctuation mark of material that is cited. The numbers are keyed to numbers in the notes. The first reference to the work contains full bibliographic information—author, title, and publication information. Subsequent references to the same work are cited in brief. The note numbers should be consecutive throughout the paper. When endnotes are used for documentation, it is usually not necessary to include a separate bibliography or *Works Cited* list in the paper.

In the text of the paper:

. . . A number of government policies and a stronger business culture have resulted in a more favorable climate for women in business.[1]

. . . "When median earnings of women are compared with those of men of a similar age and similar levels of education, major fields of study, and occupational characteristics, however, the earnings gap narrowed progressively."[2] . . . Although affirmative action litigation has significantly increased hiring of women in lower echelons of government, female representation in higher positions such as city councilors or mayors was not significantly affected.[3]

In the footnotes or endnotes:

[1] Robert L. Nelson and William P. Bridges, Legalizing Gender Inequality: Courts, Markets, and Unequal Pay for Women in America, Structural Analysis in the Social Sciences, 16 (New York: Cambridge, 1999) 10.

[2] Daniel E. Hecker, "Earnings of College Graduates: Women Compared with Men," Monthly Labor Review 121.3 (1998), EBSCOhost: Academic Search Elite, LLN (Louisiana Library Network), Baton Rouge 22 Feb. 2000 <http://search.epnet.com/>.

[3] Nelson and Bridges 6.

Caution

The use of the terms *ibid.* (in the same place), *op. cit.* (in the work cited) and *loc. cit.* (in the place cited) is no longer recommended in most style manuals. Rather, the work being cited is identified with the relevant page numbers. In most cases the author's last name is sufficient to identify the work. If two or more different titles by the same author are being cited, the citation should include a shortened form of the title after the author's last name. References to Gwendolyn Mink's *The Wages of Motherhood* and her *Welfare's End* would be cited in subsequent references as follows:

4 Mink, <u>Wages</u> 48.
5 Mink, <u>Welfare's</u> 150.

Full Bibliographic Citation in the Text

Complete bibliographical references within the text should be used only if there are one or two citations in the entire manuscript. This type of citation deprives the reader of the benefits of a list of references and interrupts the flow of the text.

Documentation at the End of the Paper

The *Works Cited* list (MLA) (see Table 2.2) or *References* list (APA) (see Table 2.3) identifies all the books, articles from periodicals, government documents, theses and dissertations, articles from reference books, information from the Internet, and other sources of information that were used in writing the paper. Each entry, referred to as a bibliographical entry, contains all the essential elements needed to identify the work—author, title, series, publication information, depending on the work being described. The *Works Cited* or *References* list is placed at the end of the paper. The term *Works Consulted* is used if the list includes additional works that were not cited in the text of the paper.

Bibliography

Another name for a list of sources is *a bibliography*. It is a broader term that encompasses other types of listings such as suggested readings on a topic. A bibliography may also list works by one author (an *author* bibliography), or it may list works on a subject (a *subject* bibliography). A *selective* bibliography includes only some of the possible references, while a *complete* bibliography lists all the references available. Bibliographies with descriptive notes about each entry are called *annotated* bibliographies. The items in a bibliography may be grouped according to their form of publication. For example, books may be listed in one group and periodicals in a second group. Within each group, the items are arranged in alphabetical order.

Table 2.2 Sample Works Cited List (MLA Style)

Works Cited

Borzekowski, Dina L., and Thomas N. Robinson. "The 30-Second Effect: An Experiment Revealing the Impact of Television Commercials on Food Preferences of Preschoolers." <u>Journal of the American Dietetic Association</u> 101.1 (2001): 42-46.

Bryant, Jennings, and Daniel R. Anderson, eds. <u>Children's Understanding of TV</u>. New York: Academic, 1982.

Chan, Kara. "Children's Perceived Truthfulness of Television Advertising and Parental Influence: A Hong Kong Study." <u>Advances in Consumer Research</u> 28 (2001): 207-212.

Table 2.2 **Sample Works Cited List (MLA Style)** *(continued)*

Works Cited (continued)

Children's Television Act of 1990. Pub. L. 101-437. 17 Oct. 1990. Stat.
    104.996.

Coon, James T. Rev. of <u>Harvesting Minds: How TV Commercials Control Kids</u>, by
    Roy F. Fox. <u>American Communication Journal</u> 4.3 (2001). 23 Jan. 2003
    <http://acjournal.org/holdings/vol4/iss3/reviews/coon.htm>.

Dorr, Aimée. <u>Television and Children: A Special Medium for a Special Audience</u>.
    Sage Commtext Series 14. Beverly Hills: Sage, 1986.

Fox, Roy F. <u>Harvesting Minds: How TV Commercials Control Kids</u>. Foreword George
    Gerbner. Westport, CT: Praeger, 1996.

Freeman, Michael. "Kids Back to Saturday AM TV in a Big Way." <u>Electronic Media</u>
    23 Sept. 2002: 2+. <u>ABI/INFORM Global</u>. ProQuest Direct. Louisiana State U.
    20 January 2003 <http:/http://www.umi.com/proquest/>.

Haefner, Margaret J. "Ethical Problems of Advertising to Children." <u>Journal of
    Mass Media Ethics</u> 6.2 (1991) 83-92.

Kunkel, Dale. "Children and Television Advertising." <u>The Handbook of Children
    and Media</u>. Ed. Dorothy G. and Jerome L. Singer. Thousand Oaks, CA: Sage,
    2000. 375-394.

---. "Children's Television Advertising in the Multichannel Environment."
    <u>Journal of Communication</u> 42.3 (1992): 134-152.

Moore, Elizabeth S., and Richard J. Lutz. "Children, Advertising, and Product
    Experiences: A Multimethod Inquiry." <u>Journal of Consumer Research</u> 27.1
    (2000):31-48. <u>InfoTrac General Reference Center Gold</u>. Gale Group
    Databases. Louisiana State U. 20 Jan. 2003 <http://www.galegroup.com/>.

"Parents Must Help Filter Out Marketing, Violent Media." <u>Clinical Psychiatry
    News</u> Sept. 2001: 25. 23 Jan. 2003 <http://www2.eclinicalpsychiatrynews.com/
    scripts/om.dll/serve>.

Pine, Karen J. and Avril Nash. "Dear Santa: The Effects of Television
    Advertising on Young Children." <u>International Journal of Behavioral
    Development</u> 26 (2002): 529-539.

Prevention Institute for the Center for Health Improvement (CHI). <u>Nutrition
    Policy Profiles: Restricting Television Advertising to Children</u> n.d. 20
    Jan. 2003 <http://www.preventioninstitute.org/CHI_food_advertising.html>.

Rowan, David. "Hard Sell, Soft Targets." <u>Times (London)</u> 18 Oct. 2002: 2, 6.
    <u>LexisNexis Academic</u>. Louisiana State U. 21 January 2003 <http://
    www.lexisnexis.com/academic/universe/academic/>.

Signorielli, Nancy, and Jessica Staples. "Television and Children's
    Conceptions of Nutrition." <u>Health Communication</u> 9.4 (1997): 289-302.

Stewart, David W., and Scott Ward. "Media Effects on Advertising." <u>Media
    Effects: Advances in Theory and Research</u>. Ed. Jennings Bryant, and Dolf
    Zillmann. Hillsdale, NJ: Erlbaum, 1994. 315-364.

Tseng, Eliana Shiao. <u>Content Analysis of Children's Television</u>. Fall 2001.
    U. Texas at Austin. 20 January 2003 <http://www.ciadvertising.org/student_
    account/fall_01/adv392/estseng/ContentAnalysis/ContentAnalysis.
    html#introduction>.

United States. Congress. House. Committee on Energy and Commerce. Subcommittee
    on Telecommunications and Finance. Children's Television: Hearing . . .
    103rd Cong., 1st sess. Serial no. 103-27. Washington: G.P.O, 1993.

Table 2.3 Sample References List

Note: APA recommends using double-spaced lines within entries. Because of space limitations here, the entries are single spaced.

References

Borzekowski, D. L., & Robinson, T. N. (2001). The 30-second effect: An experiment revealing the impact of television commercials on food preferences of preschoolers. *Journal of the American Dietetic Association, 101*(1), 42–46.

Bryant, J., & Anderson, D. R. (Eds.). (1982). *Children's understanding of TV.* New York: Academic Press.

Chan, K. (2001). Children's perceived truthfulness of television advertising and parental influence. *Advances in Consumer Research, 28,* 207–212.

Children's Television Act of 1990, Pub. L. No. 101-437, 104 Stat. 996 (1990).

Coon, J. T. (2001). [Review of the book *Harvesting minds: How TV commercials control kids*]. *American Communication Journal, 4*(3). Retrieved January 23, 2003, from http://acjournal.org/holdings/vol4/iss3/reviews/coon.htm

Dorr, A. (1986). *Television and children: A special medium for a special audience* (Sage Commtext Series No. 14). Beverly Hills, CA: Sage.

Fox, R. F. (Author), & Gerbner, G. (Foreword). (1996). *Harvesting minds: How TV commercials control kids.* Westport, CT: Praeger.

Freeman, M. (2002, September 23). Kids back to Saturday a.m. TV in a big way. *Electronic Media.* Retrieved January 20, 2003, from ABI/INFORM Global: http://www.umi.com/proquest/

Haefner, M. J. (1991). Ethical problems of advertising to children. *Journal of Mass Media Ethics, 6*(2), 83–92.

Kunkel, D. (1992). Children's television advertising in the multichannel environment. *Journal of Communication, 42*(3), 134–152.

Kunkel, D. (2000). Children and television advertising. In D. G. Singer & J. L. Singer (Vol. Eds.), *The handbook of children and media* (pp. 375–394). Thousand Oaks, CA: Sage.

Moore, E. S., & Lutz, R. J. (2000). Children, advertising, and product experiences: A multimethod inquiry [Electronic Version]. *Journal of Consumer Research, 27*(1), 31–48.

Parents must help filter out marketing, violent media. (2001, September). *Clinical Psychiatry News, 29* (9). Retrieved January 23, 2003, from http://www2.eclinicalpsychiatrynews.com/scripts/om.dll/serve

Pine, K. J., & Nash, A. (2002). Dear Santa: The effects of television advertising on young children. *International Journal of Behavioral Development, 26,* 529–539.

Prevention Institute for the Center for Health Improvement (CHI). (n.d.). *Nutrition policy profiles: Restricting television advertising to children.* Retrieved January 20, 2003, from http://www.preventioninstitute.org/CHI_food_advertising.html

Rowan, D. (2002, October 18). Hard sell, soft targets [Electronic Version]. *Times (London),* p. 2 c. 6.

Signorielli, N., & Staples, J. (1997). Television and children's conceptions of nutrition. *Health Communication, 9*(4), 289–302.

Stewart, D. W., & Ward, S. (1994). Media effects on advertising. In J. Bryant & D. Zillmann (Eds.), *Media effects: advances in theory and research* (pp. 315–364). Hillsdale, NJ: Erlbaum.

Tseng, E. S. (2001, Fall). *Content analysis of children's television.* Retrieved January 20, 2003, from U. Texas at Austin: http://www.ciadvertising.org/student_account/fall_01/adv392/estseng/ContentAnalysis/ContentAnalysis.html#introduction

United States. Congress. House. Committee on Energy and Commerce. Subcommittee on Telecommunications and Finance. (1993). *Children's television: hearing before the Subcommittee on Telecommunications and Finance of the Committee on Energy and Commerce, House of Representatives, One Hundred Third Congress, first session, March 10, 1993.* (Serial 103-27). Washington, D.C.: Government Printing Office.

Exercise 2.2

Instructor: _____ Course/Section: _____

Name: _____

Date: _____ Points: _____

Accessing Information: General to Specific

The purpose of this exercise is to help you discover strategies for narrowing or broadening a topic. Practice arranging the following topics by placing them in numbered order from 1 to 4, with 1 being the most general and 4 being the most specific.

1. agriculture
   boll weevil
   crops
   pesticides

   ① Agricultural
   ② crops
   ③ pesticides

2. history
   elections
   political history
   election of 2000

3. planets
   astronomy
   robotic exploration
   Mars dust particles

4. Vikings
   North America
   exploration
   Lief Eriksson

Each of the terms below is very specific. For each, use two other terms that are general.

5. genetically altered corn

   bioengineering

6. U.S. Naval Academy cheating scandal of 1994

   naval academy scandal
   academic cheating

Each of the terms below is very broad. For each, write two terms that would lead to a more narrow aspect of the topic.

7. higher education

8. crime

Instructor: _____ Course/Section: _____

Name: _____

Date: _____ Points: _____

Documentation Exercise

Using the information provided below, prepare a list as though you were preparing a Works Cited or a References list. (Your instructor will assign one or the other styles to follow.) Use the examples in Appendix A as a guide.

lexus nexis

1. Type publication: Chapter in a book
   Title of Chapter: Balances of Power: The Strategic Dimensions of the Marshall Plan
   Author of chapter: Michael Hogan
   Inclusive pages: 75–98
   Book title: The Cold War and Defense
   Editors: Keith Neilson and Ronald G. Haycock
   Publisher: Praeger Publishers
   Place of publication: New York
   Publication date: 1990

   http://Citationmachine.net/

2. Type of publication: Book
   Title: We Now Know: Rethinking Cold War History
   Author: John Lewis Gaddis
   Publisher: Oxford University Press
   Place of publication: Oxford
   Publication date: 1997

3. Type publication: Online scholarly work
   Title: A Cold War Conundrum
   Sponsoring agency: History Staff, Center for the Study of Intelligence, Central Intelligence Agency
   Personal author: Benjamin B. Fischer
   Publication date: 1997
   Date retrieved: February 1, 2003
   Internet address: http://www.cia.gov/csi/monograph/coldwar/source.htm

4. Type publication: E-book
   Title: The Medical Implications of Nuclear War
   Corporate author: Institute of Medicine, National Academy of Sciences
   Editors: Fredric Solomon and Robert Q. Marston
   Publisher: National Academy Press
   Place of publication: Washington, D.C.
   Publication date: 1986
   Internet address: http://www.ulib.org/webRoot/Books/National_Academy_Press_Books/
      nuclear_war/nuclear.htm
   Date viewed: 20 January 2003

5. Type of publication: Newspaper article online
   Title of newspaper: Christian Science Monitor
   Title of article: Regime Change
   Author of article: Peter Ford
   Publication date: January 27, 2003
   Date viewed: 1 February 2003
   http://www.csmonitor.com/

6. Type of publication: Article in an encyclopedia
   Article title: Cold War
   Encyclopedia title: The Columbia Encyclopedia
   Edition: 6
   Publication year: 2000
   Page: 8891

7. Type of publication: Journal article from an online subscription service
   Title of article: In from the Cold: Relations between the United States and China and Russia
   Authors of article: Robert S. McNamara and James G. Blight
   Title of journal: World Policy Journal
   Publication date: Spring 2001
   Volume/issue: 18, 1
   Pages: 667–77
   Subscribing library: Louisiana State University
   Internet address: http://infotrac.galegroup.com/
   Date viewed: 30 January 2003

8. Type of article: Article from a scholarly journal
   Title of article: The Impact of the Korean War on the Cold War
   Author of article: Robert Jervis
   Title of journal: The Journal of Conflict Resolution
   Volume/issue: 24, 4.
   Publication date: December 1980
   Pages: 563–592 (Note: Pages are numbered continuously throughout the volume.)

9. Type of article: Signed article from a weekly magazine
   Title of article: Cold War Lab Applies Strengths to New Missions
   Author of article: Michael A. Dornheim
   Title of magazine: Aviation Week & Space Technology
   Publication date: July 22, 2002
   Volume/issue: 157, 4
   Pages: 149–152

10. Publication type: Book review—signed
    Author of the review: Vincent P. Tinerella
    Title of book being reviewed: Great Debates at the United Nations: An Encyclopedia of Fifty
       Key Issues, 1945–2000
    Title of journal: Reference & User Services Quarterly
    Volume/issue: 41, 3
    Page: 287
    Publication date: Spring 2002

Search Techniques: Electronic Sources

"I don't pretend we have all the answers. But the questions are certainly worth thinking about."

Arthur C. Clarke

Introduction

It has been said that access to information has never been so easy! Computer technology makes it possible to create, store, and retrieve information quickly and effectively. However, for the novice, the retrieval process can be daunting. We now have all types of information in electronic format: library catalogs, indexes and abstracts, and full-text books and journal articles. The information is available remotely from the Internet, or locally on CD-ROM or DVD. To compound the confusion, there is very little uniformity even among electronic sources that serve the same purpose, such as indexes and abstracts. Online catalogs, too, vary in the way searches are formulated and in the way that information is presented. The Internet offers a variety of search engines to help users locate information. The search commands in one source might be completely different from those in another; the way that the information appears on the screen in one electronic source may look altogether different on another screen, depending on the producer or the vendor. However, it is possible to acquire some basic search skills that will enable you to do research effectively, regardless of the source or type of electronic source.

This chapter will acquaint you with the "why's" and "how's" of searching various sources in electronic format. It outlines the steps in planning a search and shows some basic techniques for executing the steps. Chapter 4 focuses on understanding and interpreting information in library catalogs; Chapter 5 will give you greater insight into using search engines to get information on the Internet. Subsequent chapters will introduce you to various other information sources, much of which is available in electronic format. It is expected that the searching skills discussed here will be a springboard to use the myriad of available electronic information sources.

THE SEARCH STRATEGY

In order to search a particular topic it is necessary to execute a search strategy that consists of the following steps.

Steps to Execute a Search Strategy

1. **Analyze your topic.**

   Consider the appropriate disciplines or large subject areas for your topic.

   What aspect of the topic are you looking for?

   Under what discipline does it fall?

   What are some concepts related to the topic that might cross disciplines?

2. **Identify standardized subject headings.**

   Look in *LCSH (Library of Congress Subject Headings)*.

   Check a thesaurus of discipline or subject related indexes and abstracts.

   Look for a known item in the online catalog, such as an author in a field, and use the subject headings you locate.

3. **Identify keywords and terms that are not standardized subject headings.**

   What words or terms most nearly describe the subject you are searching?

   What are some synonyms?

4. **Combine subject headings or keywords to narrow or broaden your search.**

5. **Select the appropriate electronic source to use.**

   Search the library's online catalog.

   Look at the menu on the library's home page to see if indexes, abstracts, or full-text journals are available in electronic format.

   Look at the menu on the library's home page for guides to Internet sites.

   Check any print guides to bibliographic or full-text electronic sources.

   Ask a reference librarian.

6. **Execute the search by typing in the commands on the computer's keyboard.**

7. **Evaluate the search results for appropriateness.**

   The search results are sometimes called *hits*. If your search yields too many or too few hits, you might need to go back and modify it.

8. **Revise the search in light of your results.**

   Consult a thesaurus or index (available in many electronic sources).

   Narrow the search by combining search terms.

   Broaden the search if the results are too limited.

INFORMATION IN ELECTRONIC FORMAT

Information in electronic format refers to any information that is created or stored electronically—either on a hard drive, on a disk (floppy, CD-ROM, or DVD), or on magnetic tape—and accessed by a computer. The term *online* refers to information that is stored in a remote computer that is connected to the Internet and accessed locally. Information in electronic format is available on a wide variety of subjects in all disciplines—science, social sciences, and humanities. The format of these resources varies from bibliographic citations, full text, archival collections, to images. See Tables 3.1 and 3.2 for advantages and limitations of information in electronic format. These materials are collected and presented in *databases*. Understanding the structure of databases and search techniques is the key to achieving optimal results in any search for information stored in electronic format.

Databases

A *database* is a collection of data that is organized so that its contents can easily be searched, accessed, and edited. Databases are created and maintained by special software (known as a database management system) that stores and organizes data and provides a search mechanism for its retrieval.

Table 3.1 Advantages of Information in Electronic Format

☐ **Saves time.** It takes minutes or even seconds to search an entire database or several databases covering multiple years. To search the same indexes in paper copy might take hours or even longer, as each volume of the index would have to be searched separately.

☐ **More effective than searching a printed source.** It permits the searcher to link words and terms in a way that can never be done manually. Compare, for example, searching for a book in a card catalog. The search is limited to searching by the author's name, the title of the book, or the standardized subject heading. In an index to periodicals in paper format the access points are usually by author, title, and standardized subject heading. Information in electronic databases can be searched by keying in almost any element in the record, and "mixing and matching" keywords and terms.

☐ **More flexible than searching printed indexes and abstracts.** It is possible to search for words regardless of where they appear in the record. This is called *free-text searching* or *keyword searching*.

☐ **Possible to truncate or shorten terms.** All the variations of a term can be located.

☐ **Provides access to much more information than is available in the library.** Online databases through *EBSCOhost*, *LexisNexis Academic*, or *INFOTrac* provide access to hundreds of journals; library networks provide access to the catalogs of other libraries in the network; the Internet makes available an endless amount and array of information.

☐ **Information is usually more up-to-date.** In an online catalog, records can be entered for materials as soon as they are ordered. Databases are updated frequently, sometimes daily. For example, in *LexisNexis Academic*, a full-text database that includes hundreds of newspapers, information is available almost as soon as it is produced.

☐ **Possible to print material.** It is convenient and easy to print information retrieved as a result of a search in an electronic format.

☐ **Not always necessary to come to the library to find information.** Searching and retrieving information can be done from computers both inside and beyond the library—from offices, dormitories, and homes.

Table 3.2 Limitations of Information in Electronic Format

☐ **Sometimes the "logic" in electronic searching does not work.** For example, a search for articles on apricots in a database retrieved articles on the fruit as well as on a computer named "Apricot." This kind of result is called a "false hit'" or "false drop." Free-text searching is likely to yield more false drops than searching by controlled vocabulary. Full-text databases are more likely to yield false hits than are bibliographic databases.

☐ **Many databases do not include older information.** Most of the Wilson databases (see Chapter 8) go back to 1983 for bibliographic information and even more recent for full-text articles. In many databases, the information does not go beyond the last five to ten years. For example, you could use a database for current studies showing the effects of advertising on consumer preferences, but to find articles about consumer preference in the 1950s, you should consult a printed index from that period.

☐ **Information in electronic sources lacks standardization.** The screens of an online catalog in one library may not look at all like those in another library. This is because the software that runs the online system is different. Some libraries use SIRSI software; others use DRA (Data Research Associates), Innovative Interfaces, or some other system from a commercial vendor. A number of academic libraries have developed their own systems. CD-ROM and online databases also vary greatly in the way they are searched. For example, *Readers' Guide to Periodical Literature,* available online from Ovid, does not use the same search commands as the same database available directly from the H.W. Wilson Company, its producer.

☐ **Not all of a library's electronic sources are available outside the library.** Some databases, especially those in CD-ROM or DVD formats, are available only in the library.

Types of Databases

Databases include online catalogs, information on the Internet, bibliographic indexes and abstracts, and the full text of works such as books, periodical articles, plays, poems, essays, reports, and transcripts.

☐ A library's *online catalog* lists the library's books, periodical titles, and other materials. For most of us, the online catalog is probably our first introduction to information in electronic format. Electronic library catalogs have been commonplace in libraries since the mid-1980s. A discussion of online catalogs is found in Chapter 4.

☐ The *Internet* is a network that connects computers of all types throughout the world, enabling users to communicate, find information, transfer data and program files, and access remote catalogs and databases. Information available through the Internet is made accessible through the Web (World Wide Web). It allows users to read texts as well as to see images and hear sounds. This chapter introduces you to the basics needed to understand and use search engines effectively. Chapter 5 elaborates on Internet resources and the World Wide Web, including the use of specific Internet search engines.

☐ *Bibliographic databases* provide citations or references to materials such as periodical articles, books, government reports, statistics, patents, research reports, conference proceedings, and dissertations. They can be compared to printed catalogs, indexes and abstracts.

☐ *Full-text databases* include the complete text of many different sources such as books, newspapers, periodicals, legislation, court cases, encyclopedias, research reports, and letters.

☐ *Aggregated databases* are collections of different databases containing both bibliographic and full-text records and covering many different subjects. *EBSCOhost* and *InfoTrac* are treated as aggregated databases. Chapter 8 discusses specific periodical databases, including aggregated databases.

SEARCH BASICS

To make use of information in electronic format, you need to understand a basic concept: some search systems search only certain parts of a database (such as author or title) while others search the entire contents (full-text searching). Knowing this affects not only the way you search but also your results. The other factor which impacts your search results is understanding an elementary fact about database structure: that all databases share common elements. Although different databases may look different when you see them on a computer screen, there are common elements that allow users to search and retrieve information. The most basic of these elements is *field* structure (how the data are arranged). Once you become familiar with these concepts, the mechanics of searching will become much clearer to you.

Field Searching

As with access tools in paper format, electronic records in a database are organized in a systematic way. The individual entries are called *records*. Each record has different data elements, or *fields*, each of which is labeled. Field searching is a powerful tool that allows you to restrict your searches to particular fields. Field searching enables more precise searching since the fields serve as access points to the particular information you are seeking. Searches for authors search only the author fields; title searches limit the search to the title fields.

**THE MOST COMMONLY SEARCHED FIELDS
IN AN ONLINE CATALOG ARE:**

AUTHOR

TITLE

EDITION

PUBLISHER

DATE

PHYSICAL DESCRIPTION

NOTES

SUBJECTS

**TYPICAL FIELDS IN A BIBLIOGRAPHICAL RECORD
IN A PERIODICAL DATABASE ARE:**

ACCESSION NUMBER

TITLE OF ARTICLE

AUTHOR OF ARTICLE

AUTHOR'S INSTITUTIONAL AFFILIATION

JOURNAL TITLE

INTERNATIONAL STANDARD SERIAL NUMBER (ISSN)

LANGUAGE OF THE ARTICLE

PUBLICATION YEAR

SUBJECT DESCRIPTORS OR TERMS

INTERNET PAGES, ALSO, ARE DIVIDED INTO SEARCHABLE FIELDS. THE MOST COMMON ARE:

TITLE

DOMAIN

HOST (OR SITE)

URL

LINK

IMAGE

TEXT

Full-Text Searching

With full-text searching, you can search every word or phrase in a document as opposed to searching in specific fields. This can be very effective where it is possible to search for narrow topics that might not be covered elsewhere. For example, the full text of a newspaper article might provide valuable information on events and persons that might not be mentioned in a database that only has citations to the articles but not the full text. It is possible to search the full text of electronic books (e-books) to find terms and concepts that might never appear in a printed index.

When searching you need to be wary of *false hits*, but especially in full-text searching. False hits are search results which match your search terms, but have nothing to do with the information you are seeking. For example, the word "orange" will bring up records relating to Agent Orange, the cities named Orange, the color orange, and the fruit. Many words are spelled similarly but have different meanings; for example, "desert" means a barren land, but it also can mean to abandon.

Commands

While the computer is a powerful information storage and retrieval tool, it is also a very exacting one. To retrieve information, you need to select the appropriate electronic source and then type in a search request or a *command*. A search engine then scans the source looking for an exact match of the search statement.

Although some Internet search engines recognize natural language, many online catalogs and databases do not. If the search query is "find the standard of living among people of Appalachia during the Great Depression," the search is not likely to yield anything because the computer is searching for an exact match of that statement. Some search engines on the Web allow natural language searching, but even these search only for the keywords in the statement. Most of the search engines in use today are designed in such a way as to permit searching on certain access points, to combine terms, and to limit terms.

Example

For books *by* Hemingway	Search in the author field
For books *about* Hemingway	Search in the subject fields
For books *by* and *about* Hemingway	Search all the fields

Access Points

The key to access in any electronic source is identifying the concepts and terms you wish to search and applying basic search skills to achieve the desired results.

truncating - using first part of a word

FOUR BASIC WAYS TO SEARCH AN ELECTRONIC SOURCE

- by author name
- by title of the work
- by subject of the work
- by words or keywords in the record

An explanation of each of these four methods of electronic searches follows, with examples of each. Although the commands might vary slightly, the techniques can be applied to online catalogs, online indexes and abstracts, and Internet search engines. With online catalogs and databases, you select the field or type of search from a template or pull-down menu. You then type the word or phrase in the form provided.

Author Search

An author search is restricted to searching only the author field. It necessarily involves a known element—either an author's name or part of the author's name. Some electronic sources allow you to truncate or shorten the author's name if you do not know the complete first name or correct spelling.

Example

Type [**author's last name or a portion of the last name**]

solzhenitayn or **solzhen** (for Solzhenitsyn)	
james hen	(For more common names, include at least some of the first name.)
oneill eugene	(Omit accent marks and all other punctuation in the author's name.)
unesco	(An organization as author, also called a *corporate author.*)

Title Search

A title search is also a search for a known element—you know the title of a work or enough of the title to make it distinctive. To retrieve a title you must key in the title exactly as it appears in the title field (except that initial articles are usually omitted). If the first part of a title is sufficiently distinctive, it is not necessary to type in the full title. You only need to put in the first three or four words. In some online catalogs it is not necessary to type in the entire last word.

Example

Type [**title or as much of the title of which you are certain**]

red badge of cour	(*Red Badge of Courage:* You need not include the entire title.)
man for all seasons	(*A Man for All Seasons:* Generally, omit initial articles "a," "an," "the," and foreign equivalents. Some systems accept articles.)
red white black	(*Red, White, and Black:* Omit all punctuation in the title.)
2 minutes to noon	(Write numbers in numeric form or spelled out, depending on how they appear in the original work.)
part time teacher	(Do not use hyphens; try as separate words or one word.)

Subject Search

Subject searching is usually recommended because it gives a more precise search than keyword searching. A subject search refers to using standardized subjects headings to search a record. The subject headings used in online catalogs and many other databases are established by the Library of Congress and are listed in a multivolume publication, the *Library of Congress List of Subject Headings* (*LCSH*) (see Figure 3.1). It gives alternative terms (refers from a term that is not used to one that is used), related terms, and terms used to broaden or narrow a search. The National Library of Medicine establishes headings that are appropriate for use in the medical sciences. In many periodical databases, the subject headings, or *descriptors* as they are sometimes called, are listed in a *thesaurus* or an index.

Example

Type [**standardized subject heading**]
    African American scientists

The mistake most people make with subject searching is that they think they can type in any word in the subject field and the search engine will pull up items on that subject. Although this does sometimes work, it is due more to chance than anything else. In subject searching, the terms must be keyed in exactly as they appear in the subject field(s). This may or may not be the terms you would use to describe the subject.

Example

If you want books on:	You search under:
gun collecting	**firearms--collecting**
streetcars	**cable cars (streetcars)**
vitamin B3	**nicotinamide**
themes of folktales	**folklore--classification**

So how do you know what subject heading to use for your topic? When searching the online catalog, you can look in the *Library of Congress Subject Headings*. In doing a search in a periodical database, you should consult the thesaurus or index to determine appropriate terminology to use. If you locate a record that is on target for your topic, you should check the record for additional subject headings.

Keyword Search

Keyword searching is the term used to refer to searching by words or phrases in any of the fields in a record.

Guidelines

Use keyword searching when:

☐ you are unsure about the order or spelling of all words in the title;

☐ you don't know the author's name;

☐ you don't know the precise subject heading used;

☐ you want to link terms from different parts of a record such as an author's name with a word from a title;

☐ you want to combine terms to narrow a topic or to limit a topic.

Sex discrimination (May Subd Geog)
  UF Discrimination, Sexual
      Gender discrimination
      Sexual discrimination
  BT Discrimination
      Sexism
  NT Radical therapy
      Sex discrimination against men
      Sex discrimination against women
      Sex discrimination in employment
      Sex of children, Parental preferences for
--Law and legislation (May Subd Geog)
Sex discrimination against men
(May Subd Geog)
  UF Discrimination against men
      Men, Discrimination against
  BT Sex discrimination
Sex discrimination against women
(May Subd Geog)
  UF Discrimination against women
      Subordination of women
      Women, Discrimination against
  BT Feminism
      Sex discrimination
      Women's rights
  NT Purdah
--Law and legislation (May Subd Geog)

Sex discrimination in consumer credit
(May Subd Geog)
Here are entered works on the difficulties
encountered in obtaining consumer credit
due to sex discrimination.
  BT Consumer credit
--Law and Legislation (May Subd Geog)
Sex discrimination in criminal justice
administration (May Subd Geog)
  BT Criminal justice, Administration of
      Discrimination in criminal justice
      administration
Sex discrimination in education
(May Subd Geog) [LC212.8-LC212.83]
  UF Education, Sex discrimination in
  BT Discrimination in education
  NT Sex discrimination in medical education
Sex discrimination in employment
(May Subd Geog) [HD6060-HD6060.5]
  BT Discrimination in employment
      Sex discrimination
  RT Sex role in the work environment
      Sexual division of labor
      Women--Employment

Figure 3.1 Library of Congress Subject Headings, 1995, p. 1710.

In a keyword search, the search engine looks at all the records and retrieves those that contain the word or phrase that you specify anywhere in the record. This is very important! If you type in the word "guns" in the online catalog, you are not only going to get books on guns, but also books written by Walter Guns, a book titled *Guns or Butter* about Lyndon Johnson, or any other item that has the word "guns" somewhere in its record. You can remedy this by specifying a particular field to search.

A keyword search is usually the only search that allows you to:

☐ truncate or shorten a search term;

☐ use Boolean and positional operators to combine search terms;

☐ use advance searching such as limiting a search to specific fields; or

☐ qualify a search according to certain specifications.

Keyword searching allows for flexibility in searching that you do not have with author, title, or subject searches. Below are outlined some of the techniques used in keyword searching.

Truncating Search Terms

In keyword searching it is possible to shorten (truncate) a term by using a character such as a question mark (?) or, in some online catalogs and databases, an asterisk (*). This allows you to retrieve singular or plural forms or different spellings of a word or name in a single search. Other terms for truncation are "wildcard" searching and "stemming."

Avoid over-truncating search terms. Do not enter **const?** if you're searching for the term "constitution" as it will pull up too many terms.

Boolean Searching

An effective way to search for information in a database is to combine terms together in a logical process using Boolean operators. The process, which originated with British mathematician George Boole in the nineteenth century, is based on the logical relationship among search terms. In Boolean searching terms are connected together by a Boolean operator. The three Boolean operators are the words:

- ☐ AND
- ☐ OR
- ☐ NOT

In some databases, the symbols + (plus), – (minus), and / (slash) are used in place of the words AND, OR, NOT respectively. A few search engines, most notably Google, use a space between words to imply a Boolean AND.

Boolean Operators

Boolean operators are words used to make a logical search query. They enable you to broaden or narrow your search or link terms. Most databases use the basic Boolean operators: **and**, **or**, and **not**. When using any online catalog or database you should verify whether or not Boolean operators are used. Figure 3.2 shows examples of Boolean operators.

☐ **AND** searches for occurrences of all of the search terms in a single record.

☐ **OR** searches for records that contain any of the terms.

☐ **NOT** searches for records that contain the first term but not the second term.

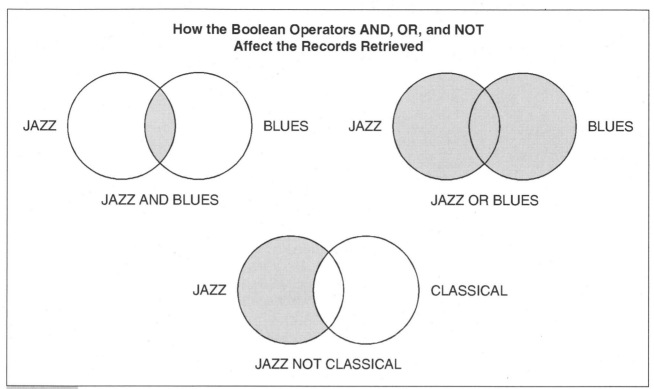

Figure 3.2 Example of Boolean operators.

Nested Searches

Nesting is used with Boolean operators to specify the order of the search. With nesting, parentheses are placed around words to make a single search statement.

Example

(fraud or evasion) and income tax

(Finds all records that have **fraud** and **income tax** and all those that have **evasion** and **income tax**.)

An un-nested search:

fraud or evasion and income tax

(Finds all the records that have **fraud** (with or without income tax) and all those that have **evasion** and **income tax** in the same record.)

Proximity Searching

Proximity searching allows you to refine a search by specifying where the search terms should be in relation to each other. This is done with the use of positional (or proximity) operators. Positional operators include: **adj**, **foll**, **near**, **with**. There are other operators depending on the particular database. The availability and use of positional operators vary from database to database. You should also be aware that positional operators are the *default* in some search engines. *Default operators* are the operators the system automatically places between search terms. These are transparent to the searcher. Not knowing the default operator can skew your search results.

ultraviolet radiation [where **adjacency** is the default operator]
(Searches all occurrences of the two words together and in that order.)

ultraviolet radiation [where **AND** is the default operator]
(Searches occurrences of the two words anywhere in the record.)

ultraviolet radiation [where **OR** is the default operator]
(Searches occurrences of either word in the record.)

The following examples illustrate typical applications of positional operators. Keep in mind that these will not apply to all databases.

☐ **ADJ** (adjacent) searches for terms that you want to occur next to one another. In some databases **ADJ** is the default operator, so there is no need to type it in. However, this is not always the case, so you need to be aware of the way positional operators are treated in the database you are searching. In many Internet search engines, the default connector is an implied AND between the words. These databases usually require quotation marks around the words that need to be next to each other. Some search engines have an option to check "this exact phrase" in an advanced search menu.

Example

liberal democrat [where adjacency is the default]
OR
liberal **adj** democrat
OR
"liberal democrat"
(Finds all the records with **liberal democrat** together in that order.)

☐ ADJ# finds terms in the order typed within a specified number of words of each other.

Example

conservative **adj3** politics
(Finds records that contain the word "conservative" within three words of the word "politics.")

☐ **FOLL** (meaning followed by) is used in some databases instead of **ADJ**.

Example

arms **foll** race
(Finds all the records that have **arms race** in that order.)

Use lowercase

☐ **NEAR** specifies that terms must be **near** one another in the record. Usually the terms can appear in any order. Some databases use ten as the default; others let you specify the number.

> ### EXAMPLE
>
> migrants **near** florida
> (Searches for the word **migrants** near the word **Florida**.)

☐ **WITH** specifies that terms are in proximity with each other. Terms can appear in any order. The **With** operator is usually used in online catalogs to search for records that contain the search terms, in any order, but in the same field.

> ### EXAMPLE
>
> tobacco **with** harvesting
> (Searches for records that contain the term **tobacco** close to the term **harvesting**.)

Limiting a Search

If your search results in too many hits or if you know beforehand that you want to apply certain limitations to your search, you can refine your search by using the limiting options available in most databases. These limiting features vary by database but may include the following:

☐ language

☐ publication date (limit to items before, after, or on a certain date)

☐ publication type (review article, case study, book review, research report)

☐ format (journal article, book, dissertation, music, map, image, computer file)

☐ articles with text (in aggregated database)

☐ refereed articles (in periodical databases)

☐ domain (in Internet search engines)

☐ file type (PDF, PostScript, Microsoft Office formats—in Internet search engines)

Most databases have features which allow you to search by keywords in specific fields. For example, if you recall that there is an article on the Surma tribe in Africa that was published in *National Geographic* but you do not recall the date, you can narrow your search to the article title field and the source (or journal) fields to locate it.

SEARCH TIPS

The preceding explanation and examples have shown you how to formulate and execute a basic online search. While there appears to be no standardization among online catalogs, bibliographic and full-text databases, and Internet search engines, there are a great number of search features that are common in most: use of Boolean logic, truncation, and the ability to limit a search. Although databases differ in the way search terms are formulated, the information you learn here should help you understand how computers translate your search request into retrieval of information. Below are a few tips to guide you into becoming a more proficient searcher.

TIPS

☐ **BE PRECISE**

If you are looking for information on a specific case involving the misdeeds by the chief executives of a particular corporation, do not search for "corporations"; rather search for the name of the company you are researching. Add Boolean operators and positional operators to refine your search. Limit the search to dates that include the time period involved in your research.

☐ **USE THE HELP MENU**

Determine which search features and options are available and how to use them. Find out if Boolean operators are used and, if so, whether or not AND, OR, NOT are spelled out, implied, or indicated by the symbols—plus, minus, slash.

☐ **AVOID THE USE OF STOPWORDS IN YOUR SEARCH STATEMENT**

Some words and abbreviations (called *stopwords*) appear so frequently in records that a keyword search system does not search for them. Some common stopwords are: **a, an, and, by, for, from, in, not, of, or, same, the, to**, and **with**. Avoid the use of all stopwords when constructing your keyword search statement. **AND, NOT, OR, WITH**, and **SAME** may be used only as Boolean or positional operators in a search.

☐ **USE THE ADVANCED SEARCH FEATURE TO FORMULATE YOUR SEARCHES**

Most search engines and directories offer both **basic** and **advanced** search options. You can refine your search by using the advanced option which provides for field searching and limiting capabilities.

☐ **AVOID SPELLING ERRORS**

The search engine is very precise. It searches for terms exactly as you type them. If you misspell a word, the computer will look for a match of the misspelled word. Thus you will not get any hits unless the word is also misspelled in the database. One major exception is the Google search engine which tries to interpret what you mean and will offer alternative search words.

Exercise 3.1

Search Techniques

Instructor: _____ Course/Section: _____

Name: _____

Date: _____ Points: _____

Review Questions

1. What is meant by the term "information in electronic format"?

2. Define database as it is used in this chapter.

3. What is the difference between a bibliographic database and a full-text database?

4. Name four advantages of using an electronic database.

   a.

   b.

   c.

   d.

5. Name three limitations of information in electronic databases.

   a.

   b.

   c.

6. Explain what is meant by "records" as applied to an electronic source.

7. What are "fields" in electronic records?

61

8. Name four basic ways to search for information in an electronic source.

   a.

   b.

   c.

   d.

9. Explain the difference between a subject search and a keyword search.

10. What is meant by the term "truncating" as applied to searching?

11. Name the three Boolean operators and define each.

   a.

   b.

   c.

12. What is meant by the term "nesting" as applied to searching an online database?

13. What are "positional operators"?

   Name three positional operators.

   a.

   b.

   c.

14. What is meant by the term "limiting a search"?

15. Name three ways you can limit a search.

   a.

   b.

   c.

Exercise 3.2

Instructor: _____ Course/Section: _____

Name: _____

Date: _____ Points: _____

Electronic Searching

In the hypothetical problems below state the command you would use to execute the search.

Use: a=for author searches
    t=for title searches
    s= or subject searches
    k=for keyword search
    * to truncate

For Questions 1–6 use Boolean or positional operators to state your commands:

Example

Find all the information on using animals in experimentation
Command:

    k=animal and experimentation

Find all the records with information on importing perfume from France
Command:

    k=perfume and import? and France

1. Find any records dealing with business ethics in the United States.
Command:

2. Find all the records that have information on business and all the records that have information on ethics.
Command:

3. Find the records that have information on ethics, but eliminate those dealing with business.
Command:

4. Find all the records where *country* appears within five words of music.
   Command:

Assume that you are using the online catalog in your library for problems 5–11.

Use the command: t=for a title search
                  a=for an author search
                  s=for a subject search
                  k=for a keyword search

5. Find the periodical: *The Economist.*
   Command:

6. Find all the works on the subject of *chemical warfare.*
   Command:

7. Find all the books by *Shirley Ann Grau.*
   Command:

8. Find all the books about *Shirley Ann Grau.*
   Command:

9. Find all books that have the word *cloning* in the record.
   Command:

10. Find all books with *cloning* as the established subject.
    Command:

11. Find a book dealing with *wealth* by an author whose last name is *Conniff.*
    Command:

Library Catalogs

"A place for everything, and everything in its place."

Samuel Smiles: Thrift V.

Introduction

A library catalog is a listing of all the items available in a particular library—whether in tangible form (printed books, periodicals, CD-ROMs, etc.) or in Web-based form. Each record in a library catalog describes a particular item (book, microform, video, map, audio tape, CD-ROM, DVD, or Internet site), and gives its location in the library or its address (URL) on the Internet. In order to provide access to its physical collections, libraries organize materials by classifying them and assigning specific location numbers or call numbers. In this way materials on similar subjects are grouped together on the shelves. This rationale has resulted in the development of uniform classification systems that are used by libraries throughout the world. Items available on the Internet are usually not given classification numbers; rather they are assigned subject headings and can be accessed by any of the searchable fields in the catalog—author, title, subject—or by keyword. This chapter will discuss some of the important things you need to know about using the catalog to find information.

CLASSIFICATION SYSTEMS

The purpose of any classification system is to bring together comparable materials in a logical arrangement so they can be found easily. This also allows library patrons to browse the shelves in a given subject classification number or letter in order to find materials on that subject grouped together. In most libraries, books are classified and shelved in stack areas, while other materials may be grouped according to format, such as books, microforms, videos, maps, audio tapes, CD-ROMs, or DVDs. These materials are usually assigned accession numbers that identify location, rather than numbers based on classification.

The two most commonly used classification systems in American libraries are the Dewey Decimal Classification System—commonly called Dewey or DC—and the Library of Congress Classification System—referred to as LC (see Figure 4.1). Public libraries and small college libraries tend to use the Dewey system while larger colleges and universities use the Library of Congress system.

Both classification systems start with a general classification and then proceed to a more specific classification. The main differences between the two are:

☐ Dewey begins with numbers while LC begins with letters.

☐ Dewey has ten major classes; LC has 21.

☐ LC allows more room for expansion than Dewey. This is important as new subjects are constantly being added to the fields of knowledge. A comparison of the two systems can be seen in Figure 4.2. Note that Dewey classifies all "engineering" in 620, while LC subdivides it into several branches, "T Technology."

The Library of Congress system is used in large libraries because its broader base allows room for expansion as new subjects are added to the fields of knowledge.

Materials covering one particular subject can be classified easily under that subject. However, when the item deals with more than one subject, it is classified under the largest subject covered or under what the catalogers feel is the most important subject. Subjects covered in the book that are not reflected in the call number selected by the cataloger are brought out by means of *subject headings*.

Example

Affirmative Action for Women: A Practical Guide
Classified : HD 6058 —the LC Classification number for:
Women—Employment—United States
It has one additional subject heading:
Sex discrimination in employment—United States

Libraries with extensive collections of materials published by the United States Government often use the *Superintendent of Documents* or *SuDocs* System to classify the publications. The system was devised by the Government Printing Office to organize the thousands of publications it issues annually.

In addition to the three major systems discussed previously, libraries may also use other systems for classifying smaller special collections such as state documents, United Nations documents, or archives.

It is not necessary to learn all the details of the classification systems in order to use the library effectively, but you do need to be able to recognize which classification systems are used in your library and to understand the basic principles of each.

MAJOR LIBRARY CLASSIFICATION SYSTEMS

DEWEY DECIMAL (DC)		LIBRARY OF CONGRESS (LC)		SUPERINTENDENT OF DOCUMENTS (SuDocs)		UNITED NATIONS SYMBOLS (UN)	
000	Generalities	A	General Works	A	Agriculture	A/	General Assembly
100	Philosophy/Psychology	B	Philosophy/Psychology/Religion	AE	Archives/Records		
200	Religion					E/	Economic & Social Council
		C	History—General	C	Commerce		
300	Social Sciences	D	History—World	C.3	Census	S/	Security Council
400	Language	E	American History	D	Defense		
		F	Local American History	E	Energy	T/	Trusteeship Council
500	Natural Science/	G	Geography/Anthropology/Sports	ED	Education		
	Mathematics			EP	Environmental Protection	ST/	Secretariat
		H	Social Sciences	FR	Federal Reserve		
600	Technology	HA	Statistics	GS	General Administration	Other:	
700	The Arts	HM	Sociology	HE	Health & Human Services		
				HH	Housing & Urban Development	CCPR/	Human Rights Committee
800	Literature/Rhetoric	J	Political Science	I	Interior		
900	Geography/History	K	Law	I19	US Geological Survey	DP/	UN Development Program
		L	Education	J	Justice		
		M	Music	JU	Judiciary		
		N	Fine Arts				
				L	Labor		
		P	Language/Literature	LC	Library of Congress		
		PR	English/Literature				
		PS	American Literature	NAS	National Aeronautics/Space		
				PR	President's Office		
		Q	Science				
		R	Medicine	S	State Department		
		S	Agriculture	SI	Smithsonian Institution		
		T	Technology				
		U	Military Science	T	Treasury		
		V	Naval Science	T22	Internal Revenue		
		Z	Bibliography/Library Science	TD	Transportation		
				VA	Veterans Administration		
				Y	Congress		
				Y4	Congressional Hearings		

Figure 4.1 Comparison of major library classification systems.

DEWEY DECIMAL CLASSIFICATION SYSTEM

000 GENERALITIES
010 Bibliographies & catalogs
020 Library & information sciences
030 General encyclopedic works
040 Unassigned
050 General serials & their indexes
060 General organizations & museology
070 News media, journalism, publishing
080 General collections
090 Manuscripts & rare books

100 PHILOSOPHY & PSYCHOLOGY
110 Metaphysics
120 Epistemology, causation, humankind
130 Paranormal phenomena
140 Specific philosophical schools
150 Psychology
160 Logic
170 Ethics (moral philosophy)
180 Ancient, medieval, Oriental philosophy
190 Modern Western philosophy

200 RELIGION
210 Natural theology
220 Bible
230 Christian Theology
240 Christian moral and devotional theology
250 Christian orders & local churches
260 Christian social theology
270 Christian church history
280 Christian denominations & sects
290 Other and comparative religions

300 SOCIAL SCIENCES
310 General statistics
320 Political science
330 Economics
340 Law
350 Public administration
360 Social services; associations
370 Education
380 Commerce, communications, transport
390 Customs, etiquette, folklore

400 LANGUAGE
410 Linguistics
420 English & Old English
430 Germanic languages, i.e., German
440 Romance languages, i.e., French
450 Italian, Romanian, Rhaeto-Romanic
460 Spanish & Portuguese languages
470 Italic languages, i.e., Latin
480 Hellenic languages, i.e., Classical Greek
490 Other languages

500 NATURAL SCIENCES & MATHEMATICS
510 Mathematics
520 Astronomy & allied sciences
530 Physics
540 Chemistry & allied sciences
550 Earth sciences
560 Paleontology, paleozoology
570 Life Sciences
580 Botanical sciences
590 Zoological sciences

600 TECHNOLOGY (APPLIED SCIENCES)
610 Medical sciences, i.e., Medicine
620 Engineering & allied sciences
630 Agriculture
640 Home economics & family living
650 Management & auxiliary services
660 Chemical engineering
670 Manufacturing
680 Manufacture for specific uses
690 Buildings

700 THE ARTS
710 Civic & landscape art
720 Architecture
730 Plastic arts
740 Drawing & decorative arts
750 Painting & paintings
760 Graphic arts, i.e., Printmaking & prints
770 Photography & photographs
780 Music
790 Recreational & performing arts

800 LITERATURE & RHETORIC
810 American literature in English
820 English and Old English literature
830 Literatures of Germanic languages
840 Literatures of Romance languages
850 Italian, Romanian, Rhaeto-Romanic
860 Spanish & Portuguese literatures
870 Italic literatures, i.e., Latin
880 Hellenic literatures, i.e., Classical Greek
890 Literatures of other languages

900 GEOGRAPHY & HISTORY
910 Geography & travel
920 Biography, genealogy, insignias
930 History of the ancient world
940 General history of Europe
950 General history of Asia & Far East
960 General history of Africa
970 General history of North America
980 General history of South America
990 General history of other areas

LIBRARY OF CONGRESS CLASSIFICATION SYSTEM

A GENERAL WORKS
General encyclopedias, ref. works

B PHILOSOPHY, RELIGION, PSYCHOLOGY
B-BJ Philosophy
BF Psychology
BL-BX Religion

C AUXILIARY SCIENCES OF HISTORY
CB History of civilization (general)
CC Archaeology
CR Heraldry
CS Genealogy
CT Biography (general)

D HISTORY GENERAL AND WORLD
D World history including world wars
DA-DR Europe
DS Asia
DT Africa
DU Oceania

E–F HISTORY OF AMERICA
E 1–143 America (general)
E 151–857 United States (general)

F UNITED STATES (STATES AND LOCAL)

G GEOGRAPHY, ANTHROPOLOGY, FOLKLORE, RECREATION
G Geography (general)
GB Physical geography
GC Oceanography
GN Anthropology
GR Folklore
GV Recreation

H SOCIAL SCIENCE
HA Statistics
HD Agriculture and industry
HF Business
HG Finance (general)
HM–HX Sociology
  HM General works. Theories
  HQ Family. Marriage. Women
  HT Urban and rural sociology
  HX Socialism. Communism. Anarchism

J POLITICAL SCIENCE
JA Political science (general)
JC Political theory
JF–JQ Constitutional history and public administration
JS Local government
JX International law

K LAW

L EDUCATION
LA History of education
LB Theory and practice of teaching
LC Special aspects of education
LD–LG Individual institutions (by country)

M MUSIC & BOOKS ON MUSIC

N FINE ARTS
NA Architecture
NB Sculpture
NC Graphic arts
ND Painting
NK Decorative arts

P LANGUAGES, LITERATURE
P Philology and linguistics (general)
PA Classical languages and literature
PC Romance languages
PD Germanic languages
PE English language
PN General and comparative literature
PQ Romance literatures
PR English literature
PS American literature
PT Germanic literatures
PZ Fiction in English, juvenile literature

Q SCIENCE
QA Mathematics
QB Astronomy
QC Physics
QD Chemistry
QE Geology
QH Natural history
  QH 301–705 Biology
QK Botany
QL Zoology
QM Human anatomy
QP Physiology
QR Bacteriology

R MEDICINE
RA Public aspects of medicine: public health, mental hygiene, medical centers
RT Nurses and nursing

S AGRICULTURE

T TECHNOLOGY
TA General engineering
TC Hydraulic engineering
TD Sanitary/municipal engineering
TH Building construction
TJ Mechanical engineering
TK Electrical, nuclear engineering
TR Photography
TS Manufactures
TT Handicrafts, arts, and crafts
TX Home economics

U MILITARY SCIENCE

V NAVAL SCIENCE

Z BIBLIOGRAPHY, LIBRARY SCIENCE, INFORMATION RESOURCES

Figure 4.2 Selected classifications from the Dewey Decimal and the Library of Congress Classification Systems. These can be used as a guide to browse the stacks.

Dewey Decimal Classification System

The Dewey Decimal Classification System was originated by Melvil Dewey in the latter part of the 19th century. The system divides all knowledge into ten different classes. These ten primary classes are further subdivided into subclasses. Decimals are used to subdivide further. The following example illustrates how the addition of each decimal number to the whole number makes the classification more precise.

Example

900	Geography and History
970	General history of North America
973	United States history
973.7	Civil War 1861–1865
973.71	Political and economic history (Civil War period)
973.73	Military operations
973.7349	Battle of Gettysburg
973.9	20th century 1901–
973.92	Later 20th century 1953–

Library of Congress Classification System

The Library of Congress Classification System was designed by the Library of Congress in the latter part of the 19th century solely for its own use. Because it is so comprehensive, it has been adopted by many other large libraries both in the United States and in other parts of the world.

The LC system has 21 different classes with numerous subdivisions under each class. Each primary class is designated by a single letter as illustrated in Figure 4.1. The first letter or group of letters is followed by a whole number that indicates a subdivision.

Example

H	**Social sciences (General)**
HA	Statistics
Economics	
HB	Economic theory. Demography
HC-HD	Economic history and conditions
HE	Transportation and communications
HF	Commerce
HJ	Finance
Sociology	
HM	Sociology (General and theoretical)
HN	Social history. Social problems. Social reform
HQ	The family. Marriage. Women
HS	Societies: Secret, benevolent, etc. Clubs
HT	Communities. Classes. Races
HV	Social pathology. Social and public welfare. Criminology
HX	Socialism. Communism. Anarchism

The initial classification number can be subdivided further as shown in the three call numbers below.

Example

HF	HF	HF
5686	5686	5686
.D7	.P3	.S75

Where HF=commerce

      5686=accounting

      .D7=drug stores

      .P3=petroleum industry

      .S75=steel industry

Although the system is based on the alphabet, not all of the letters have been used in either the main classes or the subclasses. These letters are reserved for new subjects, for the expansion of older subjects, or, in the case of **I** and **O,** to avoid confusion with the numbers one and zero.

Superintendent of Documents Classification System

The SuDocs system is used by the United States Government Printing Office to assign call numbers to government documents before they are sent to depository libraries. Libraries that serve as depositories for government publications usually establish separate collections arranged by SuDocs number. This system is an alphanumeric scheme based on the agency that issues the publication rather than on subjects, as in the case of Dewey or LC. The initial letter or letters designate the government agency, bureau, or department responsible for the publication. The letters are subdivided further to indicate subagencies.

Publications that are part of a series are assigned a number that designates a particular series. Each individual publication in the series is assigned a number or letter/number combination that identifies the individual title, volume, year, or issue number. This number follows a colon. The following example illustrates the elements in a typical SuDocs number.

Example

C 3.134/2:C 83/2/995

Where   C=Issuing Department—Commerce Department

                3=Sub-agency—Bureau of the Census

                134/2=Series—Statistical Abstract Supplement

                C 83/2/995=Title and date—*County and City Data Book*, 1995

United Nations Symbol Numbers

United Nations publications are classified by series/symbol number designed by the UN library. Figure 4.1 shows the top level of the classification scheme. The numbers are divided further to indicate departments and series. The series symbol numbers are composed of capital letters in combination with numerical notations. The elements in the numbers are separated by slash marks.

CALL NUMBERS

The *call number* assigned to an item usually indicates its subject matter (classification), author, and title. The call number, either alone or in conjunction with an added location symbol, determines the location of the item in the library.

The following example identifies each element in a Dewey Decimal number.

> **Example**
>
> 976.3
> D261lo3
> Where   976=Classification number
>   D261=Book number (author's initial and number)
>   lo=First two letters of the book title
>   3=Edition number

The example below identifies each element in a Library of Congress number.

> **Example**
>
> F369
> .D24
> 1971
> Where   F 369=Classification number
>   .D24=Book number
>   1971=Date of edition

In both the Dewey and LC systems, it is necessary to read the numbers/letters in the call numbers sequentially in order to locate books on the shelves. In Dewey, the number before the decimal point is always treated as a whole number or integer, while all of the numbers following the decimal point are treated as decimals. Although the decimal point may not appear physically in the call number, the book number is nevertheless treated as a decimal.

> **Example**
>
> 338   would be shelved before   338
> A221i   A36

The following call numbers are arranged in correct order as they would stand on the shelf.

Materials classified in LC are arranged alphabetically, then by numbers within the sequence.

Example

PN		PN
6	would be shelved before	6
.S55		.S6

In many call numbers, the date of the book is added. When call numbers are exactly the same except for dates, as in the case with multiple editions, the books are arranged in chronological order. Notice in the second and third entries in the following example that the call numbers are exactly alike except for the 1967, which is the date for a subsequent edition of this book. The call number without the date is shelved before the one with the date. The following example illustrates LC call numbers in the correct order as they would stand on the shelf.

Example

PN	PN	PN	PN	PN
6	56	56	56	57
.S55	.H63T5	.H63T5	.3	.A43L5
		1967	.N4J6	

The call numbers for U.S. documents classified in the SunDoc system are usually written horizontally unless there is not space on the spine of the book to write the numbers. In that case, the numbers are written vertically, with the break occurring at a punctuation mark.

Example

A13.106/2-2:C35

Documents with SuDocs call numbers are shelved in alphanumeric sequence. The numbers following periods are whole numbers as are the numbers following slashes or colons. The following example shows SuDocs numbers in shelf order.

Example

A 2.113:C 35	A13.92:R 59	A13.92/2:F 29	A13.103:163

While most books in the library are shelved in the stack area by call number, other factors may determine where a book is shelved. These may include size, whether the book is a reference book, or whether it is in a remote storage area or a special collection. For example, books shelved elsewhere will often have the symbols "R" or "Ref" for Reference, or "RR" for Ready Reference, or "O" for oversize.

LIBRARY CATALOGS: KEY TO ACCESS

The catalog is the key to the collections of any library. The catalog record gives the location of each item and provides a full description, including name of the author, complete title, edition, number of pages, size, publisher, place of publication, and date of publication. Thus, it is possible to learn a great deal about the item even before it is located in the library.

One of the most important elements in any cataloging record is the *subject headings*. These are terms, sometimes referred to as *controlled vocabulary*, that are assigned to each item by catalogers. They are based on the *Library of Congress Subject Headings* (*LCSH*) (see Figure 4.3), used in most academic libraries, or on *Sears Subject Headings* (*Sears*), used in many small and medium-sized libraries. The subject headings in Sears are similar to those in *LCSH*, but not as extensive. Some special libraries use subject headings that are peculiar to a particular field. For example, medical libraries use *MeSH*, a system devised by the National Library of Medicine. Periodical databases also use standardized subject headings, often referred to as *descriptors,* which are based on *LCSH* or one of the specialized lists of subject headings.

One advantage of using subject headings in searching is that it brings together all of the materials that are available on a particular topic. Another advantage of using standardized subject headings in a search is that the search results are likely to be more on target than keyword searching. This is because the professional catalogers assign the established subject headings after examining the work and determining its subject. Most of the records for non-fiction material in the library's online catalog have one or more subject headings assigned to them. These search terms are helpful in the research process because they suggest related terms to use for finding additional information on a topic.

Materials That Might Not Be Found in Library Catalogs

It is important to know what you will find in a library catalog as well as what you are not likely to find.

MATERIALS OFTEN NOT FOUND IN LIBRARY CATALOGS

☐ individual articles from magazines, journals, and newspapers;
☐ individual titles in series (although some individual titles may be cataloged);
☐ individual titles from anthologies; and
☐ government publications (varies with individual libraries).

Format of Cataloged Materials

When looking at catalog records you should recall that format is a consideration. The online catalog not only includes the books in the collection, but also identifies materials in a variety of formats. These include films, microfilm, microfiche, microprint, sound recordings, reel-to-reel tapes, videocassettes, maps, musical scores, CD-ROMs, online databases, and information found on the Internet.

The locations of material with special formats will be indicated on the catalog record. They usually have a location symbol such as "Film," "LP," "Recording," or "Tape" plus a sequence number instead of a classification number as a means of locating them. The number given with the location symbol is often an *accession number*. This means that as the materials are received by the library, they are assigned a number in-

Television
— Transmitters and transmission
  (Continued)
    Here are entered works on the technical aspects of television transmission, including television transmitters. Works on the transmission of television programs that are intended for general public reception are entered under Television broadcasting.
  UF Television transmission
  BT Image transmission
     Television—Equipment and supplies
     Television broadcasting
— Tuners
  [TK6655.T8]
  UF Television tuners
     Tuners, Television
  BT Television—Receivers and reception
— Ultrahigh frequency apparatus and supplies
  [TK6655.U6]
  UF UHF
     UHF television
     Ultrahigh frequency television
  BT Television—Equipment and supplies
— Vocational guidance (May Subd Geog)
    Here are entered works on the occupational opportunities in the field of television. Works on the portrayal of occupations on television are entered under Occupations on television.
  UF Television as a profession
     [Former heading]
     Television broadcasting—Vocational guidance
     [Former heading]
Television, Business
  USE Industrial television
     Television in management
Television, Cable
  USE Cable television
Television, Closed-circuit
  USE Closed-circuit television
Television, Color
  USE Color television
Television, Industrial
  USE Industrial television
Television, Low power
  USE Low power television
Television, Master antenna
  [TK6676]
  UF Master antenna television
     MATV
  BT Television—Antennas
  NT Satellite master antenna television
Television, Military
  USE Military television
Television, Religious
  USE Television in religion
Television, Rental (May Subd Geog)
  UF Rental television
     Television—Renting
  BT Lease and rental services
Television, Submarine
  USE Underwater television
Television, Three-dimensional
  USE Stereoscopic television
Television acting (May Subd Geog)
  UF Acting for television
     [Former heading]
     Acting for video
     Video acting
  BT Acting
Television actors and actresses
  (May Subd Geog)
  [PN1992.4]
  BT Actors
     Actresses
     Television personalities
— Credits

UF Credits of television actors and actresses
   Television credits of television actors and actresses
Television adaptations
  UF Adaptations, Television
     Literature—Film and video adaptations
  BT Literature—Adaptations
     Television plays
     Television programs
     Television scripts
  SA subdivision Film and video adaptations under individual literatures and under names of individual persons, e.g. English literature—Film and video adaptations; Shakespeare, William, 1564-1616—Film and video adaptations
Television addiction (May Subd Geog)
  UF Addiction to television
     Addictive use of television
  BT Compulsive behavior
→ Television advertising (May Subd Geog)
  [HF6146.T42]
  UF Advertising, Television
     Commercials, Television
     Television commercials
     Television in advertising
  BT Advertising
     Broadcast advertising
     Radio advertising
     Television broadcasting
  RT Television commercial films
  NT Cable television advertising
     Singing commercials
— Awards (May Subd Geog)
—— United States
    UF Television advertising—United States—Awards
       [Former heading]
    NT Clio Awards
— Law and legislation (May Subd Geog)
  BT Advertising laws
— Religious aspects
—— Buddhism, [Christianity, etc.]
— United States
—— Awards
    USE Television advertising—Awards—United States
→ Television advertising and children
  (May Subd Geog)
  BT Children
Television advertising directors
  (May Subd Geog)
  BT Television producers and directors
Television advertising films
  USE Television commercial films
Television anchors
  USE Television news anchors
Television and baseball (May Subd Geog)
  UF Baseball and television
  BT Baseball
→ Television and children (May Subd Geog)
  [HQ784.T4]
  UF Children and television
  BT Children
Television and copyright
  USE Copyright—Broadcasting rights
Television and family (May Subd Geog)
  [HQ520]
  UF Family and television
     Family in television programs
     Television programs for the family
  BT Family
Television and history (May Subd Geog)
  [PN1992.56]
  BT History
Television and Infrared Observation Satellites
  USE TIROS satellites
Television and libraries
  USE Libraries and television

Television and literature (May Subd Geog)
  [PN1992.655]
  UF Literature and television
  BT Literature
Television and motion pictures
  USE Motion pictures and television
Television and music (May Subd Geog)
  UF Music and television
  BT Music
  NT Television broadcasting of music
Television and politics (May Subd Geog)
  [PN1992.6]
    Here are entered works on the interrelations between television and political institutions. Works on the use of television as a medium of communication in the political process are entered under Television in politics.
  UF Politics and television
     Television broadcasting—Political aspects
  BT Political science
Television and propaganda
  USE Television in propaganda
Television and reading (May Subd Geog)
  BT Books and reading
     Reading
Television and sports (May Subd Geog)
  [GV742.3]
  UF Sports and television
  BT Sports
  RT Television broadcasting of sports
  NT Video tapes in sports
Television and teenagers (May Subd Geog)
  UF Teenagers and television
  BT Teenagers
Television and the aged (May Subd Geog)
  UF Aged and television
  BT Aged
Television and the arts (May Subd Geog)
  [NX180.T44]
  UF Arts and television
  BT Arts
Television and the blind (May Subd Geog)
  UF Blind and television
  BT Blind
Television and the performing arts
  (May Subd Geog)
  [PN1992.66]
  UF Performing arts and television
  BT Performing arts
Television and theater (May Subd Geog)
  UF Theater and television
  BT Theater
Television and war
  USE subdivisions Television and the war, Television and the revolution, etc. under individual wars, e.g. World War, 1939-1945—Television and the war
Television and women (May Subd Geog)
  UF Women and television
  BT Women
Television and youth (May Subd Geog)
  [HQ799.2.T4]
  UF Youth and television
  BT Youth
Television announcing
  UF Announcing for television
  BT Television broadcasting
  RT Television public speaking
  NT Voice-overs
Television antennas
  USE Television—Antennas
Television apparatus industry
  USE Television supplies industry
Television archives (May Subd Geog)
  [PN1992.16]
  BT Broadcasting archives
Television as a profession
  USE Television—Vocational guidance

Figure 4.3 A sample page from LCSH, 2002 edition, for the topic "television advertising." Several of the headings listed here would be appropriate for the topic "the effect of television advertising on children."

dicating their order of receipt. Sometimes a classification number and a location symbol are assigned to nonbook materials. Material available only on the Internet will have a note identifying the location as "Internet," "electronic resource," or some similar notation, and will include the Internet address (URL) in a separate field.

CARD CATALOG

Even though online catalogs are now the norm, the card catalog record remains a standard for understanding the information provided for each cataloged items. Traditional card catalogs consisted of index cards arranged alphabetically. A few libraries might still maintain catalogs in other non-online formats, such as COM (Computer Output Microform), and CD-ROM book catalogs.

Some libraries, because of the expense involved, cannot afford to change all of their records when they convert from one type of catalog to another. Therefore, records for older materials may be left in one system, while those for newer materials are entered into the new system. A library changing from a card catalog to an online catalog might leave all of its records for materials cataloged before a certain date in the card catalog and enter only records for materials processed after that date into the online catalog. You will need to determine which type or types of catalogs the library is using in order to locate materials. This information is generally available in the library's handbook or from a reference librarian.

Printed Cards

Card catalogs consist of multiple drawers containing 3" x 5" printed cards arranged alphabetically by author, title, subject, and added entries. Added entries include series titles or contributors such as editors, compilers, translators, illustrators, and arrangers of music. Practically every book, with the exception of fiction, has at least three cards: author (or main entry), title, and subject in the catalog. With printed cards, except for the top line, all the cards are identical. Figure 4.4 illustrates the author card for a particular work. The access points for this book are author, joint author, title, and two subject headings.

Cross reference cards are used to direct the card catalog user to the proper terminology or to additional sources of information. There are two kinds of cross reference cards—*see* and *see also*. The *see* reference directs the card catalog user from a subject heading or term that is not used to the synonymous term that is used (Figure 4.5). The *see also* reference card lists related subject headings under which more information can be found (Figure 4.6).

```
HD ——1      2 —— Jongeward, Dorothy.
6058         3 ———— Affirmative action for women:  a practical guide [by]
.J65         4      Dorothy Jongeward, Dru Scott, and contributors.  Reading, Mass.,——— 5
             6 —— Addison-Wesley Pub. Co. [1973] ————————————————— 7
             8 —— xvi, 334 p.  Illus.  22 cm.
             9 —— Includes bibliographies.


            10a ——1. Women--Employment--United States.  2.  Discrimination in ——— 10b
                   Employment--United States.  I. Scott, Dru, joint author.  II.  Title ——— 10c


            11—— HD6058.J65            331.4'0973            73-10592 ——— 14
            12—— ISBN 0-201-03293-7                          MARC ——— 15
                        international #
  Library of Congress   used for ordering 13
```

1. Call number (Library of Congress class number and book number)
2. Author (first one listed on the title page)
3. Title of the book
4. Restatement of the authors' names
5. Place of publication, including city and state
6. Publisher
7. Publication date
8. Physical description (preliminary paging, textual paging, note that it contains illustrations, height of book)
9. Notes (book includes bibliographies)

10. Tracings (traces cards in catalog for this book)
    - 10a Subject headings
    - 10b Joint author
    - 10c Title
11. Classification numbers assigned by the Library of Congress
12. International Standard Book Number
13. Classification number as assigned for Dewey Decimal
14. Library of Congress card number
15. MARC note (record available in MAchine Readable Catalog (MARC) format)

Figure 4.4 Author or main entry card from a printed card catalog.

DISCRIMINATION IN EMPLOYMENT

see

SEX DISCRIMINATION IN EMPLOYMENT

Figure 4.5 Subject cross reference.

DISCRIMINATION

see also: Age discrimination; Civil rights; Discrimination in education; Discrimination in employment; Discrimination in housing; Discrimination in public accommodation; Minorities; Race discrimination; Sex discrimination; Toleration.

Figure 4.6 See also cross reference.

Arrangement of Cards in Catalog

There are two commonly used methods of alphabetizing—*letter by letter* and *word by word*. Dictionaries use letter-by-letter filing as do some indexes and encyclopedias. Cards in the card catalog are filed word by word. You need to be aware of differences in the two methods so that you will not miss entries in reference sources. The word-by-word method treats each word in a name, title, or subject heading as a separate unit, while the letter-by-letter method treats all the words in a name, title, or subject heading as if they were one unit. In other words, in the letter-by-letter method all the words in the heading are run together as if they were one word.

Example

Word by Word	*Letter by Letter*
San Antonio	San Antonio
San Diego	Sanctuary
San Pedro	Sandalwood
Sanctuary	Sandblasting
Sand, George	Sand, George
Sandalwood	San Diego
Sandblasting	San Pedro

ONLINE CATALOGS

Today most libraries have replaced the card catalog either entirely or in part by an online catalog. Online catalogs were made possible by the advent of MARC (MAchine Readable Catalog) records in 1965 by the Library of Congress. Since that time, MARC has been universally adopted by libraries throughout the world as a means of cataloging library materials. MARC records are stored in electronic format and retrieved by the use of a computer. MARC cataloging consists of a uniform system of numbers, letters, and symbols used to encode the different data elements in a record. Each MARC record is divided into fields, such as author, title, subject, and call number, each represented by a three-character *tag*. The tags generate the access points and provide the information which is displayed to the user. The example below and Figure 4.7 illustrate the most common field tags.

Example

MARC Tags:

100 = main author

245 = title of the work

260 = publication information

300 = a description of the work

650 = subject headings

Online catalogs may be described in one of two ways: access is through a host-based mode using Telnet software, or access is Web based, directly through the Internet. With Telnet, all interaction is in the form of lines of text—hence, the term *text based* is often used to refer to this mode. In the early days of online catalogs, terminals rather than personal computers were used to access catalogs. A terminal has a screen and a keyboard but lacks a processor. A terminal can only display data sent to it from another computer. Aside from only displaying text, it is activated by a keyboard and does not respond to a mouse. Although most libraries

```
001     865481
008     740327s1973     maua     b     00010 eng  cam
010     73010592
020     0201032937
040     DLC|cDLC|dm.c.|dLDL
043     n-us---
049     LDLL, LDLR|aLLLA
050  0  HD6058|b.J65
100 10  Jongeward, Dorothy
245 10  Affirmative action for women:|ba practical guide|c[by]
        Dorothy Jongeward, Dru Scott, and contributors
260  0  Reading, Mass.,|bAddison-Wesley Pub. Co.|c[c1973]
300     xvi, 334 p.|billus.|c22 cm
504     Includes bibliographies
650  0  Women|xEmployment|zUnited States
650  0  Sex discrimination in employment|zUnited States
700 10  Scott, Dru
910     RL02Ag85jor
```

Figure 4.7 MARC record for the author card displayed in Figure 4.4. Note the 100 field indicates the author's name, the 245 field contains the title of the work, etc.

no longer use terminals, some continue to provide Telnet access, by which a computer can emulate a terminal. Most have switched to direct Internet access (or use both means of access). This type of catalog is called a WebPAC (Web Public Access Catalog), it has a graphic interface, and can be activated by a mouse. Both Telnet and WebPAC are designed to make searching a library catalog simpler and more effective than using a card catalog.

Using the Online Catalog to Find Information

Access Points

The purpose of cataloging materials in a library is to describe certain elements of each item in the collection so that it can be identified and retrieved. The elements used in describing the work are the keys to access. In card catalogs the access points are called *entries*. In online records, they are called *fields*. The main access points in any online cataloging record are author, title, subject, and keyword. Each of these is included in the discussion of basic search techniques in Chapter 3.

Searching the Online Catalog

The greatest advantage of an online catalog is that one can search for library materials by keyword as well as author, title, and subject. In addition to the public access catalog, online systems may have other capabilities. These include the ability to:

☐   update the catalog on a daily basis;

☐   provide information concerning materials on order;

☐   provide circulation information, such as whether or not material has been checked out;

☐   provide information on periodical holdings;

☐   access the database from remote locations, such as a faculty office, dormitory room, or home; and

☐   provide direct links to web sites.

Web-based catalogs have labeled fields for each record and explicit onscreen instructions and capabilities. One main advantage of a Web-based catalog is the capability of "hot links" to Internet sites. That is, if you click on the URL in the catalog record you will go directly to the Internet site. This is extremely helpful to remote users, since they can now link directly from the online catalog to a Web-based document. It is also valuable to local and in-house users who can switch back and forth from cataloged information to full-text Web sites. You can compile bibliographies by downloading or exporting information, or you can insert information from the Internet directly into a word processing document while you have the information on the screen.

Libraries throughout the world use different automated systems, each of which has its own command language. The basic search techniques discussed in Chapter 3 and the following illustrations from Conn Library at Wayne State College, should apply to searching online catalogs. Once you become familiar with searching the online catalog in your library, you should not have difficulty searching any catalog. The sample screens shown in Figures 8–20 illustrate the various features and capabilities of Innovative Interfaces Incorporated (III) used by the Nebraska State College System. Other automated systems can be seen in the Gateway to Library Catalogs listing from the Library of Congress, located at http://lcweb.loc.gov/z3950/gateway.html.

Online Catalogs (Web Based): Sample Screens

The Nebraska State College System is a consortium of three state college libraries which share their library catalogs and Interlibrary Loan services. It is typical of such cooperative efforts underway today both at the state college and university level. Chadron State College library materials are indicated by CSC; Peru State College materials, by PSC, and Wayne State College materials by WSC. Figure 4.8 depicts the initial online catalog screen.

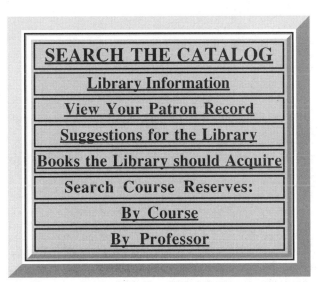

Figure 4.8 Introductory screen for a Web-based catalog at Conn Library, Wayne State College, Wayne, Nebraska. Sample of III (Innovative Interfaces Inc.)

Note that patrons can search the checkout record for overdue fines, determine which materials they have checked out, and keep track of their library materials much like an online banking system or consumer credit account. Other options include offering suggestions for library purchases and searching for materials left at the Reserve Desk by their professors. Figure 4.9 provides a guide to search commands in the online catalog.

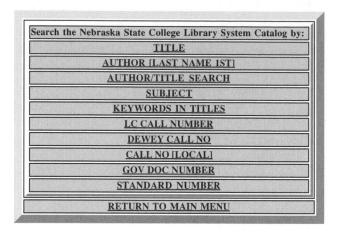

Search the Nebraska State College Library System Catalog by:

- TITLE
- AUTHOR [LAST NAME 1ST]
- AUTHOR/TITLE SEARCH
- SUBJECT
- KEYWORDS IN TITLES
- LC CALL NUMBER
- DEWEY CALL NO
- CALL NO [LOCAL]
- GOV DOC NUMBER
- STANDARD NUMBER

RETURN TO MAIN MENU

Figure 4.9 Directory describing the commands to use in searching the online catalog.

Innovative Interfaces system provides "keyword in titles" instead of a traditional "keyword" command which searches the entire text of a record for the search terms. It is useful as a starting point for electronic searching in the same way that search engines on the Web use keyword searching. (See Figure 4.10) Check the introductory screen of the online catalog in your library to determine which options are available to you.

TELEVISION is in 1711 titles.
ADVERTISING is in 367 titles.
CHILDREN is in 5146 titles.
Both "ADVERTISING" and "TELEVISION" are in 23 titles.
Adding "CHILDREN" leaves 4 titles.
There are 4 entries with ADVERTISING, TELEVISION & CHILDREN.

BRIEF DISPLAY | START OVER | ANOTHER SEARCH | LIMIT THIS SEARCH | (Univ of Nebr-Lincoln)
(Univ of Nebr-Omaha) (Univ of Nebr-Kearney) (Univ. of Nebr Med Ctr)

AUTHOR ▼

Num	Mark	Words (1-4 of 4)	Year
1		Action for children's television; [edited transcript of] the	
		WSC Stacks:AVAILABLE ; PRINTED MATL	[1971]
2		H.W. Wilson select full text [computer file]	
		WSC Network:ASK AT DESK, PSC Lib Homepage:ASK AT DESK, CSC:ASK AT DESK ; COMPUTER FILE	1994-
3		New issues in government-business relations since 1964 : con	
		WSC Stacks:AVAILABLE ; PRINTED MATL	1994
4		Research on the effects of television advertising on childre	
		WSC Government Doc:AVAILABLE ; PRINTED MATL	[1977?]

BRIEF DISPLAY | START OVER | ANOTHER SEARCH | LIMIT THIS SEARCH | (Univ of Nebr-Lincoln)
(Univ of Nebr-Omaha) (Univ of Nebr-Kearney) (Univ. of Nebr Med Ctr)

Figure 4.10 Results of a keyword (or WORD) search. Use quotation marks around your multiple word search topics (e.g. "television advertising children") to keep the terms together in resulting entries. Note the listing of a database title (H.W. Wilson), a government document, and regular books on this topic.

Figure 4.11 shows the full record for the government document listed as number 4 in Figure 4.10. It provides the subject headings "television and children" and "television advertising." Once the standardized terms are determined for your topic, it is easy to conduct a subject search to focus more directly on your needs.

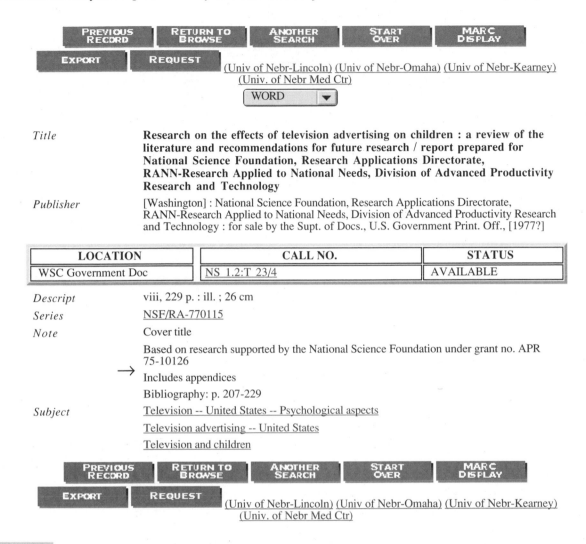

LOCATION	CALL NO.	STATUS
WSC Government Doc	NS 1.2:T 23/4	AVAILABLE

Figure 4.11   The government document retrieved from the list in Figure 4.10.

Figure 4.12 depicts several subdivisions for the subject "television and children" including abstracts, bibliography, cross cultural studies, and juvenile literature. Note that the same title appears under two different subject headings (see numbers 2 and 3). Using standardized terms found either in *LCSH* (see Figure 4.3), or in *Sears Subject Headings* produces a more focused search. If you are unsure of the exact subject heading, begin with a keyword search.

BRIEF DISPLAY	START OVER	ANOTHER SEARCH	LIMIT THIS SEARCH	SEARCH AS WORDS

(Univ of Nebr-Lincoln) (Univ of Nebr-Omaha) (Univ of Nebr-Kearney) (Univ. of Nebr Med Ctr)

SUBJECT ▼

Num	Mark	SUBJECTS (1-10 of 10)	Year
1		Television And Children	
		Action for children's television; [edited transcript of] the / **WSC Stacks:AVAILABLE** ; PRINTED MATL	[1971]
		Children and television / Cedric Cullingford / **WSC Stacks:AVAILABLE** ; PRINTED MATL	1984
		Children and the faces of television : teaching, violence, s / **WSC Stacks:AVAILABLE** ; PRINTED MATL	c1980
		Children in front of the small screen / Grant Noble / **CSC 2d Floor Stacks:AVAILABLE, WSC Stacks:AVAILABLE** ; PRINTED MATL	1975
		41 additional entries	
2	→	Television And Children Abstracts	
		Television's impact on children and adolescents / compiled b / **WSC Stacks:AVAILABLE, PSC Gen. Collection:AVAILABLE** ; PRINTED MATL	1981
3		Television And Children Bibliography	
		Television's impact on children and adolescents / compiled b / **WSC Stacks:AVAILABLE, PSC Gen. Collection:AVAILABLE** ; PRINTED MATL	1981
4		Television And Children Cross Cultural Studies	
		Television and the aggressive child : a cross-national compa / **CSC 2d Floor Stacks:AVAILABLE, WSC Stacks:AVAILABLE** ; PRINTED MATL	1986
5		Television And Children Juvenile Literature	
		Bad stuff in the news : a guide to handling the headlines / **WSC Book Exam Ctr:AVAILABLE** ; PRINTED MATL	c2002
6		Television And Children Longitudinal Studies	
		Television, imagination, and aggression : a study of prescho / **WSC Stacks:AVAILABLE** ; PRINTED MATL	1981
7		Television And Children Research Congresses	
		Television and children : priorities for research : report o / **WSC Stacks:AVAILABLE** ; PRINTED MATL	[1975?]
8		Television And Children United States	
		Children and television / by David A. England / **WSC Reavis Reading:AVAILABLE** ; PRINTED MATL	c1984
		Children's understanding of television : research on attenti / **WSC Stacks:AVAILABLE** ; PRINTED MATL	1983
		Electronic hearth : creating an American television culture / **WSC Stacks:AVAILABLE** ; PRINTED MATL	1991

Figure 4.12 First page of the result list of a *subject* search of "television and children."

Once a list of results is obtained, browse the selections and eliminate those not appropriate for your particular purpose. (Selecting materials based on currency, authorship, and other factors are discussed in Chapter 6.) Under the subdivision "Television and Children Abstracts," the title "Television's Impact on Children and Adolescents," published in 1981, appears promising. Figure 4.13 shows the full record for item number 2 in Figure 4.12. It also includes the full list of subject headings for that title.

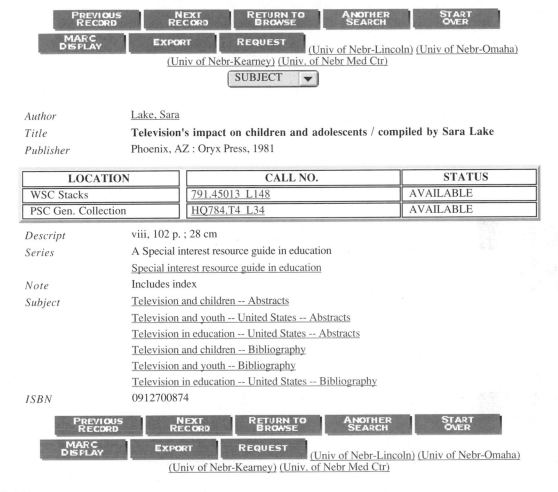

Figure 4.13 The record retrieved from the list shown in Figure 4.12, giving complete information about the work selected.

Information about the author can be useful in determining the qualifications of the writer for your particular topic. Clicking on the author's name leads to other works by the author. Figure 4.14 shows the author has compiled several books in the field of education, including "Television's Impact on Children and Adolescents," the one you have selected.

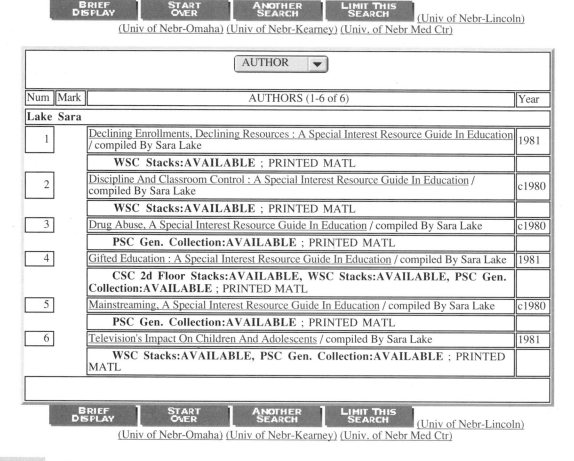

Num	Mark	AUTHORS (1-6 of 6)	Year
		Lake Sara	
1		Declining Enrollments, Declining Resources : A Special Interest Resource Guide In Education / compiled By Sara Lake	1981
		WSC Stacks:AVAILABLE ; PRINTED MATL	
2		Discipline And Classroom Control : A Special Interest Resource Guide In Education / compiled By Sara Lake	c1980
		WSC Stacks:AVAILABLE ; PRINTED MATL	
3		Drug Abuse, A Special Interest Resource Guide In Education / compiled By Sara Lake	c1980
		PSC Gen. Collection:AVAILABLE ; PRINTED MATL	
4		Gifted Education : A Special Interest Resource Guide In Education / compiled By Sara Lake	1981
		CSC 2d Floor Stacks:AVAILABLE, WSC Stacks:AVAILABLE, PSC Gen. Collection:AVAILABLE ; PRINTED MATL	
5		Mainstreaming, A Special Interest Resource Guide In Education / compiled By Sara Lake	c1980
		PSC Gen. Collection:AVAILABLE ; PRINTED MATL	
6		Television's Impact On Children And Adolescents / compiled By Sara Lake	1981
		WSC Stacks:AVAILABLE, PSC Gen. Collection:AVAILABLE ; PRINTED MATL	

Figure 4.14 A listing of other works for the author, Sara Lake, taken from Figure 4.13.

TIPS

Starting your strategy with a keyword search often results in related information not ordinarily found through just a subject search. With Web-based catalogs, it is often easier to begin with specific terms or phrases rather than guess the standardized terms. Using the *LCSH* listings would lead you directly to the correct subject headings, or standardized terms to conduct a subject search. For the topic of "effects of television advertising on children," the correct subject headings would be "television advertising," "television advertising and children," or "television and children," according to the 2002 edition of the *LCSH*. Subdivisions on the resulting pages would indicate suitable categories for you to search. (See Figure 4.3.)

Figure 4.15 shows the results of a search for the "standardized" subject heading for this topic, "television advertising and children." Note that it produced fewer entries than the keyword searches and focused more appropriately on your topic.

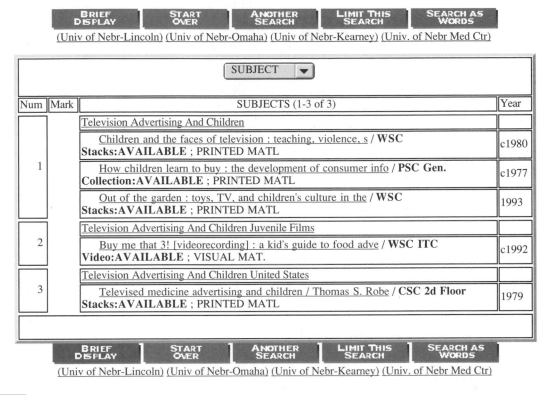

Num	Mark	SUBJECTS (1-3 of 3)	Year
		Television Advertising And Children	
1		Children and the faces of television : teaching, violence, s / **WSC Stacks:AVAILABLE** ; PRINTED MATL	c1980
		How children learn to buy : the development of consumer info / **PSC Gen. Collection:AVAILABLE** ; PRINTED MATL	c1977
		Out of the garden : toys, TV, and children's culture in the / **WSC Stacks:AVAILABLE** ; PRINTED MATL	1993
2		Television Advertising And Children Juvenile Films	
		Buy me that 3! [videorecording] : a kid's guide to food adve / **WSC ITC Video:AVAILABLE** ; VISUAL MAT.	c1992
3		Television Advertising And Children United States	
		Televised medicine advertising and children / Thomas S. Robe / **CSC 2d Floor Stacks:AVAILABLE** ; PRINTED MATL	1979

Figure 4.15 Results of search for a "standardized" subject heading.

The materials shown in Figure 4.15 include those available to students and faculty enrolled in the three state colleges in the consortium: Chadron State College (CSC), Peru State College (PSC), and Wayne State College (WSC). The title "How Children Learn to Buy" is located at Peru; "Televised Medicine" is at Chadron; the remaining works are available at Wayne. All of these materials are available to any student from the three colleges. There is no charge for borrowing materials among the three libraries. Patrons simply "Request" the item using their special student identification consisting of their social security number, campus number, and individual identity number. Materials are then transported to the appropriate library's Interlibrary Loan department, and patrons are notified to retrieve the material on their campus.

Figure 4.16 depicts a title held at Peru State College Library. To obtain this item for research, the patron would select the "Request" option from the menu and follow directions. Peru uses the Library of Congress classification system; the other two libraries use Dewey Decimal.

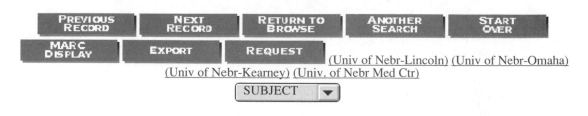

(Univ of Nebr-Lincoln) (Univ of Nebr-Omaha)
(Univ of Nebr-Kearney) (Univ. of Nebr Med Ctr)

SUBJECT ▼

Author	<u>Ward, Scott, 1942-</u>
Title	**How children learn to buy : the development of consumer information-processing skills / Scott Ward, Daniel B. Wackman, Ellen Wartella**
Publisher	Beverly Hills, Calif. : Sage Publications, c1977

LOCATION	CALL NO.	STATUS
PSC Gen. Collection	HC79.C6 W37	AVAILABLE

Descript	271 p. ; 22 cm
Series	<u>People and communication ; v. 1</u>
Note	Bibliography: p. 193-197
	Includes indexes
Subject	<u>Young consumers</u>
	<u>Television advertising and children</u>
Add author	<u>Wackman, Daniel B</u>
	<u>Wartella, Ellen</u>
ISBN	080390424X : 0803907443

(Univ of Nebr-Lincoln) (Univ of Nebr-Omaha)
(Univ of Nebr-Kearney) (Univ. of Nebr Med Ctr)

Figure 4.16 Sample of material held at another library in the system.

Another title shown in Figure 4.17 is worthy of note. The "Buy Me That 3!" is a video on food advertising and children. Read the Summary of the video shown in Figure 4.17 to determine if this is relevant to your particular treatment of this topic.

(Univ of Nebr-Lincoln) (Univ of Nebr-Omaha) (Univ of Nebr-Kearney) (Univ. of Nebr Med Ctr)

SUBJECT ▼

Title	**Buy me that 3! [videorecording] : a kid's guide to food advertising / HBO & Consumer Reports ; producer, Ellen Goosenberg Kent ; director, Edd Griles ; writer, Alan Kingsberg**
Publisher	Chicago, Ill. : Films Incorporated Video, c1992

LOCATION		CALL NO.	STATUS
WSC ITC Video	VIDEO RECORDING	659.143 B987	AVAILABLE

Descript	1 videocassette (29 min.) : sd., col. ; 1/2 in. + 1 discussion guide
Note	VHS
	Host: Jim Fyfe
	Animator, Julie Zammarchi; music, Michael Whalen
	"Partly based on Zillions magazine, the Consumer reports for kids, through December 1992."
	Discussion guide, c1993
	Ages 6 to 12
Summary	Presents children with tips to keep in mind when watching T.V. food commercials. Uses short interviews of children giving their opinions of commercials, and features a commercial maker revealing tricks for making food look appealing in T.V. advertisements
Note	Public performance rights and closed circuit broadcasting rights granted
Subject	Advertising -- Food -- Juvenile films
	Television advertising and children -- Juvenile films
	Television advertising -- Juvenile films
	Video
Add author	Fyfe, Jim
	Home Box Office (Firm)
	Consumer Reports Television (Firm)
	Films Incorporated
	Consumers Union of United States
Alt. title	Container title: Buy me that! : a kids' survival guide to TV advertising
	Kids' survival guide to T.V. advertising
	Title on label: Buy me that 3! : a kids guide to advertising
	Kids guide to advertising
Unif title	Zillions

Figure 4.17 A video catalog record.

The limitation options discussed in Chapter 3 can be seen in Figures 4.18–4.20. Select "Limit this search" from the top menu of your search screen to retrieve pull-down boxes with options for language, type of material, location, and year.

You can limit your subject search for "television advertising" to "serial" in order to locate periodical titles on this topic. Click on the "Limit" option at the top of the screen and select "serial" from the formats offered. You could also select a particular campus from among the three in this library system to limit your search even further. Figure 4.18 illustrates the screen that allows for limiting a search by selected criteria.

You searched: SUBJECT: **television advertising**
66 entries found

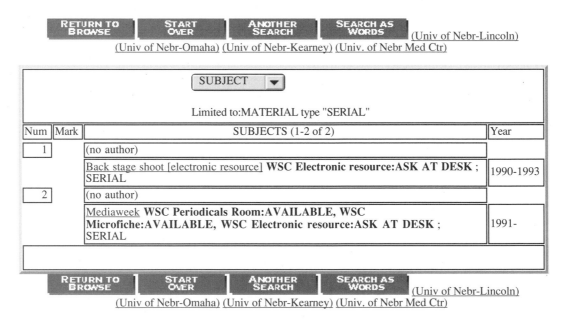

Please select criteria to limit by:

LANGUAGE: ANY ▼

MATERIAL type: SERIAL ▼

Words in the TITLE ▼

WHERE Item is located: ANY ▼

YEAR of publication: After [ ] and Before [ ]

Limit/sort items retrieved using above data

Figure 4.18 Limiting a subject search to a particular format.

The two results listed in Figure 4.19 indicate periodical titles available for this topic. In this case, all items are available online. Periodical titles can be located by searching by title in the online catalog.

RETURN TO BROWSE   START OVER   ANOTHER SEARCH   SEARCH AS WORDS   (Univ of Nebr-Lincoln)
(Univ of Nebr-Omaha) (Univ of Nebr-Kearney) (Univ. of Nebr Med Ctr)

SUBJECT ▼

Limited to:MATERIAL type "SERIAL"

Num	Mark	SUBJECTS (1-2 of 2)	Year
1		(no author)	
		Back stage shoot [electronic resource] **WSC Electronic resource:ASK AT DESK ; SERIAL**	1990-1993
2		(no author)	
		Mediaweek **WSC Periodicals Room:AVAILABLE, WSC Microfiche:AVAILABLE, WSC Electronic resource:ASK AT DESK ; SERIAL**	1991-

RETURN TO BROWSE   START OVER   ANOTHER SEARCH   SEARCH AS WORDS   (Univ of Nebr-Lincoln)
(Univ of Nebr-Omaha) (Univ of Nebr-Kearney) (Univ. of Nebr Med Ctr)

Figure 4.19 Results of limiting a subject search to "serials" format. The entry indicates holdings are available in print and bound formats in the WSC Periodicals Room, on Microfiche, and online. Specific holdings are shown in Figure 4.20.

Clicking on the title *Mediaweek* (Figure 4.19) brings up the full information for the title. It is available in print for the current two years, in microfiche, and online in two full-text databases. The note "ask at desk" indicates an online subscription.

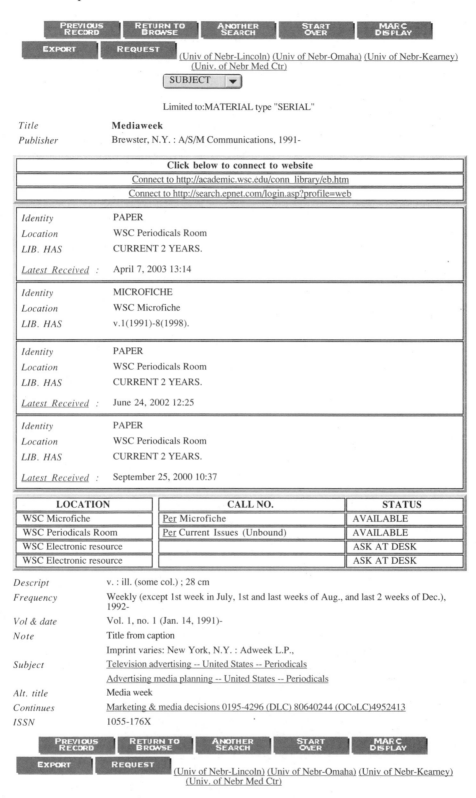

Title **Mediaweek**

Publisher Brewster, N.Y. : A/S/M Communications, 1991-

Click below to connect to website
Connect to http://academic.wsc.edu/conn_library/eb.htm
Connect to http://search.epnet.com/login.asp?profile=web

Identity	PAPER
Location	WSC Periodicals Room
LIB. HAS	CURRENT 2 YEARS.
Latest Received :	April 7, 2003 13:14

Identity	MICROFICHE
Location	WSC Microfiche
LIB. HAS	v.1(1991)-8(1998).

Identity	PAPER
Location	WSC Periodicals Room
LIB. HAS	CURRENT 2 YEARS.
Latest Received :	June 24, 2002 12:25

Identity	PAPER
Location	WSC Periodicals Room
LIB. HAS	CURRENT 2 YEARS.
Latest Received :	September 25, 2000 10:37

LOCATION	CALL NO.	STATUS
WSC Microfiche	Per Microfiche	AVAILABLE
WSC Periodicals Room	Per Current Issues (Unbound)	AVAILABLE
WSC Electronic resource		ASK AT DESK
WSC Electronic resource		ASK AT DESK

Descript	v. : ill. (some col.) ; 28 cm
Frequency	Weekly (except 1st week in July, 1st and last weeks of Aug., and last 2 weeks of Dec.), 1992-
Vol & date	Vol. 1, no. 1 (Jan. 14, 1991)-
Note	Title from caption
	Imprint varies: New York, N.Y. : Adweek L.P.,
Subject	Television advertising -- United States -- Periodicals
	Advertising media planning -- United States -- Periodicals
Alt. title	Media week
Continues	Marketing & media decisions 0195-4296 (DLC) 80640244 (OCoLC)4952413
ISSN	1055-176X

Figure 4.20 Complete holdings record for the periodical *Mediaweek*.

Library Catalogs from Around the World

Researchers have a great advantage in being able to search online catalogs from all over the world—from the Library of Congress (the national library of the United States) to the Bibliothèque Nationale (the national library of France). In many instances, they are able to find materials in a distant library that are not available locally. Most online catalogs are searched with the same search commands discussed earlier: author, title, subject, and keyword. Many have call number searching and other features. Although the search engines are not totally standardized, the search commands are easily recognized.

We have seen how the Nebraska State College Library System provides access to all of the materials held by its members to students and for all three colleges. Larger systems such as the Louisiana Library Network (LOUIS) and OhioLink have similar options. This additional access to materials provides patrons much-needed material that their local library does not have. Sharing of materials among libraries through inter-library loan programs has been in practice for many years, but the technology now allows patrons to request and receive materials directly, thus simplifying the procedures.

Taking this concept of shared resources one step further, *WorldCat,* the OCLC catalog of catalogs, is a database comprised of the holdings of more than 30,000 libraries in over 65 countries. Member libraries add cataloged materials to the database every 15 seconds, making this an excellent source for identifying and locating material. In addition to providing cataloging information for the item, *WorldCat* also lists libraries that hold the material, making interlibrary loan procedures much easier.

Instructor: _____ Course/Section: _____

Name: _____

Date: _____ Points: _____

Understanding Classification Systems

1. Use Figure 4.2 to answer these questions about the Dewey Decimal classification system.

    a. What number range would you use to find works on psychology?

    b. What number range would you use to find books on zoology?

    c. What number range would you use to find books written about plastic arts?

2. Use Figure 4.2 to answer these questions for the Library of Congress (LC) classification system.

    a. What number range would you use to find sociology books?

    b. What number range would you use to find books on nursing?

    c. In what call number range would you find periodicals on American history?

3. Use Figure 4.1 to answer these questions about the Superintendent of Documents (SuDocs) classification system.

    a. Give the names of three government agencies that are likely to publish information on drug abuse.

    b. Which agency of the government produces tax forms?

Exercise 4.3

Instructor: _____ Course/Section: _____

Name: _____

Date: _____ Points: _____

Identifying Call Numbers

Listed below are three sets of call numbers. For each set, identify the classification system used and arrange each row of numbers within the set in shelf order. Place a number under the call number indicating the order.

Classification system: _____

RM 301 .B3	RM 301 .W58 2002	RC 953.5 .G33	RM 301.15 .C67 1985	RM 300 .M57
HF 6146 .T42B34	HF 6146 .T4Y34	HF 6146 .T4F53	HF 6146 .T42S845 1986	HF 6146 .T42W53 1982
B 819 .5272 .S272	B 819 .B333	B 819 .B58	B 819 .5275D4	B 819 .S2735
G 10 .578 V21	G 25 .D19	G 7 .R693P38 1980	G 21 .K21A74 1973	G 23 .P779

Classification system: _____

532 D413F	532.005 An7P	532.05 F419c	532 Se32r	532.05 B314
792 A15s	792 A115p	792 A125	792 Ap49	792 A12

448	448	448	448	448
F848f	H870	F82t	H13m	F84cr

150	150	150	150	150
H72a	H436s	H49	H72ps	H436

Classification system:_____

J1.20/2:T27/977	I1.2:AC7/2	I1.2:B47
I1.2:A11S/2	J1.20/2/2:T27/977/supp	J1.2012:W89

C18.2:In2/2	C21.2:Au8/2	C21.2:C33
C13.77:K87	C18.2:NEB/947	C18.2:H67/a

EP1.2:AG8/6	EP1.2:AG8/7/draft	EP1.2:AG8/6/exec.sum
EP1.2:AG8/7/992	EP1.2:Ai1	EP1.2:AI5/3

Exercise 4.4 Library Catalogs

Instructor: _____ Course/Section: _____

Name: _____

Date: _____ Points: _____

Locating Material Using Classification Systems

Use Figure 4.1 to determine which type(s) of classification system(s) is/are used in your library.

1. Select a number range in an area of interest to you (e.g., education would be 370 in Dewey Decimal, L in Library of Congress).

   What number did you select?

2. Go to the book stacks in your library and select a book from this general number range. Give the following information.

   Author:

   Title:

   Call number:

3. If your library classifies periodicals, use this same general call number range to find a periodical. Give the following information.

   Title of the periodical:

   Call number (if given):

   Title of one article within the periodical:

4. Find a reference work using the same general number range. Give the following information.

   Author (if given):

   Title of the publication:

   Date of publication:

5. In the online catalog type in the call number of the book you selected in Question 2 above. What additional information did you receive about the book from the online catalog?

Instructor: _____ Course/Section: _____

Name: _____

Date: _____ Points: _____

Interpreting a Catalog Card

<table>
<tr><td></td><td>ARTIFICIAL INTELLIGENCE.</td></tr>
<tr><td>P</td><td>Moyne, John A.</td></tr>
<tr><td>37</td><td>Understanding language: man or machine / John A. Moyne.</td></tr>
<tr><td>.M69</td><td>--New York: Plenum Press, c1985.</td></tr>
<tr><td>1985</td><td>xvi, 357 p. ; ill. , 24 cm.--(Foundations of computer science)</td></tr>
</table>

        Bibliography: p. 325-345.
        Includes index.
        ISBN 0-306-41970-X

1. Psycholinguistics. 2. Linguistics--Data processing. 3. Comprehension.
4. Artificial intelligence. 5. Grammar, Comparative and general. 6. Formal
languages. I. Title. II. Series.

P37.M69 1985   401.9   85-12341
                                                                  AACR 2 MARC

Library of Congress

1. Use the information on the catalog card reproduced above to identify each of the following items. (Refer to Figure 4.4.)

   a. Call number of this book:

   b. Main classification system used:

   c. Author/authors:

   d. Complete title of the work:

   e. Physical description of the work:

2. Is the work illustrated?

   How can you tell?

3. Does it have a list of sources or references?

    How can you tell?

4. List the subject headings used for this book.

5. How are the assigned subject headings used in the research process?

6. Name four of the eight other entries you could look under in the card catalog to find this work. Give the exact words you would use.

    a.

    b.

    c.

    d.

7. Which type of entry does this card represent?

8. Write a complete bibliographic citation for this work. Use the bibliographic citation examples in Appendix A.

Exercise 4.6

Instructor: _____ Course/Section: _____

Name: _____

Date: _____ Points: _____

Using the Library of Congress Subject Headings

Use the latest edition of the *LCSH* available in your library. List the subject headings and possible subheadings that are appropriate for a topic you have chosen. Write N/A (not applicable) where no information is available.

1. Topic selected:

2. Subject heading or headings found:

3. Was there a classification letter or number following any of the subject headings? If so, list them here.

4. List up to three subdivisions found under the topic.

    a.

    b.

    c.

5. List any used for (**UF**) terms.

6. List one related term (**RT**).

7. List one broad term (**BT**).

8. List one narrow term (**NT**).

Exercise 4.7 Library Catalogs

Instructor: _____ Course/Section: _____

Name: _____

Date: _____ Points: _____

The Online Catalog

1. Look up three **authors** from the list below in your library's catalog.

Anne Rice	Virginia Woolf	Mary Higgins Clark	John Grisham
Truman Capote	Stephen King	Maya Angelou	Michael Crichton
Sidney Sheldon	James Joyce	Walt Whitman	Oscar Wilde
Benjamin Franklin	Henry L. Mencken	Bill Gates	John F. Kennedy

Give the following information for the authors you selected.

1st author (name):

Title of most recent work that you located:

Give the exact phrasing you used to look up information:

_____

2nd author (name):

Title of most recent work that you located:

Give the exact phrasing you used to look up information:

_____

3rd author (name):

Title of most recent work that you located:

Give the exact phrasing you used to look up information:

_____

2. Look up two of the following **titles** in your library's online catalog.

MLA Handbook for Writers of Research Papers   *Who's Who in America*
Twentieth Century Authors   *Julius Caesar*
Silent Spring   *Webster's New World Dictionary*
Statistical Abstract of the United States   *Arabian Nights*

Give the following information for each of the titles.

1st title:

Call number:

Give the exact phrasing you used to look up information:

_____

2nd title:

Call number

Give the exact phrasing you used to look up information:

_____

3. Look up each of the following **periodical and newspaper titles** in your library's online catalog. Write the call number next to the periodical. If your library does not receive the periodical, write NA (not available) next to the title.

Time   *People Weekly*

USA Today (newspaper)   *JAMA* (Journal of the American Medical Assn.)

The New York Times   *Jet*

_____

4. Use your library catalog to conduct a SUBJECT search for three of the following terms. *Select the most recent relevant work from the first page you retrieve.* (Note: You may be directed to a page of "additional entries" or "related subjects." If necessary, review these pages before you select your answer.)

drug abuse	computers	photography
animal rights	basketball	alcoholism
Afghanistan	solar energy	civil rights
mathematics	social security	race cars
chronic fatigue syndrome		

Give the following information for each subject you selected.

1st subject (name):

Title of most recent work:

Give the exact phrasing you used to look up information.

_____

2nd subject (name):

Title of most recent work:

Give the exact phrasing you used to look up information.

_____

3rd subject (name):

Title of most recent work:

Give the exact phrasing you used to look up information.

_____

5. Construct a keyword search phrase for each of the following concepts.

   a. How does the Chinese culture view family heritage?

   b. Do unwed teenage mothers complete their education?

   c. What statistical information is available indicating the relationship between drugs and crime, especially among young adults?

6. Select one of the above keyword searches you constructed and locate three works on the topic. Give the following information for each work you select.

   Title of the 1st work:

   Call Number:

   Date:

   Location:

   Give the exact phrasing you used to look up information.

   _____

   Title of the 2nd work:

   Call Number:

   Date:

   Location:

   Give the exact phrasing you used to look up information.

   _____

   Title of the 3rd work:

   Call Number:

   Date:

   Location:

   Give the exact phrasing you used to look up information.

   _____

Exercise 4.8

Instructor: _____ Course/Section: _____

Name: _____

Date: _____ Points: _____

Online Catalog: Record Identification

Use the following sample screen from a Web-based online catalog to respond to the questions below.

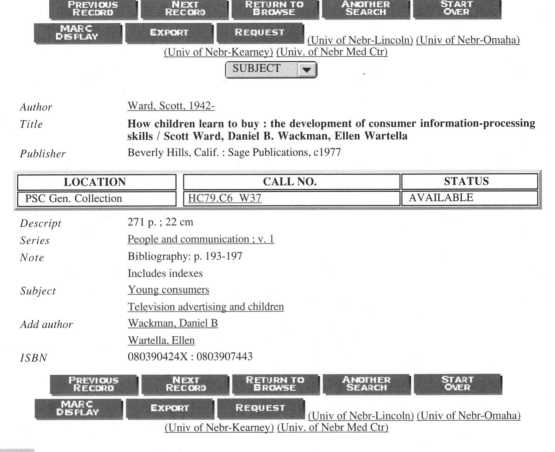

Figure 4.21 Specific record as a result of a subject search.

1. Is there an author of this work?

2. Name the publisher and the place of publication.

3. What is the date of publication?

4. What additional format is available for this title?

5. What subject headings are used for this work?

6. Is this work part of a series? If so, which one?

    How can you tell?

7. Would this work be an appropriate source for the topic "effect of television advertising on children"? Explain your answer.

8. Where is this title located in the library system?

9. Describe the steps you might follow to retrieve this work from the library indicated.

Exercise 4.9

Library Catalogs

Instructor: _____ Course/Section: _____

Name: _____

Date: _____ Points: _____

Interpreting Catalog Results

Use the following screen from a Web-based catalog to answer the questions below.

| Buttons: NEXT PAGE | BRIEF DISPLAY | START OVER | ANOTHER SEARCH | LIMIT THIS SEARCH | SEARCH AS WORDS |

(Univ of Nebr-Lincoln) (Univ of Nebr-Omaha) (Univ of Nebr-Kearney) (Univ. of Nebr Med Ctr)

SUBJECT ▼

Num	Mark	SUBJECTS (1-12 of 19)	Year
1		Television Advertising -- 2 Related Subjects	
2		Television Advertising	
		1984 CLIO awards [videorecording] / produced by Graphic Moti / **WSC ITC Video:AVAILABLE** ; VISUAL MAT.	c1984
		Addy Awards, 1984. [videorecording] / American Advertising F / **WSC ITC Video:AVAILABLE** ; VISUAL MAT.	1984
		Advertising in the broadcast media / Elizabeth J. Heighton, / **WSC Stacks:AVAILABLE** ; PRINTED MATL	c1976
		Advertising on cable : a practical guide for advertisers / D / **WSC Stacks:AVAILABLE** ; PRINTED MATL	c1985
		27 additional entries	
3		Television Advertising And Children	
		Children and the faces of television : teaching, violence, s / **WSC Stacks:AVAILABLE** ; PRINTED MATL	c1980
		How children learn to buy : the development of consumer info / **PSC Gen. Collection:AVAILABLE** ; PRINTED MATL	c1977
		Out of the garden : toys, TV, and children's culture in the / **WSC Stacks:AVAILABLE** ; PRINTED MATL	1993
4		Television Advertising And Children Juvenile Films	
		Buy me that 3! [videorecording] : a kid's guide to food adve / **WSC ITC Video:AVAILABLE** ; VISUAL MAT.	c1992
5		Television Advertising And Children United States	
		Televised medicine advertising and children / Thomas S. Robe / **CSC 2d Floor Stacks:AVAILABLE** ; PRINTED MATL	1979
6		Television Advertising Directories	
		Broadcasting & cable yearbook / **WSC Reference:LIB USE ONLY** ; PRINTED MATL	c1993-
7		Television Advertising Fiction	
		The secret life of the underwear champ / by Betty Miles ; il / **CSC Juv. Collection:AVAILABLE** ; PRINTED MATL	c1981
8		Television Advertising Films -- see --Television Commercial Films	
9		Television Advertising Juvenile Films	
		Buy me that 3! [videorecording] : a kid's guide to food adve / **WSC ITC Video:AVAILABLE** ; VISUAL MAT.	c1992
10		Television Advertising Law And Legislation United States	
		Abandoned in the wasteland : children, television, and the F / **PSC Gen. Collection:AVAILABLE** ; PRINTED MATL	1996, c1995

Figure 4.22 Results of a subject search.

1. How many total entries were found for the subject search on "television advertising"?

2. Which specific subject heading would you use to find information on each of the topics below?

    a. a general discussion of television advertising:

    b. juvenile films on children and television advertising:

    c. a listing of broadcasting and cable yearbook information:

    d. fiction works about television advertising:

    e. specific works about television advertising and children:

    f. television and children materials only in the United States:

Instructor: _____ Course/Section: _____

Name: _____

Date: _____ Points: _____

Keyword versus Subject Searching

1. Select a topic and write it here.

2. Write a sentence that describes your topic.

3. From the sentence you wrote, circle two or three of the most distinctive words.

4. Use your library catalog to search for these terms as a KEYWORD. Write each term you used and the number of entries you retrieved here.

5. Once you find a list of titles, you must evaluate those which have actual relevance to your topic and what you planned to write about the topic. Select one title that appears to be a good source for information. Write that title below.

6. Retrieve the title you select by clicking on it. Click on one of the "subjects" listed for this work. How many entries are included with this link?

7. Return to the list of titles retrieved to see if any others are of interest to you. Give the title and call number for two or three that would be useful to you for this topic.

Instructor: _____ Course/Section: _____

Name: _____

Date: _____ Points: _____

Using Remote Online Catalogs

Search the Library of Congress catalog located at http://catalog.loc.gov/ to retrieve one of the titles below.

MLA Handbook for Writers of Research Papers   *Who's Who in America*
Twentieth Century Authors   *Julius Caesar*
Silent Spring   *Webster's New World Dictionary*
Statistical Abstract of the United States   *Arabian Nights*

1. Give the title and call number of the item you select.

2. What classification system does the Library of Congress use?

3. Search the Library of Congress catalog on a subject that interests you.

   a. What subject did you use?

   b. How many entries did you find?

4. Did you have to wait to enter the Library of Congress web site? If so, how long?

5. Read "About This Catalog" on the Library of Congress home page. Why is the Library of Congress catalog useful for research?

The Internet

"I used to think that cyberspace was fifty years away. What I thought was fifty years away,
was only ten years away. And what I thought was ten years away . . .
it was already here. I just wasn't aware of it yet."

Bruce Sterling

Introduction

The Internet contains information from millions of sources and is available to anyone with a computer and connections to an Internet service provider. Information on the Internet is of all kinds and is suitable for all levels of information seekers—from pre-school children to advanced researchers. It is a rich source of information that includes primary sources which provide new and original research and secondary sources such as bibliographies, biographies, directories, atlases, encyclopedias, dictionaries, periodical articles, and books.

Accessing information on the Internet requires that you have some familiarity with computers—how to type, how to use a word processor, and how to use a mouse. In addition, you need to develop skills for finding information by using a tool that has the potential of finding exactly what you need from a resource that is virtually limitless in possibilities. The Internet is a complex system requiring many levels of expertise to tap its full range of capabilities. This chapter is only an introduction to get you launched. Your proficiency in searching the Internet will increase as you gain experience.

WHAT IS THE INTERNET?

The Internet is a vast series of networks connected via telephone lines, cables, and communications satellites. The metaphor that is most often used for the Internet is "information superhighway." It is analogous to the Interstate system in the U.S., which crisscrosses the country, connecting states and major cities. Connected to the super highways are smaller highways that are linked to rural roads and city streets. The "Interstate" highway of the Internet is a system of regional networks, which constitute the "backbone" of the system. Connected to the backbone are smaller networks serving particular geographic areas or organizations. Leading into these are small local networks and individual computers.

An Overview

The Internet originated in the 1960s when researchers from the U.S. Defense Department's Advanced Research Projects Agency (ARPA) began linking computers to each other through telephone hookup. ARPA was interested in designing a system that would support military research and at the same time provide a measure of security against partial cable outages. Previous computer networking efforts had required a single line between two computers. If something were to go wrong with the system, the entire network would be out of operation. The new system used a software program called Internet Protocol (IP) to send data in packets along a network of communication lines. Each piece of information was split into packets and transmitted from one network node to another until it reached its destination. There it could be reassembled by the computer into a readable message. With this system, researchers could exchange electronic mail (e-mail) and later were able to form discussion groups. Thus, ARPANET came into being. Much of the early research for ARPANET was done at a few select universities, where researchers soon realized what a powerful tool it was for communicating and exchanging information with other researchers throughout the country (Krol 11).

In 1985, the National Science Foundation (NSF) provided funding for the creation of additional supercomputing capabilities and the expansion and development of the Internet. Until this time, access to the Internet had been limited to researchers in universities and a few government agencies. Computing capabilities were expanded and use was extended to include thousands of colleges, research organizations, and government agencies. By 1988, the NSFNET had replaced ARPANET. In 1991, U.S. Senator Al Gore introduced the National Research and Educational Network (NREN) legislation that expanded NSFNET by extending use to K–12 schools, junior colleges, and community colleges. The legislation also included provisions for businesses to purchase part of the network for commercial use (Krol 15). The expansion of communication capabilities and the promotion of more universal usage led to the entry of commercial firms into the business of creating networks to provide Internet services. Today there are more than 100,000 networks (National Science Foundation).

By mid-1994, the U.S. government had removed itself from any day-to-day control over the Internet. The Internet does not "belong" to anyone or any company. Anyone can connect to the Internet and anyone who wishes can "publish" on the Internet. The only "authority" rests with the Internet Society (ISOC). This is a non-governmental, international organization with voluntary membership whose purpose is to promote global cooperation for the Internet and its working technologies. It is governed by a board that is responsible for setting policy and planning for the future.

The use of the Internet by individuals from every walk of life has grown tremendously since 1991. We do not know exactly how many individual users access the Internet in a year, but estimates provided by the UN indicate that the number of Internet users in the United Sates in 2001 was 142,823,000 or 49.5 users per 100 population. This compares to a worldwide total of 550,000,000 or 8.14 users per 100 population (United Nations).

How the Internet Works

Networks

The basic element of the Internet is the network. A network consists of computers that are connected one to another through a communications channel. The channel may be an ordinary telephone wire, a fiber optic cable, or a high-speed microwave or satellite communications device.

> **TWO TYPES OF NETWORKS**
>
> ☐ Local Area Network (LAN)—connects computers in a small geographic area over a single channel.
> ☐ Wide Area Network (WAN)—connects LANs, one to another over a wide geographic area.

The Internet is a WAN and is composed of three levels of networks: local, regional and national. To send or receive information over the Internet an individual must be connected to a local network that, in turn, is connected to the other levels as shown in Figure 5.1. Messages sent to individuals within the same local area are routed directly to the recipient's computer via the local network. If the message is being sent to a computer at a distant location, it will be routed through the appropriate local and regional networks until it reaches its destination.

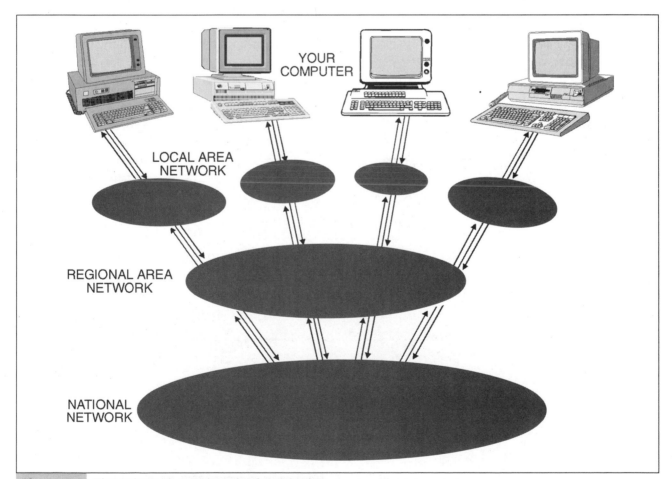

Figure 5.1 The Internet, a network of networks.

Information Transfer

The software used to send and receive information is called Transmission Control Protocol/Internet Protocol suite (TCP/IP). The Internet is often called a TCP/IP network, and for users to connect to the Internet they must connect through an Internet service provider (ISP). The other key to information sharing on the Internet is the use of the client/server model of data transfer. In the client/server model one computer serves as a "host" machine that distributes information to a "client" machine that receives information. With the client/server model, client software is installed on a personal computer to perform such tasks as displaying menus on the screen, connecting to a remote computer, and saving files. The server or remote host computer performs tasks such as searching a database and transmitting the results to the client.

How to Connect to the Internet

Virtually all college campuses provide students with Internet connections, but if you want to connect to the Internet from your home, you will need to subscribe to an Internet service provider. There are thousands of Internet service providers competing to provide Internet connections that are faster and more reliable than those of their competitors. A list of Internet providers may be found at http://thelist.internet.com. The list lets you locate providers by area codes or type of service. You also have a wide choice of technologies: cable television modem, digital subscriber lines (DSL), wireless satellite, and dial up-connection. A dial-up account is the least expensive, but it is also the slowest.

ELECTRONIC MAIL (E-MAIL)

Electronic mail (e-mail) is a feature of the Internet that allows you to send or receive mail electronically. With e-mail you can send a message to any person with an e-mail account anywhere in the world. Mail delivered in this way is extremely fast, usually arriving at its destination within seconds of having been sent. E-mail functions also support LISTSERV discussion groups where you can share information with people around the world.

Steps to Follow in Sending E-mail

1. LOGON TO THE COMPUTER AND ACTIVATE THE E-MAIL SOFTWARE.
2. THE SYSTEM WILL PROMPT YOU FOR THE ADDRESS OF THE PERSON TO WHOM YOU ARE SENDING MAIL.
3. CREATE THE MESSAGE. (BE SURE TO PROOFREAD THE MESSAGE BEFORE SENDING IT. ONCE A MESSAGE HAS BEEN SENT IT IS PROBABLY NOT POSSIBLE TO RETRIEVE IT.)
4. SEND THE MESSAGE.

E-Mail Addresses

The e-mail address is based on a user ID (assigned to you by the Internet provider) within the domain at a specific institution.

THE TOP-LEVEL DOMAINS ON THE INTERNET			
EDU	educational institution	MIL	military organization
COM	commercial organization or a business	NET	network resources
GOV	government agency	ORG	organization

LISTSERV

LISTSERVs are a combination of e-mail and discussion groups. You must formally subscribe to a LISTSERV in order to receive and send mail. Once you have subscribed you will automatically receive mail that is sent by any other member of the list. To subscribe to a LISTSERV you must first find the address of the list to which you wish to subscribe. Then send a message to that address by placing the following message in the body:

subscribe [name of LISTSERV] [your real name (not your e-mail ID)]

Usenet News

There are thousands of Usenet newsgroups that are designed to serve as electronic forums for discussion, debate, questions, and distribution of software, images, sounds, and other information. The newsgroups' messages are distributed to computer sites all over the world. Each computer site accumulates the messages and redistributes them to its own subscribers. Subscribers can read the articles posted to the Usenet newsgroups, reply to articles, post new articles, save articles, or forward them by e-mail to others. Newsgroups are listed by categories that define the subject. For example, "soc.culture.fr" deals with social issues related to French culture.

FILE TRANSFER PROTOCOL (FTP)

File transfer protocol (FTP) allows you to transfer files of all kinds over the Internet. There are special software utilities to handle file transfer. Two of the most widely used are WS_FTP and CuteFTP.

WORLD WIDE WEB

What Is It?

The World Wide Web (WWW or Web) is a facet of the Internet that was developed by scientists at CERN, a research institute located in Switzerland. The idea was to develop a tool that would be an improvement on existing technologies such as Gopher. They created Hypertext Transfer Protocol (HTTP), which standardized communication between servers and clients. With the Web, a searcher can follow a path that will lead to documents and files wherever they might be. The Web also has the capability of presenting information in graphic format: pictures, images, maps, charts, and animations. The World Wide Web is the primary Internet tool, and in fact, to most people, the Internet is the Web.

How Information on the Web Is Created

The main way that information gets on the Web is through the creation of Web sites. A Web site is any location on the Internet that contains information. Each Web site has its unique address. (See *URL* below.) A *home page*, or a *Web page*, is typically the top level of information at a Web site. A home page can also be the page that individuals, businesses, or organizations create about themselves.

Information on Web pages is created by the use of *hypertext* or *hypermedia* that allows links to and from files located on servers anywhere on the Internet. In a hypertext document, words, phrases, or images are highlighted in order to point to a different document where more information pertaining to that word can be found. When the user selects a highlighted word or phrase, a second document is opened. (To select a highlighted word or phrase using a mouse, the user places the mouse over the highlighted section and clicks the left mouse button.) The second document may contain links to other related documents. The linked documents may all be located at different sites, all of which will be transparent to users as they move through the Web.

Hypertext documents are created by using Hypertext Markup Language (HTML). With HTML the words and phrases are written as normal text but special format codes, called tags, are used to set fonts and colors and to insert images. Certain tags are also used to create links to other Web pages. Many of the pages that you see on the Web contain animation and imaginative graphic creations. These are probably created using special coding languages such as *Java*, which is a powerful tool used to exploit the graphic and audio potential of the Internet. There are a number of Web authoring software programs that allow even the novice to create imaginative and artistic Web pages. Recent versions of word processing software allow you to convert any document into hypertext. That is, you can prepare Internet-ready materials as easily as you can write a letter or an essay.

Accessing the World Wide Web

The World Wide Web is accessed by means of a browser—a powerful tool that allows you to navigate the Web by pointing and clicking on highlighted words or images (hot links or hyperlinks). The browser then retrieves the selected information from a remote computer and displays it on your screen. This information might be a picture, a movie, text, or sound, or it might be a connection to a Usenet Newsgroup, or a Telnet or FTP site. The browser uses the Uniform Resource Locator (URL), which is the address for the link selected.

Internet Explorer and *Netscape* are the most widely used Web browsers. They are easy to use and highly versatile. Both can be downloaded free from the Internet. The address for Internet Explorer is http://www.microsoft.com; for Netscape it is http://netscape.com. At the top of either screen is a standard menu bar and a tool bar with frequently used commands. The block just below the toolbar shows the Internet address (URL) of the document that is currently displayed. A new address can be typed in at any time to change the page. Beneath that is the screen with graphics and hypertext links. Both browsers have features that allow for e-mail, chat, downloading, and the creation of personal home pages.

URL

To go directly to a specific source you must know the URL (Uniform Resource Locator). The URL is a unique global Internet identifier used on the World Wide Web. It allows any document anywhere on the Internet to be accessed by any browser. The URL is comparable to someone's address that gives the country, state, city, street, and house number. URLs are composed of several parts including the Internet access protocol, the location, and the file.

Example

http://www.lib.lsu.edu/weblio.html

Where   http=Hypertext Transfer Protocol.

        www.lib.lsu.edu=domain address for the Web server at the LSU Libraries.

        Weblio.html=specific page (LSU Libraries Subject Guides).

Listings of URLs can be found in a great number of places, including subject guides and directories on the Internet. You can create a special directory to frequently visited sites on your computer. In Netscape this is called "Bookmarks." In Internet Explorer it is called "Favorites." To save the address of an Internet Explorer site that is currently displayed on the screen:

- [ ] click on the **Favorites** button on the menu bar;
- [ ] click on **Add to Favorites**.

The location of that site will be placed at the bottom of your bookmark list.
To retrieve a site from your Bookmark site:

- [ ] click on the **Bookmarks** button on the menu bar;
- [ ] move to the address you want to retrieve and click on the address.

The **Bookmarks** button in Netscape operates in a similar fashion. Keep in mind that URLs may change and even disappear, even if you accessed them recently.

USING SEARCH ENGINES TO FIND INFORMATION ON THE INTERNET

There are many ways to go about finding information on the Internet. You can search the databases to which your library subscribes, or you can search the vast amount of free information that is available on the Web. Other chapters are devoted to finding information in specific types of sources—reference works, periodical databases, and government sources. This discussion will focus on using search engines to find information that is free on the Web.

What Is a Search Engine?

A search engine is a utility that searches the entire Internet, a site, or a database for terms that you select. Although *search engine* is really a general class of programs that employs a search mechanism, the term is used here to describe systems like AltaVista, Google, and Excite that enable users to search for information on the Web. Typically, a search engine works by sending out a program called a *spider,* or a *robot,* to scan the area to be searched and to retrieve as many documents as possible that correspond to the search request.

Using a search engine to find specific information can be rewarding; at the same time it can be frustrating. Because it is searching so much information, it is likely to return an unmanageable number of results. In addition, there are many search engines and new ones appear regularly. As with any information search, it is important to plan ahead to know which tools to use to achieve the best results.

Developing a Search Strategy

Before you begin any search you should develop a search strategy.

Ask Yourself

- [ ] Is your topic likely to be found on the Internet?
  The Internet is an excellent source for information related to:

Government at all levels	Business	Computers	Engineering
Geography	Travel	Recreation	Biography
Entertainment News	Popular Culture	Arts	Literature

□ Do you need current or historical information?

Normally, you can expect to find information that is current on the Internet, but you need to be aware that this is not necessarily the case. You need to always check the date of information you find posted on the Internet. You may also find material that is in the public domain; that is, it is older than 75 years, and the copyright has expired.

□ Decide which keywords you will use to search for the information you need.

□ Decide which type of search engine is most appropriate to use for your search.

□ Evaluate any source you locate. (See the checklist in Table 6.2 for evaluating Internet information.)

Types of Search Engines

While you do not need to learn how to use every search engine, it is helpful to be able to identify some of the more popular ones and to understand the differences among them. As you begin to search the Internet, you will, no doubt, develop one or two favorites, and you will also learn which ones work best for different information needs.

There are essentially four types of search engines. See Figure 5.2 for examples of types of search engines.

□ A **mediated search engine**, also known as a **directory search engine**, searches for information by categories. It is a hierarchical search that starts with a broad subject heading and searches for more specific topics that fall within those categories. This type of search engine searches descriptors that have been placed in a predefined database established by the creators. Yahoo and Lycos are among the more popular search engines of this type.

□ A **general or keyword search engine** searches the entire Web. It sends out a spider, or a robot, that searches for keywords that appear in special fields, called *meta tags*. Since it is searching a much larger database than a directory type search engine, it will gather more information. However, it is more likely to retrieve information that is not relevant. AltaVista, Google, and Teoma are examples of keyword search engines.

□ A **meta-search engine** (sometimes called a **multi-search engine**) searches a number of search engines in tandem. The search is conducted using keywords employing commonly used operators or plain language. The program then lists the hits either by search engine or by integrating the results into a single listing. The search method it employs is known as a "meta search." It has the advantage of searching over a large number of other search engines, but it is not considered to be as effective as some of the keyword search engines. Dogpile is an example of a meta-search engine.

□ A **subject search engine** is a mediated search engine dedicated to specific broad subject areas. Findlaw and FirstGov are typical of subject specific search engines.

Performing a Search

As new search engines are being developed on a continuing basis, so are changes being made to existing search engines. The search features that one sees today could very well be gone tomorrow. However, it is true that practically all of the major search engines support searching using Boolean operators in one form or another. For example, some search engines use plus (+) or minus (–) symbols to indicate the Booleans AND and NOT, respectively. Search features of a few of the major search engines are shown in Figure 5.3. Review Chapter 3 to remind yourself of basic techniques for searching using Boolean and positional operators.

Different Types of Search Engines

Mediated or Directory	General or Keyword	Meta Search	Subject
About	AllTheWeb	Dogpile	ADAM (Architecture)
Ask Jeeves	AltaVista	DigiSearch	BPubs (Business)
AOL Search	Gigablast	Fazzle	FindLaw (Legal)
Britannica	Google	Ixquick	FirstGov (Government)
LookSmart	Hot Bot	Mamma	PsychCrawler (Psychology)
Open Directory	Lycos	MetaCrawler	SciNetScience Search (Science)
Yahoo!	MSN Search	ProFusion	SearchEdu (Education)
	Teoma	Search.com (SavySearch)	SearchMil (Military)
	WiseNut		Voice of the Shuttle (Humanities)
			WWomen (women)

Figure 5.2 Search engines by type.

Caution

The search tips below apply to most search engines, but you usually will be better served by first going to the "help" features or "search tips" of individual search engines.

Keyword Search

Guidelines

Conduct a successful keyword search

☐ Analyze your topic and be as specific as possible when choosing your keywords.

Be sure to check your spelling when you type your keywords.

For example, if you want information on the harmful effects of diet pills, you want to use all the terms in your search statement—diet/pills/harmful/effects, not just "diet" or "diet pills."

☐ Use Boolean operator AND (or the plus (+) symbol) to narrow a search.

Example

Diet and pills and harmful and effects

OR

diet +pills +harmful +effects

□ Use the Boolean operator NOT (or the minus (–) symbol) to eliminate pages that have one word on them but not another.

Example

You may want to find information about "jazz," but you want to eliminate those pages that have information on the Utah Jazz.

jazz not utah

OR

jazz - utah

Phrase Search

A search for keywords retrieves pages that have all the words in your search statement, but the words may not necessarily be near each other. For example, if you did a search on the census forms for the year 2000 (2000 +census +forms) you may get a page that mentions 2000 in one place, census in another, and forms in still another. All of the words in your search statement would appear on the page, but they still might not match your needs. You can do a phrase search to avoid this problem. With a phrase search, you tell the search engine to retrieve the terms in your search statement in the exact order in which you requested them. In most search engines, this is done by enclosing the phrase in quotation marks; others may use parentheses.

Example

"2000 census forms"

OR

(2000 census forms)

The search will retrieve pages that have all the words and in the exact order of the query. With some search engines, such as Google, the AND is implied; a search for 2000 census forms without the quotation marks would yield different results from one enclosed in quotation marks.

Natural Language Search

Natural language searching allows you to post a query in the form of a question instead of by keyword or subject. With natural language searching, you simply state your search in the form of a question. For example, if you type: Is acupuncture effective for the relief of pain?, the search engine would ignore common words such as "is," "for," "the," and "of" and find articles containing the words "acupuncture," "effective," "relief," and "pain."

With natural language searching, the search is based on:

□ the recognition and weighting of usual word combinations, such as "homeless shelters," "United States," or "third world";

□ exact matching of search terms to article titles;

□ proximity of search words in an article; and

□ the number of times the search terms occurs in each article.

Search results are usually ranked for relevancy with those meeting most of the criteria above ranked higher. Natural language searching is good for beginners and for children, but usually it is not as effective as keyword or subject searching.

More Information

Some search engines might be case sensitive, and others might not allow certain types of searches. Still others might have advanced search features that allow you to limit your search in much the same way as you would in an online catalog. For updates on search engines and their features, go to Search Engine Watch (http://searchenginewatch.com) or look at the help features on individual search engine pages.

Search Engine Features

Figure 5.3 shows some of the important features for a few of the most popular search engines. The information is current as of May, 2003. Recall that the Internet is fluid—anything listed here is subject to change.

EVALUATING INFORMATION FOUND ON THE INTERNET

The unbridled nature of the Internet represents its best and worst features. The quantity of information on the Internet is enormous and it runs the gamut from pure nonsense to the most highly respected research. Although Internet resources have the potential to be current, this is frequently not the case. Quite often individuals put information on the Internet for fun or perhaps as part of their current job responsibilities, but they have no interest in keeping it up-to-date. This problem is further complicated because it is not always possible to tell whether an electronic resource is up-to-date. Many of the resources do not give a date of publication or a copyright date as do printed publications. But a more serious problem with information resources

Search Engine Features

Search Engine	Advanced Search Forms	Boolean Searching	Proximity	Truncation	Image Searching	Multi-language Searching	Help Menu
AllTheWeb	yes	yes	yes	no	yes	yes	yes
AltaVista	yes	yes	yss	yes	yes	yes	yes
Ask Jeeves	no	no	yes	no	no	no	yes
DogPile	yes	yes	yes	no	yes	no	yes
Google	yes	yes	yes	no	yes	yes	yes
HotBot	yes	yes	yes	no	yes	yes	yes
Lycos	yes	yes	yes	no	no	yes	yes
MSN Search	yes	yes	yes	yes	no	yes	yes
Teoma	yes	yes	yes	no	yes	yes	yes
Yahoo	yes	no	yes	no	no	no	yes

Figure 5.3 Search engine features.

from the Internet is the lack of quality control. Although printed materials often have errors and inaccuracies, they are at least subjected to some measure of pre-publication evaluation by publishers. Further, librarians use established criteria for selecting printed materials for their libraries. Anyone can be a publisher on the Internet—from elementary school students to research scientists. For the most part, information on the Internet is not subject to any criteria to determine its accuracy or suitability for publication. **The user must be responsible for assessing the quality of the resources.** Table 6.2 provides criteria for evaluating any information resource and includes a checklist for evaluating resources on the Internet.

Works Cited

Krol, Ed. *The Whole Internet User's Guide and Catalog*. 2nd ed. Sebastopol, CA: O'Reilly, 1994.

National Science Foundation. Office of Legislative and Public Affairs. *Fact Sheet*. n.d. 27 Jan. 2003 <http://www.nsf.gov/od/lpa/news/media/backgr1.htm>.

United Nations. Department of Economics and Social Affairs. Statistics Division. *Millennium Indicators*. 2003. 23 Jan. 2003 <http://millenniumindicators.un.org/unsd/mi/mi_indicator_xrxx.asp?ind_code=48>.

Exercise 5.1

Instructor: _____ Course/Section: _____

Name: _____

Date: _____ Points: _____

Review Questions

1. What is the Internet?

2. Why was the Internet originally developed?

3. Who owns the Internet?

4. What are networks?

5. What is an Internet service provider?

6. What is e-mail?

7. What is a LISTSERV?

8. What is the World Wide Web?

9. Who can "publish" information on the Web?

10. What is a search engine?

11. What is a URL?

12. What is a home page?

13. Name four different types of search engines. Explain how they differ.

   a.

   b.

   c.

   d.

14. What is natural language searching?

15. Explain why it is important for users to evaluate information they find on the Internet.

Exercise 5.2 The Internet

Instructor: _____ Course/Section: _____

Name: _____

Date: _____ Points: _____

Finding Information on the Internet

The Internet Public Library (IPL) "the first public library of and for the Internet community" is an excellent site for locating specific information on the Internet. Locate the information requested below using this site as a starting point. To get there, type http://www.ipl.org in your browser's location bar.

Search for Hometown News

1. Under "Reading Room," select "Newspapers."

   From the "list of newspapers . . .," select "United States."

   From the list of states, select your home state.

   From the cities list, select your hometown (or a city near your hometown).

   Select a newspaper from your hometown.

   Give the following information.

   a. State:

   b. Hometown:

   c. Title of Newspaper:

   d. Title of one article from the newspaper:

   e. Article date:

How to Use the IPL Search Engine

2. Go back to the IPL home page. (Click on the "home" button or click on the "back" button until you get back to this page.) From the list on the left, select "Searching Tools." Click on "Search this Site." Read the "Searching Tips" and answer the following questions:

   a. Does the search engine search the text of documents?

   b. Does it do Boolean searching?

c. Which fields does it search?

d. How are the results sorted?

e. Which limiting feature does it provide?

3. Search for "native Americans" in the "Subject Collections." (Hint: Look under "Social Science," then under "Ethnicity . . ."

    a. How many hits did you get from this search?

    b. Give the title of one page that you locate on this topic.

Search for Specific Information

4. Return to the home page. Click on "Ready Reference," then on "Almanacs," and then on "Information Please Almanac." Locate the following information:

    a. People who were born on your birthday. List three.

    b. The weather report for your hometown. Give the URL.

    c. The plays holding the record for the longest runs on Broadway. List the top three.

5. Return to the IPL home page (http://www.ipl.org). Assume that you want to use one of the "Pathfinders" to find information on mutual funds. (Hint: A Pathfinder is a type of search tool.)

    a. Explain the steps you need to take to get to the page that contains links to that information.

    b. Give the URL for a site that contains useful information on the stock market.

Exercise 5.3 The Internet

Instructor: _____ Course/Section: _____

Name: _____

Date: _____ Points: _____

Comparing Search Engines

Select a topic from the list below (or use one assigned by your instructor) to answer the questions which follow.

snail darter	gold rush	country music	skyscrapers
professional wrestling	prayer in schools	DVD technology	Eiffel Tower
combating street gangs	genetically altered crops	weapons of mass destruction	pyramids
smallpox vaccine	hunger in America	Blue Grass music	Cubism

1. What topic did you select?

2. Go to http://www.lycos.com and answer the following questions.

   a. Does the page contain advertising?

   b. If so, is it annoying or obtrusive? Explain.

   c. Describe any features on the page that you find interesting or useful.

   d. Is there a list or directory of subject categories?

   e. If so, is there a category that is appropriate for the topic you selected above? If so, which is it?

   f. If you find an appropriate category for your subject, continue searching until you find a site that contains information that would be useful to you. Give the URL for the site.

   g. Select one Web document from the site that would be relevant to your topic and print out the first page. Attach the printout to your assignment, or give the URL and title of the page.

3. Go to http://www.google.com and answer the following questions.

   a. Does the page contain advertising?

   b. If so, is it annoying or obtrusive? Explain.

c. Describe any features on the page that you find interesting or useful.

d. Is there a list of subject categories?

e. If not, how would you find information on your topic?

f. Use the method you describe in Question 3.e to locate a site that contains information that would be useful to you. Give the URL for the site.

g. Select one Web document from the site that would be relevant to your topic and print out the first page. Attach the printout to your assignment.

4. Go to http://www.dogpile.com and answer the following questions.

a. Does the page contain advertising?

b. If so, is it annoying or obtrusive? Explain.

c. Describe any features on the page that you find interesting or useful.

d. Is there a list of subject categories?

e. If so, is there a category that is appropriate for your topic? If so, which category is it?

f. If you find an appropriate category for your subject, continue through different levels until you find a site that contains information that would be useful to you. Give the URL for the site.

g. Select one Web document from the site that would be relevant to your topic and print out the first page. Attach the printout to your assignment, or give the URL and title of the page.

5. Compare the three Web sites in terms of their helpfulness in finding information for your topic (e.g., ease of use or relevancy of materials found). Which of the three did you find most useful? Why?

Exercise 5.4

Instructor: _____ Course/Section: _____

Name: _____

Date: _____ Points: _____

Finding Factual Information on the Internet

Go to the LSU Libraries' home page (http://www.lib.lsu.edu) and click on "Ready Reference." From this page, select links that will provide answers to each of the questions below. For each question, write the link you selected and the URL where you found the answer.

1. Locate the link to AdmissionsOffice.com, a site designed to help students select a college or university. Under which link are you likely to find that site?

   After you locate AdmissionsOffice.com click on "School Ranking" to find sites that rank U.S. colleges and universities. Click on the latest rankings by *U.S. News and World Report*.

   What three undergraduate colleges received the top ranking among liberal arts colleges?

   Link:

   URL:

2. Find a review in *The Complete Review* of the book *The Professor and the Madman*.

   Who is the author of the review in the *Wall Street Journal*?

   Link:

   URL:

3. What is the job outlook for physician assistants?

   Link:

   URL:

4. Which movie won the 2001 Oscar for "Best Picture"?

   Link:

   URL:

5. Who said "Politics makes strange bed-fellows"?

   Link:

   URL:

6. What is the equivalent in miles of 28 kilometers? (Hint: Consult a conversion *dictionary*.)

   Link:

   URL:

7. What is the latest consumer product to be approved by the Food and Drug Administration (FDA)?

   Link:

   URL:

Instructor: _____ Course/Section: _____

Name: _____

Date: _____ Points: _____

Comparing Types of Search Engines

Assignment: Find out how to deal with identity theft.

Mediated or Directory Search Engines

1. Look up "identity theft" in the ProFusion search engine (http://www.profusion.com/). In the search box on the main page type in *identity theft*, and execute the search.

   How many hits (results) did you get?

2. On the main ProFusion page, select the "legal" category for your search. This will automatically take you to the next page where there is a list of legal sources. Select all the categories except "Web Search Engines," "Patents," "Legal Directories," and "Legal Forms." Type in the term *identity theft* in the search box and execute the search.

   How many hits did you get?

3. Give the title of one Website that you think would be useful for your assignment.

General Search Engines

4. Go to the Google search engine (www.google.com/). On the first page type *identity theft* in the search box and execute your search.

   How many hits did you get?

5. Do the same search, except this time put the phrase in quotation marks.

   How many hits did you get?

6. Explain why you got different results in the two searches.

7. Go to "Advanced Search" on the Google page. Search for *identity theft* as an exact phrase. Limit your search to occurrences only in the title and to pages updated within the past year.

   How many hits did you get?

8. Give the title of one Website that you think would be useful for your assignment.

Meta Search Engines

9. Go to the Mamma search engine (www.mamma.com/). Type *identity theft* in the search box and execute the search.

   How many hits did you get?

10. Go to "Power Search" and check all the search engines in the list. Type *identity theft* in the search box and perform the search.

    How many hits did you get?

11. Give the title of one Website that you think would be useful for your assignment.

12. Which of the three types of search engines (mediated, general, or meta) did you find most effective? Explain your answer.

Evaluating Information Sources

"This is the best book ever written by any man on the wrong side
of a question of which he is profoundly ignorant."

Thomas B. Macaulay

Introduction

Never before has there been so much information available or so many ways to disseminate and retrieve it. Even as you read this, Web sites are being created, books and newspapers are being published, and new ways of storing and retrieving information are being developed. Many have characterized what is happening as "information overload." As someone looking for information, you will need to know not only how to locate information, but also how to evaluate the information that you locate. You will find that not all information sources are suitable for your research; nor is all information reliable.

How critical are you?

□ Can you tell if the information is reliable?

□ Can you tell the difference between propaganda and fact?

□ Can you spot a hoax?

□ Can you determine whether an author is "profoundly ignorant about the wrong side of a question"?

Confronted with the wide array of print, electronic, oral, and visual resources available, you need to be able to make independent judgments about the suitability and the quality of the sources you locate. This chapter will provide you with criteria for selecting appropriate material and evaluating the material you find.

UNDERSTAND THE SOURCES

One of the first things you should be able to do as you locate and use information is to identify whether a source is a *primary* source or a *secondary* source and to understand the level of scholarship—whether the treatment of the topic is *popular* or *scholarly*. These concepts are critical to any evaluation of materials.

Primary Sources

Primary sources are firsthand accounts such as diaries, journals, letters—anything that is considered a direct source. That is, the author is actually a direct participant in or an observer of a research project or an event. It is also any raw data, such as census data or facts such as those gathered in a newspaper account. The test of whether or not something is a primary source is whether it is actual evidence without any interpretation or analysis beyond what the observer provided.

> **PRIMARY INFORMATION SOURCES**
>
> ☐ diaries, letters, family records, journals
> ☐ statistics
> ☐ surveys
> ☐ speeches
> ☐ interviews
> ☐ autobiographies
> ☐ poems, novels, short stories, films, paintings
> ☐ public documents, laws, treaties, court records
> ☐ maps

Secondary Sources

A secondary source provides an analysis, an explanation, or a restatement of a primary source. Many secondary sources use primary sources to prove a point or to try to persuade the reader to hold a certain opinion.

> **SECONDARY INFORMATION SOURCES**
>
> ☐ dictionaries
> ☐ encyclopedias
> ☐ textbooks
> ☐ books and articles that interpret or review research works

For example, an article entitled "Methods of Pay Earnings: A Longitudinal Analysis" in *Industrial and Labor Relations Review* uses data from the National Longitudinal Survey of Youth, a primary source, to show level and variance of wages among workers.

Popular and Scholarly Sources

Popular sources are intended for general audiences who are not experts in the field. The information is presented in such a way that a wide range of readers or viewers can understand it. *Scholarly* sources are intended for a more limited audience. The information is usually written by scholars or experts in a field for other researchers, scholars, or students. The authors normally use specialized vocabulary particular to the discipline which they are covering. Scholarly sources are often the result of original research and most include documentation or bibliographies of the sources consulted. For example, if you are looking for an analytical treatment of the topic "effects of television violence on viewers' aggression," you are more likely to find the information you need in the *Psychological Bulletin* than in the popular magazine *Time*. An article on the subject in *Time* will not provide in-depth coverage of the subject. Because *Time* is aimed at a different audience, its approach is to provide readers with factual reporting, mostly devoid of analysis, and to be as brief as possible in its coverage. It might summarize the results of a study but would not provide the kind of in-depth analysis you might need. The *Psychological Bulletin* is a scholarly journal; its purpose is to present the results of studies, experiments, surveys, or other types of research by its authors. An article in *Psychological Bulletin* is likely to provide an analytical approach that is backed by specific research and includes documentation. Keep in mind that each of the two levels of information might fill a different need.

Popular or scholarly sources are not limited to magazines and journals. Reference books, books that you locate in the library's catalog, and Internet sources may also be popular or scholarly. *World Book Encyclopedia*, for example, is a general encyclopedia intended for a wide audience; the *Encyclopedia of Psychology* is a very specialized subject encyclopedia that has been written by authors selected for their expertise in the field.

INITIAL APPROACH

The first step for evaluating information takes place before you begin the actual search. You must begin any search with two basic questions.

Ask Yourself

- ☐ What do I need to know?
- ☐ What sources are likely to provide the information I need?

☐ What Do You Need to Know?

It is best to approach this question by examining your information needs in light of five basic factors:

- ▫ level of specificity
- ▫ time line needed
- ▫ focus
- ▫ level of scholarship
- ▫ type of information

Figure 2.5 addresses this question in more detail.

☐ What Sources Are Likely to Provide the Information You Need?

- ▫ You should begin by examining the body of the source.
- ▫ Read the preface of a book to determine the author's purpose.
- ▫ Scan the table of contents and the index to get a broad overview of the material it covers.
- ▫ Peruse journals and magazines, reference book articles, and Internet sources to see if they contain the information you need.
- ▫ Note whether documentation and bibliographies are included that will lead to additional sources.
- ▫ Read the relevant parts of the book or article that specifically address your topic.

□ As you locate sources of information cast a critical eye on the content. Are the sources reliable, fair, objective, lacking hidden motives?

APPLYING EVALUATION CRITERIA

The ability to determine the suitability and worth of a particular source is one of the most important research skills you can acquire. It is also one of the most difficult because you are dealing primarily with unknowns. The task is further complicated by the fact that there are so many different formats to deal with—books, periodicals, reference books, CD-ROM and DVD and Internet resources. Most of the books and periodicals that you find in the library have already undergone some evaluative measures. Publishers edit books and periodicals; articles in scholarly journals are "refereed" by peers in the field; librarians employ evaluative techniques in selecting materials for their collections. Information on the Internet, on the other hand, has not undergone any such selection process, so you will have to be especially vigilant when you use information found on the Internet. There is no single test that you can apply to determine whether a work is reliable or whether the contents are accurate or truthful. Instead, you must make a judgment based on a number of clues or indicators.

Table 6.1 is a set of criteria together with questions and discussion that can serve as a checklist to help you evaluate books, periodical articles or Internet information that you locate.

EVALUATING INTERNET SOURCES

Unlike resources such as magazines, journals, and books that are subjected to some type of selection process (editing, peer review, library selection), most information on the Internet is almost totally lacking in quality control. The onus rests with the user to determine the quality and reliability of information on the Internet. In any information that is posted on the Web there are some telltale signs that should lead you to suspect the credibility of the information: poor grammar, misspelling, or inflammatory words. Beyond the obvious things you should also be able to apply some criteria to determine the quality of a work. The same criteria that are listed in Table 6.1 can be used to evaluate Internet resources; however, because of the unique nature of information on the Internet, you need to apply a slightly different checklist (see Table 6.2).

EVALUATIVE REVIEWS

You may be able to locate critical reviews of books in a reviewing source, such as *Book Review Index* or *Book Review Digest*. (See Chapter 12 to learn how to use these.) Book reviews may provide a more in-depth analysis than the one you are able to make by applying the criteria in Table 6.1. Book reviews may appear in journals dedicated solely to reviewing books, or they may appear in subject-based professional journals. Book reviews help answer such questions as whether the book makes a valuable contribution to the field, contains accurate information, or is overly biased or controversial. Articles in scholarly journals are refereed: that is, the authors' peers in the field have subjected them to critical review before publication. Many of the online databases will indicate whether or not a journal is refereed.

Evaluations of Web sites appear in many journals and magazines and in Internet rating services. Many Web pages list all of the awards they have won. For example, the page entitled "All the Virology on the WWW" has a separate page listing all of the awards it has received (http://www.virology.net/ATVaward.html). The author of this page claims to be the "single site for virology information on the Internet." The list of reviews as well as awards will help you determine whether the claim is mere hyperbole or if this is, indeed, the best source for information on virology.

Table 6.1 Evaluating Information Sources

Authoritativeness

Author
- ☐ What are the author's education, training, and level of expertise or experience in the field?
  Look for biographical information, the author's title, employment, position, and institutional affiliation.
- ☐ Are there other works in the same field by this author?
  Check the online catalog and databases on the same subject.
- ☐ What is the author's reputation or standing among peers?
  If a journal article, check to see if it is a refereed journal.
  If a signed article in a subject encyclopedia, read the preface to see how authors were selected.
- ☐ If the author is a corporation or an agency, is it one that is well known in the field?

Publisher
- ☐ Is the publisher well known in the field?
- ☐ Are there many works published by this publisher?
  Check the online catalog to find other books by the publisher.
- ☐ Does a university press publish the source?
- ☐ Is the publisher a professional organization?
  Generally one can assume that reputable publishers, professional associations, or university presses will publish high quality materials.

Comprehensiveness

- ☐ Are all aspects of the subject covered or have obvious facts been omitted?
  Examine the table of contents of books or peruse the article or Web source.
- ☐ Does the work update other sources or does it add new information?
  These questions may be difficult for the novice researcher to answer, but comparing information in one source with that in another may provide some answers. For example, compare the coverage of "black holes" in *World Book Encyclopedia* with the article on the same topic in *McGraw-Hill Encyclopedia of Science and Technology*.
- ☐ Is the source too elementary, too technical, too advanced, or just right for your needs?
- ☐ What type of audience is the author addressing?
- ☐ Is the information aimed at a specialized or a general audience?

Reliability

Objectives or Biased Treatment
- ☐ Do the facts support the author's viewpoint?
- ☐ Do you detect individual biases in the writing?
- ☐ Does the author use language that is designed to appeal to emotions and biases?
- ☐ What is the author's motive in writing the work?
  Knowing something about the author's background, training, and other works is useful in determining possible bias. Often this information can be obtained from biographical dictionaries and indexes. The periodical indexes and abstracts might be checked to see if the author has written biased literature or if there has been controversy surrounding his or her publications.

navigate   *informative*

Table 6.1 Evaluating Information Sources *(continued)*

Objectives or Biased Treatment *(continued)*

☐ Is the information that is presented fact or opinion?

It is not easy to separate fact from opinion. Facts can usually be verified; opinions, though they may be based on factual information, are based on the author's interpretation of facts. Skilled writers can manipulate their opinions so as to make you think their interpretations are facts. Note whether the work is well researched and documented.

☐ Is the work propaganda?

We can recognize propaganda when it is in a leaflet that is handed out on the street corner, but can we recognize it in other media? Propaganda is material that is systematically distributed to advocate a point of view or a strongly held interest on an issue. Its purpose is to influence and change the opinions and behavior of others. Those who use propaganda tend to capitalize on events by playing on emotions and by exploiting human weaknesses and fears. However, all propaganda is not negative, especially when it is designed to accomplish good, such as a campaign to stop the use of drugs among teenagers or to combat neighborhood crimes. Politicians use propaganda when campaigning for public office; businesses use it to sell products.

Accuracy

☐ Is the information correct, or are there obvious errors in the information?

It may be necessary to sample several sources to determine if there are inconsistencies in reporting such things as times, dates, and places. Statistical information is vulnerable to such inaccuracies, and one might do well to verify statistical information in more than one source whenever this is possible.

☐ Does the author cite the sources used?

☐ Does the author use primary or secondary sources?

Illustrations

☐ Does the work contain pictures, drawings, maps, or statistical tables that enhance its usefulness?

The use of illustrations not only makes a book or article more interesting, but also makes a significant contribution to the understanding of the materials being presented.

Currency

Date of Publication

☐ When was the work published?

☐ Is the information up-to-date or have discoveries been made or events taken place since the work was published?

To determine currency of information, you might check journal articles on the same topic to see if there have been new events or developments. On Web pages, the date of the last revision is usually at the bottom of the home page, or sometimes on every page.

☐ Is the source current or out-of-date for your topic?

Current information is needed in areas that undergo constant and frequent changes such as in the pure and behavioral sciences. On the other hand, material that was written many years ago is often more suitable for topics in history and literature than those written more recently.

Table 6.2 Evaluating Internet Information

Authoritativeness

Author
- ☐ Is the author's name listed on the page?
    In many instances Web pages are created by Web masters whose expertise is more in page design than in familiarity with the content of the page. Also beware of anonymity.
- ☐ Is the author qualified to write on this subject?
- ☐ Are his or her education, training, and/or experience in a field relevant to the topic that is covered?
    Look on the page for biographical information, such as the author's title or position.
- ☐ Has the author published in other formats?
- ☐ Is there a way to contact the author? (E-mail or other address provided?)
- ☐ If the author is an organization, is it one that is well known and respected?

Comprehensiveness

- ☐ Is this a summary of a topic or does it cover all aspects of the topic?
    It is not unusual to find postings that are just excerpts or summaries of another work in a printed source.
- ☐ Are there links? Are they annotated?
- ☐ Does the site offer a selected list of resources in a particular discipline or field or does it claim to offer a complete list?
- ☐ If a selected list is offered, does the author explain how the list of resources was chosen?
- ☐ Does the site refer to print and other non-Internet resources or just Internet resources?

Reliability

- ☐ What is the origin of the site?
    Examine the site by checking the domain in the URL (Uniform Resource Locator) or Internet address. The domain name is the last part of the URL. The most common domains are "edu" for educational institutions, "gov" for government, "com" for commercial and "org" for organization. Countries outside of the United States use country codes as their domain names: for example, "ca" for Canada, and "fr" for France. Although government and education sites tend to be more reliable, information from commercial sites may also provide valid information. But keep in mind that commercial sites are probably more interested in selling you a product than in providing unbiased information.
- ☐ Does the site describe or provide the results of research or scholarly effort?
- ☐ Can the results be refuted or verified through other means—for example, in other research tools?
- ☐ Is advertising included on the site, and if so, does it affect the contents of the page?
- ☐ Does the page contain pictures, drawings, maps, or statistical tables that enhance its usefulness?
- ☐ Are there obvious signs of poor quality, such as bad grammar, colloquial speech, misspelled words, inflammatory words?
- ☐ Does the site contain propaganda? The Internet, as no other media in history, allows individuals from every walk of life and from throughout the world to put out messages that are designed to persuade and influence others to accept their point of view. You must be able to use your best judgment to distinguish propaganda from truly objective literature.

Currency

- ☐ When was the information posted or updated?
    On Web pages, the date of the last revision is usually at the bottom of the home page, or sometimes on every page.
- ☐ What are the inclusive dates of the information?

Exercise 6.1

Instructor: _____ Course/Section: _____

Name: _____

Date: _____ Points: _____

Review Questions

1. Explain the difference between primary and secondary sources.

2. Give four examples of primary sources.

   a.

   b.

   c.

   d.

3. Give four examples of secondary sources.

   a.

   b.

   c.

   d.

4. Identify whether each of the following is a primary source or a secondary source.

   a. Biography of Woodrow Wilson
   b. Diary of a Vietnam soldier
   c. Letters of Dorothy Day
   d. An interview in *Newsweek* with the two top presidential candidates
   e. Newspaper article giving an eye-witness account of the eruption of the volcano at Mount St. Helens
   f. Journal article on the history of the labor movement
   g. A congressional hearing on AIDS research
   h. A map of the Aegean Sea

5. Explain the differences between popular and scholarly levels of information.

6. Materials that you locate in libraries (or that libraries subscribe to online) have been subjected to some degree of evaluation. Describe to what extent this statement is correct.

7. Name two sources that might help you evaluate books.

   a.

   b.

8. How would you determine if a source meets each of the following criteria?

   Authoritativeness

   Comprehensiveness

   Reliability

   Currency

9. Why is it so important that you evaluate information that you find on the Internet?

10. Name three criteria to help you determine the authoritativeness of information on the Internet.

Exercise 6.2

Instructor: _____ Course/Section: _____

Name: _____

Date: _____ Points: _____

Applying Evaluative Criteria to Internet Sites

Using one of the search engines listed on the site below, conduct a search on a topic that interests you or use one that is assigned by your instructor.

http://www.ipl.org/div/websearching/

1. Search engine used:

2. Select a Web document (not just a site) with information on your topic. Give the following information.

   URL of Web page:

   Title of the Web page:

Authoritativeness

3. Who is the author of the page?

4. What are the author's credentials?

5. In your opinion, is the author qualified to write on this subject? Explain.

6. Is there a way to contact the author? (E-mail or other address provided?)

7. If the author is an organization, is it one that is well known and respected? Explain.

8. Is the organization one that is likely to take an advocacy position on the subject covered in the page? Explain.

Comprehensiveness

9. Does this page cover the topic adequately for your purposes or is it a brief summary?

10. Does the page contain links to other sources?

   Are they annotated?

11. Does the site provide a list of resources?

   Are these helpful to your research?

Reliability

12. What is the domain (i.e., edu, com, gov) of the page?

   Is this important to your evaluation? Explain.

13. Does the search describe or provide the results of scholarly research?

14. Is advertising included on the site? If so, does it affect the contents of the page?

15. Does the page contain pictures, drawings, maps, tables, or other graphics that enhance its usefulness? If so, describe.

16. Are there obvious signs of poor grammar, colloquial speech, misspelled words, inflammatory words?

Currency

17. When was the information posted?

18. What are the inclusive dates of the information?

   Using the information you have learned while evaluating this site, briefly explain why it is (or is not) useful for your research topic. Include the aspects such as authority, reliability, bias, subject content, currency.

Instructor: _____ Course/Section: _____

Name: _____

Date: _____ Points: _____

Evaluating Books and Journal Articles

1. Locate a nonfiction book that interests you in the online catalog of your library or use a nonfiction book that you have read recently. Apply any of the evaluative criteria listed in the chapter to determine its merit.

   Give the following information.

   a. Author of the book:

   b. Title:

   c. Publisher of the book:

   d. Is this a primary or a secondary source?

   e. What is the level of scholarship? Popular or scholarly?

   f. Write a brief evaluation of the book based on the criteria listed in this chapter. For example, does the book include biographical information about the author? Is it sufficient to vouch for her or his authoritativeness? Explain.

2. Locate a journal in your library and give the following information.

    a.   Author of an article in the journal:

    b.   Title of the article:

    c.   Title of the journal:

    d.   Publisher of the journal:

    e.   Is this a primary or a secondary source?

    f.   What is the level of scholarship? Popular or scholarly?

    g.   Write a brief evaluation of the journal article based on the criteria listed in this chapter.

Reference Sources

"Knowledge is of two kinds: we know a subject ourselves, or we know where we can find information upon it."

Samuel Johnson

Introduction

Reference sources are useful in the research process for a number of reasons: they provide background information, they provide facts or specific details on a subject, and they point to other sources of information. Reference services have changed dramatically with the introduction of computers and the Internet. With access to worldwide information literally at your fingertips 24 hours a day, you might find that many of your reference questions can now be answered with the click of a button without having to visit your local library. However, in many instances, and particularly for research papers, you will find that some of the reference sources that would prove helpful are available only in the library. Libraries continue to provide access to a combination of sources—some in print and others in electronic format such as CD-ROM and DVD that are not available remotely. Any information retrieval, whether in paper or electronic format, is more effective if you are familiar with the sources that provide that information. This chapter seeks to identify the major reference sources, regardless of format, and to help you sharpen your skills in finding and using them.

WHAT ARE REFERENCE SOURCES?

Reference books are housed in a separate area in the library. They usually provide quick answers to questions or specific facts, such as the address of the local Congressional representatives, the number of alcohol-related deaths in a given year, a short biography of Malcolm X, or a brief interpretation of the poem "The Love Song of J. Alfred Prufrock" by T.S. Eliot. Certain nonbook materials are also used for reference. These include information in electronic format such as CD-ROMs, online catalogs and databases, and information in other formats such as microforms, videocassettes, and the Internet.

How can you distinguish traditional reference material from other materials in library collections?

- ☐ They are designed to be consulted rather than being read straight through (reference).
- ☐ They may provide facts and figures in an easy-to-find format.
- ☐ They may provide concise information to frequently asked questions.
- ☐ They may contain valuable information for particular subject areas.
- ☐ They may serve as guides to information.
- ☐ They do not circulate but remain in the library for access to all.

USING REFERENCE SOURCES

Reference works can serve a variety of purposes. In the beginning of the research process, general encyclopedias and dictionaries can highlight specific major aspects of a topic. A subject bibliography might provide references to information that has already been gathered on a topic. For example, the *United States Government Documents on Women, 1800–1990: A Comprehensive Bibliography* by Mary Ellen Huls would be useful in reviewing the topic of women and discrimination in employment. An article in *Compton's Encyclopedia* entitled "Women's Rights" gives a narrative of the history of women in the workforce and highlights the inequality in wages that continues to exist. Most encyclopedias give bibliographies for further reading. Subject reference books provide more in-depth information on a particular aspect of a topic. Statistics and facts are often found in one-volume reference works such as almanacs or yearbooks. While many statistical sources, periodical indexes, abstracts, databases, biographies, and works on criticism are often housed in the reference area, they will be discussed in other chapters.

Evaluation of Reference Sources

Some features of reference works that you should look for to determine their suitability for research are discussed below. In addition, the criteria for evaluating general research materials discussed in Chapter 6 can be applied to reference sources.

Scope of Coverage

The scope of the reference work must match that of the research question. Does the work include sufficient material to answer the question? Is there sufficient detail to cover all the points needed for an answer? There are several ways to determine the scope of a work.

1. The introduction, the preface, and the table of contents all tell something about the scope or coverage of the work and about the author's intent. Manuals or instruction books that accompany nonbook materials serve the same purpose as the introductory pages of books.

2. The title of a work will help to determine its scope. Subject reference works tend to give greater coverage to the topics that they cover than more general works. The title of the work often provides clues to the contents. The text itself might be perused to determine the extent of details and the type of coverage.

Timeliness

The *copyright date*, revision date, or last update notification for Web documents should be used to determine whether or not the information contained in the source is current. The contents of a reference book are about a year older than the copyright date since it takes approximately a year before a book is published. The publication date and any revised edition dates are found on the reverse side of the title page of a work. A revised edition with a new copyright may indicate only minor changes. The terms "completely revised edition" or "enlarged edition" are indicative of more extensive revisions.

Arrangement

Reference works may be arranged or organized in three ways.

1. **Alphabetically:** Subjects or words appear in simple alphabetical order. Dictionaries are typically arranged in this fashion. Some reference books arranged in alphabetical order often include a separate index to help locate subtopics within the work. For example, *Webster's New World Dictionary* has a single alphabetical arrangement without a separate index while *World Book Encyclopedia* includes a separate index volume.

2. **Topically:** Subjects are listed in order by broad categories. Reference works arranged by topics almost always have a separate index that is used to find specific subjects within the broad categories. *The Encyclopedia of Crime and Justice* and *Sociological Abstracts* are examples of this type of arrangement.

3. **Chronologically:** Subjects are listed by date or time periods. Historical works such as Langer's *Encyclopedia of World History* are arranged by time periods.

Author

Knowing something about the author can be useful for determining the reliability of information. Occasionally reference books are written by one author, but more often, they are the work of several authors under the direction of an editor. Individual articles are usually signed by the author or authors responsible. Often the author's full name is given along with a brief biographical note indicating education, professional position, and a list of the author's other works. Sometimes that information appears elsewhere in the book or even in a separate volume if the work is a multivolume one. In *The New Encyclopaedia Britannica*, for example, only the author's initials appear at the end of the article; the full name and biographical information are found in a separate volume. With Web-based documents, some authorship or ownership is usually provided on the initial page of the source or at the end of the document.

Bibliographies

Bibliographies are helpful in providing the researcher with a list of materials for further consideration. They also tell the reader that the author has researched the topic, which is an indication of the reliability of the information. Bibliographies may be found at the end of each article, at the end of a section in some topically arranged works, at the end of the entire work, or perhaps as an appendix to the work.

Cross References

Cross references include *see* and *see also* references that direct the reader to similar or related topics. The *see* reference guides the reader from a term that is not used to one that is used. A *see also* reference suggests other terms to consult for additional information. Both of these are useful in gathering information.

Types of Reference Sources

Reference sources fall into two broad categories: (1) general, and (2) subject.

General—Materials that are general in scope provide information in one source on a wide variety of topics. *The New Encyclopaedia Britannica* and *World Almanac* are examples of general reference sources. Refdesk.com is a comprehensive Web source for all types of information.

Subject—Subject reference sources cover a single subject field or a group of related subjects. The *New Grove Dictionary of Musical Instruments* and *Black's Law Dictionary* are examples of reference works that are devoted to single subject areas. *The Encyclopedia of the Social Sciences* covers education, psychology, sociology, business and other subjects. CeoExpress.com covers business information online.

Both general and subject reference sources can be further categorized as being direct or indirect sources of information. A *direct source* provides the information in such a way that it is not necessary to consult another source. An *indirect source* serves as a guide to information that is located in other sources.

DIRECT ACCESS	INDIRECT ACCESS
almanacs	abstracts
biographical dictionaries	bibliographies
dictionaries	concordances
directories	indexes
encyclopedias	
gazetteers	
guidebooks	
handbooks	
manuals	
yearbooks	

Each year thousands of reference materials are published. Librarians select those sources that will be of greatest value to their library users. The reference collection is necessarily diverse, consisting of various types of reference sources designed to yield different kinds of information. Figure 7.1 briefly defines the various types of reference sources that are standard for most libraries.

Selecting a Reference Source

As you can see from the preceding discussion the collection of materials found in a typical library and on the Internet varies widely both in content and in format. Whether you are looking for quick facts or conducting extensive research, there are several points to consider before you start.

1. Identify the research question and determine your information needs.
2. Determine the type of source(s) you'll need to meet those needs.
3. Determine the discipline (treatment) of your topic.

Figure 7.2 illustrates how to determine your information needs once a topic is selected. Figure 7.3 categorizes selected subjects within an appropriate discipline, helping you determine what aspect of the topic you might consider. Your choice of discipline affects the resources you select.

Identify Research Question and Determine Information Needs

Often just writing down a question or constructing a sentence about your topic helps formulate the type of research you want to conduct. For "the effect of television advertising on children," your thought process

TYPES OF REFERENCE SOURCES

ABSTRACT an index that lists citations of works as well as a summary of each item (ex. *Psychological Abstracts, ERIC, ABI/INFORM*)

ALMANAC usually a one-volume work with statistics and a compilation of specific facts (ex. *World Almanac and Book of Facts,* and *Information Please Almanac, Atlas and Yearbook*)

ATLAS a book of maps and geographical information (ex. *Atlas of American History*)

BIBLIOGRAPHY a compilation of sources of information; provides literature on a specific subject or by a specific author (ex. *Books in Print* and *Bibliography of Nursing*)

BIOGRAPHICAL DICTIONARY sources of information about the lives of people; short entries (ex. *Current Biography* and *Who's Who in America*)

CONCORDANCE an alphabetical listing of keywords or phrases found in the work of an author or work in a collection of writings (ex. *Strong's Exhaustive Concordance of the Bible*)

DICTIONARY defines words and terms; confirms spelling, definition, and pronunciation; used to find out how words are used; helps to locate synonyms and antonyms and to trace the origin of words (ex. *Webster's Dictionary* and *Black's Law Dictionary*)

DIRECTORY lists names and addresses of individuals, companies, organizations, and institutions (ex. *Encyclopedia of Associations* and *Foundation Directory)*

ENCYCLOPEDIA covers knowledge or branches of knowledge in a comprehensive, but summary fashion; useful for providing facts and giving a broad survey of a topic; written by specialists (ex. *Encyclopedia Americana* and *World Book Encyclopedia*)

GAZETTEER a dictionary of geographical places (no maps) (ex. *Webster's New Geographical Dictionary*)

GUIDEBOOK provides detailed descriptions of places; intended primarily for the traveler; geographical facts plus maps (ex. *Baedeker's guidebooks to various countries*)

HANDBOOK treats one broad subject in brief, or gives a brief survey of a subject (ex. *Handbook of Literature* and *Benet's Reader's Encyclopedia*)

INDEX lists citations to periodical articles, books, and proceedings, and tells where they can be found (*see* Chapter 8. ex. *Readers' Guide to Periodical Literature* and *New York Times Index*)

MANUAL a specific work that tells how to do something, such as how something operates; descriptions of the inner workings of an organization (ex. *Chilton's Car Repair, MLA Handbook,* and *U.S. Government Organizational Manual*)

YEARBOOK covers the trends and events of the previous year; may be general in coverage, limited to one subject, or restricted to one geographical area (ex. *Britannica Book of the Year*)

Figure 7.1 Types of reference sources.

TOPIC: DISCRIMINATION OF WORKING WOMEN		
Needed information		**Appropriate reference sources**
overview article	------------ consult ------------	subject or general encyclopedia
current statistics	------------ consult ------------	statistical handbook, yearbook, almanac, *Statistical Abstract of the United States*
biographical information	------------ consult ------------	biographical index or biographical dictionary, library catalog
contemporary accounts	------------ consult ------------	periodical indexes, Internet, online databases
definition of legal terms	------------ consult ------------	dictionary, legal dictionary

Figure 7.2 Sample reference sources for a selected topic.

might be something like this: "Television advertising has had a tremendous effect on children in recent years. This can be dramatically seen in the increase of children's buying habits." To pursue this, you would seek current material providing spending habits of specific children's ages, or look for statistics indicating the amount of time children spend watching television advertisements.

Determine the Type of Reference Source

Knowing something about the types of reference sources can save you from having to guess where to look for information. Many of the types of reference books listed in Figure 7.1 may already be familiar to you. The definitions will help you to become familiar with those that you have not used before. Figure 7.2 illustrates several types of sources that might be used for the topic discrimination of working women.

For "the effects of television advertising on children," you should be able to locate information about the brands advertised on television and buying habits of children. Information about television advertising marketing primarily to children should also be useful.

Determine the Subject Area (Discipline)

The next step in selecting appropriate reference sources for a topic is to determine the broad subject category. It is often necessary to examine the topic from its broadest aspect or discipline—humanities, social sciences, or sciences. For example, to find an encyclopedia article specifically about the effects of television advertising on children, you are likely to find materials that will be more on target in an encyclopedia of the social sciences than in a general encyclopedia. Further, you may need to change the search terms to consider broader aspects of the topic. For information on types of effects, you might consider the *Encyclopedia of Psychology* or the *Encyclopedia of Adolesence*. Most subjects can be grouped into broad disciplines such as those shown in Figure 7.3.

There are indexes, abstracts, and reference works in all three major subject disciplines. To select the most appropriate sources, first you must determine how the topic is to be approached. In developing a research statement, it is extremely helpful to determine the focus of your topic. For example, how would you plan to treat the topic of television advertising and children? The box following Figure 7.3 outlines three different approches that could be used.

HUMANITIES	SOCIAL SCIENCES	SCIENCE
Architecture	Anthropology	Agriculture
Art	Business	Biology
Classical Studies	Criminal Justice	Chemistry
History	Economics	Computer Science
Journalism	Education	Engineering
Literature	Geography	Environment
Music	History	Health
Philosophy	Law	Mathematics
Poetry	Management	Medicine
Religion	Political Science	Petroleum
	Psychology	Physics
	Social Work	
	Sociology	

Figure 7.3 Selected subjects within disciplines.

APPROACH	DISCIPLINE
Television and children	Social Sciences
Child psychiatry	Science
Moral and ethical obligations of television advertisers	Humanities

Finding Reference Sources

Once you have analyzed your research topic and determined the appropriate subject areas to use for finding information, the next step is to actually locate the appropriate sources.

Guidelines
Locate reference sources

☐ use the library catalog,

☐ browse the reference shelves,

☐ consult a guide to reference books,

☐ consult the reference sources on the Internet, and

☐ ask the reference librarian for assistance.

Library Catalog

Use the library catalog when you know the title of a reference source, but not its location, or to find titles of works when you know only the subject. If you do not find the topic, it may be because it is too specific or it may be that the topic is not used as a subject in the catalog.

The *Library of Congress Subject Headings (LCSH)* (see Chapter 3, Figure 3.1) suggests related terms, narrow terms, and broader terms to be used in locating topics in the library catalog. In finding reference sources, it is often necessary to broaden the topic (see Figure 7.4).

The terms "use" and "used for" in the *LCSH* indicate the proper terminology to be used in locating a subject heading. Reference books are listed in the library catalog by subject and then by the type of reference book. The examples below illustrate various subdivisions of a subject.

HISTORY--BIBLIOGRAPHY   HISTORY--HANDBOOKS, MANUALS, ETC.

HISTORY--DICTIONARIES   HISTORY--INDEXES

HISTORY--DIRECTORIES   HISTORY--YEARBOOKS

Many of the types of reference sources listed in Figure 7.1 can be located by using a keyword approach.

Example

history and dictionaries   women and biographies
science and bibliographies   bible and concordance

Figure 4.12 illustrates the result of a subject search using "television and children bibliography" on the topic "the effect of television advertising on children."

Browse the Reference Shelves

Classification numbers may be found in the library catalog or sometimes in the *LCSH*. For example, to locate reference works on the topic of children and television, you could browse the reference stacks under the general classification number range for television or television and children. Several specific encyclopedias could be useful in researching this topic. These include chapters in the following:

Encyclopedia of Psychology—"Media Effects"

Encyclopedia of Marriage, Divorce, and the Family—"Media as Role Model for Individuals and for Families"

Encyclopedia of Mental Health—"Television Viewing"

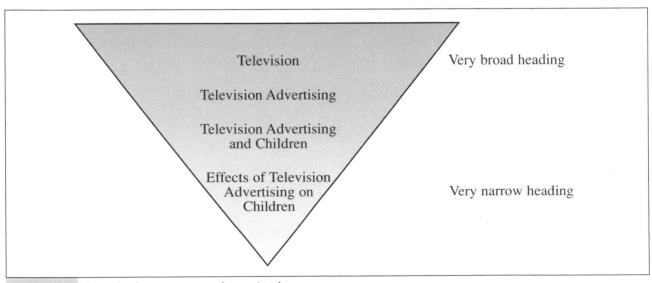

Television — Very broad heading

Television Advertising

Television Advertising and Children

Effects of Television Advertising on Children — Very narrow heading

Figure 7.4 Broadening or narrowing a topic.

Encyclopedia of Adolescence—"Television, Adolescents, and . . ."

General encyclopedias, such as the *Encyclopedia Americana*—"Television," "Social Significance of Television," and "Influence on Children."

Some reference departments keep frequently used materials on *ready reference* shelves or on special index tables, making it necessary to browse in several different areas.

Consult a Guide to Reference Books

The guides list reference sources by subject and often include subdivisions by type such as encyclopedias, handbooks, and manuals. Listed below are some of the more useful guides.

☐ *American Reference Books Annual*. Englewood, CO: Libraries Unlimited, 1970–.
  Lists both general and subject reference books. Comprehensive review of each work with author/title index and subject index.

☐ Balay, Robert, ed. *Guide to Reference Books*. 11th ed. Chicago: American Library Association, 1996.
  A comprehensive, annotated work that includes broad subject headings with further subdivisions according to type of source. Includes specific subject headings, and/or geographical subdivisions. The index incorporates author, title, subject, editors, compilers, and sponsoring bodies.

☐ Walford's *Guide to Reference Material*. 8th ed. 3 vols. London: Facet Publishing.
  Each volume is devoted to a different discipline: Science and Technology; (1999) Social and Historical Sciences, Philosophy and Religion; (2000) Generalia, Language and Literature, the Arts (1998). Each entry is annotated. Includes author/title index and a subject index in each volume.

Consult Reference Sources on the Internet

Electronic sources are becoming more numerous and more important as components of the library's reference collection. Access to CD-ROMs, online databases, and the Internet is usually available in the reference area (as well as remotely). Reference sources such as *Bartlett's Familiar Quotations*, *Webster's Dictionary*, *Roget's Thesaurus*, *800 Number Directory*, and thesauri formerly available only in paper copy are readily available on the Internet. You can also find stock market prices, subject bibliographies, directories for e-mail addresses, instructions on resume writing, current employment opportunities, and current federal and state legislation. Many types of reference sources discussed earlier in this chapter (manuals, handbooks, dictionaries, etc.) can now be found on the Internet and searched using the basic search techniques discussed in Chapter 3. Chapter 5 discusses the use of search engines to find information on the Internet. However, finding reference materials on the Internet can be frustrating, so it is advisable to use one of the many guides to reference sources that are available.

Guidelines
Finding Internet reference material

☐ type in the URL for a specific reference source

Example

http://encyclopedia.com is a free online encyclopedia.

☐ use a search engine to conduct a subject search, combining the topic with "reference"

Example

"biology reference" or "psychology resources"

Although this usually brings up a large list, you should be able to locate several relevant Web sites compiled by others on the subject.

☐ use a directory search engine like Yahoo and search on "Reference" as a category

Example

http://dir.yahoo.com/Reference/

http://www.google.com—then select "Directory" for a list of reference works.

☐ go to a college or university site and look for reference and subject guides

Example

http://www.lib.lsu.edu/ref/readyref.html—ready reference sites selected by the reference staff at the LSU Libraries

http://academic.wsc.edu/conn_library/research/online_ref/—created by Conn Library Reference Staff.

http://www.lib.umd.edu/ETC/Reference.html—for a listing of reference works from the University of Maryland's staff

☐ use a "one-stop shopping" reference site

Example

RefDesk.com (http://refdesk.com)

OR

Internet Public Library (http://www.ipl.org/)

Both provide links to reference material by topic. You can find such things as the quote of the day; what happened today in history; and links to encyclopedias, dictionaries, almanacs, movie reviews, and newspapers from around the world.

Although much information is available online, most researchers still use a combination of articles from databases, Internet documents, books, and reference sources from the library. The list of Selected Internet Sites at the end of this chapter presents a representative sampling of resources that may be used for reference purposes.

Ask the Reference Librarian for Assistance

Reference librarians are information specialists who are trained to analyze patrons' research needs and assist them in locating different sources of information. Most computers and electronic products are located near the Reference Desk. Librarians can assist patrons not only in locating information, but in providing guidance in developing search strategies for specific projects. Typical reference questions are changing from "Where do I find . . ." to "How do I log in to the campus network?" and "Which database should I use to find articles on this topic?" Because librarians have become more knowledgeable about computers and technology in general, they can serve the remote user as well as the in-house one.

Many libraries now provide *electronic mail* (e-mail) reference service, allowing patrons to submit questions. The answers are often returned by the library with complete bibliographic citations or full articles attached. This service is especially valuable for distance education and other users who cannot come to the library.

Interactive Electronic Reference allows patrons and librarians to exchange information in real time on the Web instead of the telephone. Two examples of this service can be seen at http://www.lib.uchicago.edu/e/busecon/asklibrarian.html (The University of Chicago Business and Economics guide), and at http://www.pace.edu/library/links/conveydownload/refhelp.html (Pace University Library's Reference Help page). Both of these services are available for their students and faculty only.

Document Delivery is another service provided by many libraries; patrons request printed or electronic materials, which is then delivered to them either in paper, microform, or electronic format, usually for a small fee. In most libraries, document delivery service is provided by the interlibrary loan office.

SELECTED REFERENCE SOURCES BY TYPE

Many of these sources are now available electronically on CD-ROM or on the Internet.

Almanacs and Yearbooks

Almanacs

☐ *Information Please Almanac, Atlas and Yearbook*. New York: Simon and Schuster, 1947–.
A one-volume work arranged into broad subject areas such as astronomy, economics and business, nutrition and health, religion, and science. Articles include both discussion and statistical material. Some signed articles on important issues of the period. Maps and some pictures are included. Topical arrangement with a subject index.

☐ *The World Almanac and Book of Facts*. New York: World Almanac, 1868–.
Covers a wide variety of subjects. An excellent source for statistics. Features a chronology of events that took place during the preceding year. Contains biographical information on U.S. presidents. Includes a few maps and some pictures. Index located at the front of the book.

☐ *World Factbook*. Washington: CIA, 1971–.
Created by the Central Intelligence Agency to support basic worldwide intelligence information. Includes a list of countries with reference maps, notes and definitions of terms.

Yearbooks

☐ *Americana Annual: an Encyclopedia of Events*. New York: Encyclopedia Americana, 1923–.
A supplement to the encyclopedia. Long signed articles discuss the year's political, economic, scientific and cultural developments. Includes a list of significant monthly events. Extensive biographical material on people in the news and of major figures who have died during the year.

☐ *Britannica Book of the Year.* Chicago: Encyclopaedia Britannica, 1938–.

Annual supplement to the encyclopedia. Includes several feature articles on newsworthy events. The "Year in Review" section covers the major events of the year as well as biographical information on people in the news. A separate section entitled "Britannica World Data" provides up-to-date statistical information on all countries of the world. Articles are signed and a list of contributors is provided.

☐ *Europa World Year Book.* 2 vols. London: Europa Publications, 1926–.

(Formerly Europa Year Book.) Provides information on the organization and activities of the United Nations and other international organizations. Chapters on the major countries of the world discuss such things as government, economic affairs, social welfare, education, and recent history.

☐ *Statesmen's Year Book: Statistical and Historical Annual of the States of the World.* New York: St. Martin's, 1864–.

Handy reference source for information on various countries of the world. Gives brief history, statistical information, area and population, climate, constitution and government, and natural resources. For the United States, the information is not only for the whole country, but also for each state.

☐ *Statistical Abstract of the United States.* Washington: GPO, 1879–.

Issued annually by the U.S. Bureau of the Census. Consists of a compilation of social, political, and economic statistics gathered from both private and government sources. Most tables give comparative information from prior years. Many of the statistics are from primary sources; all information is documented.

Atlases, Gazetteers, and Guidebooks

Atlases

☐ Goode, J. Paul. *Goode's World Atlas.* 20th ed. Chicago: Rand McNally, 1999.

Easy-to-use volume arranged in four major divisions: (1) world thematic maps dealing with the world's climate, raw material distribution, landform, languages, and religions; (2) regional maps that cover the political and topographical features of the continents and the countries within those continents; (3) plate tectonics and ocean floor maps; and (4) maps covering the major cities of the world. Comprehensive index.

☐ *National Geographic Atlas of the World.* 7th ed. Washington: National Geographic Society, 1999.

Published for more than 35 years, this latest edition has been expanded to include full page maps for political, physical, and satellite images. Political maps reflect wars, revolutions, treaties, elections and other events.

☐ *Rand McNally Road Atlas 2000*: United States, Canada, Mexico. Skokie, IL: Rand McNally, 2002.

Includes illustrated maps of states, provinces and counties, plus many city maps. Latest edition includes digital cartography.

☐ Shepherd, William R. *Historical Atlas.* 9th ed. rev. New York: Holt, 1980.

Collection of chronologically arranged maps of the world dating from approximately 3000 BC to the 20th century. Includes plans of Rome (350 AD) and Athens (420 BC). Contains both political and physical maps.

Gazetteers

☐ Canby, Courtlandt. *Encyclopedia of Historic Places.* 2 vols. New York: Facts on File, 1984.

Lists in alphabetical order names of places of historical significance such as battle sites, archaeological sites, shrines, cities, towns, and countries. Gives geographic location and historical significance. Cross references from former names to present ones. Some illustrations.

☐ *Merriam-Webster's Geographical Dictionary*. 3rd ed. Springfield, MA: Merriam-Webster, 2001.
Alphabetically arranged list of place names with locations and pronunciations. Entries include economic, political, and physical data. Information for each state of the U.S. includes list of counties, products manufactured, and natural resources. Other countries of the world have similar listings under the country's name. Some maps.

Guidebooks

☐ *Baedeker Guidebooks*. Englewood Cliffs, NJ: Prentice-Hall, 1828–.
One of the oldest series of guidebooks still being published. Provides information about individual countries, groups of countries, and cities. Gives the history of the area, places to see, places to stay, and restaurants. Many pictures and maps.

☐ *Fodor's Travel Guides*. New York: McKay, 1936–.
Volumes cover various regions and cities of the United States, Europe, Asia, South America, and the Caribbean. Offers suggestions for transportation to and from an area and places of interest to visit. Discusses local customs and history. Maps of cities and lists of lodging places and restaurants. Well illustrated. Frequently revised.

Bibliographies

☐ *Books in Print*. New York: Bowker, 1948–.
Lists books currently available from publishers. Contains separate author, title, subject, and publisher lists.

☐ *Cumulative Book Index*. New York: Wilson, 1898–.
Author, title, and subject listing of books published in the English language throughout the world. Bibliographic information along with standard numbers useful for ordering books.

Concordances

☐ Cruden, Alexander. *Cruden's Complete Concordance*. Grand Rapids: Zondervan, 1999.
Provides references in several translations by keyword access.

☐ Strong, James, et al. *Strongest Strong's Exhaustive Concordance of the Bible*. Grand Rapids: Zondervan, 2001.
Hailed as the best yet of Strong's Concordances. Uses computer technology and a perfected database from previous editions. Extra features include history of the Strong's Concordance project and "Nave's Topical Bible Reference System."

Dictionaries

Unabridged Dictionaries

☐ *Random House Webster's Unabridged Dictionary: Indexed*. 2nd ed. New York: Random House, 2001.
Over 1,000-entry revised New-Words; 2,400 maps and illustrations. Packaged with a CD-ROM with audio pronunciations.

☐ *Webster's Third New International Dictionary, Unabridged*. Springfield, MA: Merriam-Webster, 2002.
Comprehensive dictionary containing all the principal words used in the English language. Provides pronunciations as well as definitions. A separate pronunciation guide is found in the front.

Abridged Dictionaries

☐ *The American Heritage Dictionary*. 4th ed. Boston: Houghton Mifflin, 2000.
Dictionary designed for "American English." Definitions often accompanied by illustrations. Contains several essays on the use of language. Features a separate style manual, list of abbreviations, geographic entries, and biographical entries.

☐ *Merriam-Webster's Collegiate Dictionary*. 10th ed. Springfield, MA: Merriam, 1998.
Chronological within definitions. In some cases quotations are used to clarify the meanings of words. Contains a guide to pronunciation and explanatory notes. Lists of abbreviations, chemical symbols, foreign words and phrases, personal names, geographical names, colleges and universities, and a style manual are found in the back of the book.

Historical Dictionaries

Historical dictionaries place emphasis on the historical perspectives of words and phrases. These often contain useful information about words not found in the traditional dictionary.

☐ *Historical Dictionary of the Elizabethan World: Britain, Ireland, Europe, and America*. Phoenix: Oryx Press, 1999.
Extra features include explanatory maps of Elizabethan England and London, pictures of important figures, and tables of privy council members. Many genealogical charts, illustrations of castles, etc.

☐ *Oxford English Dictionary*. 2nd ed. 20 vols. New York: Oxford University Press, 1991.
Comprehensive record of the words used in the English language from the twelfth century to contemporary times. Quotations demonstrate how words were used during different time periods. Excellent source for quotations using words in a particular context.

Specialized Dictionaries

☐ Chapman, Robert L. *Dictionary of American Slang*. New York: Harper Collins, 1998.
Includes more than 10,000 terms ranging from the 1880s through the 1990s. Terms with definitions, parts of speech, examples, and, in some cases, the date of origin.

☐ *The Dictionary of Imaginary Places*. New York: Harcourt, 1999.
A guidebook of the make-believe. Includes places like Oz, the Odyssey, Jurassic Park, even the Beatles' Pepperland from Yellow Submarine is described. More than 1,200 realms from books and films.

☐ Kepfer, Barbara Ann. *Roget's 21st Century Thesaurus: The Essential Reference for Home, School or Office*. New York: Dell, 1999.
Based on *Thesaurus of English Words and Phrases* by Peter Mark Roget. Includes an index. Cross references words with concepts.

☐ Tennant, Richard A., et al. *American Sign Language Handshape Dictionary*. Washington, D.C.: Gallaudet University Press, 1998.
Orders signs by handshape instead of traditional methods. Effectively illustrates how to go from sign language to spoken English.

Subject Dictionaries

Subject dictionaries are devoted primarily to a subject field and give the terminology most useful in that field. Many of these dictionaries are updated frequently to keep current with changing terminology and new developments.

☐ Black, Henry Campbell. *Black's Law Dictionary*. 7th ed. St. Paul: West, 1999.
Comprehensive dictionary defining terms used in law and related subjects. Good cross references. Pronunciation guide arranged alphabetically.

☐ *Dictionary of Crime: Criminal Justice, Criminology and Law Enforcement*. New York: Paragon House, 1992.

    Includes historical slang of cops, robbers, prisoners, etc. as well as technical legal terms.

☐ *Dorland's Illustrated Medical Dictionary*. 28th ed. Philadelphia: Saunders, 1994.

    Defines medical terms giving pronunciations, alternate definitions, if any, and origin of the word. Numerous plates showing detailed drawings of parts of the human body.

Foreign Language Dictionaries

Foreign language dictionaries can be found for virtually every written language. They may be written entirely in the language covered, or they may be English-foreign language.

☐ *Collins-Robert French-English, English-French Dictionary*. 3rd ed. Glasgow: Collins, 1996.

    Emphasizes contemporary rather than classical terms in both languages. "Style labels" indicate when a term may have stylistic complexities, e.g., local idioms that cannot be literally translated. Includes phrases as well as single words.

Directories

☐ *Encyclopedia of Associations*. Detroit: Gale, 1956–.

    Multivolume directory of active organizations in the United States and Canada. Has a separate volume for international organizations. Arranged by broad subject areas with separate organization name, executive name, keyword, and geographic indexes.

☐ *Thomas' Register of American Manufacturers*. New York: Thomas Publishing, 1905/06–.

    Lists of products and services available from American companies. Includes product and brand name indexes, company profiles, and a file of company catalogs. Available online, through *Thomas' Register CD-ROM*, and as *Thomas' Register Database*.

☐ *United States Congress. Official Congressional Directory*. Washington: GPO, 1809–.

    Published for each session of Congress. Contains names, addresses, committee assignments, and biographical sketches of members of Congress. Also includes names and addresses of top officials in all government agencies, international organizations, diplomatic missions, and the press corps. Contains maps of each Congressional district. Available online through GPO access.

☐ *The World of Learning*. London: Europa, 1947–.

    Directory of research organizations, libraries and archives, colleges and universities, learned societies, museums, and art galleries found throughout the world. Arranged alphabetically by country. Includes names, addresses and some annotations.

Encyclopedias

General Encyclopedias

☐ *Encyclopedia Americana*. 30 vols. Danbury, CT: Grolier. 2002.

    The first encyclopedia published in the United States. It covers the arts and humanities as well as scientific development. Signed articles by experts in the field. Unique feature is the "century'" articles that discuss the outstanding events and trends of various time periods. Long articles contain a table of contents for easy reference. Supplemented by *Americana Annual*.

☐ *The Grolier Multimedia Encyclopedia*. Database. Danbury, CT: Grolier, c1995–.

    First of the CD-ROM encyclopedias. Full text of the printed *Academic American Encyclopedia*. Enhanced 1995 edition includes additional audio-visual effects.

☐ *The New Encyclopaedia Britannica.* 30 vols. Chicago: Encyclopaedia Britannica, 1998.
Consists of three parts with a two-volume index. Volume 30, the *Propaedia* is an "Outline of Knowledge," that serves as a topical approach to the articles in volumes 1–12, the *Micropaedia,* and in volumes 13–29, the *Macropaedia.* The twelve-volume *Micropaedia* contains brief entries with cross references to the longer articles in the *Macropaedia.* The *Macropaedia* volumes contain long comprehensive articles complete with bibliographies. Articles are signed with initials that can be identified by referring to volume 30. Supplemented by *Britannica Book of the Year. Britannica CD-ROM* includes full text of the print encyclopedia plus a version of *Merriam-Webster Dictionary and Thesaurus.*

☐ *World Book Encyclopedia.* 22 vols. Chicago: World Book, 2002.
Designed for elementary through high school students, but because of its extremely wide coverage, it is excellent for general reference. Major articles provide subject headings for related articles, an outline of the subject, and review questions. Numerous diagrams and pictures, good cross references, and signed articles. Updated by *World Book Yearbook.*

Subject Encyclopedias

☐ *Encyclopedia of Bioethics.* Rev. ed. New York: Simon & Schuster, 1995.
Lengthy signed articles with good cross references and bibliographies. Covers the ethical concerns with human problems such as abortion, aging, human experimentation, population policies, and reproductive technologies.

☐ *Encyclopedia of Psychology.* Washington: American Psychological Association, 2000.
Alphabetically arranged by specific topics. Includes bibliographical references and index.

☐ *International Encyclopedia of the Social Sciences.* 19 vols. New York: Macmillan, 1968–1991.
Long scholarly articles with bibliographies covering all aspects of the social sciences from anthropology to statistics. Treats narrow subjects within the broad subjects. Good cross references. The *Biographical Supplement* contains a classified subject list to the alphabetically arranged biographies.

☐ *McGraw-Hill Encyclopedia of Science and Technology.* 9th ed. 20 vols. New York: McGraw-Hill, 2002.
Covers all aspects of science and technology. Scholarly, yet nontechnical articles, most of which are signed. Illustrations, bibliographies, and cross references. Volume 20 contains topical and analytical indexes and a section on scientific notation. Kept up-to-date by *McGraw-Hill Yearbook of Science and Technology.*

Handbooks and Manuals

Handbooks

☐ *Benét's Reader's Encyclopedia.* 4th ed. New York: Harper & Row, 1996.
Primarily concerned with literature but useful for identifying movements and important people in art and music. Contains references to literary characters and plot summaries. International in scope, but emphasis is on American and British works.

☐ De Vries, Mary Ann. *The New Robert's Rules of Order.* 2nd rev. ed. New York: Penguin, 1998.
Guide to standard parliamentary procedure used by organizations to conduct business meetings. Introduction explains the history and development of parliamentary rules; a center section codifies procedures for conducting meetings. Other chapters explain the duties of organization officers, committee members, and board members. An index is included.

☐ *McGraw-Hill's National Electrical Code Handbook.* 23rd ed. New York: McGraw-Hill, 1998.
Based on the 1996 code, written in conversational style. Presents information in easy-to-read format for safe installation of electrical wiring and equipment.

Manuals

☐ *United States Government Manual*. Washington: GPO, 1935–.

Official guide to the organization of the United States government. Lists all of the government agencies, both official and semiofficial, along with the names, addresses, and phone numbers of their top personnel. Contains a copy of the U.S. Constitution, a list of abbreviations useful for identifying government agencies, an index of names, and an agency/subject index. Available online through GPO access.

SELECTED CURRENT EVENTS SOURCES

Following is a list of sources covering politics, contemporary issues, and news events. Many are loose-leaf services; some are shelved in Reference or Ready Reference collections.

☐ *Almanac of American Politics*. 1972–.

Surveys of congressional districts, state and national politics. Published biennially.

☐ *Congressional Digest*. 1921–.

Monthly publication that explores the pros and cons of major Congressional issues.

☐ *CQ Researcher* (formerly *Editorial Research Reports*). 1967–.

In-depth analysis of current events and issues. Provides historical background, chronology of events, and opposing views on controversial issues written by experts on the subject. Includes extensive bibliographies for further research.

☐ *CQ Weekly Report*. 1961–.

Congressional Quarterly publication that tracks the major legislation, floor action, events on Capitol Hill, and every major policy issue in Congress. Includes current bills before Congress, Supreme Court decisions, campaigns, and speeches.

☐ *Editorials on File*. 1970–.

Published twice a month. Collects newspaper editorials on topics of current interest. Provides editorials for each topic presented.

☐ *Europa World Year Book*. 1966–.

Detailed information on country politics and organizations. Includes statistical surveys and names of officials.

☐ *Facts on File Yearbook*. 1945–.

A weekly world news digest summarizing newspaper articles. Emphasis is on U.S. events and international affairs of American interest.

SELECTED INTERNET SITES

General

CNN. http://www.cnn.com
For current news information. ABC, NBC, and other networks have similar sites.

Encyclopedia.com. http://encyclopedia.com/

Free Tutorials. http://www.learn2.com/

Freeweb Central. http://www.freewebcentral.com/

Information Please Almanac. http://infoplease.com/

Internet Public Library. http://www.ipl.org/
A free online public service library. Collections include reference, associations, native authors, literary criticisms, newspapers, serials, and information for young people. Online text collection provides over 11,000 titles that can be browsed by author, title, or Dewey Decimal classification. Has forms to fill out so users can ask reference questions.

Refdesk.com. http://refdesk.com
A one-stop shopping site for locating current events and reference sites. Includes links to wire services, newspapers, magazines, columns, businesses, weather, quick reference, tutorials, and books.

Business

AnyWho Toll-Free Directory. http://anywho.com/

Better Business Bureau. http://www.bbb.org/

Bureau of Labor Statistics. http://stats.bls.gov/

Census Bureau. http://www.census.gov/

CEO Express. http://www.ceoexpress.com

Edgar. http://www.edgar-online.com
Search corporate annual reports and SEC filings.

Small Business Administration. http://www.sba.gov/

Yahoo Business and Economy. http://dir.yahoo.com/Business_and_Economy/

Zip Codes. http://www.usps.gov/ncsc/welcome1.htm

Career Guidance

Americas Job Bank. http://www.ajb.org/

Federal Jobs Digest. http://www.jobsfed.com/

JobBank-USA. http://www.jobbankusa.com

Monster Board. http://www.monster.com

Occupational Outlook Handbook. http://www.bls.gov/oco/

Riley Guide. http://www.rileyguide.com

Virtual Job Fair. http://www.burlingtonfreepress.com/adv/jobfair/

Citation Guides

http://www.lib.duke.edu/libguide/citing.htm
Easy to follow guide gives specific examples of each electronic format.

http://www.lib.umich.edu/govdocs/cite.html
Provides links to a variety of style manuals and guides.

Consumer Resources

Consumer Alert. http://www.consumeralert.org

Consumer Information Center. http://www.pueblo.gsa.gov/
Government publications online.

Consumer Resources. http://www.lib.lsu.edu/ref/consumer.html

Kelly Blue Book. http://www.kbb.com/
Automobile prices.

U.S. Consumer Gateway. http://www.consumer.gov/

U.S. Postal Service. http://www.usps.gov/
Consumer information from the U.S. Postal Service.

Grants and Funding

Catalog of Federal Domestic Assistance. http://www.cfda.gov/

Foundation Center. http://fdncenter.org/
Tutorials and guides on getting funding

Grants and Funding. http://www.grantsandfunding.com/grantsandfunding/index.html

Health

Consumer Health. HealthWeb. http://healthweb.org/

Healthfinder. http://www.healthfinder.gov

Legal

Code of Federal Regulations. http://www.access.gpo.gov/nara/cfr/index.html

FindLaw. http://www.findlaw.com

Statistics (Note additional sources in Chapter 10.)

County and City Data Book. http://fisher.lib.Virginia.edu/ccdb/

Statistical Abstract of the United States. http://www.census.gov/statab/www/

World Factbook. http://www.cia.gov/cia/publications/factbook/

Weather

Old Farmer's Almanac. http://www.almanac.com/

Weather Channel. http://www.weather.com/

Weather Underground. http://www.wunderground.com

SELECTED PRINT REFERENCE SOURCES BY SUBJECT

Agriculture

Farm Chemicals Handbook. 2002.

Handbook of Engineering in Agriculture. 3 vols. 1988.

Art and Architecture

A History of Western Architecture. 2000.

Dictionary of Art. 2002.

Encyclopedia of World Art. 1959–1987.

Gardner's Art Through the Ages. 11th ed. 2000.

The Oxford Dictionary of Art. 2001.

Biology/Botany/Zoology

Cambridge Encyclopedia of Life Sciences. 1985.

Concise Oxford Dictionary of Zoology. 1992.

A Dictionary of Botany. 1984.

A Dictionary of Plant Pathology. 1992.

Encyclopedia of the Animal World. 11 vols. 1980.

Fishes of the World. 1994.

Grzimek's Animal Life Encyclopedia. 13 vols. 1972–2002.

Grzimek's Encyclopedia of Mammals. 5 vols. 1990.

Business and Economics

Accountant's Handbook. 2000.

Data Sources for Business and Market Analysis. 1994.

Dictionary of Accounting Terms. 2000.

Encyclopedia of Business. 2nd ed. 1999.

Encyclopedia of Business Information Sources. 14th ed. 2000.

International Directory of Company Histories. 30 vols. 1988–.

Standard & Poor's Industry Surveys. 3 vols. 2002.

Standard & Poor's Register of Corporations. 3 vols. plus supplement. 1999.

Value Line Investment Survey. 3 part loose-leaf service. 1936–.

Ward's Business Directory. 2000.

Communication and Journalism

Communication and the Mass Media: A Guide to the Reference Literature. 1991.

Communication Yearbook. 1977–.

Facts on File: A Weekly World News Digest with Cumulative Index. 1940–.

The Gallup Poll: Public Opinion. 1935–.

Keesing's Record of World Events. 1931–.

What They Said: A Yearbook of Spoken Opinion. 1969–.

Computers and the Internet

Computer Glossary: The Complete Illustrated Dictionary. 1998.

Dictionary of Computer and Internet Terms. 2003.

Webster's New World Computer Dictionary. 2003.

Criminal Justice

City Crime Rankings: Crime in Metropolitan America. 2002.

Crime and the Justice System in America: An Encyclopedia. 1997.

Dictionary of Crime: Criminal Justice, Criminology & Law Enforcement. 1994.

The Encyclopedia of Child Abuse. 2001.

The Encyclopedia of Psychoactive Drugs. 25 vols. 1985–1992.

Encyclopedia of World Crime. 6 vols. 1990.

Mobspeak: The Dictionary of Crime Terms. 2003.

Education

American Educators' Encyclopedia. 1991.

Education Yearbook. 1972/73–.

Encyclopedia of Careers and Vocational Guidance. 2002.

Encyclopedia of Educational Research. 4 vols. 1992.

International Dictionary of Adult and Continuing Education. 2002.

Mental Measurements Yearbook. 1941–.

Philosophy of Education: An Encyclopedia. 1996.

Tests in Print. 1961–.

Engineering Technology

Civil Engineers Reference Book. 1989.

Electrical Engineering Handbook. 1997.

Handbook of Industrial Engineering. 2nd ed. 1991.

SAE Handbook. 2002.

Genealogy

A Dictionary of Heraldry. 1999.

A Dictionary of Surnames. 1998.

Handybook for Genealogists. 9th ed. 1998.

Source: A Guidebook of American Genealogy. 1996.

Geography

Cambridge Encyclopedia of Africa. 1981.

Cities of the World. 4 vols. 4th ed. 1993.

Dictionary of Human Geography. 2000.

Harper Atlas of World History. 1993.

Worldmark Encyclopedia of the States. 2000.

Government see Law and Government

Grants and Funding

Annual Register of Grant Support: A Directory of Funding Sources. 2000.

Foundation Center's User-Friendly Guide: A Grantseekers Guide to Resources. 1996.

Foundation Directory. 2000.

Grants and Awards. 1991–.

Grants Register. 2001.

The "How to" Grants Manual: Successful Grantseeking Techniques for Obtaining Public and Private Grants. 1995.

Health see Medicine/Health/Sports Medicine

History

Africa South of the Sahara. 29th ed. 2000.

Annals of America. 21 vols. 1976–1987.

The Annual Register: A Record of World Events. 1788–1997.

Dictionary of Indian Tribes of the Americas. 2nd ed. 1993.

Dictionary of Mexican American History. 1981.

Dictionary of the Middle Ages. 13 vols. 1982–.

Documents of American History. 10th ed. 1988.

Encyclopedia of World Facts and Dates. 1993.

Encyclopedia of World History. 2000.

Great Soviet Encyclopedia. 31 vols. 3rd ed. 1982

Illustrated Encyclopedia of World History. 1997.

International and Multicultural

African American Almanac. 2002.

Encyclopedia of Asian History. 4 vols. 1988.

Encyclopedia of Multiculturalism. 6 vols. 1999.

Encyclopedia of the Holocaust. Plus supplements. 1989–1996.

Encyclopedia of Violence, Peace, and Conflict. 3 vols. 1999.

Encyclopedia of World Cultures. 1987–.

Handbook of Hispanic Cultures in the United States. 4 vols. 1994.

Handbook of North American Indians. 1984–.

Kodansha Encyclopedia of Japan. 9 vols. Supp. 1987.

Storytelling Encyclopedia: Historical, Cultural, and Multiethnic Approaches to Oral Traditions Around the World. 1997.

Journalism see Communication and Journalism

Language and Literature

Afro-American Writing Today: An Anniversary Issue of the Southern Review. 1989.

American Folklore: An Encyclopedia of Beliefs, Customs, Tales, Music, and Art. 1997.

Bartlett's Familiar Quotations. 2002.

Cambridge Encyclopedia of Language. 1997.

Cambridge Guide to Literature in English. 1992.

Columbia Literary History of the United States. 1988.

Contemporary Literary Criticism. 8 vols. 1973–.

Folklore of American Holidays. 1991.

Harbrace College Handbook. Rev. 13th ed. With *MLA Style Manual* updates. 1998.

New Arthurian Encyclopedia. 1995–.

Oxford Companion to English Literature. 1999.

Something About the Author. 1971–.

Twentieth-Century Literary Criticism. 1978–.

Law and Government

Almanac of American Politics. 1972–.

Bieber's Dictionary of Legal Abbreviations: Reference Guide for Attorneys, Legal Secretaries, Paralegals, and Law Students. 1993.

Blackwell Dictionary of Political Science: A User's Guide to Its Terms. 1999.

Countries of the World and Their Leaders Yearbook. 1980–.

County Year Book. 1975–.

Dictionary of Government and Politics. 1998.

Dictionary of 20th Century World Politics. 1993.

Encyclopedias of Revolutions and Revolutionaries: From Anarchism to Zhou Enlai. 1996.

Illustrated Dictionary of Constitutional Concepts. 2000.

West's Encyclopedia of American Law. 12 vols. 1998.

Literature see Language and Literature

Mathematics

Concise Handbook of Mathematics and Physics. 1997.

CRC Handbook of Mathematical Science. 1962–.

Dictionary of Mathematics. 2 vols. 1997.

Elsevier's Dictionary of Computer Science and Mathematics. 1995.

Encyclopedic Dictionary of Mathematics. 2nd edition. 1987.

Medicine/Health/Sports Medicine

Alternative Health & Medicine Encyclopedia. 1997.

Anatomy of the Human Body. 1985.

Concise Dictionary of Biomedicine and Molecular Biology. 2001.

Encyclopedia of Aging: 2002.

Encyclopedia of Sports Science. 2 vols. 1997.

Merck Manual of Diagnosis and Therapy. 1899–.

Physician's Desk Reference Book. 1947–.

Stedman's Medical Dictionary. 2000.

Motion Pictures, Radio, and Television

Chronicle of the Cinema. 1997.

Film Anthologies Index. 1994.

International Television and Video Almanac. 1956–.

Radio's Golden Years: The Encyclopedia of Radio Programs, 1930–1960. 1981.

Music/Theater

American Musical Film Song Encyclopedia. 1999.

American Musical Theatre Song Encyclopedia. 1995.

ASCAP Biographical Dictionary. 1990.

Best Plays of . . . and the Yearbook of Drama in America. 1894–.

Cambridge Guide to World Theatre. 1992.

The Drama Dictionary. 1988.

The Encyclopedia of Folk, Country, and Western Music. 1984.

Historical Encyclopedia of Costumes. 1988.

New Grove Dictionary of American Music. 4 vols. 1986.

New Grove Dictionary of Jazz. 2nd ed. 2001.

Norton/Grove Concise Encyclopedia of Music. 1994.

Oxford Companion to Popular Music. 1993.

Philosophy/Religion

Cambridge Dictionary of Philosophy. 1999.

Chambers Dictionary of Beliefs and Religions. 1997–.

Dictionary of Philosophy and Religion: Eastern and Western Thought. 1998.

Dictionary of the History of Ideas. 5 vols. 1980.

Encyclopedia of American Religions. 2002.

Encyclopedia of Ethics. 2nd ed. 2001.

Encyclopedia of Judaism. 2002.

Encyclopedia of Psychology. 4 vols. 1994.

Encyclopedia of Religion and Society. 1998.

Encyclopedia of Religions in the United States: One Hundred Religious Groups Speak for Themselves. 1992.

Encyclopedia of the Paranormal. 1996.

Folklore of American Holidays. 1987.

Man, Myth, and Magic: The Illustrated Encyclopedia of Mythology, Religion, and the Unknown. New ed. 21 vols. 1997.

New Catholic Encyclopedia. 18 vols. 2002.

Routledge Encyclopedia of Philosophy. 10 vols. 1998.

Psychology

American Handbook of Psychiatry. 2nd ed. 8 vols. 1974–1986.

Encyclopedia of Adult Development. 1993.

Encyclopedia of Phobias, Fears, and Anxieties. 1989.

Encyclopedia of Psychology. 4 vols. 1994.

Encyclopedia of Relationships Across the Lifespan. 1996.

Encyclopedia of the Paranormal. 1996.

Oxford Companion to the Mind. 1999.

Religion see Philosophy/Religion

Science

Beilstein's Handbook of Organic Chemistry. 1992.

Britannica Yearbook of Science and the Future. 1968–.

Cambridge Atlas of Astronomy. 1994.

Concise Dictionary of Physics. New edition. 1990.

CRC Handbook of Chemistry and Physics. 2001.

Dictionary of the History of Science. 2001.

Encyclopedia of Astronomy and Astrophysics. 2001.

Handbook of Industrial Robotics. 1999.

International Encyclopedia of Astronomy. 1992.

International Petroleum Encyclopedia. 2002.

McGraw-Hill Concise Encyclopedia of Science and Technology. 1998.

McGraw-Hill Encyclopedia of the Geological Sciences. 2nd ed. 1988.

Van Nostrand's Scientific Encyclopedia. 7th ed. 1989.

The Weather Almanac. 2001.

Social Sciences

A Hundred Years of Anthropology. 1968.

Atlas of Archaeology. 1998.

Cambridge Encyclopedia of Archaeology. 1980.

Dictionary of Human Geography. 2000.

Encyclopedia of Adolescence. 1991.

Encyclopedia of American Social History. 1993.

Encyclopedia of Cultural Anthropology. 2001.

Encyclopedia of Homosexuality. 1991.

Encyclopedia of Human Behavior. 4 vols. 1994.

Encyclopedia of Human Evolution and Prehistory. 2000.

Encyclopedia of Social and Cultural Anthropology. 2002.

Encyclopedia of Social Work. 1995 + supplements.

Handbook of American Popular Culture. 2002–.

International Encyclopedia of Sociology. 1996.

Social Science Encyclopedia. 1999.

Sports Medicine see Medicine/Health/Sports Medicine

Statistics (Note additional resources in Chapter 10.)

America's Top-Rated Cities: A Statistical Handbook. 2000.

Demographic Yearbook. 1949–.

Handbook of Key Economic Indicators. 1998.

Illustrated Book of World Rankings. 2001.

Places, Towns and Townships. 1998.

Statistical Abstract of the United States. 1878–.

Theatre see Music

Women's Studies

International Who's Who of Women. 1992.

Statistical Handbook of Women in America. 1996.

Statistical Record of Women Worldwide. 1995.

Women: A Bibliography of Bibliographies. 1986.

Women's Studies Encyclopedia. 1999.

Exercise 7.1

Instructor: _____ Course/Section: _____

Name: _____

Date: _____ Points: _____

Review Questions

1. List three ways reference material can be distinguished from other materials in the library.

    a.

    b.

    c.

2. How are reference sources used in research?

3. Name and define three different types of reference sources.

    a.

    b.

    c.

4. What types of reference sources would you use for an overview on a topic?

5. Explain the difference between *direct* and *indirect* reference sources.

6. Which discipline would you look under to find information on each of the following?

   Topic   *Discipline*

   a. stem cell research

   b. Gulf War crisis

   c. history of the Sistine Chapel

   d. weight training in sports

   e. philosophy of ideas

   f. human cloning

7. Name five possible strategies you might consider in locating reference sources.

   a.

   b.

   c.

   d.

   e.

8. Why is it important to determine the date of the reference source being used in research?

9. Why is it important to look for signed articles in a reference book?

10. Why are bibliographies useful additions to articles found in reference sources?

11. Why is it important to have cross references in a reference source?

12. What advantages do you see in using the Internet to locate reference material?

13. If you had the choice between an in-house visit and sending an e-mail for a reference question, which would you choose and why?

Exercise 7.2

Instructor: _David Jenkins_ Course/Section: _LIBS 150 A_

Name: _Patricia Crider_

Date: _Sept 3 05_ Points: _____

Identifying Types of Reference Sources

Match the following type of reference source with the information listed below. The answers on the right may be used more than once. Write the correct answer to the left of the number.

_m_ 1. Illustrations of famous works of art.

_n_ 2. How to conduct a physics experiment.

_b_ 3. The population of Alaska.

_i_ 4. A brief description of the U.S. Department of Education.

_d_ 5. A published list of sources on sociology.

_k_ 6. Hiking trails & maps of the Great Smoky Mountains in Tennessee.

_g_ 7. Term and meanings in philosophy.

_e_ 8. Brief information about Ronald Reagan.

_a_ 9. A short summary of work providing source information.

_f_ 10. A quotation from a poem when you only know the first line.

_a_ 11. A list of articles with summaries.

_j_ 12. The latitude & longitude of the highest mountain in Tanzania.

_h_ 13. Your congressman's address in Washington, D.C. and his home state.

_f_ 14. Location of words used in Shakespeare's plays.

_h_ 15. A list of the manufacturers of air conditioners.

_c_ 16. A recent map of Afghanistan.

_o_ 17. A list of major events or trends of last year.

_i_ 18. Pictures of the U.S. flag in history.

_n_ 19. How to fix your 1985 Chevy truck.

_i_ 20. A lengthy discussion of World War II.

a. abstract

b. almanac

c. atlas

d. bibliography

e. biographical dictionary

f. concordance

g. dictionary

h. directory

i. encyclopedia

j. gazetteer

k. guidebook

l. handbook

m. index

n. manual

o. yearbook

Instructor: _____ Course/Section: _____

Name: _____

Date: _____ Points: _____

Identifying Reference Needs

1. Select one of the topics below. Which topic did you select?

drug abuse	computers	photography	race cars
animal rights	basketball	alcoholism	mathematics
Afghanistan	solar energy	civil rights	social security

2. Review the types of reference sources listed in Figure 7.1.

3. In the column on the right below, give one or two titles of reference works listed on pp. 165 through 170 that might give you the required information on your topic.

Needed information	Appropriate reference sources
overview article	
current statistics	
biographical information	
contemporary accounts	
definition of specialized terms	

Exercise 7.4

Instructor: _____ Course/Section: _____

Name: _____

Date: _____ Points: _____

Determining the Discipline

Use Figure 7.3 and the illustration following it to determine the approach and discipline for research on your topic. Sometimes a topic can be approached from more than one angle or discipline. For example, a research project on the "Gulf War" might have more than the obvious political aspects to review, such as the effect of the war on business, society as a whole, the economy, etc.

1. Select a topic for possible research. List it here.

2. Develop an approach for your topic. Fill in the form below by writing several approaches that you might take to research this topic. In the column on the right, identify the discipline under which that approach falls.

Possible Approach	Discipline

Instructor: _____ Course/Section: _____

Name: _____

Date: _____ Points: _____

Finding Sources in the Reference Collection

An understanding of your library's classification system can be useful in locating reference material in particular subject areas. Use Figure 4.2 in the text to locate a particular area of interest to you. Then examine the books in the Reference collection in that area. Answer the following questions.

1. What subject area did you select? (Give the Dewey Decimal or Library of Congress general number here.)

2. Select two works from the Reference stacks in that area. Give the title and date of each of the works you found.

    a.

    b.

3. Compare the usefulness of each work for your subject. Give a few examples of how each would contribute to a research paper on this subject.

4. Use Figure 7.1 to determine the type of reference source of each work. Briefly explain how you can determine the type of source reflected by the work.

5. Give the following information about one of the books.

    a. Title of the book:

    b. Call number and location:

    c. Single or multivolume:

    d. Arrangement of the book (alphabetical, topical, chronological):

    e. Subjects covered in the book:

    f. Title of an article or chapter on your topic:

    g. Author of article (if any):

    h. Volume number (if applicable) and inclusive pages of article:

    i. Write the correct bibliographic citation for an article you found in the reference book, or cite the book itself if it is a single volume. Use the bibliographic examples given in Appendix A.

Exercise 7.6

Reference Sources

Instructor: _____ Course/Section: _____

Name: _____

Date: _____ Points: _____

Locating Reference Books in the Online Catalog

1. Select a subject you are interested in to locate information in a reference book. What subject did you select?

2. Select one of the categories appropriate for that subject from the list of selected subject reference titles provided at the end of this chapter. Search your library catalog by title of the publication to determine which (if any) publications your library owns. Give the results of your search below.

3. Titles and dates of each of the works you found: (Use back of this page if necessary.)

    Write the exact library location next to these titles.

4. Locate one of the titles you found in Question 3 and give the following information.

    Title:

    Arrangement of the work:

    Does it have information that is appropriate for your topic? Explain.

5. Write a bibliographic citation to an article or chapter (or to the entire book if that is appropriate) for the title you located in Question 4. Use the examples in Appendix A.

6. Use your library's catalog to locate one of the guides to reference material discussed in this chapter. Locate the guide and answer the following questions.

   a. Title of a work on your topic listed in the guide.

   b. Author of the work you found on your topic.

   c. Write the correct bibliographic citation for the reference guide you use. Use the examples in Appendix A.

7. Use your library catalog to determine whether or not the source you found in Question 6a is available in your library. If so, give the call number and date of the work.

Instructor: _____ Course/Section: _____

Name: _____

Date: _____ Points: _____

Evaluating Reference Books

Select a topic of your choice. Locate information on the topic in each of the types of reference sources listed below and give the requested information about each.

Topic:

1. *Abridged dictionary*
    Title and date:

    Unabridged dictionary
    Title and date:

    Compare the two sources. How is the information similar? How does it differ?

    Write a bibliographic citation for each of the sources used. Use the examples given in Appendix A.

2. *General encyclopedia*
   Title and date:

   Subject encyclopedia
   Title and date:

   Compare the two sources. How is the information similar? How does it differ?

   Write a bibliographic citation for each of the sources used. Use the examples given in Appendix A.

3. *Subject or general bibliography*
   Title and date:

   Arrangement (alphabetically, topically, chronologically):

   Number of references in bibliography:

   Write a correct bibliographic citation. Use the examples given in Appendix A.

4. *Handbook or manual*
   Title and date:

   Write a brief summary of the information located.

   Write a correct bibliographic citation. Use the examples in Appendix A.

5. Using a state or a city as a topic, look up information in each of the types of reference sources listed below and give the requested information about each.

   Topic:

   Almanac
   Title and date:

   Population:

   Yearbook
   Title and date:

   Population:

   Compare the two sources. How is the information similar? How does it differ?

   Write a correct citation for each of the sources used. Use the bibliographic citations in Appendix A.

6. Using a country as a topic, look up information in each of the types of reference sources listed below and give the requested information about each.

Topic:

Atlas
Title and date:

Population:

Gazetteer
Title and date:

Population:

Compare the two sources. How is the information similar? How does it differ?

Write a bibliographic citation for each of the sources used. Use the examples of bibliographic citations given in Appendix A.

Instructor: _____ Course/Section: _____

Name: _____

Date: _____ Points: _____

Using Online Reference Guides

Use a college or university site, such as the three listed on page 164, or your local university or public library Web site. Find either a dictionary, encyclopedia, or other reference work for two of the following broad subjects:

history   mathematics   art   geography

1. Which site did you select?

2. 1st subject:

    a. title of work you found

    b. type of reference work (use Figure 7.1)

2. 2nd subject:

    a. title of work you found

    b. type of reference work (use Figure 7.1)

3. How does finding this type of material online compare with using the library catalog or browsing the Reference collection to find similar material?

Instructor: _____ Course/Section: _____

Name: _____

Date: _____ Points: _____

Using Major Reference Sites

Conduct a search using Refdesk.com (http://www.refdesk.com) and Internet Public Library (http://www.ipl.org/) sites to identify additional reference sources on a topic of your choice.

1. What topic did you select?

2. What site did you prefer?

3. Compare the steps you followed to find information at each of the sites.

4. What differences, if any, did you find in the type of results you found?

5. Discuss the ease, difficulty, accuracy, and speed of both sites.

Exercise 7.12

Instructor: _____ Course/Section: _____

Name: _____

Date: _____ Points: _____

Finding Legal and Business Information Online

A. *Legal Sources*

Go to *Findlaw* at http://www.findlaw.com

1. Find the constitution of your home state. Give the URL of the page you found.

2. Use the "Legal Subject Index" of *Findlaw* to select a topic.

    a. What topic did you select?

    b. Select two relevant Web sites for the topic you selected. Give the title and URL for each. Return to the *Findlaw* home page.

3. Under "U.S. State Resources," find the Nebraska Unicameral online. What exactly is a "unicameral" form of state government?

4. What types of information can you find about the Supreme Court at http://supct.law.cornell.edu/supct/

B. Business Sources

5. Using the Google search engine, search for "NAICS." Click on the first entry (not the "Sponsored Link") and answer the following questions.

   a. What does "NAICS" stand for?

   b. Click on "Ask Dr. NAICS" from the menu on the left of the page. Why is this system important for business and company information?

6. Using Google (www.google.com), find the home page of the Small Business Administration site on the Internet.

   a. What is the URL of this site?

   b. What type of information does this government agency provide for those beginning or involved in a small business?

7. Using your favorite search engine search for "fortune 500 companies."

   a. List the top five companies.

   b. Give the URL of this page.

   c. List the last five companies.

   d. When was this page updated?

Exercise 7.13

Instructor: _____ Course/Section: _____

Name: _____

Date: _____ Points: _____

Using the *American Memory* Collection at the Library of Congress

From the Library of Congress page located at http://www.loc.gov/, click on "American Memory."

1. Browse the collections listed to see what is available. Select one collection of special interest to you. Which one did you select? Why did you select this one?

2. Select an appropriate subject to search within this collection, or read the list of contents provided and select one of them. Which subject did you select?

3. Describe the results of your search. How many entries did you find? What types of information did you find? (film, text, or recordings)

Go back to the *American Memory* home page and use the search feature to locate a copy of the design of the telephone drawn by Alexander Graham Bell.

4. Does your library have a copy of this design in a printed source? How would you proceed to look for it in your library?

5. Would you use the *American Memory* collection again for research? Why?

Periodicals

"The hand that rules the press, the radio, the screen and
the far-spread magazine, rules the country."

Learned Hand

Introduction

Serials are publications that are issued on a continuing basis at regularly stated intervals. They include periodicals, newspapers, annuals and yearbooks, and the proceedings, transactions, and memoirs of societies and associations. The term *periodical* is usually used to refer to magazines and journals. Since newspapers appear periodically, for ease of discussion, this chapter will discuss magazines, journals and newspapers under the broad definition of periodicals.

Just as you may think of the library catalog as an index to its holdings, a large variety of indexes and databases serve the same purpose for the contents of individual periodical titles. Effective and critical use of information sources often depends on a mastery of these access tools for finding articles in newspapers, magazines and journals. It is the goal of this chapter to demystify this subject by describing and analyzing the major types of periodical indexes and databases and their use.

WHY USE PERIODICALS FOR RESEARCH?

Information found in periodicals is valuable in research for several reasons:

☐ Information appearing in periodicals constitutes the bulk of published information; there are thousands of periodicals published regularly, each containing an abundance of articles on different topics.

☐ The material found in newspapers, magazines, and journals is the most recent printed information you can find outside of the Internet.

☐ Information in periodicals, particularly newspapers, reflects contemporary opinion. Articles written shortly after an event occurred, whether it was in the nineteenth century, the 1930s, or the 1990s, convey what people thought of the event at the time it occurred.

☐ Periodical literature reflects the constantly evolving nature of information. No matter when an event occurred, the facts surrounding it and the event's significance are constantly being reinterpreted.

☐ Periodical literature provides comparative information for different periods. Compare, for example, the concepts of the role of women in the workplace in the 1920s with those of the 1990s.

☐ Sometimes periodical literature is the only information available—the topic may be too faddish ever to appear in a book. The findings of researchers and scholars in particular fields are usually published in journals rather than in books.

UNDERSTANDING PERIODICAL LITERATURE

As you can see, periodicals are important sources to use in the research process. How do you go about selecting appropriate periodical literature? How do you know which periodicals have the information that you need for your research purposes? You are probably familiar with a large number of periodicals—either you subscribe to one or more, or you have seen them on the display shelves at newsstands, grocery stores, or libraries. It is not unusual to stumble across information in a periodical that is exactly the answer to a research question that you might have. Although browsing is one way to find information in periodicals, it is neither the most efficient nor the most effective way. Because there are thousands of periodicals, you have to depend on something more than chance to find the most appropriate source for your needs. Finding and using periodical literature involves knowing something about the types of literature you can expect to find, the kinds of subjects covered, the formats, and the appropriate finding tools.

Types of Periodical Literature

There are two basic types of periodical literature: *popular* and *scholarly.*

Popular Periodical Literature

Magazines are designed to appeal to a broad segment of the population. They are characterized by relatively short articles written in nontechnical language, usually by staff writers. The style of writing is easy to understand and concise. The articles are especially useful for information on current events or for the contemporary treatment of a topic. Magazines are usually published weekly or monthly.

Newspapers provide short articles written in nontechnical language. Newspaper articles are usually *primary* sources of information because they provide firsthand accounts of an event. They are useful both for current and historical perspectives on a topic. Newspapers are usually published daily or weekly.

Scholarly Periodical Literature

Journals are scholarly publications intended for a more limited readership. The articles are written by scholars or experts in a field. The vocabulary is often technical, and the style of writing is more complex than that found in popular magazines. They provide research articles on specific topics, and may include charts and graphs. Journal articles usually include extensive bibliographies, reflecting the fact that the author has researched the topic. Journals are usually published monthly, quarterly, semiannually, or annually.

Subject Focus of Periodical Literature

In addition to the two types of periodical literature described above, you also need to consider the subject focus of periodical literature. Some periodicals are *general* in coverage while others are *subject* based—that is, they cover subjects that can then be categorized into broader subject *disciplines*.

THREE PRIMARY *DISCIPLINES* FOR SUBJECT-BASED LITERATURE

☐ **Humanities**—architecture, art, classical studies, history, journalism, literature, music, philosophy, poetry, and religion.

☐ **Social Sciences**—anthropology, business, criminal justice, economics, education, geography, law, management, political science, psychology, social work, and sociology.

☐ **Sciences**—agriculture, biology, chemistry, computer science, engineering, environment, health, mathematics, medicine, petroleum, and physics.

Format of Periodical Literature

Print

The traditional format of periodical literature is print on paper, although many libraries purchase microform (microfilm or microfiche) copies of newspapers and other periodicals.

Electronic

With the advent of computer technology as a storage and retrieval medium for information, we are seeing more and more periodical databases, that is indexes and abstracts and full-text periodical articles in electronic format—either on CD-ROM or via the Internet (Web based). While many periodical databases are freely available on the Web, most are fee based. Libraries subscribe to these databases in order to ensure free access to their patrons. CD-ROMs are usually used on the library's stand-alone computers. Web-based services to which the library subscribes may be restricted to use in the library, or may be available in homes and offices. Users must have a user-ID and password in order to access these subscription services from computers outside the library. In addition to the subscription services, there are numerous databases, some full text, which are available for free on the Web. These include *ERIC, FindArticles*, and *FirstGov*. Some of these are listed in this chapter under the heading "Selected Subject Indexes to Periodical Literature."

E-Journals

Electronic journals may be defined very broadly as any journal, magazine, newsletter, or newspaper that is prepared and distributed electronically. E-journals may be further distinguished as those electronic publications where complete articles are available rather than just citations or abstracts. Most often e-journals are accessed via the World Wide Web (WWW), although some are available on CD-ROM. Many e-journals have a print counterpart, and some publishers require print subscriptions along with electronic access. Some electronic versions differ from the print journal, for example, the electronic version may not have all of the graphics or supplementary materials available in the print version. E-journals may fall into any one of several categories (adapted from the Introduction to the *Vanderbilt Report on Access to Electronic Serials and Databases*, available at: http://library.vanderbilt.edu/eserials/serintro.htm):

- Individual e-journal titles—either free or subscription based
- Collections of individual journal titles, available on a subscription basis, such as *Project Muse* and *JSTOR*
- Journals in aggregated databases, such as *EBSCOhost, InfoTrac,* or *ProQuest Direct*, which link citations to full-text articles (*Aggregated* databases are collections of different databases.)
- Full-text databases, such as *LexisNexis Academic.*

How do you know where to look for an electronic version of a journal? If you are searching a database you will have direct access to the electronic version of the article. If you know the title of a journal, you can search the online catalog in your library. Many libraries catalog individual titles of e-journals, even those included in aggregated databases and collections. The record includes the URL (Internet address) for the journal. The user can click on the link and go directly to the journal or the Web site containing the journal. This type of direct link is called a *hot link.*

FINDING INFORMATION IN PERIODICALS

Finding appropriate information in periodicals is a multistep process that begins by determining a topic and deciding which subjects or keywords might be used to find articles about the topic. The second step is to determine the type of information needed—whether popular or scholarly publications would be most relevant to the topic. Next you must decide what is to be the focus of your research and which subject discipline might be most appropriate. Then you must determine which indexes or databases to use to find the information. It is a good idea in doing a thorough search of the literature to use both general and subject indexes, abstracts, and databases. Figure 8.1 outlines the steps for finding information in periodicals.

Indexes and Abstracts

The library catalog lists the library's cataloged works and gives location information. While it also includes periodical titles, and in some cases refers to specific database titles available through the individual library, it does not include individual articles in periodicals. For this you must use an *index* or *abstract*, either in print format or electronic(database). An *index* to periodical literature is a guide that provides *citations* or references to articles in periodicals. A citation includes:

- the name of the author;
- the title of the article;
- the title of the periodical; and
- the volume number, date, and pages of the periodical in which the article appears.

An *abstract* is a type of index that gives the citation and includes a summary of each item. Abstracts are important reference sources because the summary will tell you whether or not the literature is appropriate for your needs. While the summaries in abstracts vary in length, there is usually sufficient information to determine the main ideas presented in the original work.

Although many indexes and abstracts continue to be published in printed form, indexes and abstracts in electronic format (either Web-based or CD-ROM) have become the norm.

Printed Indexes and Abstracts

Although indexes to periodical literature have existed since the middle of the nineteenth century, the number of indexes to periodical literature has increased considerably over the past few years. It is necessary to acquire a basic knowledge of indexes in order to take advantage of the wealth of information they provide.

Most of the paper versions of periodical indexes are published monthly with an annual cumulation in which all of the articles included throughout the year are arranged in a single list. A section in the front of

Steps for Finding Information in Periodical Literature	
Step 1	Decide on a topic. What keywords would you use to find articles about your topic?
Step 2	Decide if the information you need will be found in popular magazines or in scholarly journals.
Step 3	Determine which discipline or broad subject area would be most suitable for the topic—humanities, science, or social science.
Step 4	Based on your approach in steps 2 and 3, select an appropriate index for your subject. Explore the various printed indexes, abstracts, and databases available at your library, or select from the lists included in this chapter. A brief selection of indexes and abstracts is listed below._x000D_

Humanities
America: History & Life
Art Index
Arts & Humanities
Citation Index
Historical Abstracts
Humanities Index
MLA International
Bibliography
Music Index

Science
ACM Guide to Computing
Agricola
Biological Abstracts
Biological & Agricultural
Index
Computer Select
Engineering Index
General Science Index
Medline
Science Citation Index

Social Sciences
ABI/INFORM
Education Index
ERIC
PsycLit
Social Sciences Index
Social Sciences Citation
Index
PAIS International

Multi-Disciplinary Sources
LexisNexis Academic; EBSCOhost Academic Search Premier; InfoTrac and _E-Library_ are all full-text databases that can be used for both popular and scholarly full-text articles in newspapers, magazines, and journals.

The reference librarian can also advise on the appropriate index to use. |
Step 5	Interpret the citation correctly. Identify the full title of the magazine or journal, the volume, issue, pages, and date for the articles you select.
Step 6	Copy, download, or print the citations or articles you need.
Step 7	If necessary, check the library catalog to see if the library has the magazine or journal title you need. Review the holdings record for the title to see the correct location for your issue.

Figure 8.1   Finding information in periodicals.

each index usually lists alphabetically all the periodical titles indexed and gives the abbreviations used in the entries.

Readers' Guide to Periodical Literature has long been a standard index to the most popular general-interest magazines published in the United States and Canada. It is one of only a few sources available for historical research. Published since 1900 by the H.W. Wilson Co., it covers current events and the popular literature in all subject areas. In some cases, *Readers' Guide* may be the only source available for contemporary information on a topic or event. For example, if you wanted to find articles on the signing of the original Panama Canal Treaty in 1903, the print copy of *Readers' Guide* would be an excellent place to start. (The electronic version of *Readers' Guide Retrospective* covers the years 1890–1982. In the current version there are about 136 full-text journals with coverage back to 1994.)

Each issue of the printed version of *Readers' Guide* is divided into several important sections. These are:

1. a list of the periodicals indexed;
2. a list of other abbreviations used in the index;
3. the main body of the index consisting of subject and author entries; and
4. a listing of book reviews by authors with citations.

Figures 8.2–8.4 show representative pages from the print version of *Readers' Guide*. These illustrations are provided to show a typical printed index to periodical literature.

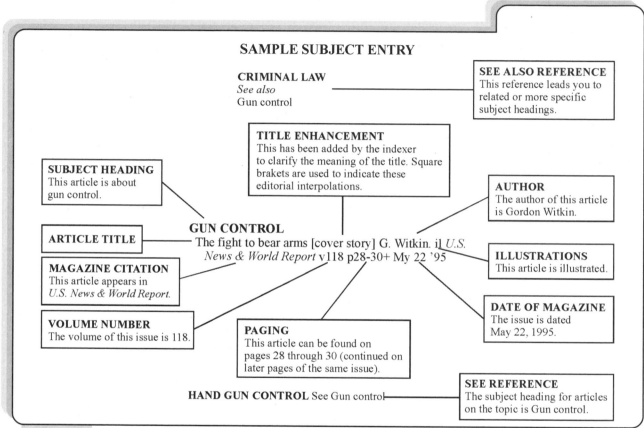

Figure 8.2 Sample subject entry from *Readers' Guide to Periodical Literature*, labeling parts of citation. (Copyright © 2000 by H.W. Wilson. Reprinted by permission.)

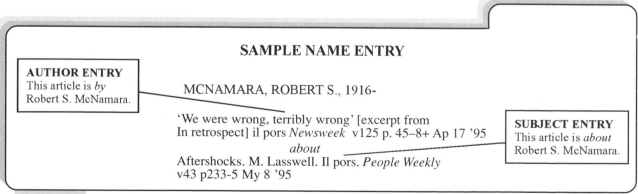

Figure 8.3 Sample name entry from *Readers' Guide to Periodical Literature*, explaining name entry. (Copyright © 2000 by H.W. Wilson. Reprinted by permission.)

TELETUBBIES (TELEVISION PROGRAM)
Teletubby trouble. H. Hendershot. il *Television Quarterly* v31 no1 p19-25 Spr 2000
TELEVEND INC.
Small change, big bucks: your pocket change is about to disappear into your PDA and cell phone [Tele Vend's Vending Automation System Technology] J. Conley. il *PC Computing* v13 no3 p52 Mr 2000

SUBJECT HEADING → **TELEVISION**
See also ← CROSS REFERENCES
Cable television
Closed circuit television
Digital television
High definition television
Interactive video
Minorities and television
Personal TV devices
Projection television
Video art
Wide screen television
History
True lies [E. Presley] E. Weiner. il por *TV Guide* v48 no1 p18 Ja 1-7 2000
Who really invented television? E. I. Schwartz. il por *Technology Review (Cambridge, Mass.: 1998)* v103 no5 p96-106 S/O 2000
Internet resources
Movies & television. C. Denton. il *Smart Computing* v11 no4 p96 Ap 2000
The shortsighted site busters [protecting intellectual property on fan Web sites; views of J. Kuzmanich] V. Postrel. il *Forbes* v166 no3 p132 Jl 24 2000
Locations
See Television program locations
Transmitters and transmission
See Television transmission
TELEVISION ACTORS AND ACTRESSES *See* Television performers
TELEVISION ADAPTATIONS
See also
David Copperfield (Television program: 2000)
Shakespeare, William, 1564-1616—Film and video adaptations
Book-based cartoons hit PBS [Bookworm Bunch] K. Raugust. il *Publishers Weekly* v247 no38 p35-6 S 18 2000
Extra ER for 'Ecco retro' [television adaptation of Fail-safe by G. Clooney spurs sales of Ecco's reprint] J. Quinn. il por *Publishers Weekly* v247 no9 p22 F 28 2000

→ **TELEVISION ADVERTISING**
See also
Cable television advertising
Computers—Television advertising use
Princeton Video Image Inc.
Product placement—Television programs
Voiceovers (Advertising)
Zapping of television advertising
Acting for justice. M. Cooper. *The Nation* v271 no10 p7, 38 O 9 2000
Ad in [abundance of tennis-themed TV advertising] K. O'Keefe. il *Tennis* v36 no2 p10-12 Mr 2000
Ad lib [C. Stone's short film Wazzzup used in Budweiser ad campaign] S. Dumenco. il por *New York* v33 no5 p22-3 F 7 2000
E-nuff! A. Ferguson. il *TV Guide* v48 no5 p54-6 Ja 29-F 4 2000
Helmers by day, hucksters by night [film directors make TV commercials] W. Berger. il *Premiere* v14 no2 p40 O 2000
Indie rock in space [M. Timony and C. Brownstein join W. Shatner for Priceline.com TV ads] M. Binelli. por *Rolling Stone* no839 p34 Ap 27 2000
Message in a beer bottle [Molson ad espousing Canadian nationalism] A. Bryant. il *Newsweek* v135 no22 p43 My 29 2000
Nike gets kinky [advertising on television and Internet] J. Walters. il *Sports Illustrated* v92 no5 p24 F 7 2000
A political nightmare: not enough airtime [political ad campaigns] L. Woellert. graph il *Business Week* no3704 p110-12 O 23 2000
Public television and the camel's nose [airing of commercials] B. S. Redmont. *Television Quarterly* v31 no1 p27-32 Spr 2000
Stuart Big [portrayal of Ameritrade's Stuart character by M. Maronna] por *People Weekly* v53 no11 p78 Mr 20 2000
TV or not TV? Not TV [Internet companies purchasing TV ad time vs. Internet ads] J. Ginsburg. il *Business Week* no3682 p114 My 22 2000
The unkindest 'cut' [New York and Los Angeles feel impact of commercial actors' strike] A. Barrett. il *The New York Times Magazine* p22 S 10 2000
Awards
See also
Clio Awards
History
How to score in advertising [Super Bowl ads] D. Enrico. il *TV Guide* v48 no5 p49-50+ Ja 29-F 4 2000
Social aspects
Boom box [impact of technology from TiVo and Replay upon TV advertising; cover story] M. Lewis. il *The New York Times Magazine* p36-41, 51, 65-7 Ag 13 2000
Time purchasing
Hey Bud, what's it to ya? [Anheuser-Busch's Super Bowl ads] M. Wells. il *Forbes* v165 no2 p70-1 Ja 24 2000

Now that's a Hail Mary play [OurBeginning.com spending $5 million on Super Bowl ads] M. Hyman. il por *Business Week* no3666 p100+ Ja 31 2000
Off the island and into the outback [ad rates for second CBS Survivor show set in Australian outback] il *Business Week* no3698 p48 S 11 2000

→ **TELEVISION ADVERTISING AND CHILDREN** ← TITLE / MAGAZINE / PAGES
Psyched out. M. K. Feldman. il *Utne Reader* no99 p16-18 My/Je 2000 ← ISSUE / DATE
The television networks kids watch most [Channel One] S. Manning. il *Columbia Journalism Review* v38 no6 p55-7 Mr/Ap 2000 ← AUTHOR
USA: commercials in the classroom. M. Walsh. il *The Unesco Courier* v53 no4 p14-16 Ap 2000

→ **TELEVISION AND CHILDREN**
See also
Television advertising and children
Television broadcasting—Children's programs
Don't give kids their own TVs. D. F. Roberts. il *Parents (New York, N.Y.)* v75 no8 p33-5 Ag 2000
Goin' down to South Park. B. S. Fagin. il *Reason* v32 no1 p38-41 My 2000
Healthy kids: limit TV for healthy bedtimes [research by Judith Owens] J. Van Tine. il *Prevention (Emmaus, Pa.)* v52 no3 p52 Mr 2000
How to tame that Trojan horse: the story the media won't tell. J. Cantor. *Television Quarterly* v30 no3 p19-22 Wint 2000
Is this too raw for kids? [watching wrestling on TV] B. Kantrowitz. il *Newsweek* v135 no6 p52 F 7 2000
Kick the TV habit. A. Dickinson. il *Time* v156 no3 p81 Jl 17 2000
The lure of the superhero. B. Solomon. il *Parents (New York, N.Y.)* v75 no4 p217-18 Ap 2000
Steve Allen's culture war. D. Kamp. por *Gentlemen's Quarterly* v70 no5 p115-18 My 2000
Tech potatoes. J. Bowen. il *Working Mother* v23 no2 p74-6+ F 2000
Teletubby trouble. H. Hendershot. il *Television Quarterly* v31 no1 p19-25 Spr 2000
Television as intelligence. T. J. Cottle. *Television Quarterly* v31 no2-3 p63-7 Summ/Fall 2000
TV under the tree? E. Allen. il *Time* v156 no26 p164 D 25 2000-Ja 1 2001
What can I watch with my kids? [special section] il *TV Guide* v48 no16 p32-56 Ap 15-21 2000
TELEVISION AND HISTORY
See also
Television broadcasting—Historical programs
TELEVISION AND LITERATURE
See also
Television adaptations
Television and reading
Going Hollywood [publishing offers opportunities for film studios' consumer products divisions] K. Raugust. il *Publishers Weekly* v247 no33 p206-7 Ag 14 2000
Hooray for Hollywood [children's properties going strong in film and on TV] S. Maughan. il *Publishers Weekly* v247 no46 p31-3 N 13 2000
It's quiz time [Hyperion's book tie-in to Who wants to be a millionaire] J. Quinn. il *Publishers Weekly* v246 no51 p19 D 20 1999
TELEVISION AND MINORITIES *See* Minorities and television
TELEVISION AND POLITICS
See also
Conservatism in television
Crossfire (Television program)
Presidential debates
Presidents in television
Television broadcasting—Government use
Vice-presidential debates
Washington week in review (Television program)
The 10 most memorable convention moments. A. Ferguson. il *TV Guide* v48 no31 p30-4 Jl 29-Ag 4 2000
15,000 journalists in search of—parties? [television coverage of Democratic and Republican national conventions] M. Frankel. il tab *Columbia Journalism Review* v39 no3 p16-19 S/O 2000
Al and Dubya after hours [late-night comics help shape the race between G. W. Bush and A. Gore] M. Peyser. il por *Newsweek* v136 no18 p38 O 30 2000
Alter-ed state [J. Alter] J. J. Miller. il *National Review* v52 no23 p26-8 D 4 2000
Anchors astray [mistakes made by networks in declaring a presidential winner] L. Menand. il *The New Yorker* v76 no35 p40 N 20 2000
Blacked out [television coverage of local government news] J. Geisler. il *American Journalism Review* v22 no4 p34-40 My 2000
Dead air [coverage of Bush and Gore campaigns] D. Plotz. il *The New York Times Magazine* p17-18 Ag 13 2000
Dead air [poor television coverage of political conventions] *The New Republic* v223 no5 p9 Jl 31 2000
Down by law [television coverage of presidential election and U.S. Supreme Court decision in Bush v. Gore] J. Poniewozik. il *Time* v156 no26 p79 D 25 2000-Ja 1 2001
Exit polls, Academy Awards, and presidential elections— [television coverage] L. K. Grossman. il *Columbia Journalism Review* v39 no1 p70, 72 My/Je 2000

Figure 8.4   Sample page, *Readers' Guide to Periodical Literature*, 2000, p. 2202, listing subject headings relating to television, advertising, and children. (Copyright © 2000 by H.W. Wilson. Reprinted by permission.)

Figure 8.4 illustrates some of the additional features of a print index. Note that on this page there are entries for "Television," "Television Advertising," "Television Advertising and Children," and "Television and Children." Cross references are included below each major subject heading to refer you to additional information should you decide to pursue the "History of Television," or the broadcasting of children's programs.

Figure 8.5 depicts a sample entry from *Communication Abstracts* for "Children and Advertising." The numbers at the end of the entry indicate the abstract number where the full description and citation will be found.

To locate the item number, you would then consult the bound volume containing entries including number 1972, in this case, the January-March portion. The full information on this article is found on page 870, under the entry number 1972, as indicated in the Index. Figure 8.6 gives the full abstract.

Selected Subject Indexes to Periodical Literature

The citations below describe the print version. All of the titles are available electronically.

Agriculture

Agricola. Beltsville, MD: National Agricultural Library, 1972–.
The holdings and index of the National Library of Agriculture. Includes agricultural literature primarily in both journals and book chapters, but also includes some monographs, series, microforms, audio-visuals, maps, and other types of materials.

Biological Abstracts. Philadelphia, PA: BIOSIS, 1989–.
Bibliographic database containing citations with abstracts to the world's biological and biomedical literature. Updated quarterly.

Biological and Agricultural Index. New York: H.W. Wilson, 1964–. (Continues *Agricultural Index*. 1916–1964.)
A cumulative subject index to 226 English-language periodicals in the fields of biology, agriculture, and related sciences.

Arts and Humanities

American History & Life. Santa Barbara, CA: ABC/CLIO, 1964–.
Scholarly material in American history and culture. Indexes journal articles, books, book chapters, films, videos, microforms, and dissertations. Citations and abstracts.

Art Index. New York: H.W. Wilson, 1933–.
Includes citations to articles in painting, sculpture, architecture, ceramics, graphic arts, landscape architecture, archaeology, and other related subjects.

Arts and Humanities Citation Index. Philadelphia: Institute for Scientific Information, 1976–.
Accesses about 6,900 journals in literature, poetry, short stories, music, film, radio, dance, and theater.

Historical Abstracts. Santa Barbara, CA: CLIO Press, 1971–.
Research in world history excluding the U.S. and Canada. Two sections: Modern History 1450–1914, and Twentieth Century 1914 to the present. Citations from journals, books, dissertations, and audio-visual materials.

Humanities Index. New York: H.W. Wilson, 1974–.
Author and subject index to articles in more than 300 English language periodicals in the humanities: archaeology, classical studies, folklore, history, language and literature, theology, and related subjects.

MLA International Bibliography. New York: Modern Language Association of America, 1981–.
Scholarly research in over 3,000 journals and series; covers relevant monographs, working papers, proceedings, bibliographies and other formats.

Business Communication, 0363, 1018, 1476, 1849

Business Development, 0032

Business Ethics, 1544

Business History, 1175

Business News, 0831

Businesses, 0219, 0635, 0702, 0727, 1252, 1344

Cable News Network, 0580, 0910

Cable Television, 0724, 0810, 0869, 1197, 1371

California, 0795, 1108, 1197, 1833, 1837, 1912

Caller Identification, 1296

Calvin and Hobbes, 0262

Campaign Coverage, 0885

Campaign Financial Reform, 1471

Campaign Techniques, 0773

Canada, 0028, 0038, 0062, 0066, 0082, 0098, 0112, 0147, 0178, 0205, 0206, 0208, 0238, 0285, 0295, 0298, 0407, 0532, 0705, 0746, 0852, 1350, 1382, 1415, 1468, 1481, 1485, 1543, 1715, 1883, 1900, 1936, 1964

Canadian Broadcasting Corporation, 0206, 0852

Canadian Content Policy, 0205

Cancer, 0098

Cancer Prevention, 0098

Candidate Information, 1801, 1816

Capitalism, 1071

Career Development, 1139, 1226

Career Preparation, 0723

Caregivers, 0102, 0730

Carmichael, Stokely, 1790

Carter Administration, 0121, 0150

Cartoons, 1872, 1888

Case Studies, 0168, 0616, 0711, 0820, 0907, 1378, 1601, 1870

Catch-22, 0331

CD-ROM, 0607

Celebrities, 0589, 1204

Cellular Telephones, 0614, 1340, 1342, 1347, 1349, 1467, 1486, 1592, 1594, 1597, 1601, 1602

Censorship, 0149, 0152, 0307, 0460, 0765, 0794, 0799, 0915, 1792, 1834, 1906, 1966

Central Americans, 0677

Central Europe, 1594

Chaffee, Steven, 1806, 1807

Chain Retail Stores, 0635

Chain Theory, 0313, 0176

Charitable Advertising, 1178

Charitable Donations, 1104

Chechen War, 0890

Chechnya, 0249, 0890

Chemistry Education, 1375

Chicago, 0226

Chief Executive Officers, 0187

Child Bearing, 0845

Child Death, 1669

Child Development, 0001, 1288, 1370, 1537

Child Online Protection Act, 0802

Child Pornography, 1101

Child Rearing, 1693

Children and Advertising, 0317, 0318, 1972   ←

Children and Television, 0576, 0850, 0872, 1068, 1355, 1363, 1367, 1371, 1383, 1384, 1455, 1457, 1498, 1504, 1507, 1513, 1514, 1515, 1523, 1528, 1537, 1875, 1878, 1886

Children and the Media, 0363, 0400, 0802, 1014, 1341, 1388, 1395, 1488, 1490, 1500, 1506, 1507, 1512, 1516, 1517, 1519, 1522, 1526, 1529, 1530, 1531, 1532, 1534, 1535, 1538, 1576, 1821, 1891

Children, 0010, 0093, 0352, 0396, 0460, 0663, 1067, 1289, 1328, 1330, 1336, 1357, 1370, 1379, 1649, 1661, 1931

Children's Television Act, 1377

Chile, 1019, 1814

China, 0203, 0223, 0244, 0408, 0480, 0586, 0687, 0783, 0787, 0790, 0849, 0883, 0888, 0900, 0901, 0914, 0915, 0917, 1086, 1533, 1714, 1885

Chinese, 1042, 1335, 1637, 1667, 1803

Chinese Americans, 1067, 1205

Chinese Language, 0849, 1067, 1205, 1667

Choice Behavior, 1780

Cholmondeley, Mary, 1892

Chomsky, Noam, 0292, 1727

Chronic Disease, 1293

Churn Charges, 0031

Cigarette Advertising, 1179, 1186

Cigarette Smoking, 1179

Cinematic History, 1501

Citizen Participation, 0221, 0734, 0735, 0737, 0742, 0743, 0751, 0753, 0757, 0763, 0768, 0772, 0775, 0777, 0778, 0779, 0781, 0782, 0805, 1099, 1106, 1237, 1409, 1430, 1431, 1584, 0515, 0539, 0696, 0701, 0735, 0743, 0750, 0751, 0753, 0757, 0772, 0775, 0777, 0779, 0782, 0872, 1409, 1727, 1930

Civic Journalism, 0084

Figure 8.5 *Communication Abstracts*, v. 24, 2001, showing the entries for works on "Children and Advertising." (*Communication Abstracts*, pp. 870 and 903, copyright © 2001 by Sage Publications. Reprinted by permission of Sage Publications, Inc.)

Advertising, Marketing, and Consumer Behavior

→ **1972**

Bringue, X. Child advertising and persuasive strategy: An analysis of contents. Zer 10:107-130, May 2001.

CHILDREN AND ADVERTISING. CONTENT ANALYSIS. PERSUASION.

This work analyzes children's dimension as infant consumers and their definition as a specific target for advertising campaigns. As an introduction, the limits of advertising communication for children are exposed, ranging from the nature of the recipient to children's behavior facing the media and the facts involved in this communication process. The second part focuses on the study of an ad sample, considered to be advertising for children. It tries to establish a classification of the persuasive strategies in these messages, with special attention to the formats and the main persuasive arguments offered to children. The article finishes with some brief conclusions on the results.

1973

Chen, S. Assessing the impact of the Internet on brands. Journal of Brand Management 8(4/5):288-302, May 2001.

BRAND MANAGEMENT. ELECTRONIC COMMERCE. INTERNET.

This paper assesses the claim that e-commerce will spell the end of brand management as we know it. Evidence from market studies is reviewed, and the paper identifies some key factors that make this scenario unlikely.

1974

Chun, R. and Davies, G. E-reputation: the role of mission and vision statements in positioning strategy. Journal of Brand Management 8(4/5):315-333, May 2001.

CORPORATE ADVERTISING. CORPORATE REPUTATION. ELECTRONIC COMMERCE. WEB SITES.

This study is concerned with the reputation-building potential of corporate Web sites. Claims have been made that companies are positioning themselves on the Internet by including mission and vision statements with their Web sites. Although many companies appear to be positioning themselves against "competence," the results show substantial differences between companies competing in the same sectors as well as differences between the profile of leading companies across sectors.

1975

Clauser, R. C. Offline rules, online tools. Journal of Brand Management 8(4/5):270-287, May 2001.

BRAND PROMOTION. MARKETING STRATEGIES. ONLINE USE.

The fundamental rules of brand building have not changed. Business should stick to the traditional tried and true rules of branding while using the new technology and strategic tools now possible with the Internet. Follow them carefully and break them cautiously. This argument is explored in relation to five offline rules and their online applications. These rules focus on brand names, consistency, customer insight, emotional connection, and brand experience.

Figure 8.6   Abstract for entry retrieved in Figure 8.5 in *Communication Abstracts*, v. 24, 2001. (*Communication Abstracts*, pp. 870 and 903, copyright © 2001 by Sage Publications. Reprinted by permission of Sage Publications, Inc.)

Social Sciences Index. New York: H.W. Wilson, 1974–.

Author and subject index for articles in more than 300 periodicals in anthropology, area studies, economics, environmental science, geography, law and criminology, political science, psychology, public administration, sociology and related subjects.

Business

ABI/INFORM. Ann Arbor, MI: UMI, 1971–.

Indexes over 1,500 business and trade journals. Citations and abstracts to articles in all business-related topics, economics, and managerial science. Allows keyword searching and several print options.

Business Index. Los Altos, CA: Gale Group, 1979–.

Provides cumulative author/subject access to over 800 business periodicals, including articles in the *Wall Street Journal, Barron's*, and the financial section of *The New York Times*. Also covers articles relating to business appearing in over 1,100 general and legal periodicals.

Business Periodicals Index. New York: H.W. Wilson, 1958–. (Continues *Industrial Arts Index.* 1913–1957.)

Magazines and journals in advertising, banking and finance, marketing, accounting, labor and management, insurance, and general business. Good source for information about an industry and about individual companies.

Education

Education Index. New York: H.W. Wilson, 1929–.

Subject index to educational literature including 339 periodicals, pamphlets, reports, and books. Includes counseling and personnel service, teaching methods and curriculum, special education and rehabilitation, and educational research.

ERIC. Rockville, MD: Department of Education, Office of Educational Research and Improvement, 1966–.

Contains a combination of the *Resources in Education* (RIE) file of ERIC document citations and the *Current Index to Journals in Education* (CIJE) journal article citations from over 750 professional journals. Includes all aspects of education.

Public Affairs

PAIS International. New York: Public Affairs Information Service, 1915–. (Previous title *PAIS Bulletin.*)

Citations to articles in international affairs, public administration, political science, history, economics, finance, and sociology. Both U.S. and UN government documents are included, as well as books, pamphlets, society publications, and periodicals. Published twice monthly; cumulated annually.

Science and Technology

Applied Science and Technology Index. New York: H.W. Wilson, 1958–. (Continues *Industrial Arts Index,* 1913–1957.)

Citations to articles in the fields of aeronautics, automation, construction, electricity, engineering, and related subjects.

Biological Abstracts. (*See* Agriculture.)

Biological and Agricultural Index. (*See* Agriculture.)

Chemical Abstracts. Columbus, OH: American Chemical Society, 1907–.

Contains literature related to chemistry appearing in books, reports, annotated documents, and about 14,000 journals and conferences.

Engineering Index. Baltimore: Engineering Index, 1984–.

    Contains abstracts of literature published in engineering journals, technical reports, monographs, conference proceedings. Issued monthly and cumulated annually. Annual volumes are divided into subject volumes and an author index volume. Available online and on CD-ROM as COMPENDEX.

GEOREF. Alexandria, VA: American Geological Institute, 1990–.

    Comprehensive coverage of more than 4,500 international journals, books, proceedings, dissertations, and maps in geology and geography. Covers 1785– (North American), 1967– (worldwide).

Index Medicus. Washington: GPO, 1960–.

    Created by the National Library of Medicine primarily for the medical professional, but it is also useful to lay persons interested in medical-related topics. Available online as *Medline.*

INSPEC. Stevage, Herts., England: Institution of Electrical Engineers, 1993–.

    Indexes scientific and technical literature in electrical engineering, electronics, communications, control engineering, computers and computing, and information technology. Covers 1969–.

MathSciNet. Providence, RI: American Mathematical Society, 1973–.

    Includes information relating to mathematics, statistics, physics, and computer science.

SCI, Science Citation Index. Philadelphia: Institute for Scientific Information, 1965–

    Bimonthly with calendar year cumulations. Published in three sections:
    Available on the Internet as *Web of Knowledge.*

Social Sciences

NCJRS Documents Database. Washington: National Institute of Justice/National Criminal Justice Reference Service, 1972–.

    Contains references to periodical articles, research reports, books and unpublished materials from private sources as well as from local, state, and national governments.

Psychological Abstracts. Arlington, VA: American Psychological Association, 1927–.

    Abstracts of journal articles, monographs, and reports on psychology and related studies arranged by major classification groups. Includes author and subject index. Issued monthly. Available online and on CD-ROM as *PsycLit* and *PsycInfo.*

Sociological Abstracts. New York: Sociological Abstracts, 1952–.

    International in scope; covers articles from journals concerned with sociology. Electronic version covers 1977–.

Newspaper Indexes/Databases

Newspapers are good sources for information on local, state, national, and international levels. Periodical indexes such as *Readers' Guide* provide references to many different publications, but a printed newspaper index usually references only one newspaper. Newspaper indexes generally have subject entries and do not give the exact title of an article; instead, they give a brief description of the article.

Many newspaper indexes and the full text of newspapers are now available electronically. One of the most comprehensive databases of full-text newspapers is *LexisNexis*. (See the description under Multidiscipline: General.) *ProQuest Direct* has an electronic collection of over 1,000 full-text newspapers. Subscribers can subscribe to a single online newspaper or can customize a database of selected newspapers. Selected indexing and full text of some newspapers are available in *EBSCOhost, InfoTrac,* and *Library.* Some newspapers are available free on the Web, including the *New York Times.* Most of the directory-type search engines have a "news" category, linking major news stories to their site. CNN.com and other services offer full articles from current newspapers. Some services include back files.

A sample page from the *New York Times Index* (Figure 8.7) is typical of the format of most newspaper indexes. Notice that in the 1996 Index there are several general articles on "advertising," including an article

Index cover
Index page
Article description
length of Article— short (S)
date & cover year
Section IV pg. 7 column 1
Subject heading
Cross reference
Index page

The New York Times

INDEX 1996

A Book of Record

The Master-Key to the News since 1851.

NYT

Inframetrics Inc, O 2
ADVENTUROUS TRAVELER BOOKSTORE (WILLISTON, VT). See also
Travel and Vacations, Jl 21
ADVERTISING. See also
Acquired Immune Deficiency Syndrome, Ja 6, Jl 12, S 25, N 21
Adelphi University, Ag 30
Agriculture, Je 4
Air Pollution, Mr 8
Airlines and Airplanes, My 13, Je 4,6,12, Jl 29, Ag 12, O 10,19,29, N 21,22, D 1,11
Alcoholic Beverages, F 9, Mr 12,19,28, Ap 11, My 3,14,15, Je 16,20, Jl 19,26, S 26, O 6,15,23, N 8,10,12,13,20,25,26, 28, D 13,24,30,31
American Express Co, Ja 25
Apparel, My 1,5, Je 6, Jl 26,31, Ag 20, S 10, N 14
Apple Computer Inc, Ja 29
Arthritis and Rheumatism, O 17
Athletics and Sports, F 7,8, Je 21, Jl 15, Ag 30, O 28, D 23
Automobile Racing, F 21
Automobiles, F 12,13,22, Mr 3,28, Ap 8,24, My 1,10,15,16, 23, Je 10,13, Jl 18, S 13,19,24,27, O 2,9,14,15,16,24,29,30, N 21, D 27
Back (Human Body Part), Je 27
Banks and Banking, O 16
Baseball, Ja 26, My 2,5,8, N 27
Basketball, F 26, Mr 13, Ap 7
Batteries, D 26
Birth Control and Family Planning, F 8
Books and Literature, Mr 31
Campbell Soup Co, S 6
Cancer, O 3
Candy, My 19
Cereals, Ja 10, Jl 8
Children and Youth, N 4
Children's Defense Fund, N 4
Christmas, D 5
Circuses, Mr 7
Citibank, F 27
Cleansers, Detergents and Soaps, F 6
Colleges and Universities, N 6
Computers and Information Systems, Ja 22,23, Mr 4,11,25, 29, Ap 22, My 5,13, Je 2,9,13,24,26,27, Jl 3,30, S 5,7,16,18, O 1, N 11,20,25,26, D 3,12,16
Convenience Stores, Ag 2
Cosmetics, F 7,11, My 29, Jl 31
Culture, Je 20
Dairy Products, Mr 3, My 8,22, Jl 10, O 4
Dating (Social), F 11
Drug Abuse and Traffic, My 9, Je 17, Jl 8
Education and Schools, F 28, My 15
Electric Light and Power, O 25

Four agencies win best of show Grand Awards at 38th annual international television advertising competition sponsored by New York Festivals; they are Dentsu Inc, Delvico Bates Barcelona, Dektor Higgins & Associates, and Saatchi & Saatchi Advertising Worldwide (S), F 1,D,9:3

Advertising column examines advertising campaigns from mainstream marketers aimed at black consumers (M), F 9, D,2:1

Thomas Hine article on how popular images become cultural icons; comments on how advertising, news and entertainment media have created and disseminated stock of images whose potency transcends local boundaries, and computer technology has made it easier for people to use and manipulate them; examples cited; photos (L), F 18,II,1:1

Special report, The Next Generation, on J Richard Smith Advertising; Long Island, New York, company is now run by founder's son, 34-year-old Michael Smith; Michael and father, Jerry Smith, discuss transition at firm; photos (M), F 18,XIII-LI,1:1

Advertising column asks 20 questions about advertising, marketing and the media (L), F 20,D,5:1

Goodby Silverstein & Partners, advertising agency that Madison Avenue considers perhaps strongest creative force in American advertising today, is raising its profile to a level more commensurate with its abilities and accomplishments; San Francisco, Calif-based agency is attracting large, high-profile accounts; Rich Silverstein and Jeff Goodby, co-chairmen and creative directors, comment; photo (L), F 23,D,2:1

J Walter Thompson Co unit of WPP Group is putting up World Wide Web site to promote Thompson to potential clients as well as reinforce ties with current clients (M), F 26,D,9:1

For the fifth consecutive year, Ogilvy & Mather Direct, unit of the WPP Group, takes top honors from judges of the John Caples International Awards for excellence in direct marketing, 18th annual ceremony, NY (Advertising column) (S), F 28,D,4:3

Stuart Elliott (Advertising) column discusses efforts of Dan Staley, one-time copywriter at New York agencies, to bring lighter side of Madison Avenue to television in program on CBS called Good Company; says Staley is co-creator and co-executive producer of series that focuses on creative team at fictitious Blanton, Booker & Hayden Worldwide Advertising (M), Mr 1,D,4:1

List of some of '100 best commercials,' as listed by Leo Burnett Company; photo (S), Mr 10,IV,7:1

Advertising New York annual benefit event sponsored by Advertising Club of New York, Advertising Women in New York and American Advertising Federation, will for the first time present three Best Corporate Citizens awards in June (S), Mr 13,D,7:4

Advertising Research Foundation's third annual David Ogilvy Award ceremony; campaign for Winterfresh brand of chewing gum marketed by Wm Wrigley Jr Co takes top honors; other winners noted (Advertising column) (S), Mr 14,D,4:4

Nonprofit groups are using parodies of advertisements by their large corporate adversaries to grab attention enemies' costly advertising campaigns have generated; photos (M), Mr 17,IV,6:1

Hitachi sign overlooking Central Park goes dark after company decides that all its advertising should include an Hitachi product, not just the logo; Artkraft Strauss Corp is negotiating with another large company to sponsor the sign, which has 2,500 light bulbs; photo (M), Mr 24,XIII-CY,6:4

Jay Chiat, Ann Fudge, O Milton Gossett, Harold Levine, Mark Rodriguez and Brandon Tartikoff receive Diversity Achievement Awards, honoring executives in advertising, marketing and the media for their work in fostering diversity; awards are presented by District 2 of the American Advertising Federation, NY (Advertising column) (S), Mr 27,D,7:1

Americans between ages of 50 and 64, caught in relative demographic obscurity between Depression-era parents and ubiquitous baby boomers, are finally getting some respect from Madison Ave, which is beginning to recognize them as distinct economic target (Market Place) (M), Mr 29,D,18:3

Advertising column discusses merger of Tucker Wayne & Co and West Group, two relatively small but well-regarded agencies, to form biggest independent shop in Southeast; says move is indicative of consolidations that are remaking the advertising industry to meet changing client needs; new shop to be named West Wayne (M), Ap 5,D,4:3

Barbara Carr, president of Carr & Associates, and Lee Nadler of the Survivors of the Shoah Visual History Foundation are awarded Crystal Prism Award by the Advertising Club of New York (S), Ap 9,D,11:2

Interview with Mason Reese, star of 75 commercials in early 1970's and today the owner of a Greenwich Village club Nowbar; photo (M), Ap 10,C,1:1

Cliff Freeman & Partners, New York, takes top honors, winning most awards at the 1996 Best of New York American Advertising Awards ceremony sponsored by the Advertising Women of New York; other winners noted (Advertising column) (S), Ap 11,D,6:3

Advertising column discusses ambitious but risky decision by British ad agency, Leagas Delaney, to open full-service office in United States, in San Francisco; Bruce Haines, chief executive at Leagas Delaney, says he is not daunted by challenges confronting cultural transplant; he notes large number of American agencies that have successful shops in London (M), Ap 12,D,6:1

Wieden & Kennedy is named National Agency of the Year by Adweek (S), Ap 15,D,10:6

Advertising column on GSD&M, Texas ad agency which just 10 years ago was small regional agency and has now hit the big time; Adweek recently named GSD&M the 'biggest gainer' of year in Southwest, citing agency's increase in billings of 43 percent, or $119 million, in 1995; Roy M Spence Jr, president of GSD&M, says he is delighted with company's success, but he has no desire to be biggest, or to relocate to New York or Chicago (M), Ap 18,D,10:1

Fallon McElligott is named United States Agency of the Year for 1995 by Advertising Age in 52d annual Agency Report issue (S), Ap 18,D,10:3

Advertising column notes that marketers are increasingly featuring interracial couples in their campaigns, as well as blending actors, models and actual customers of disparate racial and ethnic backgrounds; says such mosaic advertising can be a publicity gimmick, but these changes in advertising are profound; photo (M), Ap 19,D,6:1

DeWitt Media Inc survey finds that marketers will continue to shift advertising dollars from the broadcast

television networks to other media, including cable, direct mail, interactive media and computer on-line services, as those networks continue losing viewers (M), Ap 22,D,11:3

Advertising column notes that agenda of 1996 annual meeting of American Assn of Advertising Agencies is purposely being focused on handful of issues that have been deemed significant since 1992: the importance of demonstrating how powerful advertising can be in selling brand-name products, finding ways to help agencies exploit explosive growth of new media and assisting agencies in recruiting and retaining diverse work force; concentration of issues coincides with narrowing of audience to CEO's, with conference for agency media executives held separately in February (M), Ap 25,D,6:1

Stuart Elliott (Advertising) column on American Association of Advertising Agencies annual meeting in Indian Wells, Calif; notes that Eastman Kodak Co chairman George M C Fisher urged advertising agencies to exploit advantages of Internet (M), Ap 26,D,6:1

Advertising column notes that many companies, both big and small, old and new, are making decisions involving their accounts this month (M), Ap 30,D,9:1

Leo Burnett Co and Hunt Adkins share top honors, winning Best of Show awards at 54th annual Obie Awards ceremony for creative excellence sponsored by Outdoor Advertising Assn of America (S), My 2,D,8:6

Goodby, Silverstein & Partners in San Francisco wins most awards at Clio Awards ceremony for second consecutive year (S), My 6,D,5:1

Goldberg Moser O'Neill, independent San Francisco agency, has agreed to sell substantial minority stake to Lowe Group, unit of Interpublic Group of Cos; deal is another step in major consolidations in industry so agencies can better serve multinational marketers; Goldberg Moser O'Neill will operate separately under present management after acquisition; photo (M), My 6,D,5:1

Advertising column notes that advertisers are reviving songs and styles of 1970's; agencies are going along with popular culture, where 70's revival has been under way for some time (S), My 7,D,9:1

Cliff Freeman & Partners takes top honors at 32d annual International Andy Awards presentation for creativity sponsored by Advertising Club of New York (S), My 10,D, 4:3

Ad agency buyout binge of 1996 continues unabated; Young & Rubicam agrees to acquire Waring & LaRosa; Omnicom Group, which once owned Waring & LaRosa, agrees to purchase Creative Media Inc; acquisitions typify consolidation reshaping Madison Avenue (M), My 13,D,9:1

Advertising column discusses Information Resources Inc's decision to join forces with Univision in effort to take lead in one of biggest areas of growth in advertising: ethnic marketing; advertisers are seeking more sophisticated ways to attract America's Hispanic population, which is growing dramatically; graph (M), My 14,D,10:3

Citigate Albert Frank takes top honors at second annual Portfolio Awards ceremony honoring financial advertising, sponsored by Financial Communications Society (S), My 21,D,6:5

Goodby Silverstein & Partners wins three awards, including the $100,000 prize for general excellence, at MPA Kelly Awards competition sponsored by Magazine Publishers of America (S), My 22,D,3:3

Goodby Silverstein & Partners takes top honors for second consecutive year at One Show for creative advertising sponsored by One Club for Art and Copy (S), My 23,D,8:2

More than 40 agencies that specialize in advertising aimed at Spanish-speaking consumers form trade organization named Association of Hispanic Advertising Agencies (S), My 23,D,8:4

Advertising column: Walt Disney Co and McDonald's Corp have announced landmark, decade-long cross-promotional agreement that underscores how familiar brand names are increasingly being wielded like powerful weapons by huge global marketers; goal is to forge indelible, long-term ties between consumer products and popular entertainment and sports franchises and celebrities; such strategic alliances have raised concerns that they encourage consumerism while stimulating appetites—especially among children—for junk film and junk food; alliance between Disney and McDonald's would anoint McDonald's 18,700 food outlets as Disney's primary promotional restaurant partners, promoting Disney films, home videos, theme parks and other attractions (M), My 24,D,1:2

American Advertising Federation plans new slogan, new logo and advertising drive in bid to raise profile; represents agencies and media as well as marketers; president Wally Snyder previews plan, interview (M), My 28,D,8:3

Anderson & Lembke Inc wins top honors and most awards at Business Marketing Association's Ace Awards for business-to-business communications; Advertising Age magazine honors Wieden & Kennedy for television commercial; Public Relations Society of America's New York chapter honors New York Public Library for public relations campaign to promote its 1995 centennial celebration (S), My 28,D,8:5

Janny Scott column on the cacophony of messages blared at New Yorkers through billboard ads for briefs, Scotch and other goods (M), Je 2,XIII-CY,1:1

Ralston Purina Co wins the top prize at 28th Annual Effie Awards, given by New York chapter of American Marketing Association in recognition of effectiveness in advertising; agency is Fallon McElligott (S), Je 6,D,7:4

Bigger and bolder outdoor ads are undergoing a renaissance as agencies rediscover medium as cost-effective way to build a broad awareness for a brand; photo (Advertising column) (M), Je 7,D,4:1

BBDO Canada wins most awards at Art Directors Club ceremony, New York City (S), Je 11,D,8:5

New York Festivals honors Leo Burnett Co, Euro RSCG unit, Lewis Moberly and Wunderman Cato Johnson for print advertising and Young & Rubicam's Toronto office for radio advertising (S), Je 12,D,7:1

Cliff Freeman & Partners and Wieden & Kennedy win top awards at American Advertising Awards, sponsored by American Advertising Federation (S), Je 12,D,7:1

Goodby, Silverstein & Partners in San Francisco takes top honors, winning $100,000 prize for best commercial, at fifth annual Radio-Mercury Awards presentation sponsored by Radio Creative Fund of New York (S), Je 13,D,6:5

N W Ayer & Partners says it will be acquired by D'Arcy Masius Benton & Bowles, signaling a new crest in wave of deals that are remaking Madison Avenue for second time in a decade; photos (L), Je 19,D,1:2

Figure 8.7 Sample pages from the *New York Times Index*. Composite of the title page, an index entry (taken from p. 13 of the index), and entries from p. 14 of the index. (Copyright © 1997 by The New York Times Co. Reprinted with permission.)

described as "List of some '100 Best Commercials,'" which might be relevant to the topic of advertising and children. The description gives additional information: the length of the article, the section, page, and column where the article may be found.

Since newspaper indexes usually cover only one newspaper, the year and title of the newspaper is located only on the front cover of the index, rather than listed in each individual citation. You must be careful to record the exact year and title of the newspaper index as part of the note-taking process. Once you select an article, you will need to search the online catalog to determine whether or not the library subscribes to the publication. Remember to check the holdings record to determine the exact location of this issue. Older issues of newspapers will most likely be kept on microfilm in the library.

Following are some representative indexes to major newspapers. Many of the large city newspapers are indexed, either in print or electronic format; they will not be listed here. You should check your online catalog to ascertain whether the newspaper in your city or another major newspaper that interests you is indexed.

Index to the Christian Science Monitor International Daily Newspaper. Boston: Christian Science Monitor, 1960–.

Titles of articles are listed under subject with day, month, section, page and column noted.

Selected articles from the *Christian Science Monitor* are available at http://www.csmonitor.com/.

New York Times Index. New York: New York Times Company, 1913–.

Earlier series covers the years 1851–1912. Subject index to *The New York Times* newspaper. Published twice monthly with annual cumulations. Most general databases now include citations from *The York Times*.

USA Today. Arlington, VA: Gannett, 1982–.

Daily newspaper featuring short articles. Has widespread readership. Selected coverage available at http://www.usatoday.com.

Wall Street Journal Index. New York: Dow Jones, 1959–.

Emphasizes financial and business news. Includes *Barron's Index*, a subject and corporate index to *Barron's Business and Financial Weekly*. The online version is available by subscription only.

The Washington Post Newspaper Index. Ann Arbor, MI: UMI, 1978–.

Useful for coverage of news from the nation's capital. Selective coverage available at http://www.washingtonpost.com/.

Databases

Although the term *database* is used interchangeable with indexes and abstracts, here it is used to refer to a collection of information that is stored electronically in such a way as to provide easy and quick search and retrieval capabilities. Databases have a distinct advantage over print sources in that they can be searched more quickly and more effectively. Most of the databases are Web-based, but many are still available on CD-ROM. The entries on the CD-ROM versions usually display a labeled screen much like the catalog records discussed in Chapter 4. There are generally two types of databases, *bibliographic* and *full text.*

☐ *Bibliographic databases* are those that provide only citations to information in other sources. Currently the lines between bibliographic and full-text databases (described below) are blurred in that many databases provide both full-text and bibliographic information in a single database.

☐ *Full-text databases,* in the context of periodical literature, are those that provide, as the term implies, the full text of periodical articles along with citations and abstracts. Subscription services such as *LexisNexis Academic, InfoTrac, EBSCOhost, WilsonWeb, ProQuest Direct*, and *E-Library* include both full-text and bibliographic information. Some of the full-text articles have charts, graphs, photographs, and other images. Many full-text databases are multi-disciplinary–they cover a broad spectrum of articles. Others, such as *ABI/Inform* and *EBSCO Business Source Elite*, are limited to specific subject areas.

Database Searching

Using the various databases is relatively simple since most contain the same basic information. However, each database has its own particular search engine and search options. It is always advisable when you use a database for the first time to go to the help screen. Some libraries provide online tutorials and "quick guides" to the databases. An understanding of the options available in particular databases can save time and improve your search results. For example, a number of databases allow you to limit your search to "full-text" articles. This can be helpful in those databases that include both full-text for some articles and only citations for others. By limiting a search to "peer-reviewed" articles it is possible to retrieve only scholarly articles.

The techniques for searching discussed in Chapter 3 can be applied when searching for periodical information for the topic "the effect of television advertising on children." You might begin with a basic search for the phrase "television advertising and children," or "effects television advertising children," or even "consumer kids," for a different approach. In order to limit or narrow your search you should use the "advanced" or "guided" search features of the database where those are available.

Appropriate databases for the topic might include *EBSCOhost Academic Search Premier* (for general information), *EBSCOhost Business Source Elite* (for a business perspective), *ERIC* (for educational concerns), *PsycLit* (for psychological aspects), and *LexisNexis Academic* for laws and regulations. There are lists of multi-disciplinary databases and subject specific databases on page 228. Figures 8.8–8.14 illustrate using some of the databases in the Nebraska State College System, to search for information on the topic "effects of television advertising on children."

Figure 8.8 shows the results of a keyword search for "television and children" in *EBSCOhost Academic Search Premier.* This search found 19 entries, eight of which are shown on this screen.

Entry no. 2 in Figure 8.8 is for an article entitled "The Impact of Television Advertising on Children's Christmas Wishes." The notes on this screen indicate that Conn Library subscribes to this periodical (available in print), but that the article is also available in full text in either HTML (Web-based) format or a PDF (Portable Document Format). PDF documents are created with Adobe Acrobat or other software programs and can be viewed with Adobe Acrobat Reader or other PDF reader programs. If you select the PDF file, your computer will launch Adobe Acrobat. If the article includes images it may take longer to print.

Figure 8.9 shows the complete citation for entry no. 4 from Figure 8.8.

The "subject" field indicates the subject heading for this article.

1. The "source" field gives the complete information and physical description of the article.

2. The "author" field shows multiple authors for this article.

3. The "Abstract" describes the summary of the content of the article.

4. "An" indicates the accession number, an identification number used by the database producer.

5. "ISSN" is the International Standard Serial number, an eight-digit number which identifies periodical publications world-wide.

6. "Database" identifies the source database for this entry.

7. "Persistent link to this article" gives the URL (Internet address) for the article. Note that since it is not underlined, it cannot be activated.

8. "View links" provides a link to generate an online interlibrary loan request.

9. "Notes" field indicates that this title is not available in the local library. Conn Library has arranged with this database vendor to process interlibrary loan requests for this title. Once the article is received, the patron is notified to pick it up at the library. Normally, there is no charge for this service.

EBSCO HOST | Research Databases

Basic Search | Advanced Search | Choose Databases | Select another EBSCO service

Keyword | Subjects | Publications | Library Holdings

Images

Searched: <u>Academic Search Premier</u> for *"television advertising and children"*

Find: Television Advertising and Children

For search examples, see *Search Tips* .

▢ <u>Folder has 0 items.</u>

Refine Search | Results | To print, e-mail, or save an article or citation, add it to your folder.

◀ **1 to 10** (of 19) ▶ **Pages: 1** <u>2</u>	▢ <u>Add (1-10)</u>
1. <u>THE NEW KINCHIN LAY.</u>; By: Thomas, George., Quadrant, Jun2001, Vol. 45 Issue 6, p30, 3p **Notes:** This title is not held locally	▢ <u>Add</u>
2. <u>The Impact of Television Advertising on Children's Christmas Wishes.</u>; By: Buijzen, Moniek; Valkenburg, Patti M.., Journal of Broadcasting & Electronic Media, Summer2000, Vol. 44 Issue 3, p456, 15p, 3 charts **Notes:** Our Library Subscribes to this Periodical ▤ <u>HTML Full Text</u> ▨ <u>PDF Full Text</u> **(752K)**	▢ <u>Add</u>
3. <u>Being an effective parent requires making the time to do so.</u>; By: Heath, Dwight B.., Brown University Child & Adolescent Behavior Letter, Jul98, Vol. 14 Issue 7, p8, 1p **Notes:** This title is not held locally ▤ <u>HTML Full Text</u>	▢ <u>Add</u>
4. <u>Children's understanding of TV advertising: Effects of age, gender, and parental influence.</u>; By: Bijmolt, Tammo H. A.; Claassen, Wilma; et al., Journal of Consumer Policy, Jun98, Vol. 21 Issue 2, p171, 24p, 5 charts, 1 diagram **Notes:** This title is not held locally	▢ <u>Add</u>
5. <u>Howdydoody.com.</u>; By: Rich, Frank., New York Times, 06/08/97, Vol. 146 Issue 50817, Section 4 p15 **Notes:** Our Library Subscribes to this Periodical	▢ <u>Add</u>
6. <u>Ad hearings pushed.</u>; Electronic Media, 03/03/97, Vol. 16 Issue 10, p2, 1/9p **Notes:** This title is not held locally ▤ <u>HTML Full Text</u>	▢ <u>Add</u>

Figure 8.8 Keyword search in *EBSCOhost Academic Search Premier*. (From EBSCO Database. Copyright © 2003 by EBSCO Publishing. Reprinted by permission.)

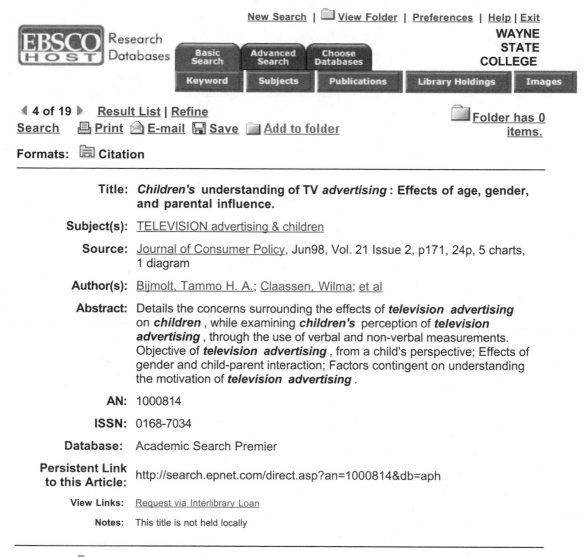

EBSCO HOST — Research Databases

Basic Search | Advanced Search | Choose Databases

Keyword | Subjects | Publications | Library Holdings | Images

WAYNE STATE COLLEGE

4 of 19 ▶ Result List | Refine

Search — Print — E-mail — Save — Add to folder

Folder has 0 items.

Formats: Citation

Title: *Children's* understanding of TV *advertising* : Effects of age, gender, and parental influence.

Subject(s): TELEVISION advertising & children

Source: Journal of Consumer Policy, Jun98, Vol. 21 Issue 2, p171, 24p, 5 charts, 1 diagram

Author(s): Bijmolt, Tammo H. A.; Claassen, Wilma; et al

Abstract: Details the concerns surrounding the effects of *television advertising* on *children*, while examining *children's* perception of *television advertising*, through the use of verbal and non-verbal measurements. Objective of *television advertising*, from a child's perspective; Effects of gender and child-parent interaction; Factors contingent on understanding the motivation of *television advertising*.

AN: 1000814

ISSN: 0168-7034

Database: Academic Search Premier

Persistent Link to this Article: http://search.epnet.com/direct.asp?an=1000814&db=aph

View Links: Request via Interlibrary Loan

Notes: This title is not held locally

Formats: Citation

Figure 8.9 Detailed record from list of citations in Figure 8.8. (From EBSCO Database. Copyright © 2003 by EBSCO Publishing. Reprinted by permission.)

Figure 8.10 depicts the detailed record for entry no. 19 (not shown in Figure 8.8) from the initial search. This article, "T.V. Ads: What Are Youngsters Buying?" is directly related to the initial topic. The "subject" field indicates both an education and psychological treatment of the topic. At the end of the citation, there are links for the citation and a PDF full-text document.

Guided searches, or advanced searches, are features available in most databases. These allow the searcher to limit or narrow a search by using the options provided on a template or on "Pull-down" menus. Figure 8.11 shows a "guided" search in *WilsonWeb*. The search is narrowed to "television advertising" in the subject field, combined (and) with "children" in the subject field, and "effects" in the text field." "Effects" may only be mentioned within the text and not be a major feature of the article, but would be an appropriate term to search. Note the limitation options: by date ("any year," "within 12 months"), "full text," "page image," and "peer reviewed."

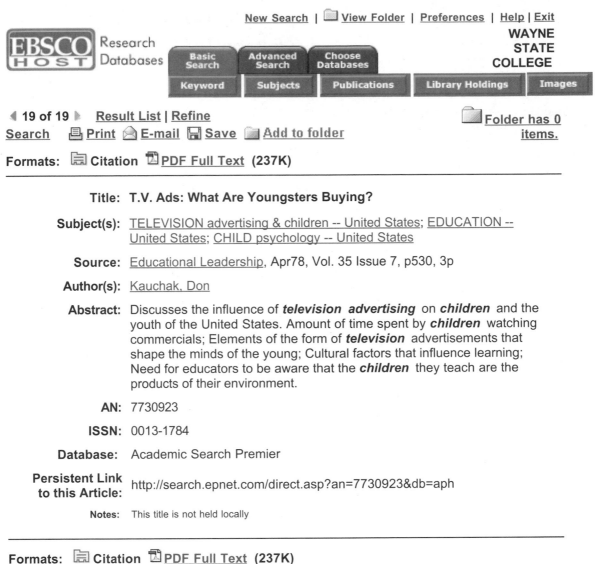

WAYNE
STATE
COLLEGE

EBSCO HOST Research Databases

Basic Search | Advanced Search | Choose Databases

Keyword | Subjects | Publications | Library Holdings | Images

◄ **19 of 19** ► **Result List | Refine**
Search 🖨 **Print** ✉ **E-mail** 💾 **Save** 📁 **Add to folder**

📁 **Folder has 0 items.**

Formats: 📄 **Citation** 📄 **PDF Full Text** (237K)

Title: T.V. Ads: What Are Youngsters Buying?

Subject(s): TELEVISION advertising & children -- United States; EDUCATION -- United States; CHILD psychology -- United States

Source: Educational Leadership, Apr78, Vol. 35 Issue 7, p530, 3p

Author(s): Kauchak, Don

Abstract: Discusses the influence of *television advertising* on *children* and the youth of the United States. Amount of time spent by *children* watching commercials; Elements of the form of *television* advertisements that shape the minds of the young; Cultural factors that influence learning; Need for educators to be aware that the *children* they teach are the products of their environment.

AN: 7730923

ISSN: 0013-1784

Database: Academic Search Premier

Persistent Link to this Article: http://search.epnet.com/direct.asp?an=7730923&db=aph

Notes: This title is not held locally

Formats: 📄 **Citation** 📄 **PDF Full Text** (237K)

© 2003 EBSCO Publishing. **Privacy Policy - Terms of Use**

Figure 8.10 Detailed record for entry no. 19 from initial search. (From EBSCO Database. Copyright © 2003 by EBSCO Publishing. Reprinted by permission.)

Figure 8.12 shows the results of the guided search in *WilsonWeb* from Figure 8.11. While some of these titles may also appear in other databases, a number of the journals indexed in *WilsonWeb* are unique to that database. If more information were needed after a general search, this would be a good choice.

To ascertain the education concerns related to the topic, a search in the ERIC database would prove useful. The *ERIC* database, administered by the National Library of Education, contains more than a million records of journal articles, research reports, curriculum and teaching guides, conference papers, and books in the field of education. In the database, the symbol "EJ" is used to indicate journal literature. Other *ERIC* documents are indicated by the symbol "ED." Many libraries subscribe to ED materials from *ERIC* in microfiche; others make them available through Interlibrary Loan E-Subscribe, an online subscription service that provides full-text ED documents from 1992 forward. Figure 8.13 illustrates the results of a search in the *ERIC* database.

Search For: television advertising   **as:** Subject(s)

and   children   Subject(s)

and   effects   Text

Sort By: ○ Date ● Relevance ○ Custom: Title   Start

Limit Dates to: ● Any Year
○ Within last 12 months
○ From Year: ___
To Year: ___

Limit to: ☐ Full Text
☐ Page Image
☐ Peer Reviewed

Document Type: All

Physical Description: All

Subject Area: All
Applied Science & Technology (AST)
Art (ART)

Figure 8.11 Preparing a guided search in *WilsonWeb* for the topic of the "effects of television advertising and children."

100% ☐ 1   Friedman, W., et. al., <u>Kids' upfront TV market loses shape</u>. *Advertising Age* v. 73 no. 9 (March 4 2002) p. 1, 64

100% ☐ 2   Schmuckler, E., et. al., <u>Fox pressing for Saturday AM deal</u>. *Mediaweek* v. 11 no. 47 (December 17 2001) p. 4-5

100% ☐ 3   Shanahan, K.J., et. al., <u>Program-length commercials and host selling by the WWF</u>. *Business and Society Review* v. 106 no. 4 (Winter 2001) p. 379-93

100% ☐ 4   Ji, M.F., et. al., <u>How Chinese children's commercials differ from those of the United States: a content analysis</u>. *Journal of Advertising* v. 30 no. 3 (Fall 2001) p. 79-92

100% ☐ 5   Baker, R. <u>Stealth TV: Channel One--and lots of advertising--seeps into America's schools</u>. *American Prospect* v. 12 no. 3 (February 12 2001) p. 28-31

100% ☐ 6   McClellan, S. <u>The scarlet R</u> [networks defend, revamp movie ad policies]. *Broadcasting & Cable* v. 130 no. 39 (September 18 2000) p. 14-5

100% ☐ 7   Freeman, M. <u>Kids upfront looking flat: Kids' WB, Cartoon Network likely to lead overcrowded market</u>. *Electronic Media* v. 19 no. 16 (April 17 2000) p. 1, 48

100% ☐ 8   Baker, R.W. <u>Changing the channel</u> [conservative backlash against Channel One]. *The New Republic* v. 221 no. 17 (October 25 1999) p. 22+

100% ☐ 9   Stewart-Allen, A.L. <u>Rules for reaching Euro kids are changing</u>. *Marketing News* v. 33 no. 12 (June 7 1999) p. 10

100% ☐ 10   Schofield, J., reviewer <u>Ads come to class</u> [Youth News Network in Canada]. *Maclean's* v. 112 no. 14 (April 5 1999) p. 69-70

Figure 8.12 Results of a guided search in *WilsonWeb*.

[Return to simple search screen] [Return to advanced search screen]

Didn't find what you are looking for? <u>Ask us</u>

[Previous] [Next]

159 documents found (25 returned) for query : *(television and advertising and effects and children)*

Score	Document Title
776	ED145499. Adler, Richard P.; And Others. Research on the Effects of Television Advertising on Children; A Review of the Literature and Recommendations for Future Research. . 1977
767	ED116820. Atkin, Charles K.. The Effects of Television Advertising on Children. Report No. 6: Survey of Pre-Adolescent's Responses to Television Commercials. Final Report. . 1975
759	EJ207855. Robertson, Thomas S.. Parental Mediation of Television Advertising Effects. Journal of Communication; v29 n1 p12-25 Win 1979. 1979
754	EJ274141. Desmond, Roger Jon; Jeffries-Fox, Suzanne. Elevating Children's Awareness of Television Advertising: The Effects of a Critical Viewing Program. Communication Education; v32 n1 p107-15 Jan 1983. 1983
744	ED123675. Atkin, Charles K.. The Effects of Television Advertising on Children: Survey of Children's and Mother's Responses to Television Commercials. Final Report. . 1975
744	ED116784. Atkin, Charles K.. The Effects of Television Advertising on Children. Report No. 2: Second Year Experimental Evidence. Final Report. . 1975
721	ED181474. Reeves, Byron; Atkin, Charles K.. The Effects of Televised Advertising on Mother-Child Interactions at the Grocery Store. . 1979
721	EJ214153. Rotfeld, Herbert J.; Reid, Leonard N.. Potential Secondary Effects of Regulating Children's Television Advertising. Journal of Advertising; v8 n1 p9-14 Win 1979. 1979
715	ED121353. Wiley, Richard E.. Current Policy Problems at the FCC. . 1976
712	ED305040. Kunkel, Dale. Children and Television Advertising: Can the Marketplace Protect the Public Interest? . 1988

EJ JOURNAL → (marks row 759)

ED FULL-TEXT DOCUMENTS → (marks row 744)

Figure 8.13 Results of an *ERIC* keyword search for "television advertising effects children."

Figure 8.14 is an example of an ED publication. This document from UNESCO expresses several concerns about children and media in general and would be useful to the topic. Note that each item has a specific number (ED449884) to identify the material. Libraries subscribing to the *ERIC* microfiche collection can retrieve the item by the corresponding number.

The illustrations in this chapter are from typical databases. The following lists of databases will help in selecting appropriate sources for your search.

Selected Multidiscipline Databases

General

The databases listed below are considered *aggregate* databases. That is they are a collection of databases. Some include only the more popular periodical titles; others include both popular and scholarly titles.

OBTAIN

ERIC_NO: *ED449884*
TITLE: News from the International Clearinghouse on Children and Violence on the Screen (ICCVOS), 2000.
AUTHOR: von Feilitzen, Cecilia, Ed.
PUBLICATION_DATE: 2000
JOURNAL_CITATION: News from ICCVOS; v4 n1-2 2000
ABSTRACT: This document is comprised of the year 2000 reports from the UNESCO International Clearinghouse on Children and Violence on the Screen. The two issues describe research findings concerning children and media violence, children's media use, and activities aimed at limiting gratuitous media violence. The first issue includes articles addressing children's media use in India, Chile, the United States, and Sweden, and adolescents' media use in Greenland. This issue also contains a section on children's TV programs on the global market. The second issue contains several articles on the media and children in Russia, along with sections on media violence, children and advertising, media for children, media literacy and children's participation, and regulation and self-regulation. Both issues contain a listing of relevant coming events. (EV)
MAJOR_DESCRIPTORS: Children; Mass Media Effects; Mass Media Use; Violence;
MINOR DESCRIPTORS: Adolescents; Advertising; Childrens Television; Foreign Countries; Mass Media; Mass Media Role; Television Viewing;
IDENTIFIERS: Chile; Greenland; India; Media Education; Russia; Sweden; UNESCO; United States
PUBLICATION_TYPE: 022; 070
PAGE: 54
CLEARINGHOUSE_NO: PS029168
AVAILABILITY: UNESCO International Clearinghouse on Children and Violence on the Screen, Nordicom, Goteborg University, Box 713, SE-405 30 Goteborg, Sweden; Tel: 46-31-773-10-00; Fax: 46-31-773-46-55; e-mail: nordicom@nordicom.gu.se; For full text: http://www.nordicom.gu.se.
EDRS_PRICE: EDRS Price MF01/PC03 Plus Postage.
INSTITUTION_NAME: BBB35926 _ United Nations Educational, Scientific, and Cultural Organization, Goteborg (Sweden). International Clearinghouse on Children and Violence on the Screen.; BBB14557 _ Nordic Documentation Center for Mass Communication Research, Aarhus (Denmark).
LEVEL: 1
LANGUAGE: English
GEOGRAPHIC_SOURCE: Sweden
GOVERNMENT: International
NOTE: For 1997-1999 issues, see ED 438 943.
ERIC_ISSUE: RIEJUL2001

OBTAIN

Figure 8.14 Sample *ERIC* document retrieved from the search in Figure 8.13.

EBSCOhost. Birmingham, AL; EBSCO Subscription Services, dates vary.

A one-stop online reference system accessible via the Internet, EBSCOhost offers multiple databases in an easy-to-use interface. Among the database selections are: *Academic Search Elite, Business Source Premier, Clinical Reference Systems, Health Source Plus* and *Newspaper Source. Academic Search Elite* has full text for over 1,250 journals with many dating back to 1990 and abstracts and indexing for nearly 2,990 scholarly journals, with many dating back to 1984.

InfoTrac. Los Altos, CA: Gale Group, dates vary.

Features full-text articles and citations on academic and general topics, and is comprised of several databases, depending on the library's subscription. Some of the databases are *General Reference Center Gold, General Business File, General Health Center, Expanded Academic Index*, and *National Newspaper Index*. Includes citations, abstracts and full-text articles from more than 1,000 popular magazines, business and professional journals, and newspapers.

E-Library. Chicago: Alacritude, LLC, dates vary.

Full-text online research service includes hundreds of magazines, journals, newspapers, and reference works. More suitable for high school level than college, but useful for transcripts and pictorial works not found elsewhere.

FirstSearch. Dublin, OH: OCLC, dates vary.

A collection of many of the online databases available from other sources. May include *ABI/INFORM, Agricola, Aids and Cancer Research, Applied Science & Technology Abstracts, Art Abstracts, Biography Index, Book Review Digest, Books in Print, CINAHL, Consumers Index, Dissertation Abstracts, OCLC, ERIC, GenderWatch, Humanities Abstracts* and many others, depending on library selection. Entries and dates of coverage vary depending on database selected. Some databases have citations only, others include full text.

WilsonWeb. New York: H.W. Wilson, dates vary.

Indexes all Wilson products in one database. Includes full-text articles in business, humanities, science, education, and the social sciences, plus *Readers' Guide to Periodical Literature*. Includes full text, depending on subscription.

Selected Subject Databases

The following databases cover multiple subjects also, but they are limited to the more scholarly journals.

Cambridge Scientific Abstracts. Bethesda, MD; CSA, dates vary.

Provides access to more than 35 databases. Includes physical sciences, biological sciences, and computer science, *Sociological Abstracts, Linguistics & Language Behavior Abstracts*, and *Medline*. Has citations and abstracts only, no full text, although there are direct links to any e-journals to which the library subscribes. May also provide local holdings information.

Ingenta. Cambridge, MA, 1988–.

Provides delivery of academic and professional content to over 5400 full-text online journals and 26,000 publications. Documents can be ordered directly or obtained through interlibrary loan. A personal account may be established for credit card purchases.

Web of Knowledge. Philadelphia: Institute for Scientific Information, dates vary.

Provides Web access to the citation indexes, a unique set of databases that indexes the cited references as well as the contents to journals in the sciences, social sciences, and humanities. Searching the citation literature allows users to search forward and backward through the literature in all the disciplines and time periods for information related to their research. It also enables users to find out how many times a particular work was cited and in which sources. The citation indexes included in the *Web of Knowledge* are:

Arts & Humanities Citation Index.

An index to 1,130 leading arts and humanities journals, as well as covering individually selected, relevant items from over 7,000 major science and social science journals. Some of the subjects covered include archaeology, linguistics, architecture, literary reviews, art, literature, Asian studies, music, classics, philosophy, dance, poetry, folklore, radio/television/film, history, religion, language, and theater.

Science Citation Index Expanded.

Covering the journal literature of the sciences, it indexes more than 5,900 major journals across 1150 scientific disciplines, including agriculture, neuroscience, astronomy, oncology, biochemistry, pediatrics, biology, pharmacology, biotechnology, physics, chemistry, plant sciences, computer science, psychiatry, materials science, surgery, mathematics, veterinary science, medicine, and zoology.

Social Sciences Citation Index.

An index to the journal literature of the social sciences, covering more than 1,700 journals spanning 50 disciplines. Some of the disciplines covered include anthropology, political science, history, public health, industrial relations, social issues, information and library science, social work, law, sociology, linguistics, substance abuse, philosophy, urban studies, psychology, women's studies, and psychiatry.

ELECTRONIC JOURNALS

Humanities

JSTOR. JSTOR, 2000.
> Retrospective collection of over 300 journal titles representing core titles in each discipline of social sciences and humanities. Available only by subscription.

Project Muse. Baltimore, MD. Johns Hopkins UP.
> Full-text articles in the humanities and social sciences: literature and criticism, history, visual and performing arts, cultural studies, education, political science, gender studies and many others. Available only by subscription.

http://www.pw.org/
> *Poets and Writers Magazine*

http://www.theatlantic.com
> *The Atlantic Online*

http://www.adage.com/
> *Advertising Age*

Social Sciences

(See JSTOR *and* Project Muse*)*

http://www.indiana.edu/~anthling/
> *Anthropological Linguistics*

http://foreignpolicy.com
> *Foreign Policy*

http://www.bea.doc/gov/bea/pubs.htm
> *Survey of Current Business*

http://chronicle.com/
> *Chronicle of Higher Education*

Sciences

http://www.egj.lib.uidaho.edu/idndex.html
> environment

http://library.gsfc.nasa.gov/
> space

http://www.amjbot/
> botany

http://www.the-scientist.com
> *The Scientist*

http://www.wired.com/news/nc_index.html
> *Wired News*

http://www.physsport.med.com
> *Physician and Sports Medicine*

Exercise 8.1

Instructor: _____ Course/Section: _____

Name: _____

Date: _____ Points: _____

Review Questions

1. Give three reasons why periodical materials are important sources for research.

    a.

    b.

    c.

2. List three different formats of periodical literature.

    a.

    b.

    c.

3. What is the difference in scope between a magazine or journal index and a newspaper index?

4. What is meant by the term "e-journal"?

5. How does an abstract differ from an index?

6. Explain the differences between a bibliographic database and a full-text database.

7. Name two electronic databases that could be useful in searching for articles in popular magazines.

   a.

   b.

8. Explain the difference between popular periodical literature and scholarly periodical literature.

9. List three multidisciplinary subject databases.

10. What is the difference between a multidisciplinary index or database and a subject index or database?

11. How would you locate periodical articles in the library after the information has been found in an index?

Exercise 8.2

Instructor: _____ Course/Section: _____

Name: _____

Date: _____ Points: _____

Using *Readers' Guide to Periodical Literature*

Answer the following questions based upon the entries taken from *Readers' Guide to Periodical Literature*, Figure 8.4, using "television" as the subject.

1. What subject heading would you use to locate additional information on television advertising?

2. Who wrote the article on "Teletubbies"?

3. Is the first article under "television and children" illustrated? How do you know?

4. In which magazines can you locate some articles on television and literature?

5. Where would you find information on the history of television?

6. List two magazines that contain information on television and politics.

7. What subject heading is used to locate articles dealing with actors in television?

8. What does p.100+ mean in the first article at the top of the right column?

9. List each step you would need to take to retrieve one of these articles from the printed index.

Exercise 8.3

Instructor: _____ Course/Section: _____

Name: _____

Date: _____ Points: _____

Using Printed Periodical Indexes

Locate a periodical index or abstract that you could use to locate information on topic that interests you or that has been assigned by your instructor. Give the following information.

Topic:

1. Describe the strategy you used to find this index/abstract. Be specific in your answer. (Used library catalog, searched under . . ., browsed reference shelves, index shelves, etc.)

2. Call number and location of index/abstract:

3. Title of index/abstract:

4. What subjects are included in this source?

5. Describe the arrangement of the source (alphabetical, topical, etc.).

6. What subject heading(s) are used in this index/abstract for your topic?

7. Write the correct bibliographic citation for this article, using the examples in Appendix A.

8. Does the library subscribe to this periodical?

9. If the library subscribes (or has this periodical in a full-text database), give the call number and location or title of the database here.

Exercise 8.4

Instructor: _____ Course/Section: _____

Name: _____

Date: _____ Points: _____

Selecting Printed Periodical Indexes

1. Select a topic of your choice, or use one provided by your instructor.

   Topic:

2. Write a preliminary thesis statement for this topic.

Examine the following printed indexes and respond to each question.

PART A. *Readers' Guide to Periodical Literature* is an example of a general, popular, periodical index. Answer the following questions using *Readers' Guide*.

1. Subject heading you used for your topic:

2. Did you find citations under this heading?
   If not, which cross references did the index send you to?

3. Write the correct citation to this article, using the examples from Appendix A.

4. Would you label this article as popular or scholarly?

5. Give two reasons why you think this would be a popular or scholarly article.

   a.

   b.

6. Describe the steps you would take to find this article in the library.

PART B. *Social Sciences Index*, *Humanities Index*, and *General Science Index* are examples of discipline-related periodical indexes. Each covers a group of related subjects in one particular area of knowledge. Answer the following questions using the appropriate discipline index for your thesis statement.

1. Title of index used:

2. Subject heading you used for your topic:

3. Did you find citations under this heading?

   If not, which cross references did the index send you to?

4. Write the correct bibliographic citation for one article on your topic. Use the examples given in Appendix A.

5. Would you label this article as popular or scholarly?

6. Give two reasons why you think this would be a popular or scholarly article.

   a.

   b.

7. How do articles in this index compare to those you found in *Readers' Guide*? Give at least two differences you noted.

8. Describe the steps you would take to find this article in the library?

PART C. Besides general indexes, such as *Readers' Guide*, and discipline-related indexes, such as *Humanities Index*, there are also many subject-specific or specialized periodical indexes on a variety of subjects, such as *Education Index*, *PAIS*, *Health Resource Center*, and *Psychological Abstracts*. Find an appropriate specialized index to develop your thesis and answer the following questions.

1. Index used for your topic:

2. Subject heading you used for your topic:

3. Did you find citations under this heading?

   If not, which cross references did the index send you to?

4. Write the correct bibliographic citation for this article, using examples from Appendix A.

5. Would you label this article as popular or scholarly?

6. Give two reasons why you think this would be a popular or scholarly article.

   a.

   b.

7. How do articles in this index compare to those you found in *Readers' Guide* and the discipline-related index? Give at least two differences you noted.

8. Describe the steps you would take to find this article in the library.

Exercise 8.6

Instructor: _____ Course/Section: _____

Name: _____

Date: _____ Points: _____

Using a Printed Newspaper Index

Use the sample page from *The New York Times Index* (Figure 8.7) to find a specific article on the subject of advertising and give the following information. (Remember, the name of the newspaper and the year are taken from the cover of the index.)

1. Month:

2. Day:

3. Year:

4. Section:

5. Column:

6. Page(s):

7. How would you locate this article in the library?

8. Write the correct bibliographic citation for this article, using the examples in Appendix A.

Instructor: _____ Course/Section: _____

Name: _____

Date: _____ Points: _____

Using Online Newspapers

Today many full-text newspapers are available online. Find a recent article from either *The New York Times* or another major newspaper and answer the following questions.

1. Give the name of the newspaper you found.

2. Give the URL for the newspaper.

3. Give the name of the author of the article, if given. If not, mark N/A for not applicable.

4. Give the exact title of the article.

5. Can you retrieve the full article, or only the headlines, without a subscription?

6. How long is the article (number of words or number of pages)?

7. Write the correct bibliographic citation for this article, using the examples in Appendix A.

8. Were there any other references listed in this article for related information?
   If so, give one other entry here.

9. How would you determine if your library receives this newspaper? Be specific in your answer.

Exercise 8.8

Instructor: _____ Course/Section: _____

Name: _____

Date: _____ Points: _____

Selecting Databases

1. Select a topic of your choice or one provided by your instructor for research.

   Topic:

2. Write a preliminary thesis statement for this topic.

PART A. *EBSCOhost* and *InfoTrac* are examples of a general database that may include both popular and scholarly articles. Answer the following questions using one of the general databases available at your library.

1. Title of the database you selected:

2. Subject heading or keyword term(s) you used for your topic:

3. If you found citations under this heading, how many were listed?

4. If none were found, did the database give you other terms to select? If so, what were the terms?

5. Select two articles relevant to your topic. Write the correct bibliographic citation for each article, using the examples in Appendix A.

6. Identify each article as "popular" or "scholarly." Give at least two characteristics for each article that determine whether it is "popular" or "scholarly."

    a. 1st article:

    b. 2nd article:

7. Does the database give just the citation, or the full text of the article?

8. How would you determine if this article is also available in the library?

PART B. There are also many subject-specific or specialized databases on a variety of subjects, such as *ERIC* (education), *ABI/INFORM* (business), and *PsycInfo* (Psychology). Select an appropriate specialized database available in your library for your topic and complete the questions below.

1. Title of database you used:

2. Subject heading or keyword used for your topic:

3. Did you find citations in this database under this heading?

    If not, which cross references did the database send you to?

4. Write the correct bibliographic citations for two articles on your topic. Use the examples in Appendix A.

5. Did this database give you the citation only, the citation and abstract, or the full text of the article you retrieved?

6. Would you consider these articles popular or scholarly?

    Give two reasons why.

    a. 1st article:

    b. 2nd article:

7. How do articles in this database compare to those you found in Part A above?

    Give at least two differences you found.

    a.

    b.

8. How would you determine if these articles are available in the library?

PART C. Retrieve one of the articles you found in either Part A or Part B. Consider each of the following points as you read the article.

1. Does the author use primary or secondary sources to write the article?

2. Would you consider the author to be knowledgeable in this field? Why?

3. How current is the material covered in the article?

4. Is the article written for a popular audience or scholarly one?

5. Is there any indication of bias on the part of the author?

6. What is the source of the author's information? (e.g., survey, personal knowledge, or interviews.)

7. If you were writing a research paper on this topic, would you consider using this article:

    a. at the beginning of your paper as an introduction?

    b. as a major point in your argument or presentation?

    c. as a supporting point of a thesis?

    d. at the conclusion of your paper?

8. Explain your choice for Question 7.

Exercise 8.9

Instructor: _____ Course/Section: _____

Name: _____

Date: _____ Points: _____

Finding E-Journals

Select one of the following sites and answer the questions below.

http://www.adage.com   http://www.wired.com

http://www.newscientist.com/   http://www.pw.org/

1. Which Web site did you select?

2. Is the site full text or does it only provide information about the journal?

3. Does the site give archival information or current issue information only? Other?

4. Is the site free to search, or do you need a subscription, or have to login?

5. Is this publication also available in print or other format?

6. Use your favorite search engine and search for "biology e-journals." Select one site.

   a. Give the title of the e-journal.

   b. Give the URL.

   c. Does the e-journal give full-text articles?

   d. Does it provide archives for older issues?

   e. What additional features are offered at this site (if any)?

Government Information

"Just be thankful you're not getting all the government you're paying for."

Will Rogers

Introduction

In the United States it is an elementary—but all important—principle that the operations of government are to be open to scrutiny and criticism. This makes it possible for citizens to participate in government and to contribute to the advancement of society. Indeed, the American political system, and to a large extent the educational system, rests on the widespread acceptance of ready and fair access to information about government and information produced by the government. This principle has led local, state, national, and even international governing bodies to produce large quantities of information. Publications produced by governing bodies encompass a broad range of topics—not only on the government itself and how it is run, but also on many subjects of interest to citizens. This chapter is designed to serve as a guide for locating government information, both in traditional and electronic format. The emphasis is on U.S. Government publications, which are more numerous than those of the other entities; there are brief introductions to local, state, and international documents.

GOVERNMENT INFORMATION IN THE RESEARCH PROCESS

Government information is useful for research in many disciplines, but especially in the social sciences and the natural sciences. Although it is possible to find government information covering topics in the humanities, that is not the norm. Aside from the intrinsic value of contributing to an informed citizenry, government publications have a number of distinctive characteristics that add to their value as information sources.

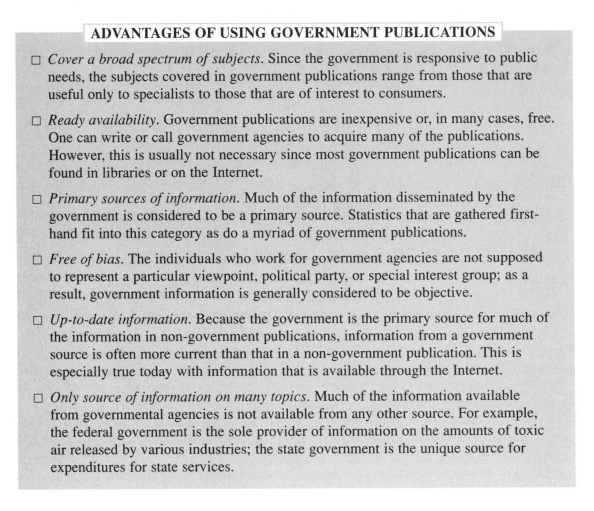

ADVANTAGES OF USING GOVERNMENT PUBLICATIONS

☐ *Cover a broad spectrum of subjects.* Since the government is responsive to public needs, the subjects covered in government publications range from those that are useful only to specialists to those that are of interest to consumers.

☐ *Ready availability.* Government publications are inexpensive or, in many cases, free. One can write or call government agencies to acquire many of the publications. However, this is usually not necessary since most government publications can be found in libraries or on the Internet.

☐ *Primary sources of information.* Much of the information disseminated by the government is considered to be a primary source. Statistics that are gathered first-hand fit into this category as do a myriad of government publications.

☐ *Free of bias.* The individuals who work for government agencies are not supposed to represent a particular viewpoint, political party, or special interest group; as a result, government information is generally considered to be objective.

☐ *Up-to-date information.* Because the government is the primary source for much of the information in non-government publications, information from a government source is often more current than that in a non-government publication. This is especially true today with information that is available through the Internet.

☐ *Only source of information on many topics.* Much of the information available from governmental agencies is not available from any other source. For example, the federal government is the sole provider of information on the amounts of toxic air released by various industries; the state government is the unique source for expenditures for state services.

As part of your search strategy, you should consider whether the information you need might be found in a government source.

Ask Yourself

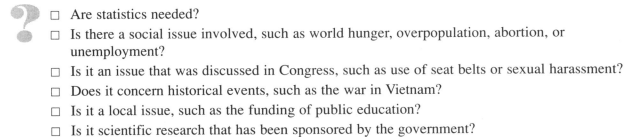

☐ Are statistics needed?

☐ Is there a social issue involved, such as world hunger, overpopulation, abortion, or unemployment?

☐ Is it an issue that was discussed in Congress, such as use of seat belts or sexual harassment?

☐ Does it concern historical events, such as the war in Vietnam?

☐ Is it a local issue, such as the funding of public education?

☐ Is it scientific research that has been sponsored by the government?

Information produced by government agencies may show up in some of the tools you use to conduct a search. For example, if government documents are included in the library's online catalog along with other materials, they will show up in the results of many subject and keyword searches. Some periodical indexes include government periodicals and reports among the sources they index. For example, *PAIS International* includes both U.S. and international government publications. A keyword search on the Internet is also likely to turn up government sources. Even so, to find specific government information you need to know what type of information is available, what formats you can expect to encounter, and which tools to use to locate the information.

UNITED STATES GOVERNMENT PUBLICATIONS

The United States government is the single largest producer of information in the world. The information sources from the federal government are as varied as they are numerous. They come in all sizes and shapes—from one-page leaflets to works of several thousand pages and many volumes. They vary in scope from highly technical scientific research reports to popular pamphlets on such topics as weight loss and caring for pets. Included in government publications are all the official documents such as laws, regulations, court decisions, presidential documents, treaties, congressional proceedings, military records, and census reports. The government issues a large number of reference books including indexes, abstracts, bibliographies, directories, atlases, handbooks, yearbooks, and almanacs. Approximately 1,200 government periodicals are published on a regular basis.

Format

The format of government information is almost as varied as its scope. Until recently, government publications were published in traditional formats: paper, microfiche, film, video and cassette tapes, photographs, maps, charts, and posters. The federal government has always been a leader in utilizing new technologies to produce, store, and retrieve information, and was the first publisher to make widespread use of the CD-ROM as a publication medium. There are thousands of government titles in CD-ROM format. These include statistical sources, maps, government regulations, and reference sources such as the *Statistical Abstract of the U.S.*

Today the Government Printing Office (GPO), which is the chief publisher of U.S. government information, is in a state of transition from a paper publisher to an electronic publisher. In 1996 Congress issued a mandate that the GPO formulate a plan to cease publishing and distributing government information in paper and microfiche format and move to electronic format. It was anticipated that before the end of the century all government information, with the exception of a few titles, would be available only in electronic format—primarily through the Internet. While this did not happen, it is true that large numbers of U.S. government publications are now available only on the Internet.

Depository Libraries

The Government Printing Office (GPO) was established in 1861 for the purpose of publishing the official publications of the federal government. Prior to that time private firms printed the official documents of the U.S. government. Consequently, we have historical documents published by authority of the federal government dating back to the Continental Congress. The GPO is still the official publisher and/or distributor of all the documents of the legislative, executive, and judicial branches of the federal government that are considered by law to be in the public interest—the Congressional debates, laws, executive orders, annual reports, court decisions, regulations, reports, and special studies.

In 1895, Congress enacted legislation that provided for the free distribution of documents to designated libraries and institutions. The libraries receiving documents free of charge from the GPO are called *depository libraries*. There are approximately 1,400 depository libraries in the United States. Of these, about 50 are *regional depository libraries,* which receive all the publications distributed by GPO. Other libraries are *selective depository libraries*, so designated because they can choose the items that they wish to receive. The depository library provides the facilities for housing documents and the staff needed to administer the collections. The only other obligations of the depository library are to assure that the materials are cared for according to guidelines established by the GPO and to make the documents available to the public.

Because government information is in a state of transition from paper and microfiche format to electronic format, the status of depository libraries is being questioned. The role of the depository library in a predominately Internet environment will no doubt change. With government information being available primarily through the Internet, the need to house and preserve government information in libraries throughout the country will cease to exist. Depository libraries will probably maintain their retrospective paper and microfiche collections, but will assume different roles with regard to current information. They will be expected to provide the means for the public to access government information on the Internet—computers, printers, and Internet connectivity. They will also continue to provide bibliographic access to all publications using catalog records in the online catalog or some other index to government publications. And librarians knowledgeable about government information sources will still be available to assist users.

Finding U.S. Government Information

Most discussions of finding government information inevitably begin by acknowledging the difficulty of identifying and locating material published by the government. In most libraries, government publications are housed in a separate collection and shelved by SuDocs number (see Figure 9.1.). This of itself is not a problem. The problem is the fact that traditionally there have been very few tools to help users identify and locate these publications. It was not until the early 1990s that libraries began including government publications in their online catalogs; many library catalogs still do not include them. Even those libraries that do include government publications in the online catalog list primarily materials published since 1976 when GPO began creating records in machine readable format. Government publications traditionally have not been included in the usual indexing tools such as *Readers' Guide* and *Social Sciences Index*. Although many of the barriers to finding government information were lifted in the 1990s when libraries began including government publications in their online catalogs and government information became available on the Internet, it is still difficult to find government information. The tools listed below are helpful in getting you started. Beyond that you should consult a librarian who is familiar with government information.

General Finding Aids

You need to be aware of whether or not your library includes government documents in its online catalog and, if so, what portion of the collection is represented. The years of coverage vary with individual libraries. Many libraries have the records for items dating back to 1976 when GPO began creating records in electronic format. The *Monthly Catalog of United States Government Publications* serves as the primary access point for government publications distributed to depository libraries.

Monthly Catalog of United States Government Publications. Washington: GPO, 1895–
>   The comprehensive index to government publications. It is used chiefly to search for retrospective government publications (pre-1976) that are not cataloged, but are shelved by SuDocs call number. The main entries are arranged alphabetically by issuing agency in the main body of the catalog. Each issue contains separate indexes for subjects, titles, title keywords, authors, series reports, contract numbers, stock numbers, and SuDocs numbers (see Figures 9.2 and 9.3). (Figures 9.4 and 9.5 are examples of an index entry and a bibliographic record from a pre-1976 *Monthly Catalog.*)

Catalog of United States Government Publications. GPO, 1994–. 2 Nov. 1999. 5 Apr. 2000 <http://www.gpo.gov/catalog>.
>   The online version of the *Monthly Catalog,* it provides direct links to online resources from federal agencies and identifies print and CD-ROM materials distributed to depository libraries. Coverage is from January 1994; new records are added daily.

Figure 9.1

Instructions for locating a U.S. government publication.

How to find a U.S. Government Publication

As a Federal Depository Library, we receive many publications issued by agencies of the U.S. Government. These publications, which may include books, maps, posters, pamphlets, and periodicals, contain information on careers, business opportunities, space exploration, health and nutrition, energy, and many other subjects.

Federal Government publications in this collection are arranged by the Superintendent of Documents classification number. Publications are grouped together by issuing agency.* To ensure that you find all of the materials available on a particular subject, be sure to check the indexes recommended by the librarian.

The example below shows how the Superintendent of Documents classification number C 61.34:987 is constructed for the publication *U.S. Industrial Outlook:*

C	61.	34:	987
Commerce Department (issuing agency)	International Trade Administration (subordinate bureau within the agency)	Number designating the title	Year of Publication (1987)

Here are the prefixes from the Superintendent of Documents classification numbers for some other agencies that you may be interested in:

A	Agriculture Department
C 3.	Census Bureau (Commerce Department)
D	Defense Department
E	Energy Department
ED	Education Department
GA	General Accounting Office
GS	General Services Administration
HE	Health and Human Services Department
I	Interior Department
I 19.	U.S. Geological Survey (Interior Department)
J	Justice Department
Ju	Judiciary
L	Labor Department
LC	Library of Congress
NAS	National Aeronautics and Space Administration
S	State Department
SI	Smithsonian Institution
T 22.	Internal Revenue Service (Treasury Department)
X, Y	Congress
Y 4.	Congressional Committees

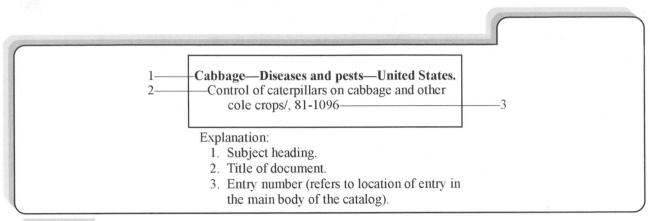

Figure 9.2 Excerpt from Subject Index in *Monthly Catalog*.

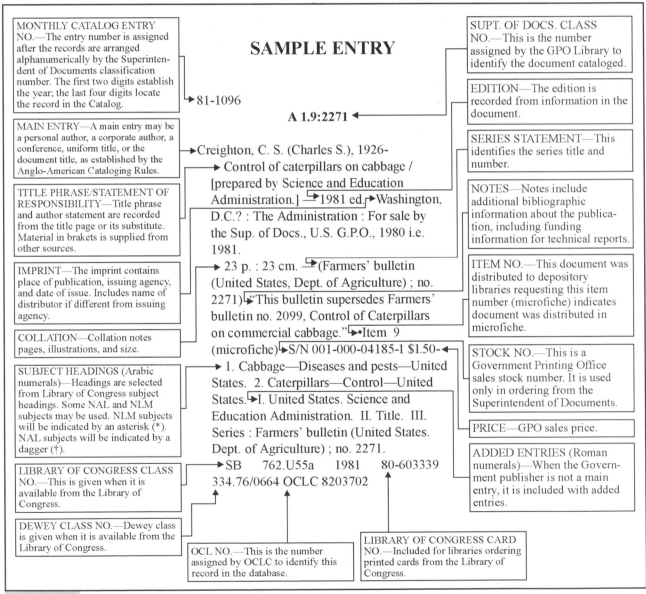

Figure 9.3 *Monthly Catalog of United States Government Publications.*

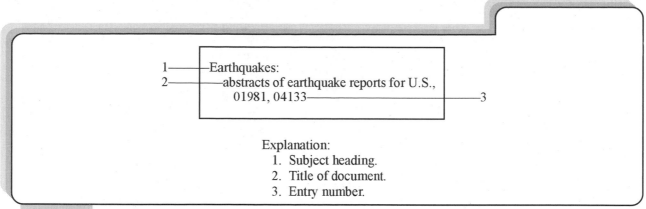

Figure 9.4 Sample entry from Subject Index of a pre-1976 *Monthly Catalog*.

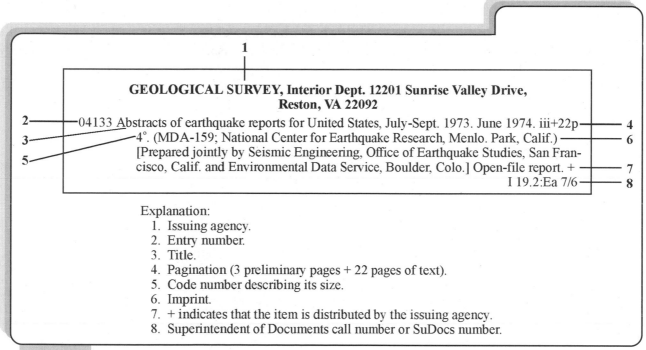

Figure 9.5 Sample entry from the main entry section of the pre-1976 *Monthly Catalog*.

Internet Sites (General)

Browse Government Resources. Library of Congress. 7 Jan. 2003. 29 Jan. 2003 <http://lcweb.loc.gov/rr/news/extgovd.html>.

A list of government sources prepared and maintained by the Serial and Government Publications Division of the Library of Congress.

Federal Government Resources on the Web. Comp. Grace York. University of Michigan Documents Center. 20 May 2002. 29 Jan. 2003 <http://www.lib.umich.edu/govdocs/federal.html>.

An excellent site for federal government information. Kept up-to-date with a "What's New" section.

FirstGov: The U.S. Government's Official Web Portal. Office of Citizen Services and Communications. U.S. General Services Administration. 30 Jan. 2003. 31 Jan. 2003 <http://www.firstgov.gov/>.

"The most comprehensive search of government anywhere on the Internet," FirstGov includes more than 51 million web pages from the federal government, local and tribal governments and foreign nations around the world.

Government Information Connection: Catalogs, Indexes, and Databases. Comp. Melody Kelly. University of North Texas Libraries. 11 Nov. 1999. 14 Apr. 2000 <http://www.library.unt.edu/govinfo/subject/catsindx.html>.

An alphabetical list to both general and subject-specific Internet catalogs, indexes, and databases.

GPO Access. GPO. 27 Jan. 2003. 2001. 29 Jan. 2003 <http://www.access.gpo.gov/su_docs/index.html>.

This comprehensive service searches more than 1,000 federal databases. A help page tells how to search *GPO Access.*

LexisNexis Academic (Formerly *Academic Universe*). LexisNexis Academic & Library Solutions. 2003. Louisiana State University. 29 Jan. 2003 <http://www.lexisnexis.com/academic/default2.asp>. Available by subscription only.

Although not devoted exclusively to government publications, *LexisNexis Academic* includes a vast amount of information, most of it full text, by and about the U.S. government, including Congressional hearings, summaries of legislative actions, committee markups, television transcripts, presidential campaign materials, tax information, laws, regulations, attorney general opinions, the U.S. Code, and the Constitution.

LexisNexis Government Periodicals Index (formerly Government Periodicals Index). LexisNexis Academic. 2003. Louisiana State University. 30 Jan. 2003 <http://www.lexisnexis.com/academic/>. Available by subscription only.

Index to articles in U.S. government periodicals from 1988 forward. Index is searchable by keyword, title, subject, author, agency, or periodical title.

U.S. Federal Government Agencies Directory. Louisiana State University Libraries. 26 Jan. 2003. 29 Jan. 2003 <http://www.lib.lsu.edu/gov/fedgov.html>.

A directory of U.S. government agencies on the Internet as represented in the *United States Government Manual.*

Retrospective Government Information (Pre-1976)

Cumulative Subject Index to the Monthly Catalog of United States Government Publications, 1900–1971. Comp. William W. Buchanan, and Edna M. Kanely. 15 vols. Washington: Carrolton, 1973–1975.

A subject index to the titles listed in *Monthly Catalog* for the years 1900–1973.

Cumulative Title Index to United States Public Documents, 1789–1976. Comp. Daniel W. Lester, Sandra K. Faull, and Lorraine E. Lester. 16 vols. Arlington: United States Historical Documents Institute, 1979–1983.

An alphabetical listing of the titles of publications distributed by the Government Printing Office. Useful for locating a pre-1976 publication if the title is known.

Congressional Information

CIS/Index to Publications of the United States Congress. Washington: Congressional Information Service, 1970–.

Paper counterpart to *CIS Index. LexisNexis Academic.*

CIS Index. LexisNexis Academic. 2003. Louisiana State University. 30 Jan. 2003 <http://www.lexisnexis.com/academic/>. Available by subscription only.

"The *CIS Index* provides bibliographic access to all regularly produced congressional publications. This includes hearings, reports, prints, and documents. The index record provides title, committee, bill number, report number, witness, and subject information, as well as an abstract to the contents of each congressional publication" (Pub. note).

Congressional Masterfile. Washington: CIS, 1789–1969.

A CD-ROM-based database, it provides most of the same information as *CIS Index,* for the earlier years.

Congressional Indexes, 1789–1969. LexisNexis Academic. 2003. Louisiana State University. 30 Jan. 2003 <http://www.lexisnexis.com/academic/>. Available by subscription only.

The same as *Congressional Masterfile*, it is available online in the LexisNexis Congressional databases.

CQ Electronic Library. Washington: Congressional Quarterly, 1998–. 30 Jan. 2003 <http://libraryip.cq.com>. Available by subscription only.

A suite of full-text databases covering public affairs. Includes The *CQ Researcher*, *CQ Weekly*, *CQ Electronic Encyclopedia of American Government*, the *Washington Information Directory (eWID)*, *CQ Public Affairs Collection*, and *CQ Insider*. Subscriptions to individual titles available.

Thomas. Library of Congress. Washington, n.d. 30 Jan. 2003 <http://thomas.loc.gov/>.

Primary point of entry for information on current U.S. federal legislative information. It is fully searchable and includes the full text of bills, laws, the *Congressional Record* (the verbatim record of sessions of the U.S. Congress), reports, and links to other government information.

Scientific and Technical Information

DOE Information Bridge. Oak Ridge: Department of Energy. 11 April 2002. 30 Jan. 2003 <http://www.osti.gov/bridge/>.

"At this site you will find over 500 databases and Web sites containing information and resources pertaining to science and technology of interest to the Department of Energy, with an emphasis on the physical sciences" (Pub. note).

Energy Files. Oak Ridge: Department of Energy. 11 Apr. 2002. 30 Jan. 2003 <http://www.osti.gov/energyfiles/>.

Home page to a vast array of information and resources pertaining to energy, science, and technology. Developed and maintained by the Department of Energy's Office of Scientific and Technical Information (OSTI), it provides searching across a number of energy-related databases.

Government Reports Announcements and Index (GRAI). Springfield, VA: National Technical Information Service, 1970–. Bimonthly.

The National Technical Information Service is a clearinghouse for government-sponsored scientific, technical, engineering, and business research. It also includes some reports from state and local government agencies and from countries outside the U.S., as well as reports from more than 200 federal agencies that are not distributed free of charge through the depository library program. *GRAI* indexes and abstracts the reports in the NTIS collection.

NTIS Library. Springfield, VA: National Technical Information Service, 1990–. 30 Jan. 2003 <http://www.ntis.gov/search/index.asp?loc=3-0-0>.

The online counterpart to the NTIS database, for the years 1990 forward.

Statistical Information

See Chapter 10.

STATE GOVERNMENT INFORMATION

State governments and the federal government have similar missions: to keep the public informed. Although state governments publish less information than the national government, they too are prolific publishers of information. Each state provides descriptions of its governmental activities, reports of special developments in industry and economics, maps, laws, and statistics on education, crime, health, employment, and business. The information found in state documents is especially useful because of its timeliness. Statistics on employment, housing construction, crime, and health, for example, are gathered by the states and published in state documents before they appear in federal documents.

Most states do not have funds to provide for widespread distribution of their publications. Rather, certain libraries are designated as depository libraries for state documents and automatically receive the state's publications. The way that depository collections are organized varies among libraries. Some libraries keep their documents in a separate state collection with other special materials on the state; others house them as a separate collection within the government documents department. Still other libraries integrate state documents with their general collection. Access to state documents varies among libraries. Many states publish checklists and bibliographies listing currently available publications; a few libraries catalog state documents along with other library materials; and many states are now publishing state documents online. Even though technology has improved access to state information, it is still difficult to identify and locate state publications. For that reason, in most libraries with state documents collections, a librarian with special training and experience is usually available to assist patrons in locating state information.

State Government Information on the Internet

FindLaw. State Resources. FindLaw, Inc. 1994–2003. 31 Jan. 2003. <http://www.findlaw.com/11stategov/>.
   A state-by-state listing of legal information on the Internet.

State and Local Government on the Net. Piper Resources. 2003. 31 Jan. 2003 <http://www.piperinfo.com/ state/index.cfm>.
   A directory of links to government resources on the Internet. Frequently updated.

State and Local Governments. Library of Congress. 17 Mar. 2000. 31 Jan. 2003 <http://lcweb.loc.gov/global/ state/stategov.html>.
   Library of Congress Web site listing state and local government information under two categories: *Meta-Indexes for State and Local Government Information* and *State Government Information.*

State Government and Politics. Comp. Grace York. University of Michigan. 9 Dec. 2002. 31 Jan. 2003 <http:// www.lib.umich.edu/govdocs/state.html>.
   A comprehensive guide to state information on the Internet.

The State Web Locator. Center for Information Law and Policy. 1995–2002. 31 Jan. 2003 <http://www.infoctr. edu/swl/>.
   A state-by-state listing for government information Web sites.

LOCAL GOVERNMENT INFORMATION

In the United States there are many local units of government—towns, cities, counties, and special districts. Although information about local governmental units appears in federal government as well as in commercial publications, most of the key information is produced by local governmental units. Publications from local governments include records of their official activities, such as charters, laws, regulations, financial reports, city plans, maps, statistics, budgets, and decisions. Local publications are an important primary source of information. These documents usually are not widely distributed, making them difficult to locate and access. One way to get information from local governments is to request it directly from the local agency. Another way is through the library. Libraries, especially college and university libraries, often serve as depositories for local documents. The way local documents are handled varies among libraries. Some libraries catalog local documents along with the other materials in the library, while others keep them in separate collections which may or may not be cataloged. Since there are no quick and easy guides to local government publications, one should ask the librarian for assistance when seeking local documents or information about a local governmental unit.

Local Government Information on the Internet

GovLinks Index: Local Government. Governing.Com. Congressional Quarterly. 2003. 31 Jan. 2003 <http:// www.governing.com/govlinks/glocal.htm>
   A guide to Internet resources for local government, including city and county home pages.

Local Government. GovEngine.com: 2002. 31 Jan. 2003. <http://www.govengine.com/localgov/index.html>
   A subset of the search engine GovEngine.com. Contains links to counties and municipalities in all of the states.

(See also sites listed under State Government Information on the Internet.)

INTERNATIONAL ORGANIZATIONS AND FOREIGN GOVERNMENTS

International government organizations (IGOs) refers to those institutions that are created as a result of formal agreements between two or more sovereign states. The agreements are designed to address and regulate (within the bounds of international law) matters of common concern to all the parties—peacekeeping, human rights, or economic development. Included in the agreements are arrangements for maintaining facilities and providing for the ongoing activities of the members. IGOs vary greatly in their goals, structures, and geographic scope. Some focus on single issues while others deal with broader concerns. There are hundreds of IGOs, the most notable being the United Nations and its allied organizations such as World Health Organization, International Labour Organization, Food and Agriculture Organization, and World Bank. Other well-known international organizations include the European Union (EU), the North Atlantic Treaty Organization (NATO), the Organization of American States (OAS), and the Organization of Petroleum Exporting Countries (OPEC).

The Internet has opened the door to finding information not only about IGOs but also about the governments of many individual countries of the world. The number of governments using the Internet to disseminate information is increasing at a phenomenal rate. Thanks primarily to government documents librarians, there are now many sites that identify international government information at all levels. A few of the sites will be identified below. Others can be found by using one of the Internet search engines. Search for the term "international government information" or the name of a country or an organization.

United Nations

The United Nations is the largest of all the international government organizations. Headquartered in New York, it issues a large quantity of documents in print and electronic formats. The primary purpose of United Nations documents is to serve the immediate needs of the delegates to the United Nations. However, publications of the United Nations and its allied agencies are of great value because they deal with important issues in international affairs. They provide statistics and other types of information gathered from all over the globe on all facets of human endeavors. They also document world problems such as hunger, illiteracy, and human rights.

The publications of the United Nations and its allied agencies may or may not be listed in the main catalog along with the other resources of a library. In either case they may be shelved in a separate collection. Libraries that serve as depository libraries for United Nations documents usually keep the publications in a separate collection shelved by the series symbol, composed of capital letters in combination with numerical notations. The elements in the numbers are separated by slash marks. The example below is the call number for the 1985 *Report on the World Social Situation.*

Example

ST/ESA/165
ST=United Nations Secretariat
ESA=Department of International and Social Affairs
165=Series number designation

International Information on the Internet

Access UN. 1956–. Readex Corp. 2002. 31 Jan 2000 <http://infoweb.newsbank.com/>. Available by subscription only.

Provides access to current and retrospective United Nations documents and publications issued since 1956. (Dates may vary, depending on individual library subscriptions.) Searchable by author, country, type of document (official record, sales publication), subject, title, text, and date. Citations are keyed to the UN symbol number or the microfiche number, for those libraries that have the collection in microfiche. It includes the full text of General Assembly plenary meetings and its committees since the 45th session. Articles appearing in UN periodicals are individually indexed. Covers topics such as peacekeeping and security, world hunger, human rights, economic development, the environment, atomic energy, and other issues addressed by the United Nations. For older publications, see:

Checklist of United Nations Documents. New York: United Nations, 1946–1949.

United Nations Documents Index. (*UNDI*). New York: United Nations, 1950–1973.

International Documents. Northwestern University Library, Government Publications and Maps. 24 Jan. 2003. 31 Jan. 2003 <http://www.library.nwu.edu/govpub/resource/internat/foreign.html>.

A listing by country name of links to official government sites. The country name links to official government portals or homepages and the list below the names links to legislative and executive branch institutions.

United Nations. New York: United Nations. 2001. 31 Jan. 2003 <http://www.un.org/>.

Excellent starting point for current information by and about the UN. Contains links to many full-text documents, databases, e-journals, maps and geographic information.

United Nations Documents and Publications. Comp. Chuck Eckman. Guide to Government Publications Series. Stanford University Jonsson Library of Government Documents. n.d. 31 Jan. 2003 <http://www-sul.stanford.edu/depts/jonsson/int/un.html>.

This site includes a comprehensive guide to the UN plus a listing of both Internet sites and print sources.

The WWW Virtual Library: International Affairs Resources. Elizabethtown College, Elizabethtown, PA. 24 Jan. 2003. 31 Jan. 2003 <http://users.etown.edu/s/SELCHEWA/vl/>.

A well-organized site for international government information at all levels.

Instructor: _____ Course/Section: _____

Name: _____

Date: _____ Points: _____

Review Questions

1. Why is government information important to the public?

2. Name four characteristics of government information that add to its value as a reference source.

   a.

   b.

   c.

   d.

3. List the ways in which U.S. government publications vary (a) in scope and (b) in format.

   a.

   b.

4. What are federal depository libraries?

   Why were they established?

5. Describe how electronic publishing has affected depository libraries.

6. Which classification system is used to classify U.S. government publications in many academic libraries?

7. What is the purpose of the *Monthly Catalog of United States Government Publications*?

8. Name two indexes that one can use to find retrospective (pre-1976) U.S. government publications.

9. Give the URLs (Internet addresses) for two Web sites that serve as general guides to U.S. government publications.

10. What is meant by "local government" publications? What is the value of these publications?

11. Why are publications of the United Nations and its allied agencies important sources of information?

12. What system is used to classify UN documents?

13. Is there a depository for U.S. documents at your institution?

    If so, what type depository is it? (Selective or regional?)

Exercise 9.2

Instructor: _____ Course/Section: _____

Name: _____

Date: _____ Points: _____

Finding Government Publications in the Online Catalog

Use the online catalog in your library to determine whether or not your library has any government documents on one of the topics below. Search by subject or keyword.

child abuse   early childhood education   groundwater pollution

Gulf War syndrome   Interstate Highway System   speleology

white collar crimes   strip mining   unidentified flying objects

Topic:

1. Give the exact word or phrase you used to look up the information.

2. Did you discover any government publications related to the topic?
   How can you tell that these are government publications?

3. What classification system was used for these sources?

4. Where are these items located in your library?

5. Locate one of the government documents you found and give the following information.

   Title of the publication:

   SuDoc number: Date:

   Author/agency of publication:

6. If you were writing a research paper, how would this publication be useful in developing your topic:

   a. as a background source? Why?

   b. as a source for developing a major point in your outline? Why?

   c. as supportive evidence? Why?

   d. as concluding remarks? Why?

7. Write the correct bibliographic citation for this work. Use the bibliographic examples in Appendix A.

Exercise 9.3

Instructor: _____ Course/Section: _____

Name: _____

Date: _____ Points: _____

Finding U.S. Government Publications Online

Visit the official U.S. Government sites below to answer questions 1–5.

American Memory: http://memory.loc.gov/ammem/amhome.html

FirstGov: http://www.firstgov.gov/

GPO Access: http://www.access.gpo.gov

Thomas: *Legislative Information on the Internet*: http://thomas.loc.gov/

U.S. Federal Government Agencies Directory: http://www.lib.lsu.edu/gov/fedgov.html

1. Go to the *American Memory* site and locate an image of Thomas Jefferson. In which collection is it located?

2. Go to the *FirstGov* site and find the official site for the U.S. Department of State. Follow the links leading to a list of U.S. Embassies and Consulates to answer the following questions.
   Who is the ambassador to Australia?

   Where is the U.S. Embassy in Australia located?

3. During each session of Congress, Senators and Representatives introduce bills on many issues of public concern, such as abortion, domestic violence, social security reform, income tax reform, and gun control. Go to *Thomas* to locate a bill or bills on child abuse that were introduced in the most recent Congressional session. Give the following information.

   Bill title:

   Bill no.:

   Date introduced:

4. The *Congressional Record* is the verbatim record of action that takes place in Congress. Locate the *Congressional Record* in *GPO Access* and find a discussion on human cloning. Give the following information.

   Search terms used in *GPO Access* to find information:

   Date of *Congressional Record* in which article appears:

   Pages:

5. Go to the *U.S. Federal Government Agencies Directory* and find the official site for the White House. What is the URL?

6. Each of the sites below contains information on tanning. Using the criteria in Chapter 6 for evaluating information on the Internet, examine each of the sites. Which do you consider to be the most reliable? Explain your answer.

   a. http://www.lotionbarn.com/tanning-facts.html

   b. http://vm.cfsan.fda.gov/~dms/cos-tan.htmlURL.

Exercise 9.4

Instructor: _____ Course/Section: _____

Name: _____

Date: _____ Points: _____

Finding State Government Information Online

Go to the State and Local Government Web site at http://www.piperinfo.com/state/index.cfm.

Click on your home state and answer the questions below.

1. Which state did you select?

2. Under what broad categories would you find information about your state?

3. Where would you find driver's license information for your state?

4. Who is the lieutenant governor of your state?

5. What is the URL for general tourist information for your state? How did you locate this link?

Exercise 9.5 Government Information

Instructor: _____ Course/Section: _____

Name: _____

Date: _____ Points: _____

Finding International Government Information Online

Go to the official United Nations site (http://www.un.org) to answer the following questions.

1. Who is the Secretary-General of the UN?

2. What is his native country?

3. Who was the first Secretary-General of the UN?

4. Name an online journal related to Africa that is published by the UN.

Go to the *International Affairs Resources* site at: http://www.etown.edu/vl/ and answer the following questions.

5. Give the name of a site that has a map of Afghanistan.

6. Which category would you click on to find information about health care in Canada?

7. What is the name of Canada's national health care program?

Instructor: _____ Course/Section: _____

Name: _____

Date: _____ Points: _____

Finding Government Information in the Documents Collection

An understanding of the Superintendent of Documents classification system (SuDocs) can be useful in locating government information on many subjects. Use Figure 5.1 in the text to locate a government agency that might have information on a topic that interests you. Browse the materials from that agency in the government documents area of your library for information on the topic. Select two documents that relate to the topic. Answer the following questions.

1. What topic did you select?

2. What is the name of the agency you selected?

3. What is the general SuDocs number for the agency?

4. Give the following information for each of the documents you selected.

   a. Title:

      SuDocs number:

      Date of publication:

   b. Title:

      SuDocs number:

      Date of publication:

5. Evaluate each of the documents for relevancy to the topic. Briefly explain how each would be useful (or not useful) for a research project on the topic.

Statistical Sources

"There are three kinds of lies: lies, damned lies, and statistics."

Benjamin Disraeli

Introduction

Many agree with the notion expressed in the quotation above. On the other hand, we know of people who believe that statistics don't lie. It is safe to say that neither of these two positions is altogether true. The fact is that statistics are used to prove and support research. It is also true that the researcher must evaluate statistical sources (just as they would any other information) as to reliability and usefulness.

There are generally two definitions of statistics: (1) the science that deals with the collection, classification, analysis, and interpretation of numerical facts and data; and (2) the actual numerical facts or data. Some sources present raw data, such as population or test scores, etc.; others have data that has been massaged, or interpreted by others, then presented to prove or verify a hypothesis. The United States government is the chief source for statistics gathered in the United States, but it is not the only source. Every level of government gathers statistics: international, national, state, and local. Organizations and businesses also collect them.

This chapter serves as a guide to finding statistical data and offers suggestions for evaluating statistical information. Many of the examples focus on the topic "effects of television advertising on children" to illustrate a search for statistical information on an actual topic.

WHY USE STATISTICS?

Statistics are a vital element in effective research:

- [ ] Scientists use statistical data to support or refute a hypothesis
- [ ] Businesses use statistics to survey market potential
- [ ] Economists analyze present conditions and forecast economic trends by using statistics
- [ ] Social scientists use statistical data to understand and predict many types of human behavior.

In the day-to-day conduct of our human activities we all use statistics in one form or another. We may want to know:

- [ ] What is the best-selling software program for word processing?
- [ ] Where are the top paying jobs in the country?
- [ ] What are the highest ranked graduate programs in business in the United States?
- [ ] Where is the best place to live in the United States?
- [ ] Which airline has the safest record?

All rankings are based on statistics—the reliability of the statistics determines whether one can rely on the rankings.

FINDING STATISTICAL INFORMATION

Statistical data covering a wide range of topics appear in many sources. Many publications are dedicated exclusively to statistical data. Other publications might include statistics along with other information. This is especially true of data in magazine and journal articles.

WAYS TO FIND STATISTICAL INFORMATION	
☐ use the Internet;	☐ use a periodical index; or
☐ use an index to statistical sources;	☐ use the library's catalog.

Use the Internet

The Internet is a great source for statistics from local, state, national, and international agencies, and from business and professional organizations. The U.S. government has begun a policy requiring that federal agencies produce and distribute information in electronic format. The result is a wealth of government-produced statistical data on the Internet.

Guidelines

Finding statistical data on the Internet

- [ ] **Go to a well-maintained Web page with links to statistical sources.**
  Search "statistic resources" on one of the search engines to locate a Web site listing statistical sources. An excellent site for statistical sources can be found on the University of Michigan Documents Center page at http://www.lib.umich.edu/govdocs/statsnew.html.

There is a list of additional sites at the end of this chapter. Use them as a starting point until you find several sites you prefer.

☐ **Go directly to a government site using the URL.**
The Bureau of Labor Statistics page provides information on labor and employment in the United States.

http://stats.bls.gov

Other levels of government also have links to statistical information (see Chapter 9).

Stat-USA: http://www.stat-usa.gov is an excellent source for statistical information. It is available in depository libraries or to individual subscribers.

☐ **Search the Internet for a specific statistical topic.**
Statistics of all kinds can be found on the Internet. Some statistics are located at specific government sites such as the Bureau of Labor Statistics. You can also use one of the search engines to locate statistical information. Chapter 3 discusses creating phrases to keep related terms together in an electronic search.

Example

"television advertising statistics"
   OR
"television statistics"

Use an Index to Statistical Sources

There are a number of indexes to statistics. Use a subject search in the online catalog to locate these.

Example

united states--statistics--abstracts
   OR
statistics--indexes
   OR
use one of the indexes listed in this chapter.

Figure 10.1 is taken from the printed Index of the 2002 edition of *Statistical Abstract of the United States*. The numbers in the Index refer to *table numbers* instead of page numbers as in most indexes. The references to tables under the subject "Television Broadcasting, Advertising Expenditures," includes Table #1253, shown in Figure 10.2, which indicates how much advertisers spend putting their products before the consumer.

The following general statistical indexes may be used as starting points.

American Statistics Index (ASI). Bethesda, MD: LexisNexis, 1973–.
A two-part (index and abstracts) guide to statistical information published by the U.S. government. Citations include the Superintendent of Documents call number as well as a microfiche reference number to the microfiche collection published by Congressional Information Service (CIS) to accompany the index.

Table

Television broadcasting (see also Cable and other pay TV services):
→ Advertising expenditures 1271
Mergers and acquisitions 743
Public confidence in media 398
Television broadcasting industry:
Earnings 609, 1119, 1121, 1123
Employees 609, 1119, 1121, 1123
Finances 1119, 1120, 1121, 1124, 1143, 1145
Gross domestic product 641, 1122
Televisions:
Consumer expenditures 1233, 1234
Households with 1126, 1375
Sales or shipments 1005, 1023
Viewing 1125, 1127
Temperature:
Cities 372, 373, 374, 377
Foreign cities 1334
States (highs and lows) 370
Temporary assistance for needy families program 519, 521, 524, 544, 545, 546, 548, 552
Tennessee. See State data.
Tennis ... 1242, 1244, 1245, 1247, 1248, 1251
Tenure. See Housing and housing units and Farms.
Tetanus 181
Texas. See State data.
Textile mills and product manufacturing:
Capital 749
Earnings 609, 972, 974, 979
Electronic commerce 974, 976
Employees 609, 972, 974, 979
Energy consumption 899
Establishments 972
Foreign trade 1306
Gross domestic product 641, 971
Inventories 982
Mergers and acquisitions 743
Occupational safety 633
Output 754
Patents 746
Productivity 612, 754
Shipments 974, 976, 981, 982
Toxic chemical releases 363
Textile mill products:
End-use 987
Foreign trade 988, 1303, 1306
Production 988
World 1326
Thai population 22
Thailand. See Foreign countries.
Theaters:
Attendance and receipts 1235, 1243
Federal aid 1237
Personal expenditures 1225, 1133
Theft. See Crime and criminals.
Theology, degrees conferred 289
Thread. See Yarn, thread, etc.
Thrift Savings Plan 529
Timber (see also Lumber and wood products):
Consumption 852
Foreign trade 852, 853
Producer prices 855, 856
Production 852
World (roundwood) 1326
Removed from national forests 848
Roundwood products 852
Volume, growth and cut 850

Table

Tin:
Foreign trade 874
Prices 870
Production 872
World 1365
Strategic and critical materials 873
Tires and tubes 1303
Titanium:
Production 868, 872, 882
Strategic and critical material 873
World production 872
Tobacco (see also Tobacco products, manufacturing, and Cigarettes):
Acreage harvested 827, 828
Consumer expenditures 657, 659, 660
Consumption and use .. 189, 191, 192, 986
During pregnancy 89, 90
Farm marketings, sales 808
Foreign countries 1363
Foreign trade ... 817, 821, 827, 1303, 1363
Prices 694, 813, 827, 828
Production . 816, 821, 827, 828, 1326, 1363
Taxes 436, 472
Tobacco manufacturing (see also Beverage and tobacco product manufacturing):
Capital 749
Earnings 609, 979
Employees 609, 979
Energy consumption 899
Foreign trade 1306
Gross domestic product 641
Inventories 982
Occupational safety 633
Price indexes 694
Productivity 612
Shipments 981, 982
Toxic chemical releases 363
Togo. See Foreign countries.
Tokyo Nikkei 225 stock market index 1382
Tomatoes 203, 706, 808, 820, 834
Tonga. See Foreign countries.
Tonnage, U.S. Flag fleet 1071
Tools. See Cutlery, etc., and Machine tools.
Tornadoes 368
Tourism, foreign (see also Travel) 1258, 1259, 1260, 1262, 1387
Townships and special districts 413, 414
Toxic material shipment 1077
Toxic-shock syndrome 181
Toys and sporting goods:
Consumer expenditures 1233
Foreign trade 1303
Price indexes 694
Sales 1023
Toys and sporting goods, manufacturing:
Earnings 609
Employees 609
Productivity 612
Shipments 1030
Track 1247, 1248
Trade (business). See Commerce, Foreign trade, Retail trade, and Wholesale trade.
Traffic fatalities 1098, 1099
Trailers (campers) 1088
Tranquilizers 189
Transit and ground transportation industry. See Passenger transit industry and subways.
Earnings 1053, 1054
Employees 1053, 1054
Establishments 1053, 1054

NOTE: Index citations refer to **table** numbers, not page numbers.

982 Index

U.S. Census Bureau, Statistical Abstract of the United States: 2001

Figure 10.1 Subject listing for "Television broadcasting" in *Statistical Abstract of the United States, 2001.*

No. 1253. Advertising—Estimated Expenditures by Medium: 1990 to 2001

[In millions of dollars (129,968 represents $129,968,000,000). See source for definitions of types of advertising]

Medium	1990	1994	1995	1996	1997	1998	1999	2000	2001
Total	129,968	153,024	165,147	178,113	191,307	206,697	222,308	247,472	231,287
National	73,638	69,124	96,933	105,054	112,809	122,271	132,170	151,664	141,797
Local	56,330	63,900	68,214	73,059	78,498	84,426	90,138	95,808	89,490
Newspapers	32,281	34,356	36,317	38,402	41,670	44,292	46,648	49,050	44,255
National	3,867	3,906	3,996	4,400	5,016	5,402	6,358	7,229	6.615
Local	28,414	30,450	32,321	34,002	36,654	38,890	40,290	41,821	37,640
Magazines	6,803	7,916	8,580	9,010	9,821	10,518	11,433	12,370	11,095
Broadcast TV	26,616	31,133	32,720	36,046	36,893	39,173	40,011	44,802	38,881
Four TV networks	9,863	10,942	11,600	13,081	13,020	13,736	13,961	15,888	14,300
Syndication	1,109	1,734	2,016	2,218	2,438	2,609	2,870	3,108	3,102
Spot (National)	7,788	8,993	9,119	9,803	9,999	10,659	10,500	12,264	9,223
Spot (Local)	7,856	9,464	9,985	10,944	11,436	12,169	12,680	13,542	12,256
Cable TV	2,631	5,209	6,166	7,778	8,750	10,340	12,570	15,455	15,536
Cable TV networks	2,000	3,885	4,500	5,695	6,450	7,640	9,405	11,765	11,883
Spot (Local)	631	1,324	1,666	2,083	2,300	2,700	3,165	3,690	3,653
Radio	8,726	10,529	11,338	12,269	13,491	15,073	17,215	19,295	17,861
Network	482	463	480	523	560	622	684	780	711
Spot (National)	1,635	1,902	1,959	2,135	2,455	2,823	3,275	3,668	2,956
Local (Local)	6,609	8,164	8,899	9,611	10,476	11,628	13,256	14,847	14,194
Yellow Pages	8,926	9,825	10,236	10,849	11,423	11,990	12,652	13,228	13,592
National	1,132	1,314	1,410	1,555	1,711	1,870	1,986	2,093	2,087
Local	7,794	8,511	8,826	9,294	9,712	10,120	10,666	11,135	11,505
Direct mail	23,370	29,638	32,866	34,509	36,890	39,620	41,403	44,591	44,725
Business papers	2,875	3,358	3,559	3,808	4,109	4,232	4,274	4,915	4,468
Out of home [1]	1,084	1,167	1,263	1,339	1,455	1,576	1,725	5,176	5,134
National	640	648	701	743	795	845	925	2,068	2,051
Local	444	519	562	596	660	731	800	3,108	3,083
Internet	(NA)	(NA)	(NA)	(NA)	800	1,383	2,832	6,507	5,752
Miscellaneous [2]	16,656	19,893	22,102	24,103	26,005	28,500	31,545	32,083	29,988
National	12,074	14,425	16,147	17,574	18,745	20,312	22,264	24,418	22,829
Local	4,582	5,468	5,955	6,529	7,260	8,188	9,281	7,665	7,159

NA Not available. [1] Prior to 2000, represents only "outdoor" billboards. Beginning 2000 includes other forms of outdoor advertising (i.e. transportation vehicles, bus shelters, telephone kiosks, etc.) previously covered under "Miscellaneous." [2] Beginning 2000, part of miscellaneous now included under "Out of home" advertising. See footnote 1.
Source: McCann-Erickson, Inc., New York, NY. Compiled for Crain Communications, Inc. in *Advertising Age* (copyright).

No. 1254. Magazine Advertising Revenue by Category: 1999 to 2001

[15,508 represents $15,508,000,000. Represents the volume of advertising in the consumer magazines belonging to the Publishers Information Bureau]

Category	Pages			Volume (mil. dol.)		
	1999	2000	2001	1999	2000	2001
Total [1]	255,146	269,016	237,613	15,508	17,052	16,214
Automotive	24,753	22,295	19,837	1,844	1,730	1,688
Automotive accessories and equipment	24,502	22,012	19,636	1,833	1,711	1,676
Technology [1]	22,009	26,536	17,426	1,385	1,736	1,236
Telecommunications	4,734	4,812	3,231	312	311	223
Computers and software	13,252	17,156	10,141	894	1,205	817
Home furnishings and supplies [1]	17,273	16,611	15,539	1,185	1,197	1,196
Household furnishings and accessories	4,709	4,597	4,056	283	272	264
Audio and video equipment and supplies	5,057	4,507	4,453	277	284	304
Toiletries and cosmetics [1]	15,857	15,741	16,696	1,143	1,218	1,401
Cosmetics and beauty aids [2]	8,484	8,781	9,304	578	640	759
Personal hygiene and health [2]	3,238	2,818	2,801	287	271	284
Hair products and accessories [2]	2,589	2,837	3,332	185	217	264
Direct response companies	22,163	19,554	19,353	1,121	1,034	1,096
Apparel and accessories [1]	24,776	26,576	25,043	1,120	1,295	1,316
Ready-to-wear	12,771	13,648	12,179	499	586	560
Footwear	3,349	4,058	4,281	158	218	221
Jewelry and watches	4,214	5,021	4,600	210	282	293
Financial, insurance and real estate	16,253	16,976	13,112	1,023	1,154	962
Financial	12,557	13,453	9,596	757	894	694
Insurance and real estate	3,697	3,524	3,516	266	260	268
Food and food products [1]	9,894	10,693	10,687	1,003	1,140	1,207
Prepared foods	1,919	1,961	1,883	194	212	223
Dairy, produce, meat and bakery goods	2,809	2,858	3,239	288	315	378
Beverages	1,854	1,981	2,086	166	197	213
Drugs and remedies	11,759	12,470	12,550	977	1,121	1,217
Medicines and proprietary remedies	10,272	10,506	10,255	850	965	1,011
Media and advertising	11,418	15,328	11,713	846	1,145	966
Retail stores [3]	15,798	19,263	15,312	826	1,056	882
Retail stores [3]	12,786	15,869	12,227	671	863	692
Public transportation, hotels, and resorts	15,231	15,421	14,947	705	743	745
Cigarettes, tobacco and accessories	6,034	4,677	3,057	481	388	256
Beer, wine and liquor	4,565	5,016	4,924	299	360	391
Liquor	3,600	3,874	3,768	235	286	307
Miscellaneous services and amusements	5,424	5,803	5,100	277	310	287
Sporting goods	10,503	13,752	13,774	240	263	279

[1] Includes other categories, not shown separately. [2] Women's, men's, and unisex. [3] Includes apparel, business, drugs and toiletries, and food and beverage.
Source: Publishers Information Bureau, Inc., New York, NY, as compiled by Competitive Media Reporting.

772 Accommodation, Food Services, and Other Services

U.S. Census Bureau, Statistical Abstract of the United States: 2002

Figure 10.2 Specific table reference located in Figure 10.1 for television advertising expenditures.

Index to International Statistics (IIS). Bethesda, MD: LexisNexis, 1983–.

A similar index to *ASI*, covering statistical sources of the United Nations and its allied agencies, foreign governments, and international government organizations.

LexisNexis Statistical. Bethesda, MD: LexisNexis, 1973–.

Provides online access to U.S. government statistics through *American Statistics Index*, including *Statistical Abstract of the United States*; *Statistical Reference Index*; and to *Index to International Statistics*.

Statistical Abstract of the United States. Washington: GPO, 1878–.

Published by the Bureau of the Census since 1878, it is considered by many to be the single most useful reference book on statistics. It provides a large number of statistics covering social and economic conditions in the United States as well as selected data for states, counties, cities and foreign countries. Although not an index in the true sense of the word, *Statistical Abstract* does serve as a guide to more extensive data that is published in reports from government and private agencies. The statistics are presented in tabular form with the source indicated below each table. *Statistical Abstract* is available in paper and CD-ROM format and on the Internet. The book is arranged by broad topics with a subject index at the end. Many of the tables provide statistical data for more than one year, usually 10 or more.

Statistical Reference Index (SRI). Bethesda, MD: LexisNexis, 1980–.

Covers statistical publications of state and local governments, professional and trade organizations, and some commercial publishers.

Statistical Universe. Bethesda, MD: LexisNexis, 1973–.

The Web-based version of the *American Statistics Index (ASI)*, the *Statistical Reference Index (SRI)* and the *Index to International Statistics (IIS)*, it abstracts and indexes federal, state and local, and international statistical publications. It fully replaces the CD-ROM version of *Statistical Masterfile*. Available by subscription only.

Use a Periodical Index

Although you could probably find statistics in a print index, it is much more effective to search for statistical sources in an electronic source. Periodical indexes, abstracts, and databases are discussed in detail in Chapter 8.

Steps to Finding Statistics in Periodicals

1. FIND AN APPROPRIATE PERIODICAL INDEX.
   EXAMPLE:
   FOR BUSINESS, USE *ABI/INFORM* OR *BUSINESS INDEX*.

2. EXECUTE A KEYWORD SEARCH:
   EXAMPLE:
   IN *EBSCO BUSINESS SOURCE ELITE*, SEARCH "TELEVISION ADVERTISING AND SALES."

Figure 10.3 depicts the results of a keyword search in *EBSCO Business Source Elite* for sales figures on television advertising. In this databases, the article is available as a full-text article. If that were not the case, you would have to check the library catalog under the title of the journal to see if your library had the periodical. Here, you have your choice of viewing the full-text article either as a Web document (HTML format) or in Adobe Acrobat format. Once it appears on the screen you can print, download, or e-mail it for later printing.

Use the Library Catalog

Statistical information can also be found in the library catalog.

Searched: Business Source Elite for *"television advertising and sales"*

Find:

For search examples, see *Search Tips* .   📁**Folder has 0 items.**

Refine Search   **Results**   To print, e-mail, or save an article or citation, add it to your folder.

◀ **1 to 9 (of 9)** ▶ **Pages: 1**

See: All Results 📖 Scholarly Journals 📖 Magazines	📁 Add (1-9)
1. Taking to TELEVISION.; By: Chilton, David., Marketing Magazine, 12/9/2002, Vol. 107 Issue 49, p11, 2p, 2c **Notes:** This title is not held locally	📁 Add
2. RETAIL.; Marketing Week (UK), 10/10/2002, Vol. 25 Issue 41, p61, 1p **Notes:** This title is not held locally 📄 PDF Full Text **(176K)**	📁 Add
3. Dir. Fleisig Signs With Propaganda. (cover story); By: DeSalvo, Kathy., SHOOT, 05/18/2001, Vol. 42 Issue 20, p1, 2p **Notes:** This title is not held locally 📄 HTML Full Text	📁 Add
4. Carat unit, IRI link up to study TV advertising.; By: Krol, Carol., **Advertising Age**, 10/20/97, Vol. 68 Issue 42, p4, 1/5p **Notes:** Our Library Subscribes to this Periodical 📄 HTML Full Text	📁 Add
5. Advertising and concentration: A survey of the empirical evidence.; By: Leahy, Arthur S.., Quarterly Journal of Business & Economics, Winter97, Vol. 36 Issue 1, p35, 16p, 3 charts **Notes:** Our Library Subscribes to this Periodical 📄 HTML Full Text 📄 PDF Full Text **(848K)**	📁 Add
6. Does TV advertising really affect sales? The role of measures, models, and data aggregation.; By: Tellis, Gerard J.; Weiss, Doyle L.., Journal of **Advertising**, Fall95, Vol. 24 Issue 3, p1, 12p, 4 charts **Notes:** Our Library Subscribes to this Periodical 📄 HTML Full Text 📄 PDF Full Text **(1.1MB)**	📁 Add

Figure 10.3   Keyword search results for "television advertising and sales" in *EBSCOhost Business Source Elite*. (From EBSCO Database. Copyright © 2003 by EBSCO Publishing. Reprinted by permission.)

Guidelines

Retrieve the type of information required

☐ Check the *Library of Congress Subject Headings* (*LCSH*).

☐ **Search the online catalog** to find the authorized subject heading. Figure 10.4 shows the authorized subject headings for "statistics." Note the "Related Subjects" and "Additional entries" references.

☐ **Use the topic with the subdivision—statistics** for a subject search in the library catalog. (Remember that statistical information in books listed in the online catalog might not be current.)

Example

education--statistics   television advertising--statistics

Nebraska State College System

| NEXT PAGE | BRIEF DISPLAY | START OVER | ANOTHER SEARCH | LIMIT THIS SEARCH | SEARCH AS WORDS |

(Univ of Nebr-Lincoln) (Univ of Nebr-Omaha) (Univ of Nebr-Kearney) (Univ. of Nebr Med Ctr)

SUBJECT ⬍

Num	Mark	SUBJECTS (1-12 of 74)	Year
→ 1		Statistics -- 31 Related Subjects	
2		Statistics	
		The 1990 information please sports almanac / edited by Mike ∮ **CSC 2d Floor Stacks:AVAILABLE** ; PRINTED MATL	c1989
		1998 information please almanac / Borgna Brunner, editor / **WSC Stacks:AVAILABLE** ; PRINTED MATL	c1997
		Against all odds [videorecording] : inside statistics / prod / **PSC Videotapes:AVAILABLE, WSC ITC Video:AVAILABLE** ; VISUAL MAT.	1989
		Applied business statistics : an elementary approach / Elam / **CSC 2d Floor Stacks:AVAILABLE** ; PRINTED MATL	[1971]
→		257 additional entries	
3		Statistics Bibliography	
		The ... Mental measurements yearbook / **PSC Reference:AVAILABLE, WSC Reference:LIB USE ONLY** ; PRINTED MATL	1941-
		The ... Mental measurements yearbook / **CSC Ready Reference:LIB USE ONLY** ; SERIAL	1941-
		The ... Mental measurements yearbook of the School of Educat / **PSC Reference:AVAILABLE** ; SERIAL	1938
		Sources of statistics / by Joan M. Harvey / **CSC 2d Floor Stacks:AVAILABLE** ; PRINTED MATL	[1971]
		Statistics sources : a subject guide to data on industrial, / **PSC Reference:AVAILABLE** ; PRINTED MATL	c1977
4		Statistics Caricatures And Cartoons	
		The cartoon guide to statistics / Larry Gonick & Woollcott S / **PSC Gen. Collection:AVAILABLE, WSC Stacks:AVAILABLE** ; PRINTED MATL	c1993
5		Statistics Charts Diagrams Etc	
		Exercises in statistical methods, by Robert E. Chaddock and / **WSC Stacks:AVAILABLE** ; PRINTED MATL	[c1928]
		Handbook of statistical tables / **CSC 2d Floor Stacks:AVAILABLE** ; PRINTED MATL	[1962]
6		Statistics Charts Diagrams Etc Periodicals Indexes	
		Charts, graphs & stats index / **CSC 2d Floor Stacks:AVAILABLE** ; PRINTED MATL	c1992-
		Charts, graphs & stats index, 1988-1991 / edited by Robert S / **CSC 2d Floor Stacks:AVAILABLE** ; PRINTED MATL	c1992

Figure 10.4 Results of a subject search for "statistics" in the Nebraska State College Library Catalog.

Figure 10.4 shows the results of a subject search for the general topic of "statistics." Note that it produced a number of "Related Subjects." Many topics are subdivided in this manner to simplify the first screen retrieved. Figure 10.5 shows a sampling of the "Related Subjects" for statistics. Additional entries are also collapsed and noted on the screen, as shown after the last entry in number 2 (255 additional entries.)

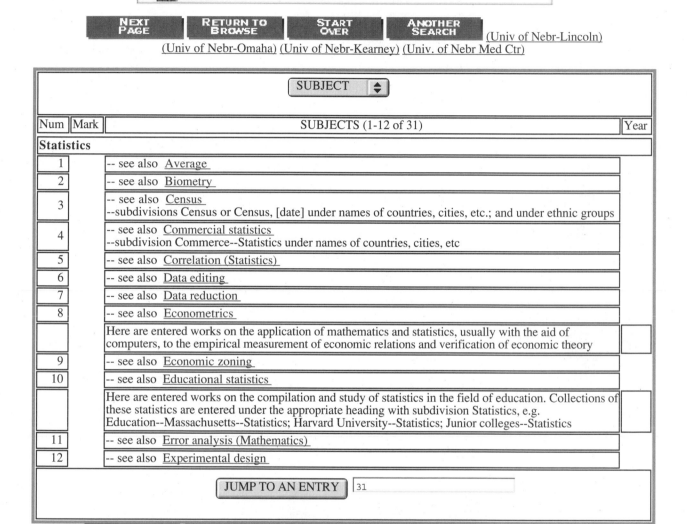

Figure 10.5 List of "Related Subjects" indicated in Figure 10.4 for "statistics."

To narrow the search you would use the more specific subject, "television advertising statistics," as shown in Figure 10.5. Note that items are held at three different libraries: Chadron State College (CSC), Peru State College (PSC), and Wayne State College (WSC).

(Univ of Nebr-Lincoln)

(Univ of Nebr-Omaha) (Univ of Nebr-Kearney) (Univ. of Nebr Med Ctr)

		SUBJECT ⬍	

Num	Mark	SUBJECTS (1-5 of 5)	Year
		Television Advertising United States	
		The Anatomy of a television commercial; the story of Eastman / **CSC 2d Floor Stacks:AVAILABLE, WSC Stacks:AVAILABLE** ; PRINTED MATL	[1970]
		Children's television commercials : a content analysis / [by / **CSC 2d Floor Stacks:AVAILABLE** ; PRINTED MATL	[1973]
1		Drive-by journalism : the assault on your need to know / Art / **WSC Stacks:AVAILABLE** ; PRINTED MATL	c2000
		Eicoff on broadcast direct marketing / Al Eicoff / **PSC Gen. Collection:AVAILABLE** ; PRINTED MATL	c1988
		10 additional entries	
2		Television Advertising United States Case Studies	
		A millionaire's notebook : how ordinary people can achieve e / **WSC Stacks:AVAILABLE** ; PRINTED MATL	c1996
3		Television Advertising United States Cost Control	
		The Bellaire guide to TV commercial cost control / Arthur Be / **CSC 2d Floor Stacks:AVAILABLE** ; PRINTED MATL	c1982
		Television Advertising United States History	
4		A&E top 10. [Greatest television commercials] [videorecordin / **WSC ITC Video:AVAILABLE** ; VISUAL MAT.	c1999
		Television's classic commercials; the golden years, 1948-195 / **WSC Stacks:AVAILABLE** ; PRINTED MATL	[1971]
5		Television Advertising United States Periodicals	
		Mediaweek / **WSC Periodicals Room:AVAILABLE, WSC Microfiche:AVAILABLE, WSC Electronic resource:ASK AT DESK** ; SERIAL	1991-

BRIEF DISPLAY START OVER ANOTHER SEARCH LIMIT THIS SEARCH SEARCH AS WORDS (Univ of Nebr-Lincoln)

(Univ of Nebr-Omaha) (Univ of Nebr-Kearney) (Univ. of Nebr Med Ctr)

INNOVATIVE INTERFACES

Figure 10.6 Results of a subject search for "television advertising statistics" in the Nebraska State College System Library Catalog.

Use Statistics as a Subdivision of a Topic

Figure 10.7 illustrates a catalog screen using United States as the subject and statistics as the subdivision. This format may be used for city, state, national, or international areas. A geographical subdivision achieves a more focused result than using a general search for "statistics."

A selected list of major statistical sources can be found using a subject search for statistics as shown in Figure 10.7. These include *Information Please Almanac*, *Almanac of the 50 States*, *The Book of American Rankings*, and *Statistical Abstract of the United States*.

Nebraska State College System

| NEXT PAGE | BRIEF DISPLAY | START OVER | ANOTHER SEARCH | LIMIT THIS SEARCH | SEARCH AS WORDS |

(Univ of Nebr-Lincoln) (Univ of Nebr-Omaha) (Univ of Nebr-Kearney) (Univ. of Nebr Med Ctr)

SUBJECT ▼

Num	Mark	SUBJECTS (1-12 of 19)	Year
		United States Statistics	
1		1998 information please almanac / Borgna Brunner, editor / **WSC Stacks:AVAILABLE** ; PRINTED MATL	c1997
		Almanac of the 50 states : basic data profiles with comparat / **PSC Reference:AVAILABLE** ; PRINTED MATL	1985
		The best, worst, least & most : the U.S. book of rankings / **PSC Gen. Collection:AVAILABLE** ; PRINTED MATL	1980, c1979
		The book of American rankings / by Clark S. Judge / **CSC 2d Floor Stacks:AVAILABLE, PSC Reference:AVAILABLE** ; PRINTED MATL	c1979
		24 additional entries	
2		United States Statistics Bibliography	
		Guide to U.S. Government statistics / **WSC Gov Doc Reference:LIB USE ONLY** ; PRINTED MATL	
		Sources of statistics / by Joan M. Harvey / **CSC 2d Floor Stacks:AVAILABLE** ; PRINTED MATL	[1971]
		State and local statistics sources : a subject guide to stat / **CSC 2d Floor Stacks:AVAILABLE** ; PRINTED MATL	c1990
		The student economist's handbook : a guide to sources / [by] / **CSC 2d Floor Stacks:AVAILABLE** ; PRINTED MATL	[1967]
3		United States Statistics Data Bases	
		1987 economic censuses [computer file] : retail trade, servi / **PSC Comp Software:AVAILABLE** ; COMPUTER FILE	1992-
4		United States Statistics Databases	
		Census mapper [computer file] : b [prototype] featuring data / **WSC Gov Doc Office:AVAILABLE** ; COMPUTER FILE	1998]
		Statistical abstract of the United States [computer file] / **WSC Gov Doc Office:AVAILABLE** ; COMPUTER FILE	1993-
5		United States Statistics Databases Periodicals	
		The American community survey [computer file] / **WSC Gov Doc Office:AVAILABLE, Gov Doc Online:ASK AT DESK** ; COMPUTER FILE	[1998?-
6		United States Statistics Juvenile Literature	
		The new view almanac : the first all-visual resource of vita / **CSC Ready Reference:LIB USE ONLY** ; PRINTED MATL	c1996
		U.S. in a nutshell. Illustrated by Arthur Wallower / **WSC ITC Young Adult:AVAILABLE** ; PRINTED MATL	[1971]

Figure 10.7 Subject search for "united states statistics."

EVALUATING STATISTICAL SOURCES

It is easy to fall into a trap with statistics—researchers tend to look for data that will support a hypothesis or a position regardless of its reliability. It is always important to evaluate any information used in research; with statistics this is even more critical. General information concerning evaluating informational sources is discussed in Chapter 6. Statistical information requires a few additional considerations.

Ask Yourself

- [ ] **Who collected the data?** Is it a business that has a "vested" interest in its publication, such as the manufacturer of a particular product who might have gathered data to support an advertising claim?

- [ ] Do the statistics reflect a **bias?** Political polls, for example, might be biased to reflect certain strengths or weaknesses of the candidates, depending on the bias of the pollsters. In this case, it is necessary to find out something about the agency conducting the poll.

- [ ] Is the data **timely?** Check the dates of coverage and the publication date.

- [ ] Is the coverage **complete?** In polls, for example, was the sample large enough?

- [ ] Has the data been **repackaged** several times so as to distort its reliability? Government data is frequently repackaged by a commercial entity and might not include all of the original data.

- [ ] Is this a "time series"? Data gathered over a long span of time is referred to as a *time series*. It is usually considered to be a reliable source. In many cases, the research project calls for data that has a timeline.

- [ ] Is the data from a *primary* or a *secondary* **source?** If it is from a secondary source (for example, a periodical article), is the source documented?

The following two examples illustrate the importance of evaluating statistical information:

> ### Example
>
> *The True But Little Known Facts About Women and Aids, with Documentation.*
> http://147.129.226.1/library/research/AIDSFACTS.htm
>
> *Feline Reactions to Bearded Men.* http://www.improb.com/airchives/classical/cat/cat.html

At first glance these sites might appear to be authentic, scholarly presentations. Upon careful examination, however, you will note errors, incorrect citation formats, and inaccurate information. These two sites are obviously designed to be used to teach the importance of evaluating statistical sites, but there are many such sites of similar merit that do not have the same honorable intention. With the wealth of information now available in a vast array of formats, it is becoming more important than ever that you are critical in selecting information sources. Statistical information, whether it is to introduce, support, or draw conclusions about your research, must be accurate, current, and appropriate for your needs to be effective.

SELECTED INTERNET SITES FOR STATISTICS
Guides

Chance. http://www.geom.umn.edu/docs/education/chance/
Information on basic statistical concepts.

Internet Glossary of Statistical Terms. http://www.animatedsoftware.com/statglos/statglos.htm
   Glossary with links to related sites.

Statistics Every Writer Should Know. http://nilesonline.com/stats/

General

Economics and Statistics. http://www.lib.lsu.edu/bus/economic.html

FedStats. http://www.fedstats.gov
   Maintained by the Federal Interagency Council on Statistical Policy. Over 70 agencies.

LexisNexis Statistical. Subscription service available from LexisNexis.

State and Local Government on the Net. http://www.piperinfo.com/state/index.cfm

Statistical Abstract of the United States. http://www.census.gov/statab/www/

Statistical Resources on the Web. http://www.lib.umich.edu/govdocs/stats.html

Statistical Universe. Subscription service available from LexisNexis.
   Index plus links to statistics pages.

STAT-USA. http://www.stat-usa.gov
   Provides economic, business, social, and environmental program data produced by more than 50 Federal sources. Available free through depository libraries.

Uncle Sam. http://www.lib.memphis.edu/gpo/statis1.htm

Selected Sites by Subject

Business and Economics

Bureau of Labor Statistics. http://stats.bls.gov/datahome.htm

Economic Statistics Briefing Room. http://www.whitehouse.gov/fsbr/employment.html
   Employment and unemployment statistics from the White House.

Regional Economic Information System (REIS). U.S. Department of Commerce, Bureau of Economic Analysis. http://fisher.lib.virginia.edu/reis/
   State, county, and metropolitan area statistics for the period 1969–1997.

Crime and Criminals

Bureau of Justice Statistics. http://www.ojp.usdoj.gov/bjs/

Crime & Justice Electronic Data Abstracts. http://www.ojp.usdoj.gov/bjs/dtdata.htm

FBI Crime Statistics. http://www.fbi.gov/crimestats.htm

NCJRS Abstracts Database. http://www.ncjrs.org/search.html

Sourcebook of Criminal Justice Statistics. http://www.albany.edu/sourcebook/

State Crime Data. http://www.ojp.usdoj.gov/bjs/datast.htm

Demographics

CIA World Fact Book. http://www.odci.gov/cia/publications/factbook/index.html

State and Metropolitan Area Data Book, 1997–98: http://www.census.gov/statab.www.smadb.html

State Population Projections. http://www.ire.org/training/vnet/stproj.htm

U.S. Census Bureau. http://www.census.gov/

Education and Youth

Condition of Education. http://nces.ed.gov/

Education at a Glance. http://www.oecd.org/els/education/ei/eag/

Youth Indicators. http://nces.ed.gov/pubs/yi/

Health

Centers for Disease Control and Prevention. http://www.cdc.gov

MMWR—Morbidity and Mortality Weekly Report. http://www2.cdc.gov/mmwr/

National Center for Health Statistics. http://www.cdc.gov/nchs/default.htm

National Institute for Occupational Safety and Health. http://www.cdc.gov/niosh/homepage.html

SAMHSA Statistical Data. http://www.samhsa.gov/
> Includes: Mental Health and Substance Use/Abuse, Treatment Services System and its Utilization, etc.

International

Eurostat. http://europa.eu.int/comm/eurostat/
> The Statistical Office of the European Communities.

United Nations Development Program. http://www.undp.org/

Public Opinion

The Gallup Organization. http://www.gallup.com

Roper Center for Public Opinion Research. http://www.lib.uconn.edu/RoperCenter/

SELECTED LIST OF PRINT STATISTICAL SOURCES

(Note: Many titles are now available electronically.)

General

Historical Statistics of the United States: Colonial Times to 1970. Washington: GPO, 1976.
> Two volume source that contains a wide range of historical statistics for the U.S. Includes economic, political, social, and demographic data. Some tables start with the colonial period.

Historical Statistics of the United States: Two Centuries of the Census, 1790–1990. Comp. Donald B. Dodd. Westport, CN: Greenwood, 1993.
> This work includes bibliographical references.

Statistical Abstract of the United States. Washington: GPO, 1878–.
> An annual summary of data collected by the government; this publication provides statistics on a vast array of topics. The documentation following each table serves as a guide to more extensive data on the topic.

World Almanac and Book of Facts 2000. New York: Primedia, 1893–.
> Contains a wide variety of statistical information.

Subject

Business and Economics

Agricultural Statistics. Washington: GPO, 1936–.
> A concise collection of data such as crop yields, market value, price, number of farms, and export/import.

Annual Energy Review. Washington: GPO, 1982–.

Detailed data on energy production, consumption, prices, imports, exports.

The Dow Jones Averages, 1885–1995. Chicago: Professional Publications, 1996.

Compilation of averages.

Economic Report of the President. Washington: GPO, 1979–.

An annual report containing detailed tables showing national income, manufacturing and commercial activity, government finance, and international trade.

Monthly Labor Review. Washington: GPO, 1918–.

In addition to employment related articles, the publication features regular compilations of data related to labor/employment. It is included in a number of indexing services.

Standard and Poor's Statistical Service. New York: Standard and Poor, 1941–.

Monthly publication with annual cumulations that contains statistics covering bank and finance, production and labor, price indexes, income and trade, building, electric powers and fuels, metals, transportation, textiles, paper products, and agricultural products. Cites data source.

Survey of Current Business. Washington: GPO, 1921–.

A monthly publication of the U.S. Bureau of Economic Analysis. Provides current and historical data on business, industry, agriculture, and manufacturing.

U.S. Exports of Merchandise. Washington: U.S. Department of Commerce, 1998–.

Monthly data, plus historical summary on separate CD-ROMs.

USA Trade. Washington: U.S. Department of Commerce. 1998–.

Monthly accumulations of tabular data for exporting. Includes country and district information and four year annual history. Includes time series analysis with four years of data. CD-ROM.

Crime and Criminals

Sourcebook of Criminal Justice Statistics. Washington: GPO, 1973–.

Tables give figures on prisons, prisoners, types of crimes, arrests, money spent on law enforcement and much more.

Uniform Crime Reports. Washington: GPO, 1930–.

Formerly known as *Crime in the United States: FBI Uniform Crime Reports.* Statistics on numbers of arrests, types of crimes, etc. Annual.

Demographics

Census of Population and Housing. GPO, 2000.

The U.S. Bureau of the Census "counts" the citizens of the United States every ten years. The data gathered includes social and economic characteristics of the population as well as head counts. The first decennial census was taken in 1790 and has continued ever since. In between the ten-year periods, the Bureau of the Census conducts surveys to obtain ongoing estimates of the population.

County and City Data Book. Washington: GPO, 1949–.

Supplement to the *Statistical Abstract of the United States*, gives a wide variety of demographic, social, and economic statistics for regions, divisions, states, counties, and SMSAs (Standard Metropolitan Statistical Areas).

Current Population Reports. Washington: GPO, dates vary.

Series of reports from the U.S. Census Bureau. P-20 series deals with population characteristics; P-23 covers special subjects.

Sourcebook of County Demographics. CACI Marketing Systems, 1990–.

Continues *Sourcebook of Demographics and Buying Power for Every County in the USA.*

Education

The Core Data Task Force Report. Washington: U.S. Department of Education, 1997.
Report prepared by the Core Data Task Force of the National Education Statistics Agenda Committee, National Forum on Education Statistics.

Digest of Education Statistics. Washington: GPO, 1975–.
Detailed coverage of public, private, vocational, and higher education statistics.

Education in States and Nations: Indicators Comparing U.S. States with Other Industrialized Countries in 1991. Phelps, Richard P. and others. Washington: National Center for Education Statistics, 1996.

Projections of Education Statistics to 2009. Ed. William J. Hussar. Washington: Dept. of Education, Office of Educational Research and Improvement, National Center for Education Statistics, 1999.

International

United Nations Statistical Yearbook. New York: United Nations, 1948–.
Statistics on a wide range of topics for countries of the world.

World Factbook. Washington: CIA, 1981–.
Information on countries of the world gathered from a variety of sources: the Bureau of the Census, Central Intelligence Agency, Department of State, and others.

World Tables. Baltimore: Johns Hopkins UP for World Bank, 1976–.
A detailed time series of data compiled from the files of the World Bank. Country statistics include balance of trade, balance of payments, and manufacturing output.

Exercise 10.1

Instructor: _____ Course/Section: _____

Name: _____

Date: _____ Points: _____

Review Questions

1. What are the two definitions of statistics?

   a.

   b.

2. Why are statistics useful in research?

3. Name four ways to locate statistical information.

   a.

   b.

   c.

   d.

4. Name three methods you might use to locate statistical information on the Internet.

   a.

   b.

   c.

5. Why would you expect to find many U.S. government statistics on the Internet?

6. Construct a search command to use in a periodical index or database to find articles containing statistical information for each of the following.

    a. Current population figures for China:

    b. Rate of crime in U.S. cities:

    c. Number of deaths by alcohol-related accidents per year:

7. Give the commands (author, title, subject, or keyword) you would use in the online catalog to find each of the following. (e.g., subject search = . . .; keyword search = . . .)

    a. Indexes to statistics

    b. Statistics about drugs

8. Give three criteria you would use to evaluate statistical sources.

    a.

    b.

    c.

Instructor: _____ Course/Section: _____

Name: _____

Date: _____ Points: _____

Finding Statistical Information Online

Use the appropriate URL from the following list to find answers to the questions below.

University of Michigan. http://www.lib.umich.edu/govdocs/stats.html

University of Wisconsin. http://dpls.dacc.wisc.edu/internet.html

Louisiana State University. http://www.lib.lsu.edu/soc/stats.html

Fedstats. http://www.fedstats.gov

1. Which site would you use to find statistics on safety?

2. Which site would be most appropriate for statistics on health?

3. Which two sites would help you locate crime statistics?

4. Which site would you use to find the current economic situation of the United States?

5. Which site would you use to find educational statistics?

6. Which site would you use to find population information about your home state?

7. Print out the first page of the last site you visited and attach it to this assignment, or give the URL and title of the page.

8. Write the correct bibliographic citation for the last web site you visited. (See examples in Appendix A.)

Instructor: _____ Course/Section: _____

Name: _____

Date: _____ Points: _____

Using *Statistical Abstract of the United States*

Use a current print copy or the online version of ***Statistical Abstract of the United States*** to find statistics on a topic you select or one assigned by your instructor. Answer the questions below. (http://www.census.gov/statab/www/)

Topic:

1. Which year of *Statistical Abstracts of the United States* did you use?

2. Which subject heading(s) did you use to look up your topic in the index?

3. Did you find listings of tables under this heading?

    If so, list the numbers of the tables here.

    If not, which cross references did the index send you to?

4. Select one table for your topic and write the number of the table here.

5. What is the title of the table you selected?

6. Does the table use primary or secondary information? How do you know?

7. Write the correct bibliographic citation to one table on your topic. (See Appendix A.)

Instructor: _____ Course/Section: _____

Name: _____

Date: _____ Points: _____

Using Statistical Indexes

Use one of the statistical indexes listed in this chapter to locate statistics on a topic of your choice, or one assigned by your instructor.

1. Topic:

2. Title of statistical index used:

3 Year of index you used:

4. Subject heading(s) you used:

5. Abstract number/accession number/table you found, if applicable:

If you used a print index volume, find the matching abstract and look for the abstract number or accession number for the publication you found.

6. Write the title of the publication you found in the abstract or table.

7. Give the date of the publication.

8. Write the correct bibliographic citation for the publication you found. Use the examples in Appendix A.

Instructor: _____ Course/Section: _____

Name: _____

Date: _____ Points: _____

Finding Statistics in the Library Catalog

1. Topic:

2. What catalog command did you use for your topic? (Keyword or subject?)

3. Identify two sources with possible information on your topic:

   a. title and date of first source

   b. title and date of second source

4. Give the call number and location of each of these sources.

5. Find one of the sources available in your library and examine it for information on your topic.

    a. Would you consider this source a popular or a scholarly source? Why?

    b. Does the source use primary or secondary materials? Give an example.

6. Find a specific reference to your topic in this source such as a chart or table. Write the correct bibliographic citation for the entry on your topic. Use the examples shown in Appendix A.

7. Explain how the statistical information found in this source would be useful in a research paper on this topic.

Instructor: _____ Course/Section: _____

Name: _____

Date: _____ Points: _____

Evaluating Statistical Information

Using an appropriate database with **full-text** articles, find two magazine (popular) or journal (scholarly) articles dealing with statistics on a topic of your choice or one assigned by your instructor. (Hint: Consider using "statistics" and your topic in the search command.)

1. Database used:

2. Write the bibliographic citation to the first article you found on your topic. Use examples in Appendix A.

3. Evaluate the data in the article in terms of:

    a. Who collected the data?

    b. Any bias present? Justify.

    c. Timely?

        Date of coverage?

    d. Complete or adequate coverage?

    e. Any distortion from repackaging?

    f. Time series (data gathered over a long span of time)?

    g. Data from primary or secondary sources?

    h. If secondary sources are used, is documentation provided?

4. Write the bibliographic citation to the second article you found on your topic. Use examples in Appendix A.

5. Evaluate the data in the article in terms of:

   a. Who collected the data?

   b. Any bias present? Justify.

   c. Timely?

      Date of coverage?

   d. Complete or adequate coverage?

   e. Any distortion from repackaging?

   f. Time series (data gathered over a long span of time)?

   g. Data from primary or secondary sources?

   h. If secondary sources are used, is documentation provided?

6. Write a brief summary in which you compare the two articles, using the criteria you used for each in Questions 3 and 5 above.

Biographical Information

"There has rarely passed a life of which a judicious and faithful
narrative would not be useful."

Samuel Johnson

Introduction

A biography is a written history of a person's life and accomplishments. Questions dealing with biographical information are among the most frequently asked in a library. People want to know about the lives of other people, both the famous and the not-so-famous. Popular literature is rich with sources that satisfy that need. Biography makes for wonderful reading, but more than that, it is an important source in the research process. We can approach research on most subjects through the lives of individuals who have shaped developments in the field. For example, to learn about the development of the polio vaccine, one must read about Jonas Salk.

Biographical information is so important to the contribution of knowledge that it can be found in most reference sources, including dictionaries, almanacs, and encyclopedias. There are many books written about people's lives; information about individuals appears in the daily newspapers and in magazines and journals. In addition, there are dictionaries devoted exclusively to presenting facts about the lives of individuals. The Internet is a rich source of biographical information. Biographical information on the Internet ranges from well-written and researched biographical articles to home pages of fan clubs and family album pages for individuals.

FINDING BIOGRAPHICAL INFORMATION

Finding biographical information on noteworthy persons is not difficult. Articles about famous persons appear in many sources, including encyclopedias and dictionaries. It is the not-so-famous that cause problems. Selecting the appropriate source requires the researcher to determine certain basic information about the person—his or her nationality and profession and whether the person is living or not. The search strategy for finding biographical information depends on the question being asked and the information needed.

Guidelines
Finding biographical information

- ☐ Search the Internet.
- ☐ Search an online database.
- ☐ Look in the appropriate biographical dictionary.
- ☐ Use a specialized biographical index such as *Biography Index* or *Biography and Genealogy Master Index*.
- ☐ Check the general and/or appropriate periodical indexes and abstracts to find articles by or about the individual.
- ☐ Consult the library catalog to see if the library owns a book by or about the individual.
- ☐ Try a reference book such as a general or subject encyclopedia.
- ☐ Ask a reference librarian for help.

Internet

The Internet is a great source for biographical information. It is possible to find information on the lives of famous composers, actors, authors, and television personalities by executing a simple name search in one of the search engines such as Google or Lycos. For a broad search on biographical information, use search phrases such as "science biography," or "biography resources." This will take you to pages with numerous links to biographical information.

There are many excellent guides to biographical information on the Web that have been created by librarians. These include the *Biography* site from the University of Michigan and the *Biography* page available from the *Ready Reference* site on the LSU Libraries' home page. (The URLs for these sites can be found in the listing at the end of this chapter.) These sites are useful in that they provide links to categories of biographical databases and Web sites. It is always a good idea to use Web-based guides that are developed by librarians because they apply standard criteria in evaluating the sites for inclusion on the pages. Some libraries catalog Web sites that the librarians select for inclusion in their online catalogs, including Web sites for biographical information.

Many reference works, including dictionaries, encyclopedias, and indexes, are now available free on the Internet. These include *Biographical Dictionary, Encyclopedia.com*, and *Biographical Directory of the U.S. Congress*.

Databases

Full-text databases often include biographical information. You can find both works written by an individual and those written about his/her life by doing a name search in one of the full-text databases such as *Academic Universe,* InfoTrac's *General Reference Center* or EBSCOhost's *Academic Search Elite*. Biographical information frequently appears in book review and literary criticism material, which are discussed in Chapter 12.

Two full-text databases devoted exclusively to biographical information are available on the Web: *Gale Biography Resource Center* and *Wilson Biography Plus*. Since these are available only by subscription, you will have to check to see if your library subscribes to either or both of these.

Figure 11.1 shows a search in the *WilsonWeb* database for information on Maya Angelou. Because *WilsonWeb* offers the option of searching more than one database at once, you can search both the regular *OmniFile Full-Text* database and the *Wilson Bios Plus III* at the same time. Use parentheses to keep the terms in a relationship (Angelou, Maya), and use the person's last name first, followed by a comma, then the first name, as instructed in the Help screens in this database. Finding multiple resources in one database saves time and effort.

As you review the titles of the works and types of publications listed in Figure 11.1, you will note that item #4 appears to be a logical choice since it includes the birth data and a photograph of the poet. Most of the other titles listed are articles or book reviews of the poet's work. Figure 11.2 shows the results of the search shown in Figure 11.1. Links to both images and other sources are provided.

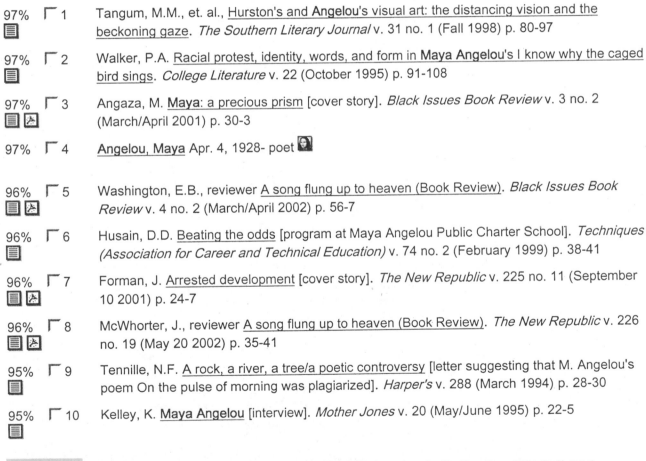

97% ☐ 1 Tangum, M.M., et. al., Hurston's and Angelou's visual art: the distancing vision and the beckoning gaze. *The Southern Literary Journal* v. 31 no. 1 (Fall 1998) p. 80-97

97% ☐ 2 Walker, P.A. Racial protest, identity, words, and form in Maya Angelou's I know why the caged bird sings. *College Literature* v. 22 (October 1995) p. 91-108

97% ☐ 3 Angaza, M. Maya: a precious prism [cover story]. *Black Issues Book Review* v. 3 no. 2 (March/April 2001) p. 30-3

97% ☐ 4 Angelou, Maya Apr. 4, 1928- poet

96% ☐ 5 Washington, E.B., reviewer A song flung up to heaven (Book Review). *Black Issues Book Review* v. 4 no. 2 (March/April 2002) p. 56-7

96% ☐ 6 Husain, D.D. Beating the odds [program at Maya Angelou Public Charter School]. *Techniques (Association for Career and Technical Education)* v. 74 no. 2 (February 1999) p. 38-41

96% ☐ 7 Forman, J. Arrested development [cover story]. *The New Republic* v. 225 no. 11 (September 10 2001) p. 24-7

96% ☐ 8 McWhorter, J., reviewer A song flung up to heaven (Book Review). *The New Republic* v. 226 no. 19 (May 20 2002) p. 35-41

95% ☐ 9 Tennille, N.F. A rock, a river, a tree/a poetic controversy [letter suggesting that M. Angelou's poem On the pulse of morning was plagiarized]. *Harper's* v. 288 (March 1994) p. 28-30

95% ☐ 10 Kelley, K. Maya Angelou [interview]. *Mother Jones* v. 20 (May/June 1995) p. 22-5

Figure 11.1 Search results for Maya Angelou in *Wilson Web*, using both the *OmniFile Full-Text* database and the *Wilson Bios Plus III* biography database.

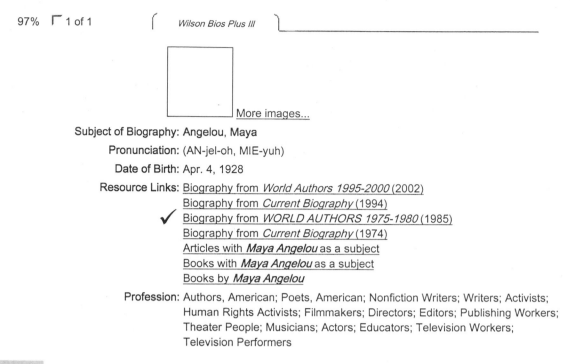

97% ⌐ 1 of 1   ⌠   *Wilson Bios Plus III*   ⌡

More images...

Subject of Biography: Angelou, Maya
Pronunciation: (AN-jel-oh, MIE-yuh)
Date of Birth: Apr. 4, 1928
Resource Links: Biography from *World Authors 1995-2000* (2002)
Biography from *Current Biography* (1994)
✓ Biography from *WORLD AUTHORS 1975-1980* (1985)
Biography from *Current Biography* (1974)
Articles with *Maya Angelou* as a subject
Books with *Maya Angelou* as a subject
Books by *Maya Angelou*

Profession: Authors, American; Poets, American; Nonfiction Writers; Writers; Activists;
Human Rights Activists; Filmmakers; Directors; Editors; Publishing Workers;
Theater People; Musicians; Actors; Educators; Television Workers;
Television Performers

Figure 11.2 List of entries found as a result of a subject search for Maya Angelou in Figure 11.1.

Figure 11.3 shows the results of clicking on the link to *World Authors* shown in Figure 11.2. *World Authors*, a reputable reference source, includes full biographical information on Maya Angelou. The article also includes a photograph and a listing of "Works by Subject" and "Works about Subject."

Biographical Indexes

One way to locate biographical information, particularly retrospective biographical information, is to use an index devoted exclusively to biographical information. *Biographical indexes* are indirect sources of information; that is, they do not contain information about people; rather they provide references to sources that do. They index the biographical literature that appears in books, periodicals, newspapers and reference sources.

Biographical indexes may be general in coverage, or they may cover a particular subject. *Biography and Genealogy Master Index* covers persons of all professions, occupations, nationalities, and time periods. *Performing Arts Biography Master Index* provides references to articles about people who are outstanding in the theater arts. The coverage of some biographical indexes is limited to certain types of literature. *People in History* indexes only history journals and dissertations, while *Biography Index* is very broad in scope and indexes both periodicals and books.

Figures 11.4 and 11.5 show excerpts from *Biography and Genealogy Master Index (BAGMI)* in print and CD-ROM formats, respectively. *BAGMI* is also available by subscription on the Internet. It offers the advantage (as does the CD-ROM version) of being able to search all years at once. For example, a search in the online version of *BAGMI* for Claudia Goldin points to 24 references that provide information about Ms.

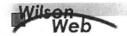

◆ Wilson BiographiesPlus Illus UPDATED AUG 7

Databases
SearchPlus
Search
Browse
History
Thesaurus
Help
Logout
QuickTour

Full Record

▶ Back ▶ Print ▶ Save ▶ Email

MORE INFORMATION
MORE IMAGES

Copyright
Copyright (c) by The H. W. Wilson Company. All rights reserved.

Article Heading
Angelou, Maya
Apr. 4, 1928-

Publication Statement
1985 Biography from WORLD AUTHORS 1975-1980

Pronunciation
(AN-jel-oh, MIE-yuh)

Full Text
ANGELOU, MAYA (April 4, 1928-), American memoirist and poet, was born Marguerite Ann Johnson in St. Louis, the daughter of Bailey Johnson, a doorman and later a naval hospital worker, and Vivian Baxter Johnson, a woman of extraordinary energy and resourcefulness. At the age of three, she and her four-year-old brother, Bailey, were sent by their parents, who had divorced, from Long Beach, California, to Stamps, Arkansas, to live with their paternal grandmother. Maya--her brother gave her the name--was brought up in this entirely segregated community (as well as for a short while in St. Louis), graduated from the Lafayette County Training School at the age of twelve, then moved with her brother back to San Francisco to live with their mother, who had remarried. She graduated from Mission High School at sixteen. Two months later, in the summer of 1944, she gave birth to a son, Guy--"the best thing that ever happened to me," she has said. "One would say of my life," she told an interviewer in 1972, "born loser, had to be; from a broken family, raped at eight, unwed mother at sixteen.... It's a fact but it's not the truth. In the black community, however bad it looks, there's a lot of love and so much humor."

She wrote eloquently of this childhood in her first volume of memoirs, I Know Why the Caged Bird Sings, a classic of American autobiography and an immediate critical and popular success. James Baldwin sensed after reading it "the beginning of a new era in the minds and hearts and lives of all Black men and women." The book, to him, "liberates the reader into life simply because Maya Angelou confronts her own life with such moving wonder, such a luminous

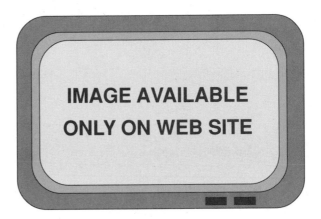

Figure 11.3 Results of an entry from Figure 11.2 showing *World Authors* as a biographical source for Maya Angelou. (From *World Authors 1975–1980.* Copyright © 1985 by The H.W. Wilson Company as appeared in Wilson Biographies online. Reprinted with permission.)

Figure 11.4

Figure 11.4   Entries from *Biography and Genealogy Master Index, 1996.* (Reprinted by permission of Gale Research, Inc.)

Goldin, Barbara Diamond 1946-
  Int Au&W93
Goldin, Claudia Dale 1946- WhoAm95,
  WhoAmW 95
Goldin, Daniel S 1940- AmMWSc95,
  BioIn18,-19,WhoAm95,WhoWor95

IntAu&W	=	International Authors and Writers Who's Who
WhoAm	=	Who's Who in America
WhoAmW	=	Who's Who of American Women
AmMWSc	=	American Men & Women of Science
WhoWor	=	Who's Who in the World

Figure 11.4   Entries from *Biography and Genealogy Master Index, 1996.* (Reprinted by permission of Gale Research, Inc.)

Goldin, Claudia Dale
1946-

American Economic Association, Directory of Members, 1974. Edited by
  Rendigs Fels. Published as Volume 64, Number 5 (October, 1974) of The
  American Economic Review.

American Men & Women of Science. A biographical directory of today's
  Leaders in physical, biological, and related sciences. 13th edition,
  Social & Behavioral Sciences. One volume. New York: R.R. Bowker Co.,
  1978.

Who's Who in America. 48th edition, 1994. New Providence, NJ: Marquis
  Who's Who, 1993.

Figure 11.5   Sample entry from *Biography and Genealogy Master Index (BAGMI)* CD-ROM. (Reprinted by permission of Gale Research, Inc.)

Goldin. With the print version it is necessary to determine which years to search and perhaps to search multiple volumes.

Most printed biographical indexes include citations to articles about individuals, including obituaries. Articles are listed alphabetically, with the individual's name as the subject. Figure 11.6 represents a sample page from *Biography Index* for Maya Angelou, and is typical of the format of this type of biographical index. Abbreviations and subheadings used in indexes are discussed in Chapter 8.

Biographical Dictionaries

Biographical dictionaries are works that contain limited information about people. They may be published either in a single volume or in multiple volumes. Some are monographs published only once, while

SEPTEMBER 2001–AUGUST 2002 17

Andre, Carl, 1935-, sculptor
Interviews
Huber, G. Carl Andre: Centre d'art contemporain. il *Art Press* no276 p70-1 Ja 2002

Andreades, Michael G., 1874-1959, Greek-American clergyman and missionary
Diaries
Farley, B. Russian orthodoxy in the Pacific Northwest. bibl f il *Pac Northwest Q* v92 no3 p127-36 Summ 2001

Andreas, G. Allen, food industry executive
Forster, J. A different kind of Andreas at ADM. il por *Bus Week* no3740 p62-4 Jl 9 2001

Andreessen, Marc, computer programmer and software executive
Lohr, S. An Internet pioneer of the 90's looks to a future in software. graph il por *N Y Times (Late N Y Ed)* p C1, C5 Je 17 2002
Juvenile literature
Tracy, Kathleen. Marc Andreessen and the development of the Web browser. Mitchell Lane Pubs. 2002 48p bibl il por

Andrei, Anda, architect
Reborn in the USA. por *O Oprah Mag* v3 no2 p140-3, 170-2 F 2002

Andreini, Isabella, 1562-1604, Italian actress and poet
Juvenile literature
Covington, Karen. Performers; actors, directors, dancers, musicians. (Remarkable women) Raintree Steck-Vaughn Pubs. 2000 p10 por

Andretti, John, 1963-, automobile racing driver
McGinn, D. Married to NASCAR. por *Newsweek* v138 no4 p46-8 Jl 23 2001

Andretti, Mario, automobile racing driver
Pund, D. My dinner with Mario. por *Car Driv* v46 no12 p34-5 Je 2001
The Scribner encyclopedia of American lives: Sports figures, v1 A-K; Arnold Markoe, volume editor; Kenneth T. Jackson, series editor in chief. Scribner 2002 p26-8 bibl por

Andretti, Nancy, wife of John Andretti
McGinn, D. Married to NASCAR. por *Newsweek* v138 no4 p46-8 Jl 23 2001

Andrew, David, Australian travel writer
Interviews
Bird man of Oz. por *Geographical* v73 no9 p98 S 2001

Andrew, E. Raymond (Edward Raymond), 1921-2001, physicist
Obituary
Phys Today por v55 no5 p78 My 2002

Andrew, Edward Raymond *See* Andrew, E. Raymond (Edward Raymond), 1921-2001

Andrew W.K., drummer and keyboardist
Heath, C. Andrew W.K. por *Roll Stone* no893 p102 Ap 11 2002
The next wave. il *Roll Stone* no889 p43-52 F 14 2002

Andrews, A. Michael, II, electrical engineer and army research official
Kumagai, J. On point for the military. por *IEEE Spectr* v39 no4 p65-7 Ap 2002

Andrews, David, religious brother
Interviews
Zyskowski, B. and O'Connell-Cahill, C. Lift your fork to help a farmer. por *U S Cathol* v67 no3 p20-3 Mr 2002

Andrews, Denzella Denise Burnside, d. 2001, art dealer and patron
Obituary
Art Nexus por no41 p38-9 Ag/O 2001

Andrews, Doug, clergyman
Health
Espinoza, G. Circle of life [J. Cross and L. Cheng, recipients of first domino liver transplant to be performed in U.S.] il por *People Wkly* v57 no1 p46-51 Ja 14 2002

Andrews, Jane, English royal assistant
Tauber, M. Breaking point. il por *People Wkly* v55 no22 p62-4 Je 4 2001

Andrews, Julie, English actress and singer
Mills, B. Julie Andrews: still supercalifragilisticexpialidocious. por tab *Biography (A&E)* v5 no7 p54-8 Jl 2001
Natale, R. Julie Andrews resonates in seventh showbiz decade. por *Variety* v384 no6 p60-2 S 24-30 2001
Who's that girl? il por *Am Girl* v9 no4 p43-4 Jl/Ag 2001
Criticism
Williams, Z. Shut your von Trapp. il por *New Statesman (Engl)* v131 p40-1 Ja 21 2002
Juvenile literature
Covington, Karen. Performers; actors, directors, dancers, musicians. (Remarkable women) Raintree Steck-Vaughn Pubs. 2000 p10 por

Andrews, Marion, French calligrapher
Interviews
Marchand, V.-M. Encounter with Marion Andrews: journey to the heart of the letter. il *Lett Art Rev* v16 no1 p2-5 2001

Andrews, Roger L., risk manager
Bradford, M. RIMS leaders renew push to boost ranks, profile. por *Bus Insur* v35 no16 p T6-T8 Ap 16 2001

Andrews, Stephen Pearl, 1812-1886, abolitionist and philosopher
Wilson, Peter Lamborn. Stephen Pearl Andrews. (In Antebellum writers in New York, second series. Gale Group 2002 p3-15) autog bibl facsim il por

Andrews, Tim, magazine publishing executive
Interviews
Gonser, S. The IndustryClick, Intertec integration [Intertec CEO] por *Folio* v30 no5 p37-8 Ap 2001

Andrews, Tina, actress and screenwriter
Jones, M. S. Tina Andrews. por *Black Issues Book Rev* v4 no3 p14-15 My/Je 2002

Andruzzi, Jimmy, firefighter
Layden, T. A Patriot's tale. il por *Sports Illus* v95 no12 p42-6 S 24 2001

Andruzzi, Joe, 1975-, football player
Layden, T. A Patriot's tale. il por *Sports Illus* v95 no12 p42-6 S 24 2001

Andsnes, Leif Ove, 1970-, Norwegian pianist
Criticism
Getting to the music's heart. por *Economist* v362 p80 F 16 2002

Anene, Mark, boxer
Clothing
Fussman, C. The pugilists. il *Esquire* v137 no2 p70-9 F 2002

Anfinsen, Christian Boehmer, 1916-1995, biochemist
Oakes, Elizabeth H. Encyclopedia of world scientists. Facts on File 2000 p12 bibl por

Angel, Albalucía, 1939-, Colombian novelist and poet
Notable twentieth-century Latin American women; a biographical dictionary; edited by Cynthia Margarita Tompkins and David William Foster. Greenwood Press 2000 p14-17 bibl por

Angeles, Dean, music teacher and conductor
Interviews
Baumer, M. A shortage of string teachers, too many performance majors. il por *Instrumentalist* v56 no1 p30-2, 86 Ag 2001

Angeletti, Roberta, 1964-, Italian illustrator
Something about the author, v124; facts and pictures about authors and illustrators of books for young people. Gale Group 2002 p9-10 bibl il por

Angell, David, d. 2001, television producer
Casualties of war [eulogies for cross section of business community lost in Sept. 11 attacks] il por *Fortune* v144 no6 p30-4 O 1 2001
Colucci, J. and others. Tribute 2001. il *TV Guide* v49 no52 p20-8, 43-4 D 29 2001-Ja 4 2002
Obituary
Advocate por p52-3 O 23 2001
N Y Times Biogr Serv v32 no9 p1507 S 2001
N Y Times (Late N Y Ed) p A25 S 14 2001
TV Guide por v49 no42 p40-3 O 20-26 2001

Angell, Roger, sportswriter
Interviews
DeCandido, G. A. Talking with Roger Angell. *Booklist* v98 no1 p36 S 1 2001

Angelo, Lillian, tap dancer
Morris, B. Dancing queen. por *Rosie* v129 no1 p54-5 N 2001

Angelos, Peter, advertising executive
Jensen, T. Angelos to D'Arcy as top creative. por *Adweek (East Ed)* v42 no23 p6 Je 4 2001

→ **Angelou, Maya, poet** ←
Angaza, M. Maya: a precious prism [cover story] il por *Black Issues Book Rev* v3 no2 p30-3 Mr/Ap 2001
Cawley, J. Celebration: American classics. por *Biography (A&E)* v5 no12 p49-89 D 2001
Pierce, P. Maya's song. por *Mod Maturity* v44r no5 p26-7 S/O 2001
Poet turned marketer. il por *Sales Mark Manage* v154 no4 p13 Ap 2002
Juvenile literature
Jones, Brenn. Learning about achievement from the life of Maya Angelou. PowerKids Press 2002 24p il
Shuker, Nancy. Maya Angelou; America's poetic voice. Blackbirch Press 2001 128p bibl

Angle, Colin, robotics industry executive
Goldman, L. Machine dreams [IRobot's C. Angle and H. Greiner] il por *Forbes* v169 no12 p149-50 My 27 2002

Angleton, Bob, bookmaker and accused murderer
Hollandsworth, S. The inmate. il por *Tex Mon* v29 no12 p42-53 D 2001

Figure 11.6 Selected reference from *Biography Index*. (Copyright © 1990 by the H.W. Wilson Company. Material reproduced by permission of the publisher.)

others are serial publications issued on a monthly, quarterly, annual, or biennial basis. The *Biographical Directory of the American Congress, 1774–1989*, is an example of a single volume monographic work; the *Dictionary of American Biography* is a monograph published in multiple volumes. *Who's Who in America* and *Current Biography* are serial publications issued biennially and monthly, respectively.

A short biography of Claudia Goldin, the author used as an example in Figures 11.4 and 11.5 was found in *Who's Who in America* (see Figure 11.7). This entry is typical of many of the "Who's Who" series of biographical dictionaries.

Some biographical dictionaries such as *Twentieth Century Authors* and *Current Biography* contain pictures of the subjects. The length of the entries in biographical dictionaries may vary. Entries in the *International Who's Who* consist of a few brief facts about the person; those in the *Dictionary of National Biography* are long, descriptive, signed articles with bibliographies. *Current Biography* usually provides a picture with a narrative of the individual being discussed. Monthly issues highlight prominent people in the news in a wide variety of occupations, including national and international affairs.

Retrospective biographical dictionaries such as *Webster's New Biographical Dictionary* include only persons who are no longer living; others such as *Contemporary Authors* contain information on persons of today. Some biographical dictionaries list both living and nonliving persons.

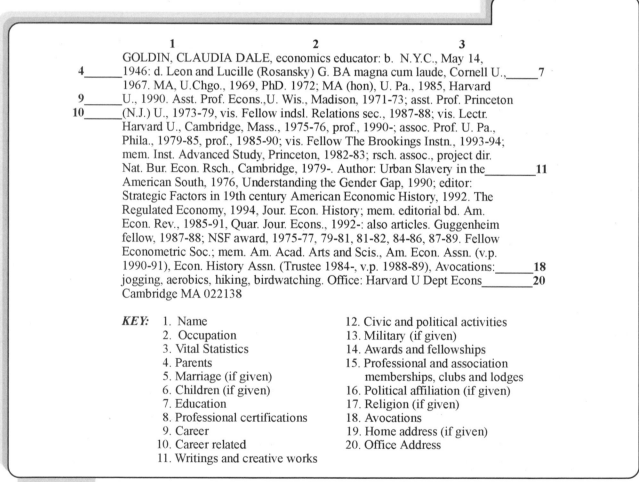

Figure 11.7 Entry from *Who's Who in America, 1996.* (Copyright © 1996, Marquis *Who's Who*, a Reed Reference Publishing Co., a division of Reed Elsevier Inc., *Who's Who in America*, 50th edition, 1996.)

Library Catalogs

The library catalog is another useful source for finding biographical works. Usually biographies about individuals are listed by the name of the individual with nothing following it. Use the individual's last name as the subject.

> **Example**
>
> SALK JONAS

Biographical dictionaries are listed under the heading:

BIOGRAPHY DICTIONARIES

Figure 11.8 illustrates a typical subject search for "women biography" in the Nebraska State College System's online catalog. Of the ten entries listed, there are several subheadings that would be useful:

—authorship

—bibliography

—dictionaries

—indexes

Bibliographies, dictionaries, and indexes are described in Chapter 7. Each of these provides different information that might be useful for a general overview of biographical sources on women.

Figure 11.9 illustrates the results found by selecting the "176 additional entries" from the list shown in Figure 11.8. It provides a list of titles on biographies of women.

Figure 11.10 gives the results of a subject search for information about Maya Angelou. Results include vertical file information, young adult literature, biographies, and videos as well as traditional books. Note that all three libraries in the Nebraska State College system have materials on this author.

Biographical information may be found in newspapers and in periodicals. Selected lists of sources for general and topical Internet sites, indexes, and dictionaries are provided at the end of this chapter.

EVALUATING BIOGRAPHICAL INFORMATION

Selecting the right source for biographical information is just as important as selecting any other type of research material. Use the criteria in Chapter 6 (Table 6.1 and Table 6.2) to evaluate any biographical material you find. Remember that some sources will be more suited to your needs than others. For example, if you need detailed information on an individual's life, the short biographies in *Who's Who* would not be suitable. It is a good practice to look at more than one biographical source to compare information.

SELECTED INTERNET SITES FOR BIOGRAPHICAL INFORMATION

Guides

Biography. The Michigan Electronic Library Reference Desk. University of Michigan. http://mel.lib.mi.us/reference/REF-biog.html

Ready Reference: Biography. Louisiana State University. http://www.lib.lsu.edu/ref/biography.html

Nebraska State College System

BRIEF DISPLAY | START OVER | ANOTHER SEARCH | LIMIT THIS SEARCH | SEARCH AS WORDS | (Univ of Nebr-Lincoln)
(Univ of Nebr-Omaha) (Univ of Nebr-Kearney) (Univ. of Nebr Med Ctr)

SUBJECT ⬍ | women biography | Search

Num	Mark	SUBJECTS (1-10 of 10)	Year
1	☐	**Women Biography**	
		The 100 most influential women of all time : a ranking past / **CSC 2d Floor Stacks:AVAILABLE** ; PRINTED MATL	c1996
		400 outstanding women of the world and costumology of their / **PSC Gen. Collection:AVAILABLE** ; PRINTED MATL	1933
		Abigail Adams / by Alexandra Wallner / **WSC Book Exam Ctr:AVAILABLE** ; PRINTED MATL	2001
		Agatha Christie : writer of mystery / Carol Dommermuth-Costa / **WSC ITC Juvenile:AVAILABLE** ; PRINTED MATL	c1997
	→	182 additional entries	
2	☐	**Women Biography Authorship**	
		Writing a woman's life / Carolyn G. Heilbrun / **WSC Stacks:AVAILABLE** ; PRINTED MATL	1989, c1988
3	☐	**Women Biography Bibliography**	
		Strong women : an annotated bibliography of literature for t / **CSC 2d Floor Stacks:AVAILABLE** ; PRINTED MATL	c1976
		Women's diaries, journals, and letters : an annotated biblio / **CSC 2d Floor Stacks:AVAILABLE** ; PRINTED MATL	1989
4	☐	**Women Biography Dictionaries**	
		A to Z of women in world history / Erika Kuhlman / **CSC Cat. Dept.:IN CATALOGING** ; PRINTED MATL	c2002
		The Continuum dictionary of women's biography / compiler and / **WSC Reference:LIB USE ONLY, PSC Reference:AVAILABLE** ; PRINTED MATL	1989
		The Norton book of women's lives / edited by Phyllis Rose / **WSC Stacks:AVAILABLE** ; PRINTED MATL	c1993
5	☐	**Women Biography History And Criticism**	
		Writing a woman's life / Carolyn G. Heilbrun / **WSC Stacks:AVAILABLE** ; PRINTED MATL	1989, c1988
6	☐	**Women Biography Indexes**	
		Index to women of the world from ancient to modern times : a / **CSC 2d Floor Stacks:AVAILABLE, WSC Reference:LIB USE ONLY** ; PRINTED MATL	1988
		Index to women of the world from ancient to modern times; bi / **CSC Ready Reference:LIB USE ONLY, WSC Reference:LIB USE ONLY, PSC Reference:AVAILABLE** ; PRINTED MATL	1970

Figure 11.8 Results of a subject search for "women biography" indicating relevant subheadings.

NEXT PAGE | **BRIEF DISPLAY** | **RETURN TO BROWSE** | **START OVER** | **ANOTHER SEARCH** | **LIMIT THIS SEARCH**

(Univ of Nebr-Lincoln) (Univ of Nebr-Omaha) (Univ of Nebr-Kearney) (Univ. of Nebr Med Ctr)

SUBJECT ⬍	women biography	Search

Num	Mark	SUBJECTS (1-12 of 186)	Year
		Women Biography	
1	☐	The 100 Most Influential Women Of All Time : A Ranking Past And Present / Deborah G. Felder	c1996
		CSC 2d Floor Stacks:AVAILABLE ; PRINTED MATL	
2	☐	400 Outstanding Women Of The World And Costumology Of Their Time, / compiled By Minna Moscherosch Schmidt ..	1933
		PSC Gen. Collection:AVAILABLE ; PRINTED MATL	
3	☐	Abigail Adams / by Alexandra Wallner	2001
		WSC Book Exam Ctr:AVAILABLE ; PRINTED MATL	
4	☐	Agatha Christie : Writer Of Mystery / Carol Dommermuth-Costa	c1997
		WSC ITC Juvenile:AVAILABLE ; PRINTED MATL	
5	☐	American Women In Civic Work / Helen Christine Bennett	1919, c1915
		CSC 2d Floor Stacks:AVAILABLE ; PRINTED MATL	
6	☐	American Women In Civic Work	1915
		WSC Stacks:AVAILABLE ; PRINTED MATL	
7	☐	America's Champion Swimmer : Gertrude Ederle / written By David A. Adler ; Illustrated By Terry Widener	c2000
		PSC Juv Nonfiction:AVAILABLE ; PRINTED MATL	
8	☐	America's Twelve Great Women Leaders During The Past Hundred Years As Chosen By The Women Of America	[c1933]
		WSC Stacks:AVAILABLE ; PRINTED MATL	
9	☐	Anne Frank : A Hidden Life / Mirjam Pressler ; Foreword By Rabbi Hugo Gryn ; Translated By Anthea Bell ; With A Note By Eva Schlo	2000
		WSC Book Exam Ctr:AVAILABLE ; PRINTED MATL	
10	☐	At Her Majesty's Request : An African Princess In Victorian England / by Walter Dean Myers	1999
		PSC Juv Nonfiction:AVAILABLE ; PRINTED MATL	
11	☐	At Her Majesty's Request : An African Princess In Victorian England / by Walter Dean Myers	1999
		WSC Book Exam Ctr:AVAILABLE ; PRINTED MATL	
12	☐	Athletes / Laurie Lindop	1996
		WSC ITC Juvenile:AVAILABLE ; PRINTED MATL	

Save Marked Records		JUMP TO AN ENTRY	186

NEXT PAGE | **BRIEF DISPLAY** | **RETURN TO BROWSE** | **START OVER** | **ANOTHER SEARCH** | **LIMIT THIS SEARCH**

Figure 11.9 Results of the additional entries found in Figure 11.8 indicating individual biographies about women.

Num	Mark	SUBJECTS (1-2 of 2)	Year
1		Angelou Maya	
		Angelou, Maya [Vertical File] / **PSC Vertical File:AVAILABLE** ; PRINTED MATL	
		I know why the caged bird sings / **CSC Biography:AVAILABLE, PSC Gen. Collection:AVAILABLE, WSC ITC Young Adult:AVAILABLE, WSC Stacks:AVAILABLE** ; PRINTED MATL	[1970, c1969]
		I know why the caged bird sings [Videorecording] / Tomorrow / **PSC Videotapes:AVAILABLE** ; VISUAL MAT.	c1986
		Maya Angelou [videorecording] : the writer/the person / prod / **WSC ITC Video:AVAILABLE** ; VISUAL MAT.	1981
		A song flung up to heaven / Maya Angelou / **CSC Biography:AVAILABLE** ; PRINTED MATL	c2002
2		Angelou Maya Biography	
		All God's children need traveling shoes / Maya Angelou / **WSC Stacks:AVAILABLE, PSC Gen. Collection:AVAILABLE** ; PRINTED MATL	c1986
		Gather together in my name / **WSC Stacks:AVAILABLE** ; PRINTED MATL	[1974]
		The heart of a woman / Maya Angelou / **WSC Stacks:AVAILABLE, PSC Gen. Collection:AVAILABLE** ; PRINTED MATL	c1981
		Singin' and swingin' and gettin' merry like Christmas / Maya / **WSC Stacks:AVAILABLE** ; PRINTED MATL	c1976

Figure 11.10 Displays the variety of formats for information retrieved on Maya Angelou.

General

Biographical Dictionary. http://www.s9.com/biography/

Biography.com. http://www.biography.com

Find a Grave. http://www.findagrave.com/

Lives. http://amillionlives.com/

Who's Alive and Who's Dead. http://www.neosoft.com/~davo/livedead/

Who's Who Online. http://whoswho-online.com/

World Biographical Index. http://www.saur-wbio.de/

Special Interests

AMG All-Music.Com Biographies. http://www.allmusic.com

Celebration of Women Writers. http://digital.library.upenn.edu/women

Faces of Science: African Americans in the Sciences. http://www.princeton.edu/~mcbrown/display/faces.html

Forbes List of the World's Richest People. http://www.forbes.com/. Select "Lists" then "Richest People"

Internet Movie Database (IMDb). http://imdb.com

Lists of US Presidents. http://www.fujisan.demon.co.uk/USPresidents/preslist.htm

Literary Menagerie. http://sunset.backbone.olemiss.edu/~egcash/

Nobel Prize Archive. http://www.nobelprizes.com/

Patron Saints Index. http://www.catholic-forum.com/saints/indexnt.htm

Political Graveyard. http://politicalgraveyard.com

Presidents of the United States. http://www.state.de.us/facts/ushist/intrpres.htm

Rock and Roll Hall of Fame and Museum. http://www.rockhall.com/

Uncle Sam: Who's Who in the Federal Government. http://www.lib.memphis.edu/gpo/whos3.htm

SELECTED PRINT SOURCES FOR BIOGRAPHICAL INFORMATION

(Some sources may also be available online.)

Indexes

General Biographical Indexes

Author Biographies Master Index. 2 vols. Gale Biographical Index Series No. 3. Detroit: Gale, 1984.
Useful source for references to biographical information on authors of all nationalities and all periods. Indexes biographical information in biographical dictionaries, encyclopedias, and directories. Includes information found in bibliographies and criticisms.

Biography and Genealogy Master Index. 2nd ed. 8 vols. Gale Biographical Index Series No.1. Detroit: Gale, 1980. *Annual Supplement*, 1981–. Also available on CD-ROM.
Name index to biographical dictionaries, subject encyclopedias, literary criticism, and other biographical indexes such as *Biography Index*. Provides names and dates of biography sources. Universal in scope.

Biography Index. New York: H.W. Wilson, 1947–.
Quarterly index to biographical information appearing in books and periodicals. Covers wide range of occupations. Arranged alphabetically, entries include birth and death dates (if available), occupation, and contributions to society. A separate index by occupations is located in the back of the book.

Historical Biographical Dictionaries Master Index. Gale Biographical Index Series No. 7. Detroit: Gale, 1980.
Alphabetically arranged index to information on prominent persons now deceased. Indexed sources include biographical dictionaries, encyclopedias, and other reference sources. Coverage is primarily American, but a few non-Americans are also included.

Marquis Who's Who Index to Who's Who Books. Wilmette, IL: Marquis, 1985–.
Annual index to the various Marquis *Who's Who* biographical dictionaries. Each volume lists names of individuals covered in the series during the prior year. If the person is listed in more than one dictionary, the references are given in chronological order. This index eliminates the need to go through all of the Marquis publications to find a particular reference.

Subject Biographical Indexes

Artist Biographies Master Index. Gale Biographical Index Series No. 9. Detroit: Gale, 1986.
   Provides references to biographical material on artists working in all aspects of art—fine arts, illustration, ceramics, craft, folk art, and architecture. Sources include biographical dictionaries, encyclopedias, directories, and indexes. Both historical and contemporary artists are included.

Business Biography Master Index. Gale Biographical Index Series No. 10. Detroit: Gale, 1987.
   Lists prominent persons in the field of business. Coverage is primarily contemporary, but includes a few historical figures. Sources include biographical dictionaries, encyclopedias, and directories. Predominately American in scope with a few international figures.

Journalist Biographical Master Index. Gale Biographical Index Series No. 4. Detroit: Gale, 1979.
   Indexes biographical information for people working in either the print or the broadcast media. Includes historical as well as contemporary journalists. Sources include biographical dictionaries and directories.

People in History: An Index to U.S. and Canadian Biographies in History Journals and Dissertations. 2 vols. Santa Barbara, CA: ABC-CLIO, 1988.
   Arranged alphabetically by name, each entry includes the author and title of the article, title of the source, and a brief abstract of the article. Volume 2 contains separate author and subject indexes.

People in World History: An Index to Biographies in History Journals and Dissertations Covering All Countries of the World Except Canada and the U.S. 2 vols. Santa Barbara, CA: ABC-CLIO, 1989.
   Each entry gives the author and title of the article, the title of the source, subject, and a brief abstract. Entries are arranged alphabetically by the subject of the article. Separate subject and author indexes in the second volume.

Performing Arts Biography Master Index. 2nd ed. Gale Biographical Index Series No. 5. Detroit: Gale, 1981.
   References to biographical information on persons working in the theater, films and television, or the concert stage. Sources indexed include biographical dictionaries, subject encyclopedias, and directories.

Twentieth-Century Authors Biographies Master Index. Gale Biographical Index Series No.8. Detroit: Gale, 1984.
   Similar to the *Author Biographies Master Index*, but includes only contemporary authors. International in scope. Indexes biographical dictionaries, encyclopedia articles, and periodicals.

Biographical Dictionaries

General Biographical Dictionaries

Current Biography. New York: H.W. Wilson, 1940–.
   Features people in the news: politicians, sports figures, entertainers, and scientists. The articles about the individuals are noncritical but comprehensive. Each article is accompanied by a photograph and a short bibliography. The annual cumulative volume includes a section of obituaries and a multiyear cumulative index.

International Who's Who. 1935–. London: Europa, 1935–.
   Contains information on people from all over the world. Articles are short and unsigned. Includes an obituary section listing those persons who have died since the preceding volume was published. Includes a list of the world's reigning royal families.

Who's Who: An Annual Biographical Dictionary. New York: St. Martin's, 1897–.
   Alphabetical listing of outstanding British subjects as well as some prominent international figures. Gives pertinent personal and professional data. Contains a list of obituaries and a list of the present royal family.

Who's Who in America. Chicago: Marquis, 1899–.
   Published biennially with a supplement issued on the off year. Lists notable Americans and some international figures. Arrangement is alphabetical with geographic, professional area, retiree, and necrology indexes. Entries are brief and noncritical.

Retrospective Biographical Dictionaries

American National Biography. Ed. John A. Garraty and Mark C. Carnes. 24 vols. New York: Oxford, 1999.
   Biographies of more than 17,400 men and women—from all eras and walks of life—whose lives have shaped the nation. An online version is also available.

Dictionary of American Biography. 20 vols. New York: Scribner, 1928–1936. *Supplements* 1–8, 1944–1988.
   Published under the auspices of the American Council of Learned Societies, this scholarly and comprehensive work provides biographical information about notable Americans no longer living. Long scholarly signed articles; extensive bibliographies. Includes noteworthy persons from the colonial period to 1970. Supplement 8 was published in two volumes and includes specialized indexes to all of the preceding volumes.

Dictionary of National Biography. 22 vols. London: Oxford, 1950. *Supplements* 2–8, 1912–1990.
   Originally published in 1895; reprinted at irregular intervals along with supplements. Premier source for historical biographical information on outstanding British subjects. Includes some non-British persons who are important in British history. Long, scholarly, signed articles with extensive bibliographies.

Merriam-Webster's Biographical Dictionary. Springfield, MA: Merriam, 1995.
   This edition contains biographical information on approximately 30,000 notable dead personages. Comprehensive coverage of non-English speaking world. Articles are short and include birth and death dates, notable accomplishments, and pronunciations of names.

Who Was Who, 1907–1980. 7 vols. New York: St. Martin's, 1929–1981.
   Companion volumes to *Who's Who;* contains reprints of articles about people listed in *Who's Who* who have died since the last compilation. Usually only the death date has been added but occasionally supplemental new material is included. Cumulative index to all seven volumes published in 1981.

Who Was Who in America. Historical Volume, 1607–1896. Chicago: Marquis, 1963.
   Short biographical sketches of both Americans and non-Americans who were influential in the history of the United States. Contains lists of the names of the early governors, the U.S. presidents and vice-presidents, Supreme Court Justices, and cabinet officers.

Who Was Who in America with World Notables, 1897–1989. Wilmette, IL: Marquis, 1942–1989.
   Compilation of the biographies of people no longer living that originally appeared in *Who's Who in America*. Death dates and, in some cases, other new information have been added. An index to all volumes of *Who Was Who in America 1607–1989* was published in 1989.

Subject Biographical Dictionaries

American Men and Women of Science. New York: Bowker, 1971–.
   Multivolume biographical dictionary listing people who are prominent in the physical and biological sciences. Articles are short and list personal data, accomplishments, and publications. Unsigned and noncritical.

Biographical Directory of the United States Congress, 1774–1989. Washington: GPO, 1989.
   Short biographical sketches of the members of Congress beginning with the Continental Congress and continuing through the 100th Congress. Some entries have bibliographies. Contains listings of the executive officers and cabinet members beginning with the administration of George Washington and going through that of Ronald Reagan. Available on the Internet with up-to-date listings at http://bioguide. congress.gov/biosearch/biosearch.asp.

Contemporary Authors. Detroit: Gale, 1962–.

Comprehensive source for biographical as well as bibliographical information on current writers of both fiction and nonfiction. Includes authors who are currently writing for newspapers, magazines, motion pictures, theater, and television. Separate annual cumulative index contains references to all previous volumes as well as other biographical sources published by Gale.

Directory of American Scholars. 10th ed. 5 vols. New York: Gale, 2001.

Contains profiles of over 24,000 American and Canadian scholars who are actively working in the humanities and the social sciences. Covers history, literature, philosophy, religion, linguistics, and foreign languages plus others. In addition to basic directory information, this new edition covers both mail and e-mail addresses for each entry. Cross references academic fields. Additional indexes include institution, discipline, and geographic information.

Twentieth Century Authors. New York: H.W. Wilson, 1941. *First Supplement*, 1955.

Universal in scope, but limited to authors working in this century. Provides photograph, list of works completed, and a bibliography of sources used to compile the article. Articles are unsigned. Alphabetically arranged by author's name.

World Authors, 1975–1980. New York: H.W. Wilson, 1985.

Continues *Twentieth Century Authors* with a similar arrangement and scope. Set includes three separately issued volumes covering the years 1950–1970, 1970–1975, and 1975–1980.

Instructor: _____ Course/Section: _____

Name: _____

Date: _____ Points: _____

Review Questions

1. Why are biographies important sources for research?

2. Name four possible steps (other than consulting the reference librarian) that you could take to find information about the lives of people.

   a.

   b.

   c.

   d.

3. What information about a person is useful in helping to select the appropriate biographical source?

4. Why is the Internet a good source for biographical information?

5. Name two biographical sources that are now free on the Internet.

6. What is the difference between a biographical index and a biographical dictionary?

7. What subject heading would be used to find a general biographical dictionary in the library catalog?

8. What subject heading would you use to find a biographical dictionary listing people in psychology?

9. How does a retrospective biographical dictionary such as the *Dictionary of American History* differ from a current one such as *Who's Who in America?*

10. What types of sources are indexed in *Biography Index?*

Exercise 11.2 Biographical Information

Instructor: _____ Course/Section: _____

Name: _____

Date: _____ Points: _____

Finding Biographies on the Internet

Locate biographical information on the Internet on two of the individuals listed below using either *Biography.com* at http://www.biography.com or *Biographical Dictionary* at http://www.s9.com/biography/.

Albert Einstein	Ann Landers	Michael Jackson
Pope John XXIII	John Lennon	Charles Schulz
John F. Kennedy	Princess Diana	Mother Teresa

1. Circle the names you selected.

2. Which Web site(s) did you use? (Give the URL.)

3. Describe the type and amount of information you found for each individual (e.g., short, detailed, references given).

Use the following sites for additional information on the same two individuals:

Who's Alive and Who's Dead http://whosaliveandwhosdead.com/
Lives http://amillionlives.com

4. Give the birth date and/or death date (if applicable) for each individual that you researched.

                                                      Birth date   Death date

   a.   Name of first individual:

   b.   Name of second individual:

5. Compare the information you found in this last group of Web sites with that found in the first group. Did you retrieve more information from this set or the first?

6. Which site was more useful? Why?

Exercise 11.3 Biographical Information

Instructor: _____ Course/Section: _____

Name: _____

Date: _____ Points: _____

Finding Biographies in Periodical Databases

Locate biographical information for one of the following individuals using either a CD-ROM or an online database such as *EBSCOhost, InfoTrac, WilsonSelect,* or *FirstSearch.*

Albert Camus	Bill Gates	Sean Connery
Bob Dole	Chuck Yeager	William (Bill) Clinton
Robert Kennedy	Whoopie Goldberg	Michael J. Fox

1. Circle the name you selected.

2. Which database(s) did you use to find information?

3. Write your search statement the exact way you typed it.

4. How many results did you find for this person?

5. Are any of the articles full text? If so, select one and print the first page, or give the title of the article here.

6. Does the list of results contain articles that are not full text?

7. Describe how you would locate a print copy of the articles in number 6 that are not full text in your library holdings.

8. Give the correct bibliographic citation for two entries you found on your individual (use the sample citations in Appendix A).

Exercise 11.4

Instructor: _____ Course/Section: _____

Name: _____

Date: _____ Points: _____

Using Biographical Indexes

Biographical indexes contain citations to articles about individuals who are outstanding or well-known for their accomplishments. Using one of the biographical indexes mentioned in this chapter or one you find in the library catalog, look up information on the life of an individual about whom you are interested or one assigned by your instructor.

Name of Person:

When you have found your reference, note the following information.

1. Title of the biographical index used:

2. Call number of the biographical index used:

3. Identify at least three publications in which you would find information about this individual. (Make sure you find the full title of the publication.)

4. Look in the library catalog to see whether your library has any of the sources you listed in Question 3. Write the call numbers you find for each of these.

5. Locate one of the articles you found. Copy the first page and return it to your instructor with this assignment or give the title of the article here.

6. Write the correct bibliographic citation for the article you found on this individual. (Use the bibliographic citation examples in Appendix A.)

Exercise 11.5 Biographical Information

Instructor: _____ Course/Section: _____

Name: _____

Date: _____ Points: _____

Using Biographical Dictionaries

Biographical dictionaries give information on the lives of individuals who are outstanding or well-known for their accomplishments. Use either the print edition of the *Biographical Directory of the American Congress, 1774–1989,* or the online version located at http://bioguide/congress.gov/biosearch.asp. Find a biography of Thomas Jefferson and give the following information.

1. What is the call number of the print edition or URL of the *Biographical Directory of the American Congress, 1774–1989?*

2. Was Thomas Jefferson the second president of the United States? If not, which one was he?

3. List three of his major achievements.

   a.

   b.

   c.

4. When did he die? Where is he buried?

5. Describe any civic involvements mentioned in the entry.

6. What educational level did he achieve?

7. From which school did he graduate?

Using a different biographical dictionary, look up information on the life of an individual in whom you are interested or one assigned by your instructor. Give the following information:

8. Name of person you selected:

9. Title of biographical dictionary used:

10. How did you find this biographical dictionary? (Library catalog, browse reference, ask for help?)

11. Call number or URL of the biographical dictionary used:

12. Identify the individual's:

   a. Place of birth:

   b. Date of birth, and death if not living:

   c. Occupation or profession:

13. Write a bibliographic entry for the article you have found. Use the examples in Appendix A.

14. Write a brief paragraph giving a few facts about the person's accomplishments.

Exercise 11.6

Instructor: _____ Course/Section: _____

Name: _____

Date: _____ Points: _____

Finding Biographies in the Online Catalog

Use your library's online catalog to find biographical information on one of the following individuals. Circle the name of the individual you look up.

Malcolm X	John Keats	Frank Lloyd Wright
Simon Bolivar	Genghis Khan	Benjamin Franklin
Ralph Bunche	Jawaharial Nehru	Cleopatra
Adolf Hitler	Carl Schurz	Joseph Stalin
Sitting Bull	Ho Chi Minh	

1. Locate at least one work **about** the individual you selected. Record the title and call number.

2. What command did you use to find the biography of this individual?

3. Retrieve one biography of the individual above. Write a bibliographic citation to the work that you locate. (Use the examples given in Appendix A.)

4. Briefly describe a few of the major accomplishments of that individual.

Book Reviews, Literary Criticism, and Literature in Collections

"What we become depends on what we read after all of the professors have finished with us.
The greatest university of all is a collection of books."

Thomas Carlyle

Introduction

Have you ever looked for a poem that you learned when you were a child but have not seen in print since? Or a short story that you read several years ago but can't recall where it appeared? Or a review of a current book? Or a critique of a novel? This chapter reviews a variety of sources that would help you find this type of information.

Just as you use indexes to find individual articles in magazines, journals, and newspapers, so also must you use special finding aids to find book reviews, individual poems, stories, essays, plays, speeches, and articles or essays that criticize or analyze an author's literary work. Becoming familiar with some key finding aids for these types of materials is extremely useful.

BOOK REVIEWS

Reviews of most new books and of forthcoming books are published in newspapers and magazines and on the Internet. Written by critics and journalists, book reviews provide descriptions and critical evaluations of books. The success or failure of a book's sale frequently depends on whether or not it receives positive reviews.

Guidelines
Finding book reviews

- ☐ Search the Internet.
- ☐ Use an index to book reviews.
- ☐ Search a periodical index or database.

Internet

An advantage of the Internet over printed sources for book reviews is that book reviews often appear online before they appear in print. Following are sites to help locate book reviews on the Internet.

ACQWEB's Directory of Book Reviews on the Web. ACQWEB. 1994–2000. 12 Feb. 2003 <http://www.library. vanderbilt.edu/law/acqs/bookrev.html>.
   Extensive list of sites for book reviews, arranged by categories.
Amazon.com. Amazon.com, c1996–2000. 12 Feb. 2003 <http://www.amazon.com/>.
   Often includes a table of contents, editorial reviews, and customer reviews of books available for sale.
BookReviews.net. n. d. 12 Feb. 2003 <http://www.bookreviews.net/>.
   Provides general links, children's books, newspaper book reviews, etc. Includes many links for librarians and others for book review sources online. Included are nonbook sites as well as subject links.
Book Spot. StartSpot Mediaworks. 1997–2000. 12 Feb. 2003 <http//www.bookspot.com/reviews/>.
   Links to book reviews for current titles in *Booklist*, the *New York Times*, and *New York Review of Books*, among others. Includes a list of top choices for the year.

Indexes to Book Reviews

Indexes to book reviews are good sources for reviews of books appearing in periodicals and newspapers. Some of these indexes have excerpts from the reviews, while others only list the sources.

To find book reviews in an index, you must have the publication date and either the author's name or title of the work. Three sources for book reviews are:

Book Review Digest. New York: H.W. Wilson, 1905–.
   An alphabetical listing by authors of books. Each entry includes the title of the book, bibliographical information, and publisher's note. The publisher's note is followed by references to the reviews that appear in periodicals. Some of the references include excerpts from the book reviews. Also includes a subject and title index. A list of periodicals indexed is located in the front. Issued monthly with annual cumulation.
Book Review Index, a Master Cumulation. Detroit: Gale, 1955–.
   Provides citations for book reviews and includes both author and title indexes. Includes list of abbreviated journal titles.

Combined Retrospective Index to Book Reviews in Humanities Journals, 1802–1974. Ed. Evan Ira Farber.
10 vols. Woodbridge, CT: Research Publications, 1983–1984.
An author and title access to about 500,000 reviews from 150 humanities journals. Names of reviewers are also given. Volume 10 has a title index.

Figure 12.1 illustrates a page from *Book Review Index* with citations to reviews of Claudia Goldin's work, *Understanding the Gender Gap.*

Note that a review of *Understanding the Gender Gap* is in *American Historical Review (AHR)* and *Journal of Literary History (JLH).* A list of abbreviations for the journals listed in the entries can be found at the beginning of *Book Review Index.*

The title entry for the book, *Understanding the Gender Gap,* is shown in Figure 12.2.

Sample pages from *Book Review Digest* are shown in Figures 12.3–12.5. Figure 12.3 illustrates how to use *Book Review Digest.* Figure 12.4 is a page from the subject/title index of *Book Review Digest* showing entries for the subject "women—employment." Note the citation to a review of the book, *Gender & Racial Inequality at Work* by D. Tomaskovic-Devey.

Once you identify the full title of the periodical in which a review appears you can search the library catalog to see if it is in your library. Use a title search for the title of the periodical. Check the holdings screen for the specific issues you need. These steps are discussed in Chapter 8.

Example

booklist
choice

Fire! The Beginnings of the Labor Movement (Illus. by James Watling)
c BL - v88 - My 1 '92 - p1600 [51-250]
c CCB-B - v45 - Ap '92 - p206 [51-250]
c HB - v68 - Jl '92 - p474 [51-250]
c KR - v60 - My 15 '92 - p677 [51-250]
c LT - v5 - S '92 - p23 [51-250]
c SLJ - v38 - Jl '92 - p73 [51-250]
Just Enough Is Plenty
c Inst - v101 - N '91 - p23

Goldin, Claudia - *Strategic Factors in Nineteenth Century American Economic History*
Choice - v30 - S '92 - p185 [51-250]
Understanding the Gender Gap
AHR - v96 - O '91 - p1271
JEL - v29 - S '91 - p1153
JIH - v22 - Win '92 - p477
JPE - v99 - D '91 - p1332
J Soc H - v25 - Win '91 - p430
Signs - v17 - Aut '91 - p220

Goldin, Grace - *Speak Out for Age*
Bloom Rev - v12 - Mr '92 - p23 [251-500]
Goldin, Ian - *Agricultural Trade Liberalization*
Econ Bks - v18 - Sum '91 - p91
Golding, Sue - *Gramsci's Democratic Theory*
UPBN - v4 - Je '92 - p25 [1-50]
Golding, William - *Lord of the Flies*
y BIC - v20 - O '91 - p26
y BL - v88 - F 15 '92 - p1100 [1-50]
GW - v145 - S 29 '91 - p25
The Paper Men
GW - v145 - S 29 '91 - p25
The Pyramid
GW - v145 - S 29 '91 - p25
Rites of Passage
GW - v145 - S 29 '91 - p25
The Spire
GW - v145 - S 29 '91 - p25
Goldman, Alan H - *Empirical Knowledge*
Phil R - v101 - Ap '92 - p428+ [501+]
Goldman, Albert - *Elvis*
Choice - v29 - Ap '92 - p1192+ [501+]
Ladies and Gentlemen–Lenny Bruce!!
Trib Bks - F 2 '92 - p8
The Lives of John Lennon
Choice - v29 - Ap '92 - p1192+ [501+]
Sound Bites
y BL - v88 - My 15 '92 - p1653 [51-250]
y BL - v88 - My 15 '92 - p1669 [1-50]
BW - v22 - Ag 9 '92 - p6 [251-500]
KR - v60 - Ap 15 '92 - p530 [51-250]
LJ - v117 - My 1 '92 - p83 [51-250]
PW - v239 - Ap 13 '92 - p51 [51-250]
Goldman, Alvin I - *Liaisons: Philosophy Meets the Cognitive and Social Sciences*
Choice - v29 - Jl '92 - p1693 [51-250]
Goldman, Ari L - *The Search for God at Harvard*
CC - v109 - Ja 1 '92 - p19
Ch Today - v35 - N 25 '91 - p35
Comt - v92 - O '91 - p54
NL - v74 - N 4 '91 - p23
NYTBR - v97 - Je 14 '92 - p32 [51-250]
PW - v239 - Ap 20 '92 - p51 [1-50]
TT - v48 - O '91 - p338
Goldman, Benjamin A - *The Truth about Where You Live*
r BL - v88 - F 1 '92 - p1058
r Choice - v29 - My '92 - p1427 [51-250]
r LJ - v117 - Ap 1 '92 - p110+ [51-250]
r New Age - v9 - My '92 - p102 [51-250]
Goldman, Bob - *Death in the Locker Room*
yr BL - v88 - Jl '92 - p1932 [51-250]
Goldman, Francisco - *The Long Night of White Chickens*
BL - v88 - My 15 '92 - p1660 [51-250]
Boston R - v17 - S '92 - p38 [501+]
BW - v22 - Je 7 '92 - p9 [501+]
CSM - v84 - Jl 24 '92 - p14 [501+]
Esq - v117 - Je '92 - p42 [51-250]
KR - v60 - Ap 15 '92 - p484 [51-250]
LATBR - Jl 19 '92 - p3+ [501+]
LJ - v117 - Je 1 '92 - p176 [51-250]
NYTBR - v97 - Ag 16 '92 - p20 [501+]
PW - v239 - Ap 13 '92 - p42+ [51-250]
VV - v37 - Jl 21 '92 - p90+ [501+]

KR - v60 - Ja 15 '92 - p91
LJ - v117 - F 15 '92 - p169
NYTBR - v97 - Jl 12 '92 - p18 [51-250]
Obs - Ag 30 '92 - p51 [51-250]
PW - v239 - F 3 '92 - p74
W&I - v7 - S '92 - p419+ [501+]
Goldman, Judith - *The Early Pictures 1861-1964 (Illus. by James Rosenquist)*
LJ - v117 - Ag '92 - p98 [51-250]
Goldman, Lawrence - *The Blind Victorian*
AHR - v96 - D '91 - p1651
VS - v35 - Aut '91 - p90
Goldman, Marshall I - *What Went Wrong with Perestroika*
BL - v88 - O 15 '91 - p404
BW - v21 - N 10 '91 - p12
Choice - v29 - Mr '92 - p1152 [51-250]
CSM - v83 - N 8 '91 - p14
Econ - v322 - Mr 21 '92 - p97 [501+]
LJ - v116 - O 15 '91 - p102
NYRB - v38 - N 7 '91 - p53
NYTBR - v97 - F 2 '92 - p15
Goldman, Martin E - *The Handbook of Heart Drugs*
BL - v88 - Ag '92 - p1985 [51-250]
r LJ - v117 - Jl '92 - p76 [51-250]
Goldman, Martin S - *Nat Turner and the Southhampton Revolt of 1831*
y B Rpt - v11 - S '92 - p58 [51-250]
y KR - v60 - Ap 1 '92 - p465 [51-250]
y SLJ - v38 - Je '92 - p145 [51-250]
y VOYA - v15 - Je '92 - p123+ [501+]
Goldman, Nahum - *Online Information Hunting*
r BWatch - v13 - My '92 - p3+ [1-50]
Goldman, Nathan C - *Space Policy*
SciTech - v16 - Ag '92 - p35 [1-50]
Goldman, Ralph M - *From Warfare to Party Politics*
Pers PS - v21 - Spr '92 - p124 [501+]
The National Party Chairmen and Committees
APSR - v86 - Mr '92 - p237+ [501+]
Goldman, Robert - *Mapping Hegemony*
Choice - v29 - Jl '92 - p1671 [51-250]
Goldman, Robert M - *A Free Ballot and a Fair Count*
JSH - v58 - Ag '92 - p552+ [251-500]
Goldman, Roger - *Thurgood Marshall: Justice for All*
LATBR - Ag 9 '92 - p1+ [501+]
LJ - v117 - Jl '92 - p104 [51-250]
PW - v239 - Je 1 '92 - p47+ [51-250]
Goldman, Steve - *Vibration Spectrum Analysis*
New TB - v76 - N '91 - p1571 [51-250]
Goldman, Steven L - *Science, Technology, and Social Progress*
Isis - v83 - Mr '92 - p168+ [501+]
Goldman, William - *Hype and Glory*
Books - v5 - N '91 - p21+ [51-250]
Obs - O 20 '91 - p61
Goldmann, Nahum - *Online Information Hunting*
SciTech - v16 - Je '92 - p4 [1-50]
Goldoni, Luca - *Maria Luiga Donna in Carriera*
BL - v88 - My 15 '92 - p1667 [1-50]
Goldratt, Eliyahu M - *The Goal: A Process of Ongoing Improvement*
Mgt R - v81 - Ja '92 - p63 [51-250]
Goldreich, Gloria - *Years of Dreams*
BL - v88 - Ap 15 '92 - p1502 [51-250]
KR - v60 - F 1 '92 - p131
PW - v239 - F 3 '92 - p62
Goldring, Roland - *Fossils in the Field*
r New Sci - v134 - My 9 '92 - p40+ [501+]
SciTech - v15 - S '91 - p19 [1-50]
Goldsborough, Robert - *The Crain Adventure*
R&R Bk N - v7 - O '92 - p37 [1-50]
Fade to Black
Arm Det - v25 - Spr '92 - p251 [51-250]
y Kliatt - v26 - Ap '92 - p6 [51-250]
Fade to Black. Audio Version
Arm Det - v24 - Fall '91 - p500
y Kliatt - v26 - Ap '92 - p58 [51-250]
Silver Spire
KR - v60 - Ag 15 '92 - p1019 [51-250]
PW - v239 - Ag 31 '92 - p67 [51-250]

CS - v21 - Jl '92 - p444+ [501+]
CS - v21 - Jl '92 - p445+ [501+]
JMF - v54 - My '92 - p464+ [501+]
Wom R Bks - v9 - D '91 - p16
Goldschmidt, Arthur, Jr. - *A Concise History of the Middle East. 4th ed., Rev. and Updated*
MEJ - v46 - Win '92 - p122
R&R Bk N - v6 - D '91 - p5 [1-50]
Goldschmidt, Bertrand - *Atomic Rivals*
T&C - v33 - Ja '92 - p177+ [501+]
Goldschmidt, Georges-Arthur - *Die Absonderung*
TLS - Mr 6 '92 - p22 [251-500]
WLT - v66 - Spr '92 - p331 [251-500]
Goldschmidt, Walter - *The Human Career*
A Anth - v93 - D '91 - p977
Goldsmith, Alix - *Celebritest: Intimate Profiles of Seventy Celebrities*
FIR - v43 - Mr '92 - p130+ [51-250]
Goldsmith, Andrea - *Modern Interiors*
Aust Bk R - S '91 - p15
Goldsmith, Arnold L - *The Modern American Urban Novel*
MFS - v37 - Win '91 - p760 [251-500]
Goldsmith, Arthur A - *Building Agricultural Institutions*
Pac A - v65 - Spr '92 - p116+ [501+]
Goldsmith, Barrie - *Monitoring for Conservation and Ecology*
Choice - v29 - N '91 - p468
ECOL - v73 - Je '92 - p1134+ [501+]
New TB - v76 - S '91 - p1290+ [51-250]
QRB - v67 - Je '92 - p228 [251-500]
Goldsmith, Colin - *Extensions of Calculus*
TES - O 11 '91 - p44
Goldsmith, Deward - *The Earth Report*
HMR - S '90 - p9
Goldsmith, Donald - *The Astronomers*
y B Rpt - v10 - N '91 - p51
y WLB - v65 - Je '91 - p162
Goldsmith, Edward - *The Way: An Ecological World View*
TLS - S 11 '92 - p5 [501+]
Goldsmith, Elizabeth C - *Writing the Female Voice*
Can Lit - Aut '91 - p156+ [501+]
Goldsmith, Emanuel S - *The American Judaism of Mordecai M. Kaplan*
Choice - v29 - D '91 - p652
Goldsmith, John A - *Autosegmental and Metrical Phonology*
MLJ - v76 - Sum '92 - p259 [501+]
Goldsmith, Lynn - *Circus Dreams*
Ant & CH - v96 - N '91 - p45
Goldsmith, Olivia - *The First Wives Club*
BL - v88 - Mr 15 '92 - p1335+ [51-250]
BW - v22 - Mr 1 '92 - p12 [1-50]
KR - v59 - D 15 '91 - p1549
LJ - v117 - Ja '92 - p174
NYTBR - v97 - My 10 '92 - p17 [251-500]
PW - v239 - Ja 6 '92 - p48
Trib Bks - Mr 22 '92 - p6 [51-250]
The First Wives Club. Audio Version
LJ - v117 - My 1 '92 - p132 [51-250]
PW - v239 - My 4 '92 - p26 [51-250]
Goldsmith, Timothy H - *The Biological Roots of Human Nature*
Choice - v29 - Je '92 - p1568 [51-250]
Goldstaub, Sylvia - *Unconditional Love*
Advocate - Je 16 '92 - p117 [51-250]
Lam Bk Rpt - v3 - My '92 - p46 [1-50]
Goldsteen, Raymond L - *Demanding Democracy after Three Mile Island*
AJS - v98 - Jl '92 - p197+ [501+]
Choice - v29 - Ap '92 - p1290 [51-250]
CS - v21 - Jl '92 - p487 [251-500]
Goldstein, Allan L - *Combination Therapies*
SciTech - v16 - Je '92 - p17 [51-250]
Goldstein, Avery - *From Bandwagon to Balance-of-Power Politics*
Choice - v29 - N '91 - p515
Goldstein, Bobbye S - *What's on the Menu? (Illus. by Chris L Demerest)*
c BL - v88 - Ap 15 '92 - p1534 [51-250]
c SLJ - v38 - Jl '92 - p68 [51-250]
Goldstein, Darra - *A Taste of Russia*

Figure 12.1 Entries from *Book Review Index*. (Reprinted by permission of Gale Research, Inc.)

Understanding the Fourth Gospel - Ashton,
John
Understanding the Gender Gap - Golding,
Claudia

Figure 12.2 Title Index, *Book Review Index*, 1992, p. 1470. (Reprinted by permission of Gale Research, Inc.)

Periodical Indexes and Databases

Periodical indexes and databases, discussed in Chapter 8, can be useful in finding book reviews. To find reviews of books on certain topics, you might search a database by using the search phrase "[subject] and book review." If you know the author of the book you might search for "[author] and book review." A search in *EBSCOhost* for "book review and literature" lists book reviews in a variety of publications on topics dealing with literature. You can also search by the title of the book.

Other databases useful for finding book reviews include:

Arts & Humanities Citation Index (Web of Knowledge). Philadelphia: ISI, 1989–.
  Updated weekly. Contains data on items from more than 1,144 journals, including individually selected relevant items from more than 6,800 science and social sciences journals. Searches can be limited to book reviews as a document type. Available by subscription only.
Humanities Abstracts. New York: H.W. Wilson, 1984–. Available from *WilsonWeb*, *FirstSearch*, *Ovid*, and others.
  Updated monthly. Indexes more than 300 key humanities publications, including reviews of books, plays, ballets, musicals, and television and radio programs.
Readers' Guide Abstracts. New York: H.W. Wilson, 1984–. Available from *WilsonWeb*, *FirstSearch*, *Ovid*, and others.
  Comprehensive abstracting and indexing for periodicals with full text of selected periodicals back to January 1994. Includes book reviews as well as reviews of movies and plays.

LITERARY CRITICISM

Works of literary criticism contain articles or essays that evaluate, judge, describe, analyze, or compare an author's novel, poem, play, short story, or other literary work.

Defining Terms

Definitions are sometimes needed for particular literary terms, such as "allusion," "satire," etc. Below are three useful sources for this type of information.

Murfin, Ross C. *The Bedford Glossary of Critical and Literary Terms*. New York: St. Martin's Press, 2003.
Cuddon, J. A. *A Dictionary of Literary Terms and Literary Theory*. New York: Blackwell, 1998.
Harmon, William, and Hugh C. Holman. *A Handbook to Literature*. New York: Simon & Schuster, 1999.

Sample Entry

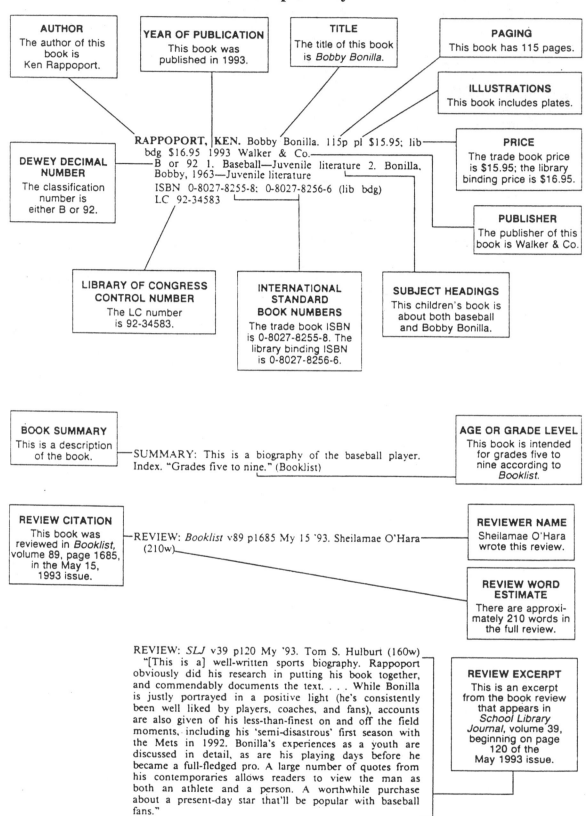

AUTHOR
The author of this book is Ken Rappoport.

YEAR OF PUBLICATION
This book was published in 1993.

TITLE
The title of this book is *Bobby Bonilla*.

PAGING
This book has 115 pages.

ILLUSTRATIONS
This book includes plates.

DEWEY DECIMAL NUMBER
The classification number is either B or 92.

PRICE
The trade book price is $15.95; the library binding price is $16.95.

PUBLISHER
The publisher of this book is Walker & Co.

RAPPOPORT, KEN. Bobby Bonilla. 115p pl $15.95; lib bdg $16.95 1993 Walker & Co.
B or 92 1. Baseball—Juvenile literature 2. Bonilla, Bobby, 1963—Juvenile literature
ISBN 0-8027-8255-8; 0-8027-8256-6 (lib bdg)
LC 92-34583

LIBRARY OF CONGRESS CONTROL NUMBER
The LC number is 92-34583.

INTERNATIONAL STANDARD BOOK NUMBERS
The trade book ISBN is 0-8027-8255-8. The library binding ISBN is 0-8027-8256-6.

SUBJECT HEADINGS
This children's book is about both baseball and Bobby Bonilla.

BOOK SUMMARY
This is a description of the book.

SUMMARY: This is a biography of the baseball player. Index. "Grades five to nine." (Booklist)

AGE OR GRADE LEVEL
This book is intended for grades five to nine according to *Booklist*.

REVIEW CITATION
This book was reviewed in *Booklist*, volume 89, page 1685, in the May 15, 1993 issue.

REVIEW: *Booklist* v89 p1685 My 15 '93. Sheilamae O'Hara (210w)

REVIEWER NAME
Sheilamae O'Hara wrote this review.

REVIEW WORD ESTIMATE
There are approximately 210 words in the full review.

REVIEW: *SLJ* v39 p120 My '93. Tom S. Hulburt (160w)
"[This is a] well-written sports biography. Rappoport obviously did his research in putting his book together, and commendably documents the text. . . . While Bonilla is justly portrayed in a positive light (he's consistently been well liked by players, coaches, and fans), accounts are also given of his less-than-finest on and off the field moments, including his 'semi-disastrous' first season with the Mets in 1992. Bonilla's experiences as a youth are discussed in detail, as are his playing days before he became a full-fledged pro. A large number of quotes from his contemporaries allows readers to view the man as both an athlete and a person. A worthwhile purchase about a present-day star that'll be popular with baseball fans."

REVIEW EXCERPT
This is an excerpt from the book review that appears in *School Library Journal*, volume 39, beginning on page 120 of the May 1993 issue.

Figure 12.3 Sample entry from *Book Review Digest*. (Copyright 1994 by the H.W. Wilson Company. Reprinted by permission.)

The wine-dark sea. O'Brian, P.
Winged victory. Perret, G.
Wingfield, George, 1876-1959
Raymond, C. E. George Wingfield
The wings of a falcon. Voigt, C.
Wings of hope and daring. Stenberg, E.
Winik, Marion
Winik, M. Telling
Winn-Dixie Stores, Inc.
Staten, V. Can you trust a tomato in January?
The winner within. Riley, P.
Winnicott, D. W. (Donald Woods), 1896-1971
Phillips, A. On kissing, tickling, and being bored
Winnicott, Donald Woods See Winnicott, D. W. (Donald Woods), 1896-1971
Winning the grand award. Iritz, M. H.
Winning ugly. Gilbert, B.
Winslow, Marcella Comès
Winslow, M. C. Brushes with the literary
Winter
      Juvenile literature
Honda, T. Wild horse winter
Maass, R. When winter comes
Winter camp. Hill, K.
Winter fox. Brutschy, J.
The Winter Prince. Wein, E. E.
Winter sports
      See also
   Sleds and sledding
Winter's orphans. Farentinos, R. C.
Wipe your feet!. Lehan, D.
Wiretapping
      See also
   Eavesdropping
Wisconsin
      History
Apps, J. W. Breweries of Wisconsin
      Politics and government
Woliver, L. R. From outrage to action
      Rural conditions
Pederson, J. M. Between memory and reality
Wise, Isaac Mayer, 1819-1900
Temkin, S. D. Isaac Mayer Wise, shaping American Judaism
The wish for kings. Lapham, L. H.
Wishbones. Wilson, B. K.
Wit and humor
      See also
   American wit and humor
   Comedy
   Jokes
   Tall tales
Grizzard, L. I took a lickin' and kept on tickin'
James, S. The adventures of Stout Mama
White, B. Mama makes up her mind
      Juvenile literature
Talbott, H. Your pet dinosaur, an owner's manual
Witchcraft
Gragg, L. D. The Salem witch crisis
Hester, M. Lewd women and wicked witches
The witches and the singing mice. Nimmo, J.
The witch's face. Kimmel, E. A.
Witch's fire. Butler, B.
With a Black platoon in combat. Rishell, L.
With liberty and justice for some. Kairys, D.
With teeth in the earth. Tussman, M. H.
With women's eyes
Within reach
Without consent or contract
Without remorse. Clancy, T.
Without sin. Klaw, S.
Witness against the beast. Thompson, E. P.
Witness for freedom
Witness to disintegration. Hixson, W. L.
A witness to genocide. Gutman, R.
Wives
      See also
   Abused women
   Widows
The wives of Bath. Swan, S. E.
The wizard next door. Glassman, P.
A wizard's dozen
Woiwode, Larry
Woiwode, L. Acts
Wojnarowicz, David, 1954-1992
Wojnarowicz, D. Memories that smell like gasoline
Wole Soyinka revisited. Wright, D.
Wolf, Hugo, 1860-1903
Youens, S. Hugo Wolf

Wolf, Lucien, 1857-1930
Levene, M. War, Jews, and the new Europe
The wolf. Bradshaw, J.
The wolf & the raven. Paxson, D. L.
Wolf at the door. Corcoran, B.
Wolf children See Wild children
Wolf whistle. Nordan, L.
Wolfe, Michael, 1945-
Wolfe, M. The hadj
Wolfpack (Basketball team) See North Carolina State Wolfpack (Basketball team)
Wollstonecraft, Mary, 1759-1797
      Fiction
Sherwood, F. Vindication
Wolves
      Juvenile literature
Bradshaw, J. The wolf
Brandenburg, J. To the top of the world
Greene, C. Reading about the gray wolf
Patent, D. H. Dogs
Simon, S. Wolves
Wolves. Simon, S.
Woman at the edge of two worlds. Andrews, L. V.
A woman at war. Moore, M.
Woman changing woman. Rutter, V. B.
A woman doctor's guide to menopause. Jovanovic-Peterson, L.
The woman reader, 1837-1914. Flint, K.
A woman unafraid. Colman, P.
A woman's book of choices. Chalker, R.
The woman's heart book. Pashkow, F. J.
A woman's view. Basinger, J.
A woman's worth. Williamson, M.

Women ──────────────── SUBJECT HEADING
      See also
   Abused women
   Black women   ⎫── CROSS
   Jewish women   ⎬   REFERENCES
   Social work with women ⎭
   White women
Heidensohn, F. Women in control?
      Bibliography ──────── SUBDIVISION
Bindocci, C. G. Women and technology
      Biography
Boyer, R. M. Apache mothers and daughters ── AUTHOR AND TITLE OF BOOK
Notable Hispanic American women
Shepherd, N. A price below rubies
      Dictionaries
Mahoney, M. H. Women in espionage
The Norton book of women's lives
      Books and reading
Flint, K. The woman reader, 1837-1914
Turner, C. Living by the pen
      Civil rights
      See also
   Pro-choice movement
   Pro-life movement
Alonso, H. H. Peace as a women's issue
Costain, A. N. Inviting women's rebellion
Daniels, C. R. At women's expense
Ferraro, G. A. Changing history
      Dictionaries
Franck, I. M. The women's desk reference
      Diaries
Clarke, P. Life lines
      Diseases
      See also
   Women—Health and hygiene
Confronting cancer, constructing change
Helfant, R. H. Women, take heart
Lockie, A. The women's guide to homeopathy
McGinn, K. A. Women's cancers
Pashkow, F. J. The woman's heart book
      Education
Powers, J. B. The "girl question" in education
Unsettling relations
      Employment
Agonito, R. No more "nice girl"
Amott, T. L. Caught in the crisis
Cook, A. H. The most difficult revolution
Driscoll, D.-M. Members of the club
Glazer, N. Y. Women's paid and unpaid labor
Murphy, T. A. Ten hours' labor
Sokoloff, N. J. Black women and white women in the professions
Strom, S. H. Beyond the typewriter
Tomaskovic-Devey, D. Gender & racial inequality at work
Turbin, C. Working women of collar city

Figure 12.4 Subject and Title Index from *Book Review Digest, 1994*, p. 2545. (Copyright 1994 by the H.W. Wilson Company. Reprinted by permission.)

TOLKIN, MICHAEL—*Continued*
mall. In addition, Tolkin has no sense of humour at all. .
. . [The novel] is consistently, stultifyingly dull, despite its
graphic descriptions of trolleys of unmatched limbs, barrels
of human viscera in the air-crash morgue. [It] might make
a good film. As a novel, however, it is still-born."

TOLLEFSON, JAMES W. The strength not to fight; an
oral history of conscientious objectors of the Vietnam
War. 248p $22.95 1993 Little, Brown
    959.704   1. Vietnam War, 1961-1975—
Conscientious objectors
    ISBN 0-316-85112-4   LC 92-36335

SUMMARY: The author examines the "experiences of cor
scientious objectors (CO) during the Vietnam War. The pei
sonal histories resulting from the author's interviews . .
discuss why people resisted the war, how they were able t
gain CO status, and what were the consequences of their ac
tions." (Libr J) Bibliography.

REVIEW: *Choice* v31 p664 D '93. R.E. Marcello (180w)
"Tollefson, himself a conscientious objector during th
Vietnam War, has written this book based on in-depth ir
terviews with 40 anonymous men who shared his convic
tions about that conflict. He does not pretend to have use
a scientific sampling in selecting his subjects. Tollefson use
a clever format. Instead of writing a series of separate, ind
vidual stories, he organized the book around the major ex
periences of the conscientious objectors. His purpose
through these highly personal and sometimes emotional ac
counts, is to understand and convey accurately the exper
ences of his interviewees. . . . He makes no judgment:
neither praising nor apologizing for nor condemning his ir
terviewees. Good bibliography of secondary sources on cor
scientious objection."

REVIEW: *Libr J* v118 p154 Je 1 '93. Robert Favini (110w
"[Tollefson] lets the collective power of many varied stc
ries provide a chronicle of the men who sought CO statu
as well as the society in which they lived. This book wi
serve as a fine complement to Christian Appy's oral history
Working-Class War: American Combat Soldiers and Viet
nam [BRD 1993]. The extensive bibliography renders th
book even more valuable. Recommended for all libraries.

TOLLISON, ROBERT D. The National Collegiate Athleti
Association. See Fleisher, A. A.

TOM, LINDA C., il. Random House American Sig
Language dictionary. See Costello, E.

TOMASKO, ROBERT M. Rethinking the corporation; th
architecture of change. 213p il $22.95 1993 AMACOM
    658.4   1. Corporations 2. Management 3. Organiza
tional change
    ISBN 0-8144-5022-9   LC 93-9246

SUMMARY: This book argues against "the unstructured reduction of managerial staff. . . . Downsizing for the purpose
of saving funds without significant planning and consideration of human needs and aspirations, Tomasko asserts, can
lead to long-term problems. Jobs within the enterprise need
to be meaningful to the workers—especially to one of the
corporation's most valuable resources, the middle manager.
Tomasko stresses the necessity for teamwork in planning, a
diminution of hierarchy, and the use of professional as well
as managerial career paths." (Libr J) Index.

REVIEW: *Bus Horiz* v37 p87 My/Je '94. Henry H. Beam
(1200w)

REVIEW: *Choice* v31 p644 D '93. G. Klinefelter (170w)
"Tomasko focuses on two groups of readers; those in the
organization who have the power and responsibility to
bring about change and those who are on the receiving end
of change. A renowned consultant in organizational structure and architectural structure, he approaches the subject
of organizational planning from the perspective of an archi-

tect, covering such topics as construction of stable structures, dealing with constraints, and effectively combining
several components into a unified entity. . . . An interesting
and creative approach to an important topic for managers
as they guide their organizations into the 21st century."

REVIEW: *Libr J* v118 p148 Je 1 '93. Littleton M. Maxwell
(150w)
"Tomasko (Downsizing: Reshaping the Corporation,
1990) . . . recommends a corporate structure that is strong
and economical, but, above all, not too rigid. This thought-
provoking book is recommended for public, academic, and
corporate collections."

TOMASKOVIC-DEVEY, DONALD. Gender & racial in
equality at work; the sources & consequences of job segre
gation. (Cornell studies in industrial and labor relation:
no27) 212p $38; pa $16.95 1993 ILR Press
    331.13   1. Discrimination in employment 2. Sex dis
crimination 3. Race discrimination 4. Women—
Employment 5. Blacks—Employment
    ISBN 0-87546-304-5; 0-87546-305-3 (pa)
    LC 93-16551

SUMMARY: This study is based on data from the 198'
North Carolina Employment and Health Survey. The au
thor examines black-white and male-female inequalities i:
employment and job-level segregation by race and sex
"Within economic and sociological frameworks, he theo
rizes about such organizational and public policy issues a
comparable worth and affirmative action." (Booklist) Bibli
ography. Index.

REVIEW: *Booklist* v89 p2019 Ag '93. David Rouse (150w
"Librarians need no reminder that one sex or the other i
usually predominant in many jobs or professions. But i
they are looking for empirical, scholarly evidence of botl
some of the sources and many of the consequences of so
called job segregation, Tomaskovic-Devey provides it. /
North Carolina State University sociology professor, he use
a 1989 North Carolina employment and health survey
unique because it included a random sample of all occupa
tions from the general population, to develop and suppor
his conclusions. . . . Recommended for research-oriente(
collections."

REVIEW: *Choice* v31 p877 Ja '94. E. Hu-DeHart (180w)
"Tomaskovic-Devey's study is a valuable contribution t<
what can be termed 'glass ceiling research'—that is, an in
quiry into job segregation and subsequent barriers to up
ward mobility for groups of workers (as opposed t<
individuals) in the workplace. . . . [His] conclusions abou
race, however, are based on research concerning blacl
workers only. Further, Tomaskovic-Devey does not thor
oughly explore the intersection of gender and race. . . . De
spite the obviously relevant and timely nature of this topi
for the majority of American workers (women and minori
ties), those uninitiated in the technical discourse of socia
science research will not find this book very accessible."

CITATION TO BOOK BEING REVIEWED

PUBLISHER'S SUMMARY

CITATION TO REVIEW

EXCERPT FROM REVIEW

TOMASSI, NOREEN, ed. Money for international
exchange in the arts. See Money for international exchange in the arts

TOMB, HOWARD, 1959-. MicroAliens; dazzling journeys
with an electron microscope; [by] Howard Tomb and
Dennis Kunkel; with drawings by Tracy Dockray. 79p il
$16 1993 Farrar, Straus & Giroux
    578   1. Microorganisms—Juvenile literature 2. Elec-
tron microscope and microscopy—Juvenile literature
    ISBN 0-374-34960-6   LC 93-1403

SUMMARY: In this book, text and photographs taken with
an electron microscope examine such items as bird feathers,
fleas, skin, mold, and blood. "Grades four to eight." (SLJ)

Figure 12.5   Main entry section, *Book Review Digest, 1994*, p. 2074. (Copyright 1994 by the H.W. Wilson Company. Reprinted by permission.)

Another excellent guide is found on the Internet Public Library site, located at http://www.ipl.org/ Under "Searching Tools," select "Pathfinders," then "Literary Criticism." The explanations provide an overview of literary criticism, a discussion of terms and concepts, and general and specific finding aids.

Finding Literary Criticism

Since many of the finding aids for literary criticism are arranged by time periods, by type of literature, or other criteria, you must consider the following questions.

Ask yourself

- ☐ Is the author living or dead?
- ☐ Where and when did the author live?
- ☐ What genre of literature is he/she known for: short stories, drama, poetry, novels, plays?
- ☐ What is the primary language of his/her writings?

To find literary criticism, you can search the Internet, use a database, search the online catalog, find a biography of the author that includes criticism, or use an index to literary criticism.

Internet

Under "Special Collections" on the Internet Public Library home page, located at http://www.ipl.org/ you'll find an "Online Literary Criticism Collection" after clicking on the link "Special Collections." The guide provides links to both literary criticism and summaries of many works.

EXAMPLE

A general search for "Maya Angelou criticism" (with the quotation marks) brings up 63 hits. The same search, without the quotation marks, results in 7 hits that are organized in "folders" such as: Maya Angelou—criticism, biographical sites, other sites. Figure 12.6 displays the categories found in the general search.

Literary Index, produced by Gale Publishing Company, is a free online index to forty of Gale's printed sources. It can be found at http://www.galenet.com/servlet/LitIndex. The entries include location information only; no textual information is available. However, it is a quick and easy way to locate biographies of authors and critical essays on their writings found in the Gale literary series.

Figures 12.7–12.11 reflect the results of a search for Maya Angelou in Gale's *Literature Resource Center*. Each figure represents different types of information available for this author.

the Internet Public Library

Online Literary Criticism Collection

Maya Angelou (1928 -)

Nationality: American

Periods:
American: 20th Century

author of *I Know Why the Cage Bird Sings*

<u>Critical Sites</u> | <u>Biographical Sites</u> | <u>Other Sites</u>

Also See:
Sites about these
individual works by
Maya Angelou

<u>Collected Poems of
Maya Angelou</u>

<u>I Know Why the Caged
Bird Sings</u>

Criticism about Maya Angelou

<u>Maya Angelou: A Bibliography of Literary Criticism</u>
http://www.geocities.com/ResearchTriangle/1221/Angelou.htm A list of critical articles on
Maya Angelou and her works. **Contains:** Bibliography **Author:** Jay Brandes

<u>Maya Angelou : Annotated Bibliography</u>
http://falcon.jmu.edu/~ramseyil/angeloubib.htm "A bibliography of book and nonbook media by
and about Angelou including autobiography, poetry, essays, juvenile works and literary
criticism." **Contains:** Bibliography, Works List **Author:** Inez Ramsey, Professor Emeritus
From: *Internet School Library Media Center*

Biographical sites about Maya Angelou

<u>An Interview with Maya Angelou</u>
http://www.newsun.com/angelou.html Transcript of Frost's PBS interview with Angelou. Topics range from her life, to her
poetry and personal philsophies. **Contains:** Interview **Author:** David Frost

<u>Maya Angelou</u>
http://www.poets.org/poets/poets.cfm?prmID=88 Provides a brief biographical sketch of the poet, and the full text of
several poems. **Contains:** Sketch, Pictures, Bibliography, Webliography **Author:** Academy of American Poets

<u>Visions: Maya Angelou</u>
http://www.motherjones.com/mother_jones/MJ95/kelley.html Write-up of a 1995 interview with Angelou. Topics include
President Clinton, artists fights against conservatives, spirituality, and literacy. **Contains:** Interview **Author:** Ken Kelley
Keywords: Bill Clinton, art, politics, religion

<u>Voices from the Gaps: Maya Angelou</u>
http://voices.cla.umn.edu/authors/MayaAngelou.html Site contains a biography, a selected bibliography with critical
summaries of the works, general commentary on her life and works, and some web links. **Contains:** Extensive Bio, Pictures,
Commentary, Bibliography, Webliography, Criticism **Author:** Sharon Burt **Keywords:** Women writers of color, "I Know Why
the Caged Bird Sings"

Figure 12.6 Results of a keyword search for "Maya Angelou criticism" at the IPL site. (From
www.ipl.org. Copyright © 2003 by Internet Public Library. Reprinted by permission.)

Literature
Resource Center

| Home | | | | | | | | | |

mava angelou   Search   Clear Form

Current Results

Your search, Maya Angelou, returned results in the following categories:

News
Click Here for Recent Update on this Author.

| Biographies | Literary Criticism, Articles, & Work Overviews | Bibliographies | Additional Resources | Literary-Historical Timeline |

Maya Angelou
(1928-)

Variant(s): Marguerite Johnson; Marguerita Annie Johnson; Marguerite (Annie) Johnson; Marguerite Annie Johnson; Marguerita Johnson
Nationality: American
Genre(s): Autobiographies; Novels; Plays; Poetry; Essays; Film scripts
Literary Movement/Time Period: American postmodern literature

Page: 1

Below are items 1-6 of 6 found.

Update Marked List

☞ Add to Mark List

☐

Angelou, Maya (1928-)
"Maya Angelou." *Writers for Young Adults* . 3 vols. Ted Hipple, editor. Charles Scribner's Sons, 1997.

☐ Angelou, Maya
"Maya Angelou," in *Contemporary Authors.* (A profile of the author's life and works)

☐ Angelou, Maya
"Maya Angelou," in *Contemporary Literary Criticism-Select* . (A brief review of the author's life, works, and critical reception)

Angelou, Maya
"Maya Angelou," in *Dictionary of Literary Biography, Volume 38: Afro-American Writers After 1955: Dramatists and Prose Writers* . A Bruccoli Clark Layman Book. Edited by Thadious M. Davis, University of North Carolina at Chapel Hill and Trudier Harris, University of North Carolina at Chapel Hill. The Gale Group, 1985, pp. 3-12.

Figure 12.7 Biographies found for Maya Angelou in the *LRC* database, Nebraska State College System. (Copyright © 2003 by Nebraska State College Systems. Reprinted by permission.)
From *Galenet: Literary Resource Center* by Gale Group. Reprinted by permission of The Gale Group.

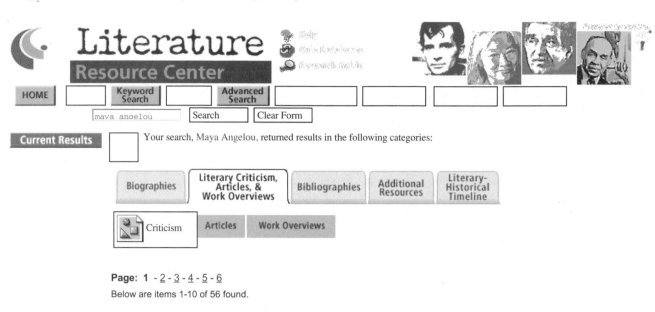

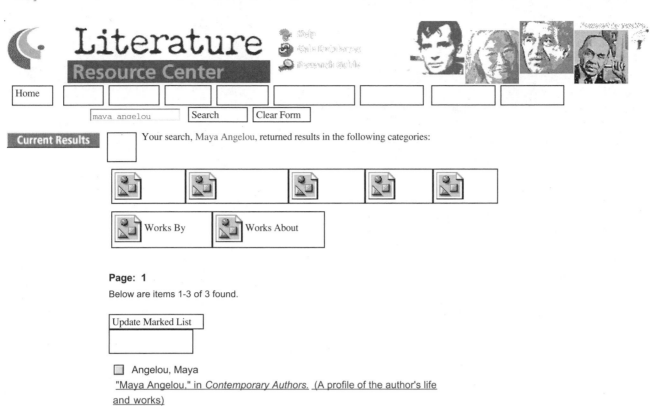

Figure 12.9 Bibliographies found on Maya Angelou from *LRC*. (Copyright © 2003 by Nebraska State College Systems. Reprinted by permission.)

From *Galenet: Literary Resource Center* by Gale Group. Reprinted by permission of The Gale Group.

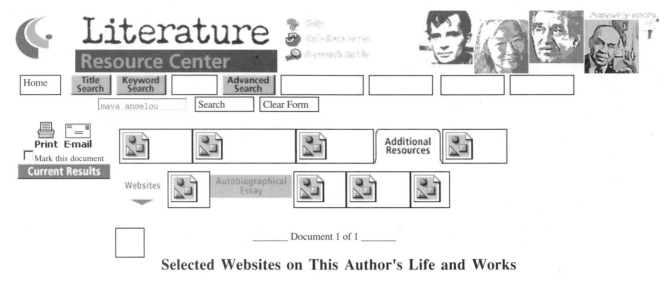

Selected Websites on This Author's Life and Works

Select any of the websites below to explore Internet resources on this author's life and works

Maya Angelou: A look into her life, her poetry
http://www.spydersempire.com/webdoc3.htm

Maya Angelou Criticism
http://www.geocities.com/ResearchTriangle/1221/Angelou.htm

Voices from the Gaps, Women Writers of Color: Maya Angelou
http://voices.cla.umn.edu/authors/MayaAngelou.html

The Academy of American Poets Poetry Exhibits: Maya Angelou
http://www.poets.org/poets/poets.cfm?prmID=88

Wired for Books: Audio Interview with Maya Angelou
http://wiredforbooks.org/mayaangelou/

NOTE: Each website included in the Literature Resource Center was reviewed and selected by a team of Internet researchers using specific editorial criteria. Chief among these criteria is the presence of substantive biographical, bibliographical, and critical information about the author; hyperlinks from the website to related authors and/or literary topics; and the update frequency of the website. To return to GaleNet after viewing the website, use the BACK button on your browser.

Gale is not responsible for the content of the websites selected for the Literature Resource Center. Further, Gale is not responsible for the conduct of website providers who offer electronic texts that infringe on the legal rights of copyright holders.

Source Database: Literature Resource Center

Home | Help | Search Tips | Research Guide | Gale Databases | Contact Gale | Comments

Copyright © 2003 Gale Group. All rights reserved.

Figure 12.10 Selected websites found on Maya Angelou from *LRC*. (Copyright © 2003 by Nebraska State College Systems. Reprinted by permission.)

From *Galenet: Literary Resource Center* by Gale Group. Reprinted by permission of The Gale Group.

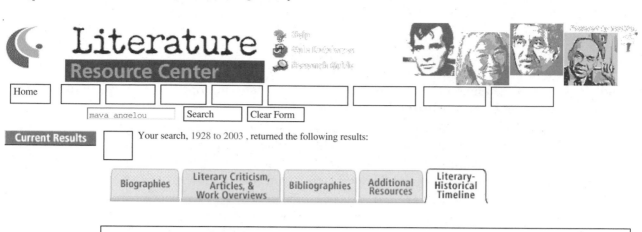

Literature
Resource Center

| Home | | | | | | | | |

mava anaelou   Search   Clear Form

Current Results   Your search, 1928 to 2003 , returned the following results:

Biographies | Literary Criticism, Articles, & Work Overviews | Bibliographies | Additional Resources | Literary-Historical Timeline

Classical Antiquity | Middle Ages | 1500-1659 | 1660-1797 | 1798-1834 | 1835-1881 | 1882-1903 | 1904-1918 | 1919-1929 | 1930-1950 | 1951-1965 | 1966-present

Maya Angelou's lifespan, 1928-

Start date: 1928   A.D. ⬍   End date: 2003   A.D. ⬍   **Search**

Page: 1 - 2 - 3 - 4 - 5 - 6 - 7 - 8 - 9 - 10 - 11 ▶

Below are items 1-10 of 3481 found.

c.1880-c.1960 Existentialism flourishes as a literary and philosophical movement in Europe

1885-1940 The Irish Literary Renaissance flourishes

1898-c.1940 The Generación del 98 flourishes in Spain

c.1900-c.1940 Symbolism flourishes in the world of British and American letters

1909-1944 Italian Futurism flourishes as a literary and artistic movement

c.1910-c.1933 Expressionism flourishes as a literary form in Germany, France, Britain, and elsewhere

c.1913-c.1939 Modernism flourishes as an English, Irish, and American literary movement

1919-1929 The Jazz Age flourishes in the United States

1920-1933 The Eighteenth Amendment is enacted, oulawing the manufacture, sale, and consumption of alcoholic beverages in the U.S; the Prohibition Era sees the rise of organized crime, as opportunistic gangsters manufacture and sell spirits to a willing public

1922-1936 Roger Martin du Gard publishes his eight-part novel *Les Thibault*

Page: 1 - 2 - 3 - 4 - 5 - 6 - 7 - 8 - 9 - 10 - 11 ▶

Home | Help | Search Tips | Research Guide | Gale Databases | Contact Gale | Comments

Figure 12.11   An interesting feature of *LRC* is the timeline, spanning the life of the author. (Copyright © 2003 by Nebraska State College Systems. Reprinted by permission.)

From *Galenet: Literary Resource Center* by Gale Group. Reprinted by permission of The Gale Group.

Other Internet sources will be identified with the finding aids discussed below.

Databases

Contemporary Authors. Gale Group, continuous updating. Web access.

Covers more than 100,000 modern authors from a wide range of media who were active prior to 1960 and whose works continue to influence contemporary literature. Information is drawn from the entire *Contemporary Authors* print series. Available by subscription only.

Literature Resource Center. Gale Group, continuous updating. Web access.

Provides access to the full text of biographies, bibliographies, and critical analysis of authors from every age and literary discipline. It combines three of Gale's most used literary sources—*Contemporary Authors Online*, including more than 100,000 writers; *Contemporary Literary Criticism Select*, with entries on all authors appearing in *CLC* since vol. 95 of the print series and complete profiles of 266 most studied authors from editions prior to vol. 95; and the *Dictionary of Literary Biography Online*, which includes more than 10,000 critical essays on authors and their works written by academic scholars. It is searchable by author, title, genre, literary movement or literary themes. Available by subscription only.

WilsonWeb New York: H.W. Wilson, dates vary. Web access.

Library Catalog

Commentaries, criticisms, interpretations, and explanatory information about all kinds of literature can be found through the online catalog. Use the author of the original work and selected subheadings of the work. Figure 12.12 shows the results of a keyword, or in the Nebraska State College System, a "Word" search for Maya Angelou. The 27 results provide a range of essays, biographical, and visual materials held at the three libraries. A listing of works written by the author can be found under an author search, as shown in Figure 12.13.

Nebraska State College System

ANGELOU is in 34 titles.
MAYA is in 130 titles.
Both "ANGELOU" and "MAYA" are in 27 titles.
There are 27 entries with ANGELOU & MAYA.

NEXT PAGE	BRIEF DISPLAY	START OVER	ANOTHER SEARCH	LIMIT THIS SEARCH

(Univ of Nebr-Lincoln) (Univ of Nebr-Omaha) (Univ of Nebr-Kearney) (Univ. of Nebr Med Ctr)

WORD ⬍   angelou maya   [Search]

Num	Mark	Words (1-12 of 27)	Year
1	☐	The African-American century : how Black Americans have shap	
		WSC Stacks:AVAILABLE ; PRINTED MATL	c2000
2	☐	American writers; a collection of literary biographies. Leon	
		WSC Reference:LIB USE ONLY ; PRINTED MATL	1974-
3	☐	Angelou, Maya [Vertical File]	
		PSC Vertical File:AVAILABLE ; PRINTED MATL	
4	☐	Black American women poets and dramatists [electronic resour	
		EBOOKS	c1996
5	☐	Challenges in reading / Nancy D. Padak, Timothy V. Rasinski,	
		CSC 2d Floor Stacks:AVAILABLE ; PRINTED MATL	1990
6	☐	The complete collected poems of Maya Angelou	
		CSC 2d Floor Stacks:AVAILABLE ; PRINTED MATL	c1994
7	☐	Great American writers : twentieth century / R. Baird Shuman	
		CSC 2d Floor Stacks:AVAILABLE ; PRINTED MATL	2002
8	☐	Maya Angelou [videorecording] : the writer/the person / prod	
		WSC ITC Video:AVAILABLE ; VISUAL MAT.	1981
9	☐	Maya Angelou, rainbow in the clouds [videorecording] / WTVS	
		WSC ITC Video:AVAILABLE ; VISUAL MAT.	c1992
10	☐	Nature's ban : women's incest literature / [compiled by] Kar	
		PSC Gen. Collection:AVAILABLE ; PRINTED MATL	c1996
11	☐	The Norton book of women's lives / edited by Phyllis Rose	
		WSC Stacks:AVAILABLE ; PRINTED MATL	c1993
12	☐	PORTRAIT OF MAYA ANGELOU	
		PRINTED MATL	

[Save Marked Records]   [JUMP TO AN ENTRY] [27]

NEXT PAGE	BRIEF DISPLAY	START OVER	ANOTHER SEARCH	LIMIT THIS SEARCH

(Univ of Nebr-Lincoln) (Univ of Nebr-Omaha) (Univ of Nebr-Kearney) (Univ. of Nebr Med Ctr)

Figure 12.12 Keyword search results for Maya Angelou. (Copyright © 2003 by Nebraska State College Systems. Reprinted by permission.)

| NEXT PAGE | BRIEF DISPLAY | START OVER | ANOTHER SEARCH | LIMIT THIS SEARCH |

(Univ of Nebr-Lincoln) (Univ of Nebr-Omaha) (Univ of Nebr-Kearney) (Univ. of Nebr Med Ctr)

| AUTHOR ◆ | | |

Num	Mark	AUTHORS (1-12 of 19)	Year
Angelou Maya			
1		All God's Children Need Traveling Shoes / Maya Angelou	c1986
		WSC Stacks:AVAILABLE, PSC Gen. Collection:AVAILABLE ; PRINTED MATL	
2		And Still I Rise / Maya Angelon	c1978
		WSC ITC Young Adult:AVAILABLE ; PRINTED MATL	
3		The Complete Collected Poems Of Maya Angelou	c1994
		CSC 2d Floor Stacks:AVAILABLE ; PRINTED MATL	
4		Down In The Delta / [Videorecording]	[1999?]
		WSC ITC Video:AVAILABLE ; VISUAL MAT.	
5		Gather Together In My Name	[1974]
		WSC Stacks:AVAILABLE ; PRINTED MATL	
6		The Heart Of A Woman / Maya Angelou	c1981
		WSC Stacks:AVAILABLE, PSC Gen. Collection:AVAILABLE ; PRINTED MATL	
7		I Know Why The Caged Bird Sings	[1970, c1969]
		CSC Biography:AVAILABLE, PSC Gen. Collection:AVAILABLE, WSC ITC Young Adult:AVAILABLE, WSC Stacks:AVAILABLE ; PRINTED MATL	
8		I Know Why The Caged Bird Sings [Videorecording]	c1986
		PSC Videotapes:AVAILABLE ; VISUAL MAT.	
9		I Shall Not Be Moved / Maya Angelou	1991
		PSC Gen. Collection:AVAILABLE ; PRINTED MATL	
10		Kindred Spirits Contemporary African-American Artists / [Videorecording] : Produced By KERA-TV And North Texas Public Broadcasting ; Clayton Corrie, Produce	c1992
		PSC Videotapes:AVAILABLE ; VISUAL MAT.	
11		Maya Angelou, Rainbow In The Clouds / [Videorecording] / WTVS Detroit ; Produced And Directed By Bill Jersey	c1992
		WSC ITC Video:AVAILABLE ; VISUAL MAT.	
12		Oh Pray My Wings Are Gonna Fit Me Well / Maya Angelou	[1975]
		CSC 2d Floor Stacks:AVAILABLE, PSC Gen. Collection:AVAILABLE ; PRINTED MATL	

| JUMP TO AN ENTRY | 19 |

| NEXT PAGE | BRIEF DISPLAY | START OVER | ANOTHER SEARCH | LIMIT THIS SEARCH |

Figure 12.13 Results of an author search showing the total titles by Maya Angelou at the three college libraries. (Copyright © 2003 by Nebraska State College Systems. Reprinted by permission.)

350   *Chapter Twelve*

Author Biographies

Biographies of authors frequently provide analyses and criticisms of their works. In addition to the biographical sources discussed in Chapter 11, biographies of authors can also be found on the Internet.

Author Guides: Webliography. LSU Libraries. 1995–2000. 24 Apr. 2000 <http://www.lib.lsu.edu/hum/auth-main.html>.
  Typical of university libraries' web pages for author information. Includes links to author and publication information.

Contemporary Authors: A Bio-bibliographical Guide to Current Writers in Fiction, General Nonfiction, Poetry, Journalism, Drama, Motion Pictures, Television and Other Fields. Detroit: Gale, 1963–.
  Print version that includes articles and references to other sources for criticism.

Dictionary of Literary Biography. Gale Group, continuous updating. Web access.
  Updated periodically. Outlines the lives and careers of authors from all eras and genres and summarizes the critical response to their work. Each entry contains personal information, a list of principal works and further readings about the author. Available by subscription only.

Online Literary Criticism Collection. Internet Public Library. 28 Apr. 2000 <http://www.ipl.org/ref/litcrit/>.
  A selected list of over 3,000 Web sites providing biographies and criticisms. Can be browsed by author, title, or by nationality of authors.

Yahoo! Authors. Yahoo. 2000. 24 Apr. 2000 <http://dir.yahoo.com/Arts/Humanities/Literature/Authors/>.
  Access to selected author biographies and criticisms of their works.

Indexes to Literary Criticism

Some of the following guides are limited to literature of a specific nationality, while others are international in their coverage. Both the titles and the annotations indicate in some measure the scope of the guide.

General

Contemporary Literary Criticism. Detroit: Gale, 1973–.
  Covers living writers and those who died after 1960, includes excerpts and citations from mystery and science fiction authors. Provides extensive annotated bibliographies.

Essay and General Literature Index. New York: H.W. Wilson, 1900/1933–.
  An excellent source for criticism of all types of literature.

Magill, Frank Northern. *Magill's Bibliography of Literary Criticism; Selected Sources for the Study of More than 2,500 Outstanding Works of Western Literature.* 4 vols. Englewood Cliffs, NJ: Salem, 1979.
  Criticisms in books, parts of books, and periodicals of poetry, drama, and fiction.

Modern Language Association International Bibliography. 1921–. CD-ROM version called *MLA* (database). Also available on the Internet.
  Coverage for the online version began with 1981 and is updated quarterly. Includes criticism of many literary works.

Nineteenth-Century Literary Criticism. Detroit: Gale, 1981–.
  Similar to *CLC* and *TCLC*, except it is limited to writers who lived between 1800 and 1900.

Twentieth-Century Literary Criticism. Detroit: Gale, 1978–.
  Similar to *CLC* and *NCLC* above, except it covers authors who died between 1900 and 1960.

Novels

Abernethy, Peter L., Christian J.W. Kloesel, and Jeffry R. Smitten. *English Novel Explication. Supplement. Supplement VII 1998–2000*. Hamden, CT: Shoe String, 2002.
> This work supplements and updates the Palmer and Dyson guide. Extends *English Novel Explication series* to 1998.

Gerstenberger, Donna, and George Hendrick. *The American Novel, a Checklist of Twentieth Century Criticism on Novels Written Since 1789*. 2 vols. Denver: Allan Swallow, 1961–1970. Vol. 1, *The American Novel 1789–1959*. Vol. 2, *Criticisms Written 1960–1968*.
> Criticisms are listed under major authors by titles of works. Includes citations from books and periodicals.

Kearney, E.I., and L.S. Fitzgerald. *The Continental Novel, a Checklist of Criticism in English 1967–1980*. Metuchen, NJ: Scarecrow, 1988.
> Critical entries are organized under the following categories: the French novel, the Spanish and Portuguese novel, the Italian novel, the German novel, the Scandinavian novel, and the Russian and East European novel.

Palmer, Helen H., and Anne Jane Dyson. *English Novel Explication: Criticisms to 1972*. Hamden, CT: Shoe String, 1973.
> Cites criticisms found in books and periodicals in English and foreign languages from 1958 to 1972.

Plays (Drama)

Breed, Paul F., and Florence M. Snideman. *Dramatic Criticism Index: A Bibliography of Commentaries on Playwrights from Ibsen to the Avante-Garde*. Detroit: Gale, 1972.
> Includes critical articles from over 200 periodicals and 630 books. Main entries under authors. Includes a title and a critic index.

Eddleman, Floyd Eugene. *American Drama Criticism: Interpretations, 1890–1977*. 2nd ed. Hamden, CT: Shoe String, 1979. *Supplement I*, 1984. *Supplement II*, 1989. *Supplement III* 1992. *Supplement IV* 1996.

Palmer, Helen H. *European Drama Criticism 1900–1975*. 2nd ed. Hamden, CT: Shoe String, 1977.
> A source book to critical writings of representative European plays in selected books and periodicals. Information is organized in three parts: (1) alphabetical list of playwrights with critical articles that appear in periodicals and books, (2) a list of books used as sources and a list of periodicals searched, and (3) an author-title index.

Palmer, Helen H., and Anne Jane Dyson. *American Drama Criticism Interpretations, 1890–1965, Inclusive of American Drama since the First Play Produced in America*. Hamden, CT: Shoe String, 1967. *Supplement I*, 1970. *Supplement II*, 1976. *Supplement III*, 1990. *Supplement IV* 1996.
> Lists critical articles of American plays located in periodicals, books, and monographs. Arrangement is alphabetical by playwright.

Poetry

Alexander, Harriet Semmes, comp. *American and British Poetry: A Guide to the Criticism*. 1979–1990 Athens, OH: Swallow Press/Ohio University Press, 1995.
> Indexes criticisms located in 170 journals and 500 books published between 1925 and 1990. Volume 1 covers the years 1925–1978; volume 2 covers 1979–1990.

Cline, Gloria Stark, and Jeffrey A. Baker. *An Index to Criticisms of British and American Poetry*. Metuchen, NJ: Scarecrow, 1973.
> Cites critical articles on poetry published in periodicals and books between 1960 and 1970. List of abbreviations of periodicals used in entries and a bibliography of books cited are found in the back of this work.

Gray, Richard. *American Poetry 20th Century*. New York: Longman Publishing Group, 1990.

Shields, Ellen F. *Contemporary English Poetry: An Annotated Bibliography of Criticism to 1980*. New York: Garland, 1984.

Short Stories

Aycock, Wendell M. *Twentieth Century Short Story Explication: 1997–98*. Hamden, CT: Shoe String Press, 2002.

Short Story Criticism. Detroit: Gale. 1988–. Annual.
  Criticisms are listed in chronological order. Cumulative author and title indexes are included.

Walker, Warren S. *Twentieth-Century Short Story Explication: Interpretations 1900–1975 of Short Fiction since 1800*. 3rd ed. Hamden, CT: Shoe String, 1977. Supplements, 1961–1991.
  Analysis of short stories appearing in books, periodicals, and monographs.

LITERATURE IN COLLECTIONS (ANTHOLOGIES)

The term *anthology* refers to any collection of varied literary compositions. Anthologies can also include works from a period of history or works devoted to a particular subject or theme. Most anthologies include works of varied authorship, but it is not uncommon to have representative works of one author selected by an editor and collected in an anthology. The outstanding characteristic of an anthology is that it includes many different titles of shorter works under one title.

Finding Works Included in Anthologies

Library catalogs usually list the titles of anthologies that the library owns, but they do not include titles of the shorter works in the anthologies. For example, the title, *Ten Modern Masters: An Anthology of the Short Story*, would be listed in the catalog, but the short story, "I'm a Fool," which is included in the anthology, probably would not be listed. The Internet is an excellent source to locate materials that might be included in anthologies—short stories, poems, plays, or essays—or just to find individual titles of shorter literary works. Most of the materials from anthologies that are being published on the Internet are older, so there are no copyright restrictions prohibiting free public access. However, some newer materials are also included. The other way to find materials in anthologies is to use one of the indexes available for that purpose.

Internet

Many sites on the Internet might be considered "virtual anthologies," in that texts of individual writers or texts devoted to specific subjects are collected on one site. A "virtual anthology" can be found at http://4poetry.4anything.com/4/0,1001,5666,00.html. A collection of some of the works of Edgar Allen Poe can be found at http://www.pambytes.com/poe/poe.html. Science fiction buffs can find a collection of short stories at http://www.sfwriter.com/stindex.htm. Some universities' and special collections' sites now provide digitized full-text versions of short stories, biographies, and other literary works. The Electronic Text Center at the University of Virginia (http://etext.lib.virginia.edu/features.html) has digitized a number of collected works and made them available to the public.

The sites below contain general collections of literary works.

ARTFL Project: American and French Research on the Treasury of French Language. U of Chicago P. n.d. 24 Apr. 2000 <http://humanities.uchicago.edu/ARTFL/ARTFL.html#general>.

Collection of nearly 2,000 texts, ranging from classic works of French literature to various kinds of non-fiction prose and technical writing. Includes eighteenth, nineteenth and twentieth century works and some seventeenth century texts as well as some medieval and Renaissance texts. Genres include novels, verse, theater, journalism, essays, correspondence and treatises. Subjects include literary criticism, biology, history, economics and philosophy. Available by subscription only.

Bartleby.com: Great Books Online. Bartleby.com. 2000. 28 Apr. 2000 <http://www.bartleby.com/>.

Full-text short stories and poetry. Available free.

LION: Literature Online. Chadwyck-Healey. 2000. 23 Apr. 2000 <http://lion.chadwyck.co.uk/html/homenosub.htm>.

A fully searchable library of over 250,000 full-text works of English and American literature. Includes several literary databases of poetry, plays and fiction as well as general reference works and links to other Internet sites. Available by subscription only.

Indexes

Besides the Internet, indexes to literature in collections can be found in a number of sources. The selected guides below are listed by type of literature.

Essays

Essay and General Literature Index is an index to essays and articles from anthologies and collections published in English. It is available both in paper and electronic format. The focus is primarily on the humanities and social sciences, with coverage of topics in history, political science, economics, and philosophy. It also includes criticism of literary works, drama, and film. The titles that are indexed are mostly monographs, but some annuals and serial publications such as *Proceedings of the American Antiquarian Society* and the *Dickens Studies Annual* are included. It is arranged alphabetically by subject and includes an author index and a "List of Books Indexed." Figure 12.14 is a sample page from the subject index showing a citation to an appropriate essay for the topic of "women and employment."

Note the work listed under the heading "women" and the subheading "employment" by R.L. Coser entitled "Power Lost and Status Gained: A Step in the Direction of Sex Equality." This essay is found in a work entitled *The Nature of Work*, edited by K. Erikson and S. P. Vallas. To retrieve this essay, you would conduct a title search in the library catalog for "nature of work," or search for "coser r l" as the author. The essay will be found on pages 71 through 87.

Individual essays can also be found under the author's name in *Essay and General Literature Index.* Figure 12.15 shows a citation to a work coauthored by Claudia Goldin and Stanley L. Engerman. Figure 12.16 illustrates the full entry listed under the author Engerman in the same index.

Short Stories

To find a short story you should consult *Short Story Index* published by the H.W. Wilson Company. This index provides references to short stories written in or translated into English that have appeared in collections and selected periodicals. The periodicals are those indexed in *Readers' Guide to Periodical Literature* and *Humanities Index*. There is also an electronic version of the *Short Story Index*. It covers the years 1983 forward and includes links to some full-text short stories.

The print version includes both a subject and an author index. Figure 12.17 illustrates an example under the subject "women." To find the source where the short story can be found, consult the author index. An example is shown in Figure 12.18.

Women—Continued

Crime

See Female offenders

Crimes against

See also Rape

MacKinnon, C. A. Crimes of war, crimes of peace. (*In* On human rights; ed. by S. Shute and S. Hurley p83-109)

Morgan, R. A massacre in Montreal. (*In* Morgan, R. The word of a woman p199-205)

Segel, L. Does pornography cause violence? The search for evidence. (*In* Dirty looks: women, pornography, power; ed. by P. C. Gibson and R. Gibson p5-21)

Diseases

See also Gynecology; Women—Health and hygiene

Education

Bee, B. Critical literacy and the politics of gender. (*In* Critical literacy; ed. by C. Lankshear and P. L. McLaren p105-31)

Harris, S. K. Responding to the text(s): women readers and the quest for higher education. (*In* Readers in history; ed. by J. L. Machor p259-82)

Great Britain

Wolff, J. The culture of separate spheres: the role of culture in nineteenth-century public and private life. (*In* Wolff, J. Feminine sentences p12-33)

Ireland

Innes, C. L. 'Groups rather than individuals': women in politics and education. (*In* Innes, C. L. Woman and nation in Irish literature and society, 1880-1935 p110-27)

Middle East

Abadan-Unat, N. The impact of legal and educational reforms on Turkish women. (*In* Women in Middle Eastern history; ed. by N. R. Keddie and B. Baron p177-94)

Berkey, J. P. Women and Islamic education in the Mamluk period. (*In* Women in Middle Eastern history; ed. by N. R. Keddie and B. Baron p143-57)

Education (Higher)

Heilbrun, C. G. The politics of mind: women, tradition, and the university. (*In* Gender in the classroom; ed. by S. L. Gabriel and I. Smithson p28-40)

Kramarae, C., and Treichler, P. A. Power relationships in the classroom. (*In* Gender in the classroom; ed. by S. L. Gabriel and I. Smithson p41-59)

Lee, E. B. Reflections on the education of women. (*In* The Liberal arts in a time of crisis; ed. by B. A. Scott p135-40)

Emancipation

See Women's rights

SUBHEADING

Employment

See also Sex discrimination in employment

Coser, R. L. Power lost and status gained: a step in the direction of sex equality. (*In* The Nature of work; ed. by K. Erikson and S. P. Vallas p71-87)

ESSAY

SOURCE

California

Hossfeld, K. J. "Their logic against them": contradictions in sex, race, and class in Silicon Valley. (*In* Women workers and global restructuring; ed. by K. Ward p149-78)

Developing countries

Tiano, S. Maquiladora women: a new category of workers? (*In* Women workers and global restructuring; ed. by K. Ward p193-223)

Great Britain

Dupree, M. The community perspective in family history: the Potteries during the nineteenth century. (*In* The First modern society; ed. by A. L. Beier, D. Cannadine and J. M. Rosenheim p549-73)

Greece

Hadjicostandi, J. "Façon": women's formal and informal work in the garment industry in Kavala, Greece. (*In* Women workers and global restructuring; ed. by K. Ward p64-81)

Ireland

Pyle, J. L. Export-led development and the underemployment of women: the impact of discriminatory development policy in the Republic of Ireland. (*In* Women workers and global restructuring; ed. by K. Ward p85-112)

Italy

Cammarosano, S. O. Labouring women in northern and central Italy in the nineteenth century. (*In* Society and politics in the age of the Risorgimento; ed. by J. A. Davis and P. Ginsborg p152-83)

Japan

Carney, L. S., and O'Kelly, C. G. Women's work and women's place in the Japanese economic miracle. (*In* Women workers and global restructuring; ed. by K. Ward p113-45)

Java

Wolf, D. L. Linking women's labor with the global economy: factory workers and their families in rural Java. (*In* Women workers and global restructuring; ed. by K. Ward p25-47)

Taiwan

Gallin, R. S. Women and the export industry in Taiwan: the muting of class consciousness. (*In* Women workers and global restructuring; ed. by K. Ward p179-92)

United States

Gabin, N. F. Time out of mind: the UAW's response to female labor laws and mandatory overtime in the 1960s. (*In* Work engendered: toward a new history of American labor; ed. by A. Baron p351-74)

Kessler-Harris, A. Law and a living: the gendered content of "free labor". (*In* Gender, class, race and reform in the Progressive Era; ed. by N. Frankel and N. S. Dye p87-109)

Enfranchisement

See Women—Suffrage

Health and hygiene

See also Clothing and dress

Jacobson, J. L. Improving women's reproductive health. (*In* State of the world, 1992 p83-99)

Figure 12.14 Sample page from *Essay and General Literature Index, 1990–1994*, p. 1794. (From *Essay and General Literature Index, 1990–1994*. Copyright © 1995 by H.W. Wilson. Reprinted by permission.)

Goldhurst, William
  Of mice and men; John Steinbeck's parable
  of the curse of Cain. (*In* The Short novels
  of John Steinbeck: ed. by J. J. Benson
  p48-59)
Goldin, Claudia
  (jt. Auth) See Engerman, Stanley L.,
  and Goldin, Claudia

Figure 12.15 Excerpt from author index, *Essay and General Literature Index, 1990–1994*, p. 658. (From *Essay and General Literature Index, 1990–1994*. Copyright © 1995 by H.W. Wilson. Reprinted by permission.)

Enger, John Van
  Faith as a concept of order in medieval
  Christendom. (*In* Belief in history;
  ed. by T. Kselman p19-67)
Engerman, Stanley L., and Goldin, Claudia
  Seasonality in nineteenth-century labor
  markets. (*In* American economic development
  in historical perspective; ed. by T. Weiss
  and D. Schaefer p99-126)

Figure 12.16 Excerpt from author index, *Essay and General Literature Index, 1990–1994*, p. 495. (From *Essay and General Literature Index, 1990–1994*. Copyright © 1995 by H.W. Wilson. Reprinted by permission.)

To retrieve the short story "A Child's Play" by Alice Adams, conduct an author search in the library catalog under "adams alice" or a title search under "after you've gone," the larger work that includes the short story.

Plays

Inter-Play: An On-line Index to Plays in Collections, Anthologies, and Periodicals. Comp. Robert Westover and Janet Wright. Portland State University. 3 Jan. 2003. 3 Jan. 2003 <http://www.lib.pdx.edu/systems/interplay/>.
Index to approximately 19,000 citations to plays in several languages, many of which are not included in the standard printed play indexes such as *Ottemiller's Index to Plays in Collections* or H. W. Wilson's *Play Index*. The authors have not included separately published plays or works by familiar authors such as Shakespeare as these can be located through local library catalogs. The sources indexed range from the late 19th century through the current year. The database is frequently updated.

ACTORS—*Continued*

Besant, Sir W., and Rice, J. The case of Mr. Lucraft
Bioy Casares, A. Cato
Bloch, R. Show biz
Boyd, W. Not yet, Jayette
Breen, J. L. Starstruck
Burns, C. Also starring
Crumley, J. The heavy
Goldman, E. S. Nelly Fallower's *Streetcar*
Goldsmith, O. Adventures of a strolling player
Hagedorn, J. T. Film noir
Hall, M. M. The pool people
Lombreglia, R. Jungle video
Mori, T. Japanese Hamlet
Nakayama, C. Good afternoon, ladies
Onetti, J. C. A dream come true
Palacio Valdés, A. Drama in the flies
Paul, B. Close, but no cigar
Runyon, D. Broadway complex
Saroyan, W. The man with the heart in the highlands
Schmidt, H. J. The honored guest
Slesar, H. Starring the defense
Spencer, D. Our secret's out
Spencer, S. Credit
Stoker, B. A criminal star
Thomas, G. An ample wish
Urbánek, Z. For dreams that now have ceased
Villanueva, M. The insult
Villiers de l'Isle-Adam, A., comte de. The desire to be a man
Zinnes, H. Wings

The actors company. Finney, E. J.
Actress. Oates, J. C.

ACTRESSES

See also Motion picture actors and actresses; Theater life

Aickman, R. The visiting star
Alcott, L. M. Hope's debut
Alcott, L. M. La Jeune; or, Actress and woman
Alcott, L. M. A laugh and a look
Alcott, L. M. The romance of a bouquet
Allen, S. The interview
Brennan, K. Jack
Carroll, J. The lick of time
Carter, A. The merchant of shadows
Cather, W. Coming, Aphrodite!
Cheever, J. The fourth alarm
Cliff, M. Screen memory
Compo, S. The continuity girl
DePew, A. Rita and Maxine
Fitzgerald, F. S. Last kiss
Frame, R. Switchback
Ganina, M. Stage actress
Haslam, G. W. Joaquin
Hébert, A. The first garden
Ingalls, R. The end of tragedy
Kinder, R. M. Witches
Kress, N. With the original cast
Lewis, S. As P. T.
Mason, B. A. A new-wave format
McGahern, J. Peaches
Minot, S. Île Sèche
Munro, A. Simon's luck
Nakayama, C. Star time
Norman, H. Whatever Lola wants
Oates, J. C. Actress
Onetti, J. C. Hell most feared
Orr, M. The wisdom of Eve
Palacio Valdés, A. Clotilde's romance
Poniatowska, E. Park Cinema

Pritchett, V. S. The chain-smoker
Salter, J. The cinema
Tagore, Sir R. Resistance broken
Tokareva, V. Thou shalt not make . . .
Turchi, P. Magician
Uvarova, L. Be still, torments of passion
Verlaine, M. J. The nude scene
Vidal, G. Erlinda and Mr. Coffin
Vivante, A. The last kiss
Walker, C. Z. The very pineapple
Wallace, D. F. My appearance
Whitebird, J. Mrs. Bruja

Acts of contrition. Binstock, R. C.
Acts of kindness. Wagner, M. M.
Acts of mercy. Coleman, J. C.
Actual oil. Steinbach, M.
Ad astra per aspera. Compo, S.
Adam, Christina
Fires
Birch Lane Press presents American fiction #3
Adam, one afternoon. Calvino, I.
Adamidou, Irena Ioannidou See Ioannidou Adamidou, Irena

Adams, Alice, 1926- ◄———— AUTHOR
1940: fall
Adams, A. After you've gone
Prize stories, 1990
After you've gone
Adams, A. After you've gone
Legal fictions; ed. by J. Wishingrad
Prize stories, 1989
Alaska
The Oxford book of American short stories; ed. by J. C. Oates
Alternatives
American stories II: fiction from the Atlantic monthly
Beautiful girl
The Invisible enemy; ed. by M. Dow and J. Regan
Child's play ◄———— SHORT STORY
Adams, A. After you've gone ◄ SOURCE
Earthquake damage
The New Yorker v66 p44-9 My 7 '90
Prize stories, 1991
The end of the world
Adams, A. After you've gone
Favors
Adams, A. After you've gone
Fog
Adams, A. After you've gone
The islands
Prize stories, 1993
The Sophisticated cat; comp. by J. C. Oates and D. Halpern
The last lovely city
The Best American short stories, 1992
The New Yorker v67 p33-9 Mr 11 '91
Prize stories, 1992
Lost cat
Adams, A. After you've gone
The Company of cats; ed. by M. J. Rosen
Love and work
Southwest Review v77 p466-79 Aut '92
Molly's dog
The Literary dog; ed. by J. Schinto
The oasis
The Rough road home; ed. by R. Gingher
Ocracoke Island
Adams, A. After you've gone

Figure 12.17 Author search, *Short Story Index*. (From *Short Story Index*. Reprinted by permission of H.W. Wilson.)

WOMEN

See also Black women; Jewish women; Muslim women; Single women

Adams, A. Child's play

Adams, A. The end of the world

Adams, A. Molly's dog

Adams, A. Return trips

Figure 12.18 Excerpt from Subject Index, *Short Story Index, 1989–1993*, p. 960. (From *Short Story Index*. Reprinted by permission of H.W. Wilson.)

Keller, Dean H. *Index to Plays in Periodicals*. Metuchen, NJ: Scarecrow, 1971. Supplements, 1973, 1979, 1990.

Indexes about 10,000 plays located in 267 periodicals in one volume with supplements to 1990.

Ottemiller's Index to Plays in Collections, an Author and Title Index Appearing in Collections Published between 1900 and Early 1985. Rev. and enlarged by John M. Connor and Billie M. Connor. 7th ed. Metuchen, NJ: Scarecrow, 1988.

Index to full-length plays appearing in books published in England and the United States. It is divided into three sections: (1) author index with titles and dates of performance, (2) list of collections analyzed with key to symbols, and (3) title index.

Play Index. New York: H.W. Wilson, 1949–.

The key index in eight volumes covering the years 1949–1952, 1953–1960, 1961–1967, 1968–1972, 1973–1977, 1978–1982, 1983–1987, and 1988–1992. Each volume indexes thousands of plays for the time period covered. The index is divided into four parts. Part I lists plays under authors' names and anthologies in which the plays are found. Part II includes the cast analysis by number of male and female characters needed. Part III lists anthologies with full bibliographic information. Part IV includes a directory of publishers and distributors.

Poetry

American Poetry Index: An Author and Title Index to Poetry by Americans in Single Author Collections. Vol. 1, 1981–1982. Vol. 2, 1983. Vol. 3, 1984. New York: Grander Book Co., 1983.

An alphabetical index to authors and titles of over 10,000 poems published in 190 collections, which are identified by number after author's name in main index.

Caskey, Jefferson D., comp. *Index to Poetry in Popular Periodicals, 1955–1959*. Westport, CT: Greenwood, 1984.

Indexes 7,400 poems by title appearing in American periodicals from 1955 to 1959. Also includes a first-line index, author index, and subject index.

_____. *Index to Poetry in Popular Periodicals, 1960–1964*. Westport, CT: Greenwood, 1988.

An update of the earlier title.

The Columbia Granger's Index to Poetry. 11th ed. New York: Columbia UP, 1997.

Continues *Granger's Index to Poetry*. Indexes over 100,000 poems appearing in over 400 anthologies.

Granger, Edith. *Granger's Index to Poetry, 1970–1981*. Ed. William James Smith. 7th ed., completely rev. and enl., indexing anthologies published through December 31, 1981. New York: Columbia UP, 1982. First published in 1904, this is considered the standard index to poetry. Each edition enlarges on the previous one, omitting some anthologies and adding new ones. Later editions arranged by sections as follows: (1) title and first-line index, (2) author index, and (3) subject index.

Poems: Research Guide. U of Delaware Library. 25 Oct. 1999. 28 Apr. 2000 <http://www2.lib.udel.edu/subj/engl/resguide/poems.htm>.

Poetry Archives. E-mule.com, 1997–2000. 28 Feb. 2000 <http://www.emule.com/poetry/>. Large collection of free classical poetry on the Internet. Searchable by author, title, and first line of poem.

Speeches

History Channel. http://historychannel.com/speeches/index.html Provides audio and text for important speeches.

Mitchell, Charity. *Speech Index: An Index to Collections of World Famous Orations and Speeches for Various Occasions*. Metuchen, NJ: Scarecrow, 1982. *Supplement*, 4th ed., 1966–1980. Alphabetical arrangement of speeches by author, subject, and type of speech.

Representative American Speeches. H.W. Wilson, 1938–. Annual. Collection of speeches. Has cumulative author index: 1937–1960 in 1959/60 volume; annual index since 1960/61.

Speech Resources. Virginia Commonwealth University. 23 Feb. 2000. 28 Apr. 2000 <http://www.library.vcu.edu/guides/speeches.html>. Good site for identifying print and online sources for speeches. Includes: Indexes, Original Print Sources, Finding Speeches Online, Selected Speech Sites on the Web.

Vital Speeches of the Day. New York: City News, 1934–. Excellent source for speeches on current issues and social trends in the United States and other countries. Published twice a month. Annual index published in November issue. Also indexed in *Readers' Guide* and in *ABI/INFORM*. Also has a 25-year (1934–1959) author/subject index. Web access at http://www.vold.com/

Exercise 12.1   Book Reviews, Literary Criticism, and Literature in Collections

Instructor: _____ Course/Section: _____

Name: _____

Date: _____ Points: _____

Review Questions

1. List the three types of sources discussed in this chapter.

   a.

   b.

   c.

2. What is the importance of using a book review for an author's work?

3. What is the difference between a book review and a literary criticism?

4. Name two book review indexes that would be useful.

5. What is the advantage of having book reviews available on the Internet?

6. Give the URLs for two Internet sites that have book reviews.

7. Can book reviews be located through periodical indexes? Justify your answer.

8. How does one locate book reviews or articles on literary criticism in the library after the reference to a review has been found in an index?

9. Name two sources you could use for finding literary criticism of a particular writer.

   a.

   b.

10. What is an anthology?

11. How would you locate a short story that is not listed in the online catalog?

12. Name an index you would use to find chapters or essays in books.

Exercise 12.2 Book Reviews, Literary Criticism, and Literature in Collections

Instructor: _____ Course/Section: _____

Name: _____

Date: _____ Points: _____

Finding Book Reviews

Reviews of books may be obtained from *Book Review Index, Book Review Digest* or any other sources containing book reviews. Choose one of the reviews listed in Figure 12.5, *Book Review Digest, 1994*, and answer the following questions:

1. Analyze one reference you found by giving the following information.

    a. Author of book selected:

    b. Title of the book:

    c. Author of review (if unsigned, mark NA):

    d. Give the following information about the source in which the review appears.

        (1) Complete title of the magazine or journal:

        (2) Volume:

        (3) Pages:

        (4) Date:

        (5) Number of words in review:

        (6) How many other references to reviews were given?

Use your library catalog to determine whether or not your library subscribes to the magazine or journal in which the review appears. If your library subscribes to the magazine or journal, answer the following questions.

2. What is the call number of the magazine or journal?

Retrieve the review article.

3. Read the complete review. Is this a book you would want to read? Justify your answer.

4. Write a bibliographic reference to the review. Use the bibliographic citations examples given in Appendix A.

Exercise 12.3 Book Reviews, Literary Criticism, and Literature in Collections

Instructor: _____ Course/Section: _____

Name: _____

Date: _____ Points: _____

Finding Literary Criticism

Using a source described in this chapter, locate a reference to a criticism of a novel, poem, play, or short story that you have read, or select from the list below. Locate the criticism, read it, and complete the following questions.

For Whom the Bell Tolls by Ernest Hemingway
The Road Not Taken by Robert Frost
The Pit and the Pendulum by Edgar Allan Poe
The Client by John Grisham
Pet Sematary by Stephen King

1. Give the author and title of the literary work you selected.

2. What is the title of the index or other source you use to locate the criticism?

3. How did you locate the index or other source for Question 2?

4. Give the following information about the criticism.

    a. Title of the work in which criticism appears:

    b. If a periodical, give the date and volume of the periodical and the pages on which it appears.

    c. Indicate if a full-text database or another online source is used.

5. What is the call number of the book or periodical in which the criticism appears (if not full text)?

6. Briefly summarize some of the major points the author of the criticism makes about the work.

7. Write a bibliographical citation for the criticism you found. Use the bibliographic citations given in Appendix A.

8. Do you agree or disagree with the critic's assessment of the work? Justify your answer.

Exercise 12.4 Book Reviews, Literary Criticism, and Literature in Collections

Instructor: _____ Course/Section: _____

Name: _____

Date: _____ Points: _____

Using *Essay and General Literature Index*

The *Essay and General Literature Index* is an index to materials in anthologies. Consult the index for information on a topic you select or one assigned by your instructor. After you have found your reference, answer the following questions.

1. What is the call number of the *Essay and General Literature Index?*

2. Give the date of the volume used.

3. Give the complete subject heading under which you located your topic.

4. Analyze the reference you located by giving the following information.

   a. Author of the article:

   b. Title of the article:

   c. Editor or author of the book (circle one or the other and record the name).

   d. Name of the book in which the article appears:

   e. Pages in the book in which the article appears:

   f. Place, publisher, and copyright or publication date of the book:

5. Does the library own the book? If so, what is the call number?

6. Write a bibliographic reference to the article you have found. Use the bibliographic citations examples in Appendix A for citing an essay in a collection or an anthology.

7. Would this article be a good reference for your topic? Justify your answer.

Exercise 12.5   Book Reviews, Literary Criticism, and Literature in Collections

Instructor: _____ Course/Section: _____

Name: _____

Date: _____ Points: _____

Exploring Literary Collections Online

Go to the Electronic Text Center at the University of Virginia at http://etext.lib.virginia.edu/features.html

Click on Poe Archives (http://etext.lib.virginia.edu/poe/).

Click on "About Poe" and read the "Brief Biography" located at http://etext.lib.virginia.edu/poe/poebiog.html. Then answer the following questions.

1. What were the occupations of Poe's parents?

2. Where did Poe attend college?

3. How long did he serve in the U.S. army?

4. Did he attend West Point? Why didn't he graduate there?

5. What was the title of his first attempt at publishing?

6. How did Poe die and where is he buried?

7. Are any references given here for further research on Edgar Allan Poe? If so, give one title and author.

At the bottom of the biography, click on "Fiction" to see a list of full-text works available at this site for the author. Scroll down to the list of short stories beginning with *The Assignation*. Select one that you would like to look at.

8. What is the title you selected?

9. When was this title published?

10. What it the title of the anthology in which this story originally appeared?

11. Click on the "Header" of this story and print out the page. Attach it to this assignment.

12. How does reading the story online compare with reading it in book form?

13. If given a choice of full-text online, cassette, or traditional book formats, which would you prefer and why?

Return to the home page for Poe. Select "Search the Poe Archives" to find a specific term in Poe's works.

14. Using the search engine on the page, find out how many times the words "despair" and "love" are mentioned in all the texts and summaries in the Poe Archives and answer the following questions.

Number of times in which the word "despair" appeared:

Total number of works in which the word "despair" appeared:

Number of works in which the word "love" appeared:

Total number of times the word "love" appeared:

Explain how this feature is useful to someone who might be doing research on Poe. Describe how this feature compares with a printed text of short stories.

Appendix A-1

DOCUMENTING SOURCES (MLA STYLE)

Works Cited

The bibliographic entries below provide guidance for citing some of the more common sources in a *Works Cited* list. The examples are based on the *MLA Handbook*. For additional help, consult the *MLA Handbook* or one of the other style manuals listed in Chapter 2 (if you use another style).

Items in the *Works Cited* section of the paper should be arranged alphabetically according to the last name of the author. If a work has more than one author, only the first name listed is inverted. If an item is listed by title rather than author, it is placed alphabetically by words in the title, excluding the initial articles *a*, *an*, or *the*. For example, *The Encyclopaedia Britannica* would be alphabetized by *Encyclopaedia*. If two or more entries have the same author, the author's name is not repeated. A three space line is used to indicate the omission of the name. The first line of each entry is placed in hanging *indentation*. That is, it begins five spaces to the left of the following lines in the entry. An example of a *Works Cited* list for a research paper is provided in Table 2.2.

Citation examples are provided for the following categories of materials.

1. Books
2. Reference Books
3. Periodical and Newspaper Articles
4. Unpublished Dissertations and Theses
5. Class Lectures
6. Interviews
7. Sound Recordings
8. Videotapes
9. Microforms
10. Television or Radio Programs
11. Government and Legal Publications
12. Electronic formats

1. Books

Items to include in documenting a book:

☐ Author's full name. When there are one, two, or three authors, all of the authors' names are included. When there are four or more authors, cite the first one listed on the title page followed by "et al." or by "and others."

☐ Title of part of the book if only citing one chapter, one section, etc.

☐ The title of the book as it appears on the title page. In preparing a manuscript for publication, use italics to highlight titles of published works; underline titles in papers that are not being prepared for publication.

☐ Editor, translator, compiler (if any).

☐ The edition if other than the first.

☐ Volume if part of a multivolume set.

☐ The series (if any).

- ☐ Publication information.
    - ▫ The city of publication. If more than one place is listed on the title page, only the first one listed is used. The name of the state is included if the city is not well known.
    - ▫ The publisher. The shortened name of the publisher is used unless there is confusion in identification. The shortened forms of publishers' names are found in the *MLA Handbook* (6.5).
    - ▫ The date of publication. The publication date is found on the title page. If there is no publication date given, the latest copyright date (usually found on the back of the title page) is used. If neither a publication date nor a copyright date is given, the abbreviation, n.d., is used.

Note that the first line of each entry begins at the left margin. Subsequent lines in each entry are indented five spaces to the right.

1.1. Book by one author

Kaufman, Martin. *Homeopathy in America: the Rise and Fall of a Medical Heresy*. Baltimore: Johns Hopkins UP, 1971.

1.2. Book by two or three authors

Powers, Scott K., and Stephen L. Dodd. *Total Fitness: Exercise, Nutrition, and Wellness*. 2nd ed. Boston: Allyn, 1999.

1.3. Book by two or more authors with the same last name

Durant, Will, and Ariel Durant. *A Dual Autobiography*. New York: Simon, 1977.

1.4. Book by four or more authors

Davis, James, et al. *Society and the Law: New Meanings for an Old Profession*. New York: Free, 1962.

Note: May also use Davis, James, and others, or give all names in full.

1.5. Two or more books by the same author

Mink, Gwendolyn. *The Wages of Motherhood: Inequality in the Welfare State*. Ithaca: Cornell UP, 1995.

---. *Welfare's End*. Ithaca: Cornell UP, 1998.

Note: When citing two or more books by the same author, give the author's name in the first entry. Use three hyphens followed by a period in place of the author's name in subsequent entries.

1.6. Book by an organization (corporate author)

Center for the Study of Democratic Institutions. *Natural Law and Modern Society*. Contrib. John Cogley, et al. Cleveland: World, 1973.

1.7. Book that is an edited work

Green, Phillip, and Michael Walzer, eds. *The Political Imagination in Literature: A Reader*. New York: Free, 1969.

1.8. Book that is part of a series

Hunt, Lacy H. *Dynamics of Forecasting Financial Cycles: Theory, Technique, and Implementation*. Contemporary Studies in Economic and Financial Analysis. Greenwich: JAI, 1976.

1.9. Book that is one volume of a multivolume work, one author, each volume a different title

Malone, Dumas. *Jefferson and the Ordeal of Liberty*. Boston: Little, 1962. Vol. III of *Jefferson and His Time*. 6 vols. 1948-1981.

1.10. Book that is one volume of a multivolume work with one general title

Warren, Charles. *The Supreme Court in United States History*. Rev. ed. 2 vols. Boston: Little, 1926.

1.11. Book that is a translation of an author's work

Nietzsche, Frederick. *The Birth of Tragedy and the Genealogy of Morals*. Trans. Francis Golffing. Garden City: Doubleday, 1956.

1.12. Short story in a collected work (anthology)

Faulkner, William. "Dry September." *Ten Modern Masters: An Anthology of the Short Story*. Ed. Robert G. Davis. New York: Harcourt, 1953. 339-50.

Note: Elements cited are author of short story, title of short story, title of book in which story appears, editor of book, publication information, pages on which story appears.

1.13. Essay or article in a collected work (anthology)

Barker, James D. "Man, Mood, and the Presidency." *The Presidency Reappraised*. Ed. Rexford G. Tugwell and Thomas E. Cronin. New York: Prager, 1974. 205-14.

Note: Elements cited: author of article, title of article, title of book in which article appears, editors of book, publication information, pages on which article appears in book.

2. Reference Books

Items to include when citing articles from encyclopedias, yearbooks, biographical dictionaries, and other well-known reference books:

☐ The author of the article, if known.

☐ The title of the article as it appears in the book.

☐ The title of the book in which the article appears.

☐ The edition, if other than the first, and the date of publication.

□ The volume number if one of a multivolume set, unless entire set is alphabetically arranged.

□ The inclusive paging of the article. If articles are arranged in alphabetical order in the work, page numbers should be omitted.

If the reference is not well known, or if there is confusion about the title, give full publication information.

2.1. *Article from a multivolume general reference book*

Vandam, Leroy D. "Anesthetic." *The New Encyclopaedia Britannica: Macropaedia*. 15 ed. 1987.

2.2. *Article from a single volume general reference book*

Betancourt, Romulo. "Latin America, Its Problems and Possibilities." *Britannica Book of the Year, 1966*. 1967.

2.3. *Article from a multivolume subject reference book*

Flexner, Eleanor. "Woman's Rights Movement." *Dictionary of American History*. Ed. Joseph G.E. Hopkins and Wayne Andrews. 6 vols. New York: Scribner's, 1961. VI, Supp. 1: 301-43.

Note: When citing less familiar reference books, give full publication information.

2.4. *Article from a biographical dictionary (unsigned)*

"Sellers, Peter (Richard Henry)." *Who's Who 1976-1977*. 1976.

Note: Full name of subject of article is used as title of article.

2.5. *Article from a biographical dictionary (signed)*

Cole, Arthur C. "Webster, Daniel." *Dictionary of American Biography*. 1936.

2.6. *Book of quotations*

Johnson, Samuel. "He who praises everybody praises nobody. . ." *The Oxford Dictionary of Quotations*. 5th ed., 1999.

3. Periodical and Newspaper Articles

Items to include when citing articles from periodicals:

□ The author of the article if it is a signed article.

□ The title of the article.

□ The title of the periodical.

□ The volume number and issue number (if it is a scholarly journal).

□ The date of the periodical.

□ The inclusive pages of the article. If an article is not printed on consecutive pages, that is, if it begins on one page and continues on later pages, cite the beginning page followed by a "+."

3.1. *Article from a monthly magazine, author identified*

Starr, Roger. "A Kind Word about Money." *Harper's* Apr. 1976: 79-92.

Note: For a monthly magazine, cite only the date and pages.

3.2. *Article from a monthly magazine, no author indicated*

"First National Data on Reading Speed." *Intellect* Oct. 1972: 9.

3.3. *Article from a weekly magazine, author identified*

Meindl, James D. "Microelectronics and Computers in Medicine." *Science* 12 Feb. 1982: 792-97.

3.4. *Article from a weekly magazine, no author indicated*

"Behind the Threat of More Inflation." *Business Week* 18 Nov. 1972: 76-78.

3.5. *Article from a journal with continuously numbered pages throughout the volume*

Runkle, Gerald. "Is Violence Always Wrong?" *Journal of Politics* 38 (1976): 247-91.

3.6. *Article from a journal with separately numbered pages in each issue*

Martin, Jay. "A Watertight Watergate Future: Americans in a Post-American Age." *The Antioch Review* 33.2 (1975): 7-25.

Note: 33.2 indicates volume 33, issue number no. 2.

3.7. *Book review, author identified*

Sherrill, Robert. Rev. of *The Time of Illusion*, by Jonathan Schell. *New York Times Book Review* 18 Jan. 1976: 1-2.

Note: Elements cited are the author of review, title of book, author of book, periodical in which review appears, date, page(s).

3.8. *Book review with title, author identified*

Hughes, Robert. "The Sorcerer's Apprentice." Rev. of *Journey to Ixtlan*, by Carlos Castaneda. *Time* 6 Nov. 1972: 101.

3.9. *Book review, no author indicated*

Rev. of *Cuneiform to Computers*, by William A. Katz. *AB Bookman's Weekly* 15 June 1986: 1611-3.

3.10. *Newspaper article, author identified*

Goldstein, Tom. "New Federal Tax Law Could Foster Growth of Plans to Provide Pre-paid Legal Services." *New York Times* 28 Sept. 1976, eastern ed.: A36.

3.11. *Newspaper article, no author indicated*

"College Enrollment Decline Predicted for South in '80's." *Morning Advocate* [Baton Rouge] 28 Sept. 1976: B7.

3.12. *Editorial from a newspaper*

"Takeovers Yes, Hold-ups No." Editorial. *New York Times* 28 Nov. 1986, eastern ed.: A26.

4. Unpublished Dissertation and Thesis

Bolden, Anthony J. "All Blues: A Study of African-American Resistance Poetry." Diss. Louisiana State U, 1998.

Vogel, Amanda E. "Body Image by Association: Women's Interpretations of Aerobics and the Role of the Fitness Instructor." Thesis (M.A.). U of British Columbia, 1998.

5. Class Lecture

Wilson, John. "Women in the Labor Force." Sociology 101. Louisiana State U, Baton Rouge, LA. 18 Feb. 1996.

6. Interview

Harris, Michael. Personal interview. 3 Feb. 1996.

7. Sound Recordings

Monk, Thelonious. *Live at the It Club*. 2 compact discs. Sony Music Entertainment, 1998.

Wayne, Jeff. *The War of the Worlds: Rock Musical*. Narr. Richard Burton, with soloists, vocal and instrumental ensembles. LP. Columbia, n.d.

Note: Citation includes performer, title of recording, type of recording, producer, date.

8. Videotape

Our National Parks. Videocassette. Prod. Wolfgang Bayer Productions. National Geographic Book Service, 1989.

9. Microform

Spalter-Roth, Roberta M., and Heidi I. Hartmann. *Increasing Working Mothers' Earnings*. Washington: Institute for Women's Policy Research, 1991: ERIC Microfiche ED 370825.

10. Television and Radio Programs

Items to include when citing a television or radio program:

- ☐ Title of the episode (enclose in quotation marks).
- ☐ Title of the program (underline).
- ☐ Name of performers, narrators, etc. of the particular episode, if applicable.
- ☐ Title of the series, if any (do not use quotation marks or underlining).
- ☐ Name of producers, directors, etc., if applicable.
- ☐ Name of network.
- ☐ Identification of the station and the city where viewed or heard.
- ☐ Date broadcast.

"Sports, Fitness and the Brain." *Gray Matters*. Prod. Mary Beth Kirchner and Robert Rand. Radio series produced for Public Radio International, in association with the Dana Alliance for Brain Initiatives. PRI. WUMB-FM, Boston. 5 Mar. 1999.

11. Government and Legal Publications

Government publications are issued by many different types of government agencies from local to international. Often the names of the authors are not provided in the document. Generally the following items are included in a citation to a government publication.

- ☐ Author—if individual author is not given, cite the name of the government entity (a city, a state, a national government, or international organization) followed by the particular agency that is responsible for the publication.
- ☐ Title of the publication.
- ☐ Any publication information necessary for identification of the publication, such as special reports or parts of series.
- ☐ Publication information. (The Government Printing Office (GPO) is usually cited as the publisher for most U.S. government publications, regardless of the branch or agency that issues them.).

Note: Cite government periodicals as you would periodicals from commercial publishers.

The citation examples below are for various types of United States government publications.

11.1. Agency publication

Reid, William J., Jr., and F.P. Cuthbert, Jr. *Aphids on Leafy Vegetables: How to Control Them*. Agricultural Research Service, Farmers' Bulletin No. 2148. Washington: GPO, 1976.

11.2. Reference book

"Number of Workers with Earnings . . ." *Statistical Abstract of the United States, 1991*. Table 656.

11.3. Congressional hearings, reports, documents

> United States. Cong. House. Committee on the Judiciary. *Opposing the Granting of Permanent Residence in the United States to Certain Aliens*. Report to accompany H. Res. 795. 95th Cong., 1st sess. H.R. no. 691. Washington: GPO, 1977.
>
> ---.---. Senate. Committee on Indian Affairs. *Providing for Business Development and Trade Promotion for Native Americans, and for Other Purposes*. Report to accompany S. 401. 106th Cong., 1st sess. S. Rept. 106-149. Washington: GPO, 1999.
>
> ---.---.---. Committee on Agriculture, Nutrition, and Forestry. *Better Nutrition and Health for Children Act of 1993, Hearings: March 1, 1994, May 16, 1994, June 10, 1994, and June 17, 1994*. 103 Cong. 2nd sess. S. 1614. Washington: GPO, 1995.

Note: The entries appear in the order as they would in a *Works Cited* list. When citing more than one work by the same government agency, use three hyphens in place of the name of the agency in the next entry and any following one(s). In the second entry above, the author is the United States Congress, Senate, Committee on Indian Affairs. The author in the next entry is the United States Congress, Senate, Committee on Agriculture.

11.4. Laws, decrees, etc.

> PL 96-511 (Dec. 11, 1980). Paperwork Reduction Act of 1980. 94 Stat. 2812.

Note: Citation to the *Statutes at Large*. Elements included in citation in the order given are: public law number, date approved, title of law, volume number of the *Statutes at Large*, abbreviation for *Statutes at Large*, page number.

> 20 U.S.C. 238 (1980).

Note: Citation to the *United States Code*. Elements in citation are number of code, abbreviation of *United States Code*, section number, and edition date.

11.5. Court case

> Brewer v. Williams, 430 U.S. 389 (1977).

Note: Name of case, volume 430 of *U.S. Reports*, page 389, year of publication.

11.6. Congressional Record

> *Cong. Rec.* 121 (1975): 40634.

Note: Elements in citation are abbreviation of *Congressional Record*, volume number, year, and page.

12. Electronic Format

When listing a source in electronic format originally printed in a book, journal, or other printed format, use the general guidelines you would use to cite the printed form. In addition, add the information that identifies the particular kind of format and, for Internet sources, the date of access and the Internet address.

12.1. CD-ROM

United States. Dept. of Commerce. Bureau of the Census. Data User Ser. Div. *1990 Census of Population and Housing: Equal Employment Opportunity File*. CD-ROM. Disc. 1. Washington: Dept. of Commerce, 1993.

Dead Sea Scrolls Revealed. CD-ROM. Tel Aviv : Pixel Multimedia; London : A. Witkin; Oak Harbor, WA: Logos Research Systems, 1994.

"Dabble." *The Oxford English Dictionary*. 2nd ed. CD-ROM. Oxford: Oxford UP, 1992.

Woolf, Virginia. "The Captain's Death Bed." *The Complete Works of Virginia Woolf Including Variant and Hard-to-Find Editions*. Ed. Mark Hussey. CD-ROM . Woodbridge, CT: Primary Source Media, 1997.

Weninger, Robert. Rev. of *Passage Through Hell*, by David L. Pike. *The German Quarterly* 72.2 (1999): 194-95. *Humanities Abstracts FTX*. CD-ROM. SilverPlatter. Dec. 1999.

12.2. Internet

Because there are no standards for what is placed on the Internet, citing the sources can be confusing. Generally, you should include the following elements.

- ☐ Author, if given.
- ☐ Title of article, if it appears to be part of a larger work (in quotations).
- ☐ Title of work or Web Page (underlined).
- ☐ Title of the project (if any).
- ☐ Publication information: date of publication and name of sponsoring organization, if applicable.
- ☐ Date of access.
- ☐ Web address (URL).

In citing a service to which the library subscribes, you should complete the information as for the print source followed by the name of the database or service used (underlined); the library; the date of access; and the URL for the site (if it is too long, cite the vendor's home page).

12.2.1. Scholarly works

Lerman, Robert I. "Meritocracy without Rising Inequality?" *Economic Restructuring and the Job Market*. Policy and Research Report, no. 2. The Urban Institute. 2000. 23 Feb. 2000 <http://www.urban.org/econ/econ2.htm>.

United States. Dept. of Agriculture. Agriculture Research Service. Human Nutrition Information Service. *Provisional Table on the Vitamin K Content of Foods*. Prep. John L. Weihrauch and Ashok S. Chatra. HNIS-PT-104. Feb 1994. 23 Feb. 2000 <http://www.nal.usda.gov/fnic/foodcomp/Data/Other/pt104.pdf>.

Imel, Susan. "Change: Connections to Adult Learning and Education." ERIC Digest No. 221. ERIC Clearinghouse on Adult Career and Vocational Education Columbus OH. Nov. 2000. 4 Aug. 2001 <http://www.ed.gov/databases/ERIC_Digests/ed446252.html>.

12.2.2. Books and selections from books

Twain, Mark. *A Double Barrelled Detective Story*. [New York: Harper, 1902]. The Naked Word Electronic Edition. 16 Jan. 2000. 23 Feb. 2000 <http://sr8.xoom.com/etcollective/nakedword/htmltext/dbdstory.html>.

Boswell, James. "Selections." *Life of Samuel Johnson*. Oxford, 1904. Ed. Jack Lynch. 23 Feb. 2000 <http://newark.rutgers.edu/~jlynch/Texts/BLJ/b272.html>.

12.2.3. Journal articles

Kuang, Wembo. "The Development of Electronic Publication in China." *LIBRES: Library and Information Science Research* 9.1 (1999). 23 Feb. 2000 <http://aztec.lib.utk.edu/libres/libre9n1/wenbo.htm>.

Johnson, Glen M. Rev. of *Huckleberry Finn as Idol and Target*, by Jonathan Arac. *The Mark Twain Forum* 4 Nov. 1997. 23 Feb. 2000 <http://web.mit.edu/linguistics/www/forum/reviews/arac1.html>.

12.2.4. Subscription services

Gartner, Scott Sigmund, and Gary M. Segura. "War, Casualties, and Public Opinion." *Journal of Conflict Resolution* 42.3 (1998): 278+. *Electronic Collections Online*. OCLC. Louisiana State U Lib., Baton Rouge. 23 Feb. 2000 <http://firstsearch.oclc.org/html/eco_frames.html>.

Lubove, Seth. "Subprime Borrower." *Forbes* 7 Feb 2000: 58. *ABI/INFORM Global*. ProQuest Direct. Delgado Community College Lib., New Orleans. 23 Feb. 2000 <http://proquest.umi.com/pqdweb>.

"Farming on the Edge of Chaos." *Whole Earth*. Summer. 1999: 72. *Health Source Plus*. EBSCOhost. Wayne State College, Wayne, NE. 23 Feb. 2000 <http://search.epnet.com/>.

Fiero, John W. "Anne Rice: Overview." *Contemporary Novelists*. 6th ed. 1996. *Literature Resource Center*. Gale Group. Wayne State College, Wayne, NE. 23 Feb. 2000 <http://www.galenet.com/servlet/LitRC?&u=LRC&u=CA&u=CLC&u=DLB>.

12.2.5. Newspaper article

"Screening Newborns Can Defeat Hereditary Diseases." *New York Times on the Web*. 25 Feb. 2000. 26 Feb. 2000 <http://www.nytimes.com/library/national/science/health/022600hth-newborn-screening.html>.

12.2.6. Personal or professional home pages

Martin, Jan. *English Springer Spaniel*. 23 Feb. 2000. 26 Feb. 2000 <http://www.teleport.com/~ariel/essfaq.html>.

Immunization Action Coalition. Home Page. 25 Feb. 2000. 26 Feb 2000 <http://www.immunize.org/index.htm>.

12.2.7. E-mail

Sokolowski, Denise. "Re: textbook." E-mail to the authors. 1 June 1999.

12.2.8. Bulletin boards and other online discussions

Lange, Andre. "Anthology of Early Texts on Television." Online posting.
4 Feb. 2000. Broadcast News Forum. 25 Feb. 2000 <http://
www.delphi.com/ab-broadcastnws/messages/?msg=235.1&ctx=1>.

Tomczak, Diane. "Re: Dyslexia and Laptops." Online posting. 23 Sept.
1999. ECPROFDEV-L: Early Childhood Professional Development
Listserv. 24 Feb. 2000 <http://ericeece.org/listserv/ecprof-l.html>.

Appendix A-2

DOCUMENTING SOURCES (APA STYLE)

The guidelines and the bibliographic entries below provide a basic introduction to APA citation style. For additional help, consult the *Publication Manual of the American Psychological Association* (5th ed., 2001).

Reference List

The *reference* list at the end of your paper identifies the sources used in writing the paper and provides the necessary information for a reader to locate and retrieve the sources.

1. All sources included in the References section must be cited in the body of the paper; also each source cited in the text must be listed in the references at the end of the paper, **except personal communications such as interviews, letters, and personal e-mail**. See the *APA Style Manual* for citing this type of material within the text of the manuscript.

2. Begin the reference list on a separate page from the text of the paper under the heading References (with no quotation marks, underlining, etc.).

3. The entries should be double spaced.

4. Use a hanging indent entry. That is, the first line of each entry begins at the left margin. Subsequent lines in each entry are indented five spaces to the right.

5. Arrange the entries in alphabetical order by author's last name or by the first significant word if the author is a corporate author or if the work is listed by the title rather by an author or authors.

6. If there are several works by the same author, repeat the author's name in each citation. Entries by the same author are arranged by year of publication beginning with the earliest year.

Examples

Citation examples are provided for the following categories of materials.

A1. Books (including reference books)

A2. Periodical and Newspaper Articles

A3. Dissertations and Theses

A4. Audiovisual Media

A5. Technical and Research Reports

A6. Electronic Formats

A7. Government and Legal References

A1.   Books

In documenting a book cite the following items in the order given:

☐ Author. Give the author's last name and initials, including any coauthor. If there is more than one, but less than seven authors, all of the authors' names are included. When there are more than six authors, give the names of the first six and abbreviate the seventh and all others as "et al." (not italicized and with a period after the "al."). Use commas to separate the names of the authors; use an ampersand (&) before the name of the last author.

□ Publication date. Place parentheses around the year the work was copyrighted, or, for unpublished works, the year the work was produced. If no date is available, use n.d. in parentheses.

□ Title. Capitalize only the first word of the title and of the subtitle of a book or chapter or article in a book. Italicize the titles of books.

□ Edition. If other than the first, place the edition in parenthesis following the title.

□ Volume. Place volume numbers of a multivolume work in parentheses following the title.

□ Publication information.

  ▫ Place. Give the city and, if the city is not well known or would be confused with another location, the state or country. Use the U.S. Postal service abbreviation for states. Place a colon after the place.

  ▫ Publisher. Give the name of the publisher in as brief a form as possible for identification.

A1.1. Book by one author

Kaufman, M. (1971). *Homeopathy in America: The rise and fall of a medical heresy.* Baltimore: Johns Hopkins.

A1.2. Book by two authors

Powers, S. K., & Dodd, S. L. (1999). *Total fitness: Exercise, nutrition, and wellness* (2nd ed.). Boston: Allyn.

A1.3. Book by two or more authors with the same last name

Durant, W. & Durant, A. (1977). *A dual autobiography.* New York: Simon.

A1.4. Book by more than six authors

James, A., Malinowski, B., Singer, C., Aliotta, A. Eddington, A. S., Brown, W. et. al. (1925). *Science, religion and reality.* New York: Macmillan.

A1.5. Two or more books by the same author

Mink, G. (1995). *The Wages of motherhood: Inequality in the welfare state.* Ithaca: Cornell University Press.

Mink, G. (1998). *Welfare's end.* Ithaca: Cornell University Pres.

Note: When citing two or more books by the same author, put in order by date with earliest date first.

A1.6. Book by an organization (corporate author)

Center for the Study of Democratic Institutions. (1967). *The university in America.* Santa Barbara: Author.

Note: When the author and publisher are identical, do not repeat the name; rather use the word "Author" in place of the name.

A1.7. Book that is an edited work

> Green, P., and Walzer, M. (Eds.)(1969). *The Political imagination in literature: A reader.* New York: Free Press of Glencoe.

A1.8. Chapter in a volume in a series

> Gelman, R., & Baillargeon, R. (1983). A review of some Piagetian concepts. In P. H. Mussen (Series Ed.), & J. H. Flavell & E. Markman (Vol. Eds.), *Handbook of child psychology*: Vol. 3. *Cognitive development* (167-230). New York: Wiley.

Note: The series editor is listed first, followed by the volume editor, the title of the series, and the title of the volume being cited.

A1.9. Book that is one volume of a multivolume work, one author, each volume a different title

> Malone, D. (1948-1982). *Jefferson and his time*: Vol. 3. *Jefferson and the ordeal of liberty.* Boston: Little, Brown.

Note: Elements cited are authors of the work, inclusive dates of publication for all the volumes, title of the work, title of the volume that is referenced, place of publication, and publisher.

A1.10. Book that is one volume of a multivolume work with one general title

> Warren, C. (1926). *The Supreme Court in United States history.* (Rev. ed., 2 Vols.) Boston: Little Brown.

A1.11. Book that is a translation of an author's work

> Nietzsche, F. (1956). *The birth of tragedy and the genealogy of morals.* (F. Golffing, Trans.) Garden City: Doubleday.

A1.12. Article or a chapter in an edited book

> Barker, J. (1974). Man, mood, and the presidency. In R. G. Tugwell & T. E. Cronin (Vol. Eds.), *The presidency reappraised* (pp. 205-214). New York: Prager.

Note: Elements cited: author of article, date of publication, title of article, editors of the book in which article appears, title of the book in which article appears, pages on which the article appears in the book, place of publication, and publisher.

A1.13. Article in an encyclopedia

> Goldblatt, H.C., & Nienhauser, W. H., Jr. (2002). Chinese literature. In *The new encyclopaedia Britannica* (Vol. 16, pp. 231-240). Chicago: Encyclopaedia Britannica.

Note: Elements cited: authors of the article, date of publication, title of the article, title of the encyclopedia, volume and page numbers of article, place of publication, publisher. If an entry has no byline, place the title in the author position.

A1.14. *Article from a multivolume subject reference book*

```
Flexner, E. (1961). Woman's rights movement. In J. G. Hopkins &
    W. Andrews (Vol. Eds.), Dictionary of American history (Vol. 6,
    Supp. 1, pp. 301-343). New York: Scribner's.
```

A2. Periodical and Newspaper Articles

Items to include when citing articles from periodicals:

☐ Author. Give the author's last name and initials, including any coauthor. If there is more than one, but less than seven authors, all of the authors' names are included. When there are more than six authors, give the names of the first six and abbreviate the seventh and all others as "et al." (not italicized and with a period after the "al."). Use commas to separate the names of the authors; use an ampersand (&) before the name of the last author.

☐ Publication date. Place the date in parentheses. For magazines, newsletters, and newspapers, where no volume number is indicated, give the year followed by the exact date of the publication (month or month and day). If no date is available, write n.d. in parentheses.

☐ Title of the article. Capitalize only the first word of the title and of the subtitle, if any, and proper nouns. Do not use italics or enclose the article titles in quotation marks.

☐ Title of the periodical. Give the full title of the periodical; capitalize words in the titles except articles (excluding initial articles) and prepositions. Italicize the title of the periodical and the volume and issue number, if any.

☐ The volume number and issue number. Give the issue number in parentheses immediately after the volume number.

☐ Inclusive pages of the article. Use the abbreviation for page(s) (p(p). before the page numbers in citations for newspaper articles.

A2.1. *Article from a journal with continuously numbered pages throughout the volume*

```
Runkle, G. Is violence always wrong? (1976). Journal of Politics, 38,
    247-291.
```

A2.2. *Article from a journal with separately numbered pages in each issue*

```
Martin, J. (1975). A watertight Watergate future: Americans in a post-
    American age. The Antioch Review, 33(2), 7-25.
```

A2.3. *Journal article with more than six authors*

```
Heim, S., Kaufmann, J., Fuechter, I., Eulitz, C., Pantev C, Lamprecht-
    Dinnesen, A., et al. (2000). Dyslexia and differences in the func-
    tional organization of the auditory cortex: Evidence from event-
    related magnetic fields. Journal of Psychophysiology, 14(1): 63-64.
```

A2.4. *Article from a monthly magazine, author identified, no volume indicated*

```
Starr, R. (1976, April). A kind word about money. Harper's, 79-92.
```

A2.5. *Article from a weekly magazine, author identified, volume indicated*

```
Meindl, J.D. (1982, February 12). Microelectronics and computers in
    medicine. Science, 215, 792-797.
```

A2.6. Article from a weekly newsletter, no author indicated

Analysis: Powerful start for media smart: Teaching children to think critically about what's on television. (2002, November 21). *Marketing*, 15.

A2.7. Newspaper article, author indicated

Goldstein, T. (1976, September 28). New federal tax law could foster growth of plans to provide pre-paid legal services. *The New York Times* [eastern ed.], p. A36.

A2.8. Newspaper article, no author indicated

Cloning's future. (1998, July 28). *The Christian Science Monitor*, p 20.

A2.9. Editorial from a newspaper

Takeovers Yes, Hold-ups No. (1986, November 28). [Editorial] *The New York Times* [eastern ed.] p. A26.

A2.10. Book review with title, author identified

Frick, R. (2003). And you thought shopping was fun. [Review of the book *I want that!*]. *Kiplinger's Personal Finance Magazine, 57*(3), 30.

Note: Review by R. Frick, entitled "And you thought shopping was fun," of the book *I want that*, in *Kiplinger's Personal Finance Magazine*, vol. 57, issue 3, page 30.

A2.11. Book review, author identified, no title

Sherrill, R. (1976, January 18). [Review of the book *The time of illusion*]. *New York Times Book Review*, pp. 1–2.

Note: Since the review is untitled, the information in brackets is retained in place of the title to identify the medium (book) and the title of the work.

A3. Dissertations and Theses

☐ If a manuscript copy of the dissertation was obtained from a university, the year of the dissertation as well as the volume and page numbers of *Dissertation Abstracts International* (*DAI*) are included.

☐ For an unpublished master's thesis, give the name of the city and the state, unless it is included in the name of the university.

☐ For an unpublished master's thesis from outside the United States give the name of the university and the location of the university, including the city, province or state (if applicable) and the country.

A3.1. Dissertation

Bolden, A. J. (1998). All blues: A study of African-American resistance poetry. (Doctoral dissertation, Louisiana State University, 1998). *Dissertation Abstracts International*, 58-08A, 2976.

A3.2. *Master's thesis (unpublished)*

Vogel, A. E. (1998). *Body image by association: Women's interpretations of aerobics and the role of the fitness instructor*. Unpublished master's thesis, University of British Columbia, Vancouver, British Columbia, Canada.

A4. Audiovisual Media

A4.1. *Sound recording*

Items to include when citing a sound recording

- ☐ Author or performer
- ☐ Copyright date
- ☐ Title of song, if applicable
- ☐ Recording artist (if different from author), in brackets [On title of album]
- ☐ Medium of recording (CD, record, cassette), in brackets
- ☐ Location
- ☐ Recording label
- ☐ Recording date if different from original copyright date

Kennedy, J. F. (1962). The Cuban missile crisis. On *Great Speeches of the 20th century* [CD]. Rhino Records. (1991)

Monk, T. (1998). *Live at the It Club* [CD] New York: Sony Music Entertainment.

Wayne, J. (Writer), & Burton, R. (Narrator) (1978). *The war of the worlds: Rock musical* [LP]. New York: Columbia.

A4.2. *Videotapes*

- ☐ Give the name of the primary contributors and, in parentheses, their function (narrator, director, producer, etc.)
- ☐ Identify the type of work immediately after the title.

Jennings, P. (Narrator) & Goodman, R. (Director). (1992). *Prejudice: Answering children's questions* [videocassette]. Oak Forest, IL: MPI Home Video.

Wolfgang Bayer Productions. (Producer). (1989). *Our national parks* [videocassette]. Washington, D.C.: National Geographic Book Service.

A4.3. *Television and radio broadcasts*

Items to include when citing a television or radio program

- ☐ Name and (in parentheses) the function of the originator or primary contributor
- ☐ Date of the program
- ☐ Title of the episode (if applicable) or program
- ☐ Type of program (in brackets immediately following the title)
- ☐ Title of series (if applicable)
- ☐ Distributors name and complete address unless the organization is well-known

Hogan, P. (Producer). (2001, June 19). *Bill Moyers reports: Earth on edge* [Television series]. New York: WNET.

Kirchner, M. B. & Rand, R. (Producers). (1999, March 5). Sports, fitness, and the brain [Radio series episode]. In *Gray matters.* Boston: PRI, WUMB-FM.

A5. Technical and Research Reports

Items to include when citing a research report

- ☐ Report authors
- ☐ Date of publication
- ☐ Report title
- ☐ Report number assigned by the issuing organization
- ☐ Organization, agency, office, etc. that published the report
- ☐ For reports available from a document deposit service (e.g., NTIS or ERIC), give the document number in parentheses at the end of the entry. Do not use a period after the document number.

A5.1. *Report available from the Government Printing Office (GPO)*

National Institute of Mental Health. (1996). *Obsessive-compulsive disorder: Decade of the brain* (NIH publication No. 96-3755). Washington, D.C. U.S. Government Printing Office.

Reid, W. J., Jr., & Cuthbert, F. P., Jr. (1976). *Aphids on leafy vegetables: How to control them* (Agricultural Research Service, Farmers' Bulletin No. 2148). Washington, D.C.: GPO.

A5.2. *Report available from the Educational Resources Information Center (ERIC)*

Spalter-Roth, R. M., & Hartman, H. I. (1991). *Increasing working mothers' earnings.* Washington, D.C.: Institute for Women's Policy Research. (ERIC Document Reproduction Service No. ED 370825)

A6. Electronic Format

When listing a source in electronic format originally printed in a book, journal, or other printed format, use the general guidelines you would use to cite the printed form. In addition, add the information that identifies the particular format and for Internet sources, the date of access and the Internet address (URL).

A6.1. *CD-ROM*

See also examples of citations to CD-ROM sound recordings at A4.1.

Dead Sea Scrolls revealed. [CD]. (1994). Tel Aviv : Pixel Multimedia; London : A. Witkin; Oak Harbor, WA: Logos Research Systems.

United States. Dept. of Commerce. Bureau of the Census. Data user Services. (1993). *1990 census of population and housing: Equal employment opportunity file* [CD, Disc 1]. Washington, D.C.: Dept of Commerce.

Weninger, R. (1999). [Review of the book *Passage through Hell*]. *The German Quarterly* [CD], 72 (2), 194-195.

Wolf, V. (1997). The captain's death bed. In M. Hussey (Ed.), *The complete works of Virginia Wolf, including variant and hard-to-find editions*. [CD]. Woodbridge, CT: Primary Source Media.

A.6.2. Internet

Because there are no standards for what is placed on the Internet, citing the sources can be confusing. Generally, you should include the following elements.

- ☐ Author, if given.
- ☐ Date of publication
- ☐ Title of article, if it appears to be part of a larger work
- ☐ Title of work or page
- ☐ Title of the project (if any)
- ☐ Publication information (name of sponsoring organization, if applicable)
- ☐ Date of access, if applicable
- ☐ Web address (URL). If you need to break a line of a URL, do so after a slash or a period. Do not place a period after the URL

A6.2.1. Periodical articles based on a print source

Lubove, S. (2000, February 7). Subprime borrower [Electronic version]. *Forbes, 165*(3), 58.

Note: Articles retrieved from online publications that are exact duplicates of print versions can be cited as you would cite the print source, with the addition of the notation [Electronic version] after the article title.

Gartner, S. S., & Segura, G. M. (1998). War, casualties, and public opinion. *Journal of Conflict Resolution, 42*(3). Retrieved February 23, 2000, from Electronic Collections Online: http://firstsearch.oclc.org/html/eco-frames.html

Note: If you reference an article that you believe is different from the print version or for which there are no pages available, you should give the date you retrieved the article and the URL.

Shields, P. G. (2002). Tobacco smoking, harm reduction, and biomarkers. *Journal of the National Cancer Institute*, 94, 1435-1444. Retrieved March 10, 2003, from LexisNexis Academic database.

Note: When citing material retrieved from an aggregated database, follow the form appropriate for the material. Add a statement giving the retrieval date and the name of the database.

A6.2.2. Articles in an Internet-only journal

Johnson, G. M. (1997). [Review of Huckleberry Finn as idol and target]. *The Mark Twain Forum*. Retrieved February 23, 2000, from http://web.mit.edu/linguistics/www/forum/reviews/aracl.html

Kuang, W. (1999). The development of electronic publication in China. *LIBRES: Library and Information Science Research, 9*(1). Retrieved February 23, 2000, from http://aztec.lib.utk.edu/libres/libre9n1/wembo.htm

A6.2.3. Newspaper articles

Screening newborns can defeat hereditary diseases. (2000, February 25). *The New York Times on the Web*. Retrieved February 26, 2000, from http://www.nytimes.com/

A6.2.4. Abstract of a periodical article retrieved from a database

Oates, C., Blades, M., & Gunter, B. (2002). Children and television advertising: When do they understand persuasive intent? *Journal of Consumer Behaviour*, 1(3): 238-245. Abstract retrieved March 10, 2003, from PsycINFO database.

A6.2.5. Nonperiodical documents on the Internet

Lerman, R. I. (2000). Meritocracy without rising inequality? *Economic Restructuring and the Job Market* (The Urban Institute Policy and Research Report, No. 2). Retrieved February 23, 2000, from http://www.urban.org/econ/econ2.htm

Martin, J. (2000, 23 February). *English Springer Spaniel*. Retrieved February 26, 2000, from http://www.ariel-ess.com/essfaq/#toc

A6.2.6. U.S. Government reports

United States. Dept. of Agriculture. Agriculture Research Service. Human Nutrition Information Service. Weihrauch, J. L., & Ashok, C. S. (Preparers). (1994, February). *Provisional table on the vitamin K content of foods* (HNIS-PT-104). Retrieved February 23, 2000, from http://www.nal.usda.gov/fnic/foodcomp/Data/Other/pt104.pdf

United States. Council of Economic Advisors. *Changing America: Indicators of social and economic well-being by race and Hispanic origin* (Report prepared by the Council for the President's Initiative on Race). Retrieved March 10, 2003, from the Council of Economic Advisors vis GPO Access: http://w3.access.gpo.gov/eop/index.html

A6.2.7. ERIC report

Imel, S. (November 2000). *Change: Connections to adult learning and education* (ERIC Digest No. 221). Retrieved August 4, 2001, from http://www.ed.gov/databases/ERIC_Digests/ed446252.html

A6.2.8. Abstract of a technical report retrieved from the Internet

Aidman, A. (1997). Television violence: Content, context, and consequences (Report No. EDO-PS-97-26). Abstract retrieved March 10, 2003, from http://ericir.syr.edu

A6.2.9. Online books and selections from books

```
Twain, M. (2002, January 16). A double barrelled detective story [The
    Naked Word Electronic Edition]. Retrieved February 23, 2000, from
    http://sr8.xoom.com/etcollective/nakedword/htmltext/dbdstory.html
    (Original work published 1902)

Boswell, J. (n.d.) Selections. In J. Lynch (Ed.) Life of Samuel Johnson
    (Based on R. W. Chapman's 1904 Oxford edition). Retrieved 23
    February, 2000, from http://newark.rutgers.edu/~jlynch/Texts/BLJ/
    b272.html

Wilson, M. S. (2002). James D(ewey) Watson: A profile of the author's
    life and works. In Contemporary Authors. Retrieved March 10, 2003,
    from Literature Resource Center, GaleNet database.
```

A7. Government and Legal and References

For most government publications APA recommends using the APA format described in other sections of Appendix A-2 and in the *APA Style Manual*. For references to legal materials which include court cases, statutes, and other legislative material, APA recommends using *The Bluebook: A Uniform System of Citation* (17th ed. Cambridge, MA: Harvard Law Review Association, 2000). The examples below illustrate some of the more common forms of citations to legislative materials using *The Bluebook*.

A 7.1. Congressional hearings

```
Better Nutrition and Health for Children Act of 1993: Hearings before
    the Committee on Agriculture, Nutrition and Forestry. 103d Cong.,
    2nd Sess., (1994).
```

Note: The full title of the hearing is cited first. It includes the names of the committee and subcommittee (if any) before which the hearing was held. Next comes the number of Congress and session number and finally, the year.

A7.2. Congressional reports and documents

```
S. Rept. No. 106-149 (1999).
```

Note: Reference is to a report submitted to the Senate from the Committee on Indian Affairs.

A7.3. Laws, decrees, etc.

```
Paperwork Reduction Act of 1980. Pub. L. No. 96-511, 94 Stat. 2812
    (1980).
```

Note: Citation to the *Statutes at Large*. Elements included in citation in the order given are: Title of the law, public law number, volume number of the *Statutes at Large*, abbreviation for *Statutes at Large*, page number.

```
20 U.S.C. 238 (1980).
```

Note: Citation to the *United States Code*. Elements in citation are number of code, abbreviation of *United States Code*, section number, and edition date.

A7.4. Court case

Brewer v. Williams, 430 U.S. 389 (1977).

Note: Name of case, volume 430 of *U.S. Reports*, page 389, year of publication.

A7.5 Congressional Record

121 Cong. Rec. 40634 (1975).

Appendix B

GLOSSARY

abstract A type of index that gives the location of an article in a periodical or a book and a brief summary that includes author, title, source, and subject headings or descriptors.

Acceptable Use Policy (AUP) A policy for Internet users that defines the accepted use of the server and the network. Internet providers, both commercial and non-commercial, frequently have AUPs.

address Internet address that refers to the e-mail address or the IP (Internet Protocol) address.

analog Data that is encoded in continuous signals over a range or interval of values—for example, the signals transmitted via a telephone line as opposed to data on a digital computer that uses binary coding.

annotated bibliography A list of works with descriptions and a brief summary or critical statement about each.

annotation Critical or explanatory note about the contents of a book or article.

anthology Any collection of varied literary compositions; includes many different titles of shorter works under one title.

appendix Section of a book or other literary work containing supplementary materials such as tables or maps.

article A complete piece of writing that is part of a larger work.

ASCII (American Standard Code for Information Interchange) Standard character-to-number encoding widely used in the computer industry.

authentication The verification of the identity of a person or process, most often associated with the login (username) and password verification process for computer use. (*See also* authorization.)

authorization The process of granting or denying access to an Internet resource. Most computer security systems use a two-step process: (1) authentication, which verifies that a user is who he or she claims to be, and (2) authorization, which allows the user access to those resources to which he or she is entitled, depending on the preassigned privileges associated with the user's identity.

backbone On the Internet, the top level in a hierarchical network; it connects regional and local networks.

barcode A code and number appearing on each piece of library material used to charge, discharge, and renew materials in an online computer system.

bibliographic citation All the necessary information to find a particular source, for example, author, title, place of publication, publisher, and date for books and author of article, title of article, publication, volume, issue, date, and pages for periodical articles.

bibliography List of sources of information such as books, journal articles, essays, and Internet sites on a particular subject. Includes information such as author, title, date, place of publication, publisher, page numbers, URL and database.

binary A code used in computing based on numbers. Once data is entered into a computer, it is converted into binary numbers consisting of the two digits 0 and 1 (bits).

bit Binary digit, the smallest amount of information that may be stored in a computer.

book number Last letter/number combination in a call number. Stands for the author of the book and sometimes the title.

Bookmark A page on the Netscape browser on which you can lists URLs or Web addresses. Bookmarks serve as links for easy access to Web addresses. In Internet Explorer such a page is called "Favorites."

Boolean A field of mathematical logic developed in the mid-19th century by the English mathematician George Boole; logic is applied in keyword searching in electronic sources by combining concepts using three commands or operators.

Boolean operators The terms **and, or, not** used in keyword searching to broaden, narrow or limit a search.

Boolean search A keyword search that uses Boolean operators to obtain a precise definition of a query.

browser The software that allows you to locate, display, and use Web documents. Netscape and Internet Explorer are the most widely used browsers.

browsing Refers to a search in a directory-type search engine on the Internet. Also, casually looking for information on the Internet.

Bulletin Board Service (BBS) An Internet service that typically provides electronic mail services, exchange of ideas, data files, and any other services or activities of interest to the bulletin board system's operator. May be operated by hobbyists, government agencies, or educational and research institutions.

byte One character of information, usually eight bits wide.

call number The identification number that determines where a book or other library material is located in the library.

card catalog Library holdings recorded on 3" x 5" cards, filed alphabetically.

CD-ROM (compact disk, read only memory) A compact disk containing text and/or images that is accessed by computers.

Chat (Internet Relay Chat) A world-wide "party line" protocol that allows individuals to converse with others in real time. (*See also* Talk.)

circulation desk The library service desk where materials are checked out and returned.

citation A reference to an information resource; usually includes author, title, date, pages, and any other information needed to identify the source.

class number Top part of call number that stands for subject matter of the book.

client A computer system or process that requests a service of another computer system or process.

client-server A common way to describe the relationship between the computer that requests information (client) and the computer that houses the information (server).

commands Symbols and/or terms used to retrieve computer-stored information.

concept search A search for the broad meaning of a term, rather than its narrower aspect.

consortium A group of libraries forming a cooperative for the purpose of sharing services and individual collections.

contemporary Belonging to the same time period in history.

controlled vocabulary Standardized or established terms used in databases or catalogs as subject headings or descriptors.

copyright The legal right to control the production, use, and sale of copies of a literary, musical, or artistic work.

cross reference A reference from one term or word in a book or index to another word or term.

cumulation An index that is formed as a result of the incorporation of successive parts of elements. All the material is arranged in one alphabet.

current   Existing at the present time.

cyberspace   A term used to refer to the universe of computers and networks. Originally coined by William Gibson in his fantasy novel *Neuromancer*.

database   Units of information that are stored in machine readable form and retrieved by use of a computer.

depository library   Specially designated libraries that receive government publications free of charge.

descriptors   A term used in some indexes or databases to represent subject headings.

dialup   A temporary, as opposed to dedicated, connection between computers established over a standard phone line.

digital   Data transmitted as discrete and non-continuous pulses (off and on) in the form of binary digits 0 and 1 known as bits, as opposed to *analog* or continuous representation.

digital library   A collection of information in digital (machine-readable) format, rather than on paper or microform. (*See also* virtual library.)

digitization   The process of converting text or images to digital format so that they can be displayed on a computer screen.

direct source   Information presented in such a way that is not necessary to consult another source.

directory search engine   A search engine that presents information in broad subject categories and proceeds through increasingly more specific topics or subjects. It provides a means of focusing more closely on the object of the search. (*See also* mediated search.)

discipline   A branch of knowledge (e.g., humanities, social sciences, or science).

dissertation   Research that is completed in partial fulfillment of the requirements for a doctoral degree.

document delivery   Service provided by libraries to deliver copies of materials from other libraries or vendors to users, usually for a fee. The service is often administered by the interlibrary loan department. In some libraries, document delivery consists of the physical or electronic delivery of materials to the office or place of business of a library user.

documentation   A reference to a source used or consulted in research.

domain   A domain, also known as a "domain name," is a unique name that identifies places on the Internet. An example of a domain name is webcrawler.com. Domains can be used as part of a Web site address (e.g., www.domain.com) or they can form part of an e-mail address (e.g., support@domain.com). Domain names are registered for use to avoid duplication of addresses. They allow the use of descriptive words that better enable people to remember Web sites or e-mail addresses.

download   To transfer data or program files from one computer to another for storage on a hard-drive, floppy disk, or other storage device.

DVD (digital versatile disk or digital video disk)   A small disk used for storing text, images, and sounds; similar to a CD-ROM, except that it holds much more information—enough for a full-length movie—and is much faster.

edition   All copies of a book printed from a single typesetting.

e-journal   Periodical published in electronic format; may require a subscription or login ID to use.

E-mail (electronic mail)   A system whereby a computer user can exchange messages with other computer users (or groups of users) via a communications network.

endnotes   Identification of sources used in a text, placed at the end of the text or, in a book, at the ends of chapters.

entry   Description of individual sources of information.

FAX   *See* facsimile transmission.

facsimile   A reproduction or copy of a work that replicates the exact appearance of the original.

facsimile transmission (FAX)   Transmission of text or images, over telephone lines from one location to another, with output printed as a facsimile of the original. Requires a FAX machine with a scanner, a printer, and a modem that is connected to a telephone line.

field   The different elements or access points by which records are retrieved in an online catalog or a database.

File Transfer Protocol (FTP)   A protocol that allows a user on one host computer to transfer and access files to and from another host over a network.

finger   A program that displays information about a particular user, or all users, logged on the local system or on a remote system. It typically shows full name, last login time, idle time, terminal line, and terminal location (where applicable).

flame   A strong opinion and/or criticism of something, usually as a frank inflammatory statement, in an electronic mail message.

footnotes   Identification of sources used in a text, placed at the bottom of the page.

format   The manner in which information is provided, displayed, or retrieved; i.e., print, audio, electronic.

free-text search   A search for words regardless of where they appear in a record.

full-text database   Database that provides the complete text of material from the original source.

FTP   *See* File Transfer Protocol

gateway   A communications device/program that passes data between networks on the Internet.

glossary   A list with definitions of technical or unusual terms used in the text.

Gopher   A menu-driven client-server computer information system. Gopher uses a simple protocol that allows a single Gopher client to access a Gopher server.

hacker   A person who is skilled in the internal workings of computers and networks. The term usually refers to individuals who use this knowledge to penetrate systems to cause mischief.

hits   A list of documents that are returned in response to a computer search; also called matches.

holdings   A field in a record which indicates which years and volumes of materials (periodicals, yearbooks, videos, etc.) owned by a particular library.

home page   The top level of information at a Web site.

host   A computer that allows users to communicate with other host computers on a network, such as by electronic mail, Telnet, and FTP.

hot links   Links within a text on the internet that connect directly to another site.

HTML (Hypertext Markup Language)   A standardized document-formatting language used in creating documents on the World Wide Web. With HTML, tags are embedded in the text to instruct the client how to display the document.

HTTP (Hypertext Transfer Protocol)   The client-server protocol used to transfer HTML documents from one site to another on the Web.

hypertext   Text that contains pointers, or links, to documents on other servers or to parts of the same document. Words or phrases in the document are highlighted, or underlined, to indicate links. The user can click on the highlighted word to display the document.

humanities   Fields of knowledge concerned with human culture, such as art, philosophy, literature, and religion.

icon   A small image or symbol on a computer screen representing a software program, a file, or other data element that is opened when clicked on with a mouse.

imprint   Place of publication, publisher, and either publication or copyright date.

index   Alphabetical list of the subjects discussed in a book with corresponding page number; also a separate publication that points to information found in other sources.

indirect source   A guide to information that is located in other sources, such as an index.

information   Knowledge in the form of ideas, facts, or data created by the human mind.

information processing   All of the ways that humans transmit, record, store, retrieve and use information.

integrated catalog   An online system that provides bibliographic records for periodical indexes in the same database as the online catalog.

interface   The process that allows the user to communicate with the software program to perform certain operations; includes the screen display that tells the user how to communicate with the software system.

Internet   A world-wide network that connects computers to one another, allowing for the free flow of information among them. Consists of a three level hierarchy—national (backbone) networks, regional networks, and local networks.

Internet Explorer   A widely-used Internet browser.

introduction   Describes the subject matter and gives a preliminary statement leading to the main contents of a book.

IP (Internet Protocol)   The protocol that allows a packet to travel through multiple networks on its way to its final destination.

IP address   The address identifying the host computer.

italic   Kind of type in which the letters usually slope to the right and which is used for emphasis.

journal   Scholarly periodical usually issued monthly or quarterly.

keyword   A term that a computer uses as the basis for executing a search.

keyword search   "Free-text searching"; electronic searching using nonstandardized headings.

LAN (Local Area Network)   A data network intended to serve a small area, usually users in close proximity.

library network   Libraries linked together via telecommunication facilities for the purpose of sharing resources.

link   A word or an image, which, when clicked, connects to a site on the Internet.

LISTSERV   An e-mail distribution system in which mail is automatically distributed to all subscribers.

logon   The process of identifying yourself and connecting to a computer system.

magazine   A general interest periodical giving news, current events, and popular material.

MARC   Machine-readable cataloging records.

mediated search engine   A search engine that has direct human intervention. Starts with a broad subject category and proceeds through increasingly more specific topics or subjects. It provides a means of focusing more closely on the object of the search. (*See also* Directory Search Engine.)

meta search   A search that uses a number of search engines in parallel to provide a response to a query.

meta tag   HTML tag that provides information about a Web page. Unlike normal HTML tags, meta tags do not affect how the page is displayed. Instead, they provide information such as who created the page, how often it is updated, what the page is about, and which keywords represent the page's content. Many search engines use this information when building their indexes; also used to catalog Web pages.

microfiche   Microimages of text and other materials printed on a small plastic sheet, usually about 3" x 5" in size. Images must be viewed and printed using a special reader/printer. Magazines, journals, and many government documents are stored in this format.

microfilm   Microimages of text printed on a roll of film, allowing greater storage and archiving of materials. Requires special readers to view and/or print this material.

microform   Printed materials that are reduced in size by photographic means and can only be read with special readers.

Mosaic   A graphics Internet browser developed at the University of Illinois for use with Macintosh, Windows, and UNIX operating systems; has been superseded by Netscape and Internet Explorer.

multi-engine search   *See* meta search.

Netscape   A widely-used Internet browser.

network   A communications system that connects computers at different sites.

notes   Identification of sources used in a text; also explanatory material.

online   Databases stored on a remote computer and accessed locally.

online catalog   Library catalog records in machine readable form which are accessed by use of computers.

online search   A search that is carried out by means of a computer.

OPAC (online public access catalog)   A computer-based source describing the holdings of a particular library; sometimes offers access to periodical databases and catalogs from other libraries.

packet   A small parcel of data by which information is transmitted over the Internet.

pamphlet file   A cardboard, plastic, or metal file for storing pamphlets, loose issues of periodicals, newspaper clippings, and other materials unbound materials. (*See also* vertical file.)

parenthetical references   Citations placed in the text and keyed to the list of *Works Cited* or *References*.

peer-reviewed journal   *See* refereed journal.

periodical   A publication issued at a regular interval; includes magazines and journals.

periodical holdings list   A list found in some libraries of the periodical titles it owns. *See also* holdings.

PDF (Portable Document Format)   A file format developed by Adobe that displays a file on the screen exactly as it looks in the original paper format.

plagiarism   Appropriation of ideas or the copying of the language of another writer without formal acknowledgment.

popular sources Material targeted for the masses; magazines and newspaper articles, books for the general public, etc.

positional operators Terms used to refer to the order in which words appear in a record–"adj," "adj#," "with," and "same."

preface A part of a book that gives the author's purpose in writing the book and acknowledges those persons who have helped in its preparation.

primary source A firsthand or eyewitness account of an event.

prompt A message on a computer screen that asks the user for information or a command.

query A search request consisting words or phrases that define the information that the user is seeking.

record Individual entries in an online catalog or database.

refereed journal A journal in which the articles are reviewed and selected by external reviewers (i.e., persons not on the journal staff) prior to publication. The external reviewers are persons selected because of their knowledge in the field.

reference A department within the library where library staff can provide assistance in locating information or in the research process; a selection of materials such as encyclopedias, dictionaries, indexes, etc. designated to remain in the library for ready access.

reference librarian A specialist in information retrieval who holds a Master's Degree in library science or information science. Many reference librarians have additional subject degrees and serve as subject specialists.

relevance The usefulness of a response to a computer-based query. Most search engines rank their hits from the best match to the query to the poorest.

reprint Copies of the same edition printed at a later time.

robot The software for indexing and updating Web sites. It operates by scanning documents on the Internet via a network of links. A robot is also known as a *spider*, *crawler*, or *indexer*.

route The path that a message takes on the Internet from its source to its destination.

router A device that forwards traffic among networks.

scholarly sources Material produced by experts in a specific field for a limited audience; includes journal articles, papers read and presented at conferences, and books on specialized topics.

sciences Fields of knowledge covering general truths especially as obtained and tested through scientific method; also fields of knowledge concerned with the physical world and its phenomena; includes chemistry, biology, physics, and medicine.

scope The range of information covered in a book, article, or other information source.

search engine A computer program that conducts searches in an electronic source.

search statement Words or phrases that make up the search terms used to look up information in an electronic source.

search strategy Logical steps used to plan and conduct research. Includes identifying the information need, selecting and evaluation of appropriate sources, and documenting the sources.

secondary source Literature that analyzes, interprets, relates, or evaluates a primary source or other secondary sources.

***see also* reference** A listing of additional headings to consult for information.

see reference   A reference from a term that is not used to one that is used.

serial   Publications issued on a continuing basis at regularly stated intervals.

series   Publications similar in content and format.

short-title   First part of a compound title.

site   *See* Web site.

social sciences   Fields of knowledge dealing with human social relationships, such as political science, anthropology, education, and criminal justice.

spider   The software that scans documents on the Internet and adds them to the search engine's database. A spider is the same as a robot.

stacks   Groups of shelves on which books are placed in a library.

stemming   The ability for a search engine to search for variations of a word based on its stem. For example, entering "catalog" might also find "catalogs" and "cataloging," depending on the search engine.

subheading   A subdivision of a major heading.

subject heading   A word or phrase assigned by catalogers to materials indicating the primary subject matter covered in the work. Subject headings allow the organization of similar materials by topic.

subject search   A search using controlled vocabulary (such as *LCSH*) to search a record.

subtitle   Second part of a compound title that explains the short-title.

surfing   Exploring sites on the Internet.

table of contents   A list of chapters or parts of a book in numerical order with the pages on which they are located.

Talk   A protocol that allows two or more people on remote computers to communicate in real-time fashion.

TCP   *See* Transmission Control Protocol.

TCP/IP (Transmission Control Protocol over Internet Protocol)   The abbreviation that refers to the suite of protocols sustaining the Internet.

Telnet   Software that allows the user to logon to a remote computer and use its software as if onsite. Telnet is designed to transmits ASCII text and is used in many libraries to provide access to text-based library catalogs. (*See also* WebPac.)

terminal   An computer device consisting of a keyboard and a monitor that can be used to enter or display data from a larger computer (a minicomputer or a mainframe), but is not capable of independent processing of information. Sometimes called a "dumb terminal."

thesis   A research project completed in partial fulfillment of the requirements for the master's degree.

thesis statement   A statement of purpose in a research paper.

title page   Page in front of a book that gives the official author, title, and often the imprint.

Transmission Control Protocol (TCP)   Internet standard transport protocol.

truncation   Abbreviation of words in the commands given to search an online database. An asterisk (*), question mark (?) or pound sign (#) are usually used to indicate truncation.

tunneling   The process by which data is transferred between domains on the Internet.

URL (Uniform Resource Locator)   The address of any resource on the Internet.

USENET   A collection of thousands of topically named newsgroups to which people contribute. Not all Internet hosts subscribe to USENET.

user friendly   Format which is easy for the computer user to interpret and understand.

vendor   One who markets databases to subscribers.

vertical file   Files containing ephemeral materials such as pamphlets, pictures, and newspaper clippings.

virtual library   A library in which the collection is in electronic format rather than in a tangible form, such as paper or microform. Some libraries use the term to refer to that portion of their collection available on the Internet. (*See also* digital library.)

virus   A program that is spread by replicating itself on any computer system with which it comes in contact.

volume   Written or printed sheets put together to form a book. One book of a series. All the issues of a periodical bound together to make a unit.

WAN   *See* Wide Area Network

Web   *See* World Wide Web

WebPAC   A Web-based OPAC (online public access catalog) with a graphics-based interface accessible through the Web, as opposed to a text-based catalog accessible via Telnet.

Web page   A Web document with a URL or Internet address. Also, a page within a Web site. When Web pages are part of the same document, they are also collectively known as a Web site.

Web site   A location on any server that contains hypertext documents.

Wide Area Network (WAN)   A network that covers a large geographic area.

wild card   In a query, a symbol that replaces a portion of a word to indicate that other word constructions are applicable.

World Wide Web (WWW, Web)   A hypertext-based, distributed information system that allows users to view, create, or edit hypertext documents. Documents are viewed using a browser.

WWW   *See* World Wide Web.

Definitions relating to the Internet were adapted from Gary Scott Malkin and Tracy LaQuey Parker, *Internet User Glossary*, http://www.kanren.net/kanren/internet_user_glossary.html; and David Wuolu, "Basic Internet Terminology." Unpublished paper (Baton Rouge: Louisiana State University), 1995. An excellent, frequently updated, glossary of Internet terms is Enzer Matisse, *Glossary of Internet Terms*, available at http://www.matisse.net/files/glossary.html.

Appendix C

Instructor: _____ Course/Section: _____

Name: _____

Date: _____ Points: _____

Topic and Outline

1. Select a topic you might want to use in a ten-page research paper.

    Topic:

2. Write three questions or statements you can make about this topic based on what you already know
    about it.

    a.

    b.

    c.

3. Compile a thesis statement using your responses to Question 1 as a basis. (See Chapter 2 for example.)

4. Write a preliminary outline for your paper. To do this you should look for background information on
    this topic in sources such as a general encyclopedia, a magazine, or on the Internet. (See Chapter 2 for
    guidance.)

Instructor: _____ Course/Section: _____

Name: _____

Date: _____ Points: _____

Developing a Search Strategy

Using the thesis statement and outline from Project 1.1, develop a search strategy for your research project. Answer the following questions. (For online assignments, skip no. 3.)

1. Would you approach this topic from a humanities, social science, or science perspective? Explain.

2. What subject headings do you propose to use to find books in your library catalog on your topic?

3. Look up the headings from Question 2 in the *LCSH* on this topic. List those that you locate. Also list any alternative subject headings in the *LCSH*.

4. What keywords do you propose to use to find additional books on the topic in your library catalog?

5. Which periodical indexes or databases will you use to locate citations for magazine or journal articles? Why did you choose these for your topic?

    What terms will you use in these indexes or databases?

6. Will you be searching for popular or scholarly articles?

   Explain.

7. List other sources you would consult as part of your search strategy and explain why you would consult each. (For example: statistical source—to find the number of . . .)

Project 1.3

Project 1.3   The Research Project

Instructor: _____ Course/Section: _____

Name: _____

Date: _____ Points: _____

Works Consulted or References

After you have selected your topic, compiled an outline (Project 1.1), and defined a search strategy (Project 1.2), you are ready to locate sources that support your thesis statement and the points in your outline. At a minimum you should have:

1 reference work that provides background information, a definition, or an overview of your topic;

3 sources from the library's catalog (books or government documents);

2 Internet sources that you locate by using different search engines;

4 articles from magazines or journals

2 additional sources such as a reference book, biographical information, or book reviews.

1. As you identify and locate your sources, complete a Research Project Worksheet (p. 415) for each.

2. After you have located all of your sources, prepare a Works Consulted list that is to be turned in along with your worksheets. The list is to be typed using either MLA or APA style documentation. See the examples in Appendix A-1 or A-2 and the Works Cited or References lists in Chapter 2.

Instructor: _____ Course/Section: _____

Name: _____

Date: _____ Points: _____

Research Project Worksheet

Use copies of this form to record information on the sources you locate for your research project. Items which do not apply should be labeled N/A. (Make a copy of the form to use with each source that you locate.)

1. Title of the source:

2. How did you locate the source? (library catalog, index or abstract, database, Internet)

3. Give the subject heading, keyword, or other command you used to locate the source.

4. If this is a reference work, give the subject heading used within the work.

5. If this is an article from a periodical, give the name of the index, abstract, or database you used to locate the article.

   What subject headings or keywords did you use to locate the article?

6. If this is an item you located on the Internet, give the name of the search engine you used to locate the article.

What search command did you use to locate the information?

7. If this is a print source, what is the call number and library location?

8. How does the information in this source support your thesis statement and outline? Give the headings in your outline which apply.

9. Write a bibliographic citation for this source. Use the examples in Appendix A.

10. Write a brief evaluation of the source using the criteria found in Chapter 6.
(Use a separate sheet of paper if necessary.)

11. Write any notes you wish to take from this source. Paraphrase the words of the author or use direct quotes if needed for emphasis or authoritativeness. Enclose direct quotes in quotation marks. Record page numbers of materials used.

Instructor: _____ Course/Section: _____

Name: _____

Date: _____ Points: _____

A pathfinder is a guide to information on a topic. It should help the reader identify information sources and the correct terminology to use to locate information. It also directs the reader to good books, the best indexes and databases, appropriate reference sources, information on the Internet, and other pertinent literature. (For online assignments, skip no. 4.)

Create a pathfinder for a topic you select or one that is assigned by your instructor. Use the form below to record your information. You may wish to include more than the minimum number of sources requested. Cite each source that you select using the MLA style for documentation (see Appendix A).

Note: Write complete citations for any books, articles in reference books and periodicals, and Internet sites; it is not necessary to give complete citations for finding aids.

If you are unable to locate information in any of the categories, see your instructor.

_____

1. Topic:

2. Write a brief summary of your topic in two or three sentences. The statements should reflect the scope of your research and which aspects of the topic are to be included with your pathfinder.

3. An introduction to the topic appears in:
   (Use a general or subject encyclopedia or another reference source such as a handbook, almanac, yearbook, a journal or magazine article, or information on the Internet. **(Cite at least one source.)**

4. Subject heading to use for finding information on this topic are:
   (Use the *LCSH (Library of Congress Subject Headings)* to find appropriate subject headings.)

   Broader term(s) (BT):

   Narrower term(s) (NT):

   Related term(s) (RT):

5. Some relevant books on this topic are: **(Cite at least three books.)**

6. Some reference books which contain information on this topic are:
   (Your sources must actually contain information on the topic, such as that found in manuals, texts, handbooks, gazetteers, atlases, subject dictionaries, or encyclopedias. <u>Do not use Indexes or bibliographies</u>. **(Cite at least two sources.)**

7. Indexes or databases to use for identifying articles in magazines or journals on this topic are:

   a. **(List at least two)**

   b. Search term(s) to use in these indexes or databases to find information on the topic are:

   c. Some relevant articles from these indexes or databases are: **(Cite at least four articles.)**

8. Search engines that can be used to locate free information on the Internet on this topic are: (Use at least two different search engines.)

    a.   1st search engine (name):

    b.   search term(s) used:

    c.   Some relevant Web sites found by using this search engine are: **(Cite at least two Web sites.)**

    d.   2nd search engine (name)

    e.   search term(s) used:

    f.   Some relevant Web sites found by using this search engine are: **(Cite at least two Web sites.)**

9. Find at least two government documents on the topic.

    a.   Finding aid used:

    b.   Search term(s) used:

    c.   Two government documents with information on this topic are:

10. Good sources for statistics on this topic are: **(Cite at least two.)**

11. One article with biographical information on an individual who has written on this topic or who is prominent in this field is: **(Cite at least one.)**

12. A review of a book on this topic appears in: **(Cite at least one.)**

Project 3

Instructor: _____ Course/Section: _____

Name: _____

Date: _____ Points: _____

The assignment below is designed to have you select and evaluate sources of information for a research paper. Identify library sources and the correct terminology to use in a literature search for information that you could use in a research paper on the topic. Any of the sources you use can be in electronic format or in paper. (For online assignments, skip no. 4.)

Write complete bibliographic citations for each appropriate entry below. Use the examples in Appendix A for all bibliographic citations. **(If you are unable to locate material in any of these categories, see your instructor.)**

1. Select a **topic** for a hypothetical 10-page research paper, in which you will use a variety of sources.

   Topic:

2. Give a **brief summary** of your topic in two or three sentences. Define your subject as specifically as possible. The statement should reflect the scope of your research and which aspects of the topic are to be included in the search. It may include questions you would like to answer.

3. Use a general or subject encyclopedia to find an **introduction** to the topic. Alternate sources include handbooks or good general books on the subject. Give the correct bibliographic citation for the source you found.

4. Use the *LCSH (Library of Congress Subject Headings)* books to find terms dealing with your topic. Include a few of each of the following if found:

Broader term(s) (BT):

Narrower term(s) (NT):

Related term(s) (RT):

5. Find at least three books that are relevant to your topic. Write the correct bibliographic citations below.

6. Find two **reference books** which contain information on this topic.
(Choose your sources from the library catalog, by browsing in the reference stacks, or with the help of a librarian. Your sources must actually contain information on the topic, such as that found in manuals, texts, handbooks, gazetteers, atlases, subject dictionaries, or encyclopedias. <u>Do not use Indexes or bibliographies</u>.)

Write the correct bibliographic citations for these works.

7. Give the names of two or three appropriate indexes or databases for your topic.

    a.

    b.

    c.

    d.

Write the search term(s) you used in each one to get an article on your topic. (The letters below correspond to those in Question 7.)

    a.

    b.

    c.

    d.

8. Find four relevant articles from the indexes or databases you listed in Question 7. Print or copy the first page of each of the articles and attach the pages to this assignment. Write the correct bibliographic citations for each of the articles below. (The letters below correspond to the indexes or databases listed in Question 7.)

    a.

    b.

    c.

    d.

9. For each article you found, write a brief evaluation. Indicate whether the article is popular or scholarly. Give specific examples to justify your answer. Indicate whether the article is a primary or a secondary source.

    a.

    b.

    c.

    d.

10. Use two different search engines to find two Web sites that are relevant to your topic.
    1st search engine used:

    search term(s):

    results (number of "hits"):

    Write the correct bibliographic citation for each source you select.

2nd search engine used:

search term(s):

results (number of "hits"):

Write the correct bibliographic citation for the sources you select.

11. Compare the two search engines in terms of ease of use, accuracy, and results.

12. Which Web source was more appropriate for your topic? Why?

13. Find two government documents relevant to your topic.
    Which aid or index did you use? (Internet, library catalog, *Monthly Catalog*, *GPO Access*, etc.)

    Search term(s) used:

    Write the correct bibliographic citations for each document.

14. You may select additional sources, such as statistics, biographies, or book reviews, that have not been included in the questions above. Write a correct bibliographic citation for each.

15. Select two of the best sources you located and give a brief evaluation of their usefulness to your topic. Use the evaluation criteria in Chapter 6 to formulate your evaluation comments.

16. Compile a Works Consulted list (a bibliography) from the sources you locate. Do not cite the finding aids you used to locate information such as online catalogs, indexes and databases, and the Internet. Rather, cite only the actual sources of information. The Works Consulted list is to be typed on a separate sheet. Use the Works Cited list in Chapter 2 as an example.

Instructor: _____ Course/Section: _____

Name: _____

Date: _____ Points: _____

For this assignment you will work in groups of 2–5 persons to use various library tools (reference books, indexes, abstracts, databases, the online catalog, or the Internet) to gather information on a topic of your choice.

Each group will turn in the results of its research to the instructor, make a 5 to 10 minute presentation to the class, and prepare a Works Consulted list.

The group must decide how to divide up the work so that each member can make a meaningful contribution to the project. You are encouraged to include more than the minimum number of sources suggested in the instructions.

Each member of the group will receive the same grade for the project. Participation by each group member is required.

In your oral presentation, you should explain:

☐ why you selected the topic,

☐ what search strategy was used to find the various sources, and

☐ why you selected the particular sources.

Grading will be based on: The appropriateness of your topic
The search strategy used
The suitability of the sources you select for your topic
Proper documentation of sources
Class presentation

Select a broad topic such as literature, business, biology, agriculture, psychology, or music and narrow it down to a manageable topic. Use *LCSH*, the online catalog, or a general or subject encyclopedia.

1. Identify the subject/topic you selected and tell why you selected it.

2. Find background information on this topic. List the sources you used to find the information.

3. Write a focused thesis statement describing the exact angle you are using to pursue your research.

4. Use the online catalog to locate three books on your topic. Write a citation for each below. (Follow the examples in Appendix A-1.)

   What command(s) did you use in the online catalog to locate the books?

5. Use an index or database to locate articles from magazines and/or journals.

   a. What indexes or databases did you use?

   b. What search terms did you use to look for information on your topic?

   c. Locate at least four relevant articles and write a citation for each. (Follow the examples in Appendix A-1.)

Find any of the following that applies to your thesis statement:

6. Statistics to support your thesis. (Cite the table or article you find.)

7. Biographical information, either on an author of one of your works, or on a person well known in your subject area. Write a citation for this biography.

8. Two Internet sites on your topic. (Write the citation for each.)

   a. Which search engines did you use?

   b. What search terms did you use?

9. Discuss the results of your search for this topic. Would you have enough information to write a 10 page research paper? Which source(s) would you use for:

   a. The introduction to your paper?

   b. The main points of your paper?

   c. The conclusion?

10. Compile a Works Consulted list (a bibliography) from the sources you located.

    a. Do not cite the finding aids you used to locate information such as online catalogs, indexes and databases, and the Internet. Rather, cite only the actual sources of information.

    b. Type the Works Consulted list on a separate sheet. Use the Works Cited list in Chapter 2 as an example.

Instructor: _____ Course/Section: _____

Name: _____

Date: _____ Points: _____

An annotated bibliography is a list of books, journal articles, Web sites, or other sources with descriptive or evaluative paragraphs. It provides information concerning the content, authority, accuracy, relevance, and quality of sources found during research.

Review Chapter 2 of your text, especially "Selecting a Topic," "Formulating a Thesis," and "Preparing an Outline."

Instructions:

Select a topic of interest to you which hasn't been discussed in the text. You will not write an actual paper, but gather the resources for a Reference list.

1. Planning for Research

    a. Complete Project 1.1, "Topic and Outline."

    b. Complete Project 1.2, "Developing a Search Strategy."
        (For online assignments, skip no. 3 in Project 1.2.)

2. Proper Documentation and Justification

    a. Compile a list of a minimum of 10 sources on your topic. Include at least one online Reference source, two relevant Web sites, and four full-text articles from magazines or journals.

    b. Use the MLA format from Appendix A. List all sources in alphabetical order with correct format, then provide a brief description of each of your sources, including:

        —How you found the source (search engine, index title, library catalog, etc.)

        —Why you selected the source for your topic (describe special features, uniqueness, relevancy, etc.)

        —How you would use the source to write a research paper (as part of an introduction, major point, conclusion, etc.)

Grading will be according to the following criteria:

- Appropriateness of topic
- Search strategy used for developing the topic and description of steps
- Suitability of sources selected
- Proper documentation and annotation as required

Index